REWARDING
CREATIVE
BEHAVIOR

PRENTICE-HALL INTERNATIONAL, INC., *London*
PRENTICE-HALL OF AUSTRALIA, PTY., LTD., *Sydney*
PRENTICE-HALL OF CANADA, LTD., *Toronto*
PRENTICE-HALL OF INDIA (PRIVATE) LTD., *New Delhi*
PRENTICE-HALL OF JAPAN, INC., *Tokyo*

REWARDING CREATIVE BEHAVIOR

experiments in classroom creativity

E. PAUL TORRANCE
University of Minnesota

PRENTICE-HALL, INC.
Englewood Cliffs, N.J.

Current printing (last digit):

11 10 9 8 7 6 5 4 3

Library of Congress Catalog Card No.: 65-16335

Printed in the United States of America
78066-C

PREFACE

When the studies described in this book were conceived, I was fully aware of the fact that many of the problems we were attacking are bigger than we would be able to solve through a few experiments and descriptive studies. I was convinced, however, that we could learn enough about these problems through such scientific approaches to provide some practical guidance to classroom teachers. I believed that we could bring some of these problems and discussions about them "out of the clouds" and the realm of pure speculation and make enough progress to enable others to pursue in an infinite variety of settings the hundreds of clues we would discover. Already the limited reporting of the results of these studies has inspired hundreds of practical experiments by classroom teachers—some of them systematic and well-controlled, others just simple tests of ideas in specific situations. It is hoped that the publication of some of the results in the present form will contribute to the multiplication of such classroom experiments.

In the first chapter, I try to show why educators should be legitimately concerned about encouraging creative behavior and developing in children the skills, motivations, and abilities necessary for creative achievement. An honest attempt is made to deal with the bothersome problem of definition. I hope that the reader will be able to accept my definition of creative behavior, at least tentatively. If not, I hope that he will create his own label for what I have defined. Otherwise, the reading of this book will not be very rewarding. Some might prefer such terms as constructive behavior, divergent behavior, or productive behavior. Thus far, I still prefer the term "creative behavior."

In the second chapter, an effort has been made to outline a strategy for investigating problems related to the rewarding of creative behavior. In the third chapter, attempts are made to deal with the basic problems of measuring creative behavior and to describe our efforts to cope with such problems. The appendix includes descriptions of the instruments for measuring the kinds of creative performance studied. As much of the reliability and validity data as seems practical has been included. Many readers will require more, but what they require will itself take another book.

Through the first set of studies, an attempt was made to find out what we could about the ways the immediate environment rewards creative behavior. In these investigations, we tried to discover what happens when teachers deliberately try to apply simple principles for rewarding creative behavior in the classroom; how the creative and critical motivations of teachers influence the creative growth of pupils; the role of creative activities; and the differential rewards for boys and girls insofar as creative behavior is concerned.

In the second set of studies, a similar attempt is made to study some of the issues about the evaluative behavior of the classroom teacher. First, some rather clear demonstrations are offered to show that children tend to develop along whatever lines they find rewarding, even in the matter of originality of thinking. Then, an attack is made upon such age-old problems as: competition; unevaluated versus evaluated practice; critical and creative peer evaluation; conversations with children about their creative productions; the effects of peer pressures in homogeneous and heterogeneous groups; positive, negative, and troubleshooting evaluations; and cultural differences in the way creative characteristics are evaluated.

The final study deals with an attempt to help children value more positively their own original ideas. The final chapter sets forth what I regard as some of the more important practical applications of these studies. It is hoped that the reader will see others that may be more important to him. An additional appendix includes a collection of rather specific ideas for developing the creative thinking abilities through the language arts. This will give the reader a better idea of just what was done in some of the experiments and perhaps some ideas for his own experimentation. Similar collections of ideas could be developed for science, social studies, mathematics, art, music, physical education, and the like.

I am greatly indebted to the former members of the staff of the Bureau of Educational Research of the University of Minnesota who accompanied me at various stages of the adventure from which this book has grown. Contributions of special importance were made by R. E. Myers, now on the faculty of the University of Oregon; Kaoru Yamamoto, now on the faculty of Kent State College; and Dietmar P. Schenitzki, now on the faculty of the State University of New York College at Geneseo. Important contributions were also made by Dorolese Wardwell, Kevser Arsan, John E. Bowers, Gordon R. Eastwood, Roberta Hiller, Noel Iverson, Vincent Johnson, P. R. Krishniah, Balderaj Luther, Necla Palamutlu, and Herman J. Radig.

I am of course immeasurably indebted to the various sources of financial support which made these studies possible: the Cooperative Research Branch of the United States Office of Education of the Department of Health, Education, and Welfare (contract for Project 725, Role of Evaluation in Creative Thinking); the regular budgets of the Bureau of Educational Research and other departments of the College of Education; the Numerical Analysis Center of the University of Minnesota; and those groups which have provided me with honorariums for conducting workshops or lecturing.

I am also grateful to the individuals and publishers who have granted permission without charges to use materials from their publications. These include: J. P. Guilford of the University of Southern California; Jules Henry of Washington University; Fred E. Berger and the University of Minnesota Center for Continuation Study; Hastings House, Publishers, Inc.; Allyn and Bacon, Inc.; and my collaborators, R. E. Myers, Kaoru Yamamoto, and Dietmar Schenitzki.

Perhaps our greatest indebtedness is to the approximately 17,000 subjects who participated in these studies and to the principals and teachers who gave so liberally of their creative energies to the conduct of these studies. All of the royalties which may accrue from the sale of this book will be placed in a special fund for the conduct of additional studies of creative behavior. From the over 20,000 children and young people who have been administered the Minnesota Tests of Creative Thinking by the Bureau of Educational Research, I hope to be able to select 1,000 of the more promising and follow their careers for 15 or 20 years and see what we can learn from their struggle to make creative contributions.

E. P. T.

CONTENTS

REWARDING
CREATIVE
BEHAVIOR

THE
NEED
FOR
REWARDING
CREATIVE
THINKING

1

"What is honored in a country will be cultivated there" (Plato). Plato was neither the first nor the last teacher to discover that people tend to learn and develop along whatever lines they consider rewarding. The truth of Plato's assertion has been validated by dozens of experiments employing modern methods of research. Thus, if we want to develop the creative thinking potential of today's school children, it is reasonably certain that we must somehow learn to reward creative thinking. The problem is not nearly as simple, however, as it would at first appear. Although there is considerable agreement that the educational environment should place a high value upon creative behavior, little is known about the principles whereby such an environment can be created in classrooms, laboratories, and conference rooms.

The purpose of the studies described in this volume has been to search out, formulate, develop, and test principles for (a) creating an environment which places a high value on creativity; (b) guiding the evaluative behavior of teachers, counselors, and administrators; and (c) helping children develop evaluative behavior conducive to creative thinking.

Some believe that a school's grading system, awarding of honors and scholarships, and entire status system should give recognition to creative achievement. Others believe that such practices would disrupt creative processes and that the rewards must come from the enjoyment of the creative process itself.

Concerning evaluative behavior, some authorities maintain that all external evaluation must be absent from the environment which nurtures successfully creative behavior. Others insist that all negative evaluation be made taboo, and still others emphasize the importance of using positive and negative evaluation in order to stimulate and develop creative thinking.

Concerning the evaluative behavior of the creative personality, some advocate a "freewheeling," abandoned, uncritical attitude. Others stress the importance of sensitivity to deficiencies, and still others consider the key to be an attitude of constructive criticism.

From such diverse and virtually untested ideas competing with one another, I formulated the experimental approaches which will be reported in this volume in an attempt to gain information which might contribute in some small way to the resolution of these issues.

Since the term "creative thinking" means such diverse things to different people and since the goals for developing the creative thinking abilities are so frequently forgotten or misunderstood, I shall attempt in this chapter to explain what creative thinking meant to us and what we regard as the goals for developing creative talent.

What Is Meant by Creativity?

DIVERSE DEFINITIONS

Quite justifiably, creativity may be defined in many ways. It is usually defined as a kind of person, product, or process. It may also be defined in terms of an environmental condition. Rhodes (1961) has referred to these four kinds of definitions as the "Four P's of Creativity" (Person, Process, Press, and Products). In attempting to combine these four approaches, Rhodes has defined the word "creativity" as "a noun naming the phenomenon in which a person communicates a new concept (which is the product)" (p. 305). He explains that mental activity (or mental process) is implicit in the definition and that no one could conceive of a person living or operating in a vacuum, so the term "press" is also implicit. He admits that the definition begs the question as to how new the concept must be and to whom it must be new.

NEWNESS AS A CRITERION

The production of something new is included in almost all the definitions given by those who have investigated creative behavior. Thurstone (1952) argued that it does not make any difference whether society regards an idea as novel. He maintained that an act is creative if the thinker reaches the solution in a sudden closure which necessarily implies some novelty for him. To Thurstone, the idea might be artistic, mechanical, or theoretical. It might be administrative if it solves an organizational problem. It might be a new football play, a clever chess move, or a new slogan. Stewart (1950) shares Thurstone's view on this issue, maintaining that productive thinking may occur even though the idea produced may have been produced by someone else at an earlier time. He points out that by this definition productive thinking may take place in the mind of the humblest workman as well as in the most distinguished statesman, artist, or scientist.

Stein (1953), contrary to Thurstone and Stewart, insists that creativity must be defined in terms of the culture in which it appears. To him, "novelty" or "newness" means that the creative product did not exist previously in the same form. It may involve a reintegration of existing materials or knowledge, but it must contain new elements. Stein also believes that to be creative the novel work must be "accepted as tenable or useful or satisfying by a group in time" (1953, p. 322). He hypothesized that studies of the creative person may reveal a sensitivity to the gaps that exist in his own culture and that his creativity may be manifest in calling attention to these gaps. In addition to sensitivity, Stein notes, as characteristics of the creative person, tolerance of ambiguity and ability to maintain direction as hypotheses are tested and refined.

CREATIVITY VERSUS CONFORMITY

A number of investigators (Crutchfield, 1962; Wilson, 1956) have defined creativity by contrasting it with conformity. In general, creativity has been seen as contributing original ideas, different points of view, and new ways of looking at problems. Conformity has been seen as doing what is expected and not disturbing or causing trouble for others. Although Crutchfield (1962) does not attempt to equate independent thinking (which he contrasts with conformity) with creative thinking, he sees the former as necessary for the latter. In his experiments, Crutchfield found that the independent thinkers were able to function effectively under stress, relatively unsusceptible to generalized anxiety, relatively free of feelings of inferiority and inadequacy, open and free in emotional processes, ascendant in relations with others, persuasive, able to mobilize resources easily and effectively, active and vigorous, natural and free from pretense, expressive, and able to seek and enjoy aesthetic and sensuous impressions.

TRUE, GENERALIZABLE, AND SURPRISING: TRIPLE REQUIREMENTS

Selye (1962) in his definition requires that basic discoveries or creative contributions possess to a high degree and simultaneously three qualities. He states, "They are true not merely as facts but also in the way they are interpreted, they are generalizable, and they are surprising in the light of what was known at the time of the discovery" (1962, p. 402).

H. H. Anderson (1959) also emphasizes the search for the truth and living truthfully as part of his definition of creativity. He is especially insistent that the creative environment must provide freedom for each person to respond truthfully with his whole person as he sees and understands the truth.

To Ferren (1953) the creative product must represent a successful step into the unknown. Bartlett (1958) employs the term "adventurous thinking," which he defines as "getting away from the main track, breaking out of the mold, being open to experience, and permitting one thing to lead to another" (1958, p. 203).

DEFINITIONS INVOLVING PROCESS

A number of approaches have been suggested by those who have studied creative thinking as a mental process. Spearman (1930), for example, saw creative thinking basically as a process of seeing or creating relationships, with both conscious and subconscious processes operating. According to one of his principles, when two or more precepts or ideas are given, a person may perceive them to be in various ways related (near, after, the cause of, the result of, a part of, etc.). Another principle held that when any item and a relation to it are cognized, then the mind can generate in itself another item so related.

Ribot (1906) and others after him have emphasized the capacity of thinking by analogy as the essential, fundamental element of creative thinking. He maintains that the process of analogizing gives rise to the most unforeseen and novel combinations, but he warns that it produces in equal measure absurd comparisons and very original inventions. Recognizing the nonrational aspects of creative thinking, a number of investigators have called attention to the exercise of discrimination and choice as a part of the creative process. Barchillon (1961), for example, says that the thinking processes involved in creation are of two kinds: *cogito*, to shake and throw things together; and *intelligo*, to choose and discriminate from many alternative possibilities and then synthesize and bind together elements in new and original ways. What he has in mind by *cogito* is apparently similar to what Kubie (1958) conceptualizes as taking place in the "preconscious system." The preconscious is apparently able to scan quickly experiences and memories, to condense, join opposites, and find relationships at speeds impossible to obtain in the conscious system. The resulting intuitions, however, are not very precise and are subject to the primary process type of thinking.

MENTAL ABILITIES APPROACH

Guilford (1956, 1959b, 1960) has conceptualized creativity in terms of the mental abilities involved in creative achievement. In his well-known structure of the intellect, he sees creative thinking as clearly involving what he categorizes as divergent production. He defines divergent production as the generation of information from given information, where the emphasis is upon variety of output from the same source (innovation, originality, unusual synthesis or perspective). Included in the divergent thinking category are the factors of fluency, flexibility, originality, and elaboration. He has concluded, however, that creative thinking cannot be equated with divergent thinking. He believes that the redefinition abilities and sensitivity to problems are also important in creative thinking. The redefinition abilities involve transformations of thought, reinterpretations, and freedom from functional fixedness in deriving unique solutions. Sensitivity to problems seems to be essential in getting the creative thinking process in motion.

LEVELS OF CREATIVITY

I. A. Taylor (1959) has sought to reconcile some of the apparent differences in opinion concerning creativity by suggesting that we think of creativity in terms of various levels. He suggests the following five levels:

1. *Expressive creativity.* Independent expression where skills, originality, and the quality of the product are unimportant, as in the spontaneous drawings of children
2. *Productive creativity.* Artistic or scientific products where there is a tendency to restrict and control free play and develop techniques for producing finished products
3. *Inventive creativity.* Inventors, explorers, and discoverers, where ingenuity is displayed with materials, methods, and techniques

4. *Innovative creativity.*   Improvement through modification involving conceptualizing skills
5. *Emergentive creativity.*   An entirely new principle or assumption around which new schools flourish

Taylor points out that many people have this fifth level in mind when they talk about creativity. Since this fifth level of creative behavior is so rare, the lower levels have usually been involved in most of the investigations concerning creative behavior. Taylor also objects to the frequent confusion of creativity and prevalent interpretations of traditional logic, scientific method, and intelligence. He maintains that fantasy associations and relaxation for unconscious play are so essential for creative thought that creativity cannot be subjected to the same interpretations as logic and scientific method.

Inventive creativity, Taylor's third level, has perhaps been subjected to more systematic definition and specification of criteria than any of the other levels. Inventors' rights to their discoveries are specified by Article 1, Section 8, of the Constitution of the United States. Thus, we have patent laws, passed by Congress and implemented by the U. S. Patent Office, which have made an effort to spell out the criteria by which the inventive level of a patent application can be assessed (Cochran, 1955). The Patent Office grants patents only for invention. This means that newness itself is not enough. The thing must not have been known before and must be useful. It must amount to an invention or discovery. In general, one is considered to have invented something if he has originated a thing of merit which others skilled in the art or science to which it relates would not have thought of or would not have known how to achieve if they had thought of it. The originator is entitled to a patent only if he discloses an invention which is not already within the knowledge of the public. The following are some criteria which have been decided upon as indicating lack of novelty or lack of invention:

1. Changes requiring only mechanical skill
2. Change in size
3. Duplication of parts of a device
4. Omission of an element of a device or step of a method
5. Reversal of parts
6. Change of material
7. Use of old process or method to a different but analogous object or material
8. Making a device adjustable
9. Change in an element of an old combination
10. Aggregation of elements

Exceptions occur in almost all of these general negative tests, if the device overcomes prior failure or some special difficulty, offers something remarkable or surprising, overcomes prior skepticism about possible success, or meets an unfulfilled need. It should be apparent that most of these criteria can be adapted to apply to a variety of creative products. In fact, they have been adapted for evaluating some of the products involved in certain experiments described in this report.

APPROACHES THROUGH STUDIES OF CREATIVE PERSONS

Using a rather elaborate approach, MacKinnon (1962) and his associates identified highly creative people in such diverse fields as architecture, writing, mathematics, and industrial research. They then did elaborate personality studies of these highly creative people contrasting them with their less creative peers.

MacKinnon has characterized the highly creative architect as follows: dominant, possessed of those qualities and attributes which underlie and lead to the achievement of social status, poised and spontaneous in personal and social interaction, not especially sociable or participative, outspoken and sharp-witted, aggressive and self-centered, persuasive and verbally fluent, self-confident, self-assured, and relatively uninhibited in expressing worries and complaints. He is relatively free from conventional restraints and inhibitions, not preoccupied with the impressions he makes on others, and able to recognize and admit unusual and unconventional self-views. He is highly motivated to achieve in situations where independence in thought and action are required and less highly motivated than his peers to achieve in situations requiring conforming behavior. He is also more flexible psychologically and cognitively and more feminine in his interests than architects in general. He is highly perceptive, open to richness and complexity of experience, and has a preference for perceptual complexity. He has a greater tolerance of complexity and disorder and a stronger preference for perceiving than for judging. He prefers intuitive perception over sense perception and is more likely to be introverted than extroverted. He cares little about being included in a group and in general prefers to be left alone, yet tends to act in a dominant manner in social interaction. His dominant values, as measured by the Allport-Vernon-Lindzey *Study of Values*, are theoretical and aesthetic.

CHOICE OF A RESEARCH DEFINITION

An analysis of the diverse ways of defining creativity which have been cited thus far will reveal that these definitions do not divide them-

enulion

selves neatly into the categories of "person, process, product, and press." It is true that some definitions emphasize one or the other of these categories, but almost all somehow spill over into more categories. Thus, it seems inevitable to me that a thorough understanding of creativity must involve the study of all four aspects of creativity (person, process, product, and press). It is obvious that an investigator must at any one time focus on one aspect and then on another, always being alert to the other three aspects of creativity. As the focus of thinking, I have chosen a process definition, but in the experiments described in this volume the focus of investigation has been on the "press" or environment. If we define creativity as a process, we can then ask what kind of person one must be in order to engage most successfully in the process, what kinds of environment he needs in order to function most successfully, and what kinds of products result from the process.

I have tried to describe creative thinking as taking place in the process of sensing difficulties, problems, gaps in information, missing elements; making guesses or formulating hypotheses about these deficiencies; testing these guesses and possibly revising and retesting them; and finally in communicating the results. I like this definition because it describes such a natural process. Strong human needs appear to be at the basis of each of its stages. If we sense any incompleteness, something missing or out of place, tension is aroused. We are uncomfortable and want to do something to relieve the tension. As a result, we begin investigating, asking questions, manipulating things, making guesses, and the like. Until the guesses or hypotheses have been tested, modified, and retested, we are still uncomfortable. Then, even when this has been accomplished, the tension is usually unrelieved until we tell somebody what we have discovered. Throughout the process there is an element of responding constructively to existing or new situations, rather than merely adapting to them. Such a definition places creativity in the realm of daily living and does not reserve it for ethereal and rarely achieved heights of creation.

To illustrate this process, I sometimes give an audience as it assembles one of the tests we have developed for assessing the creative thinking abilities, such as the Incomplete Figures Test. After a while, I check with them to find out what has happened. Most of them will admit that the incompleteness or some other quality of the figures had made them uncomfortable. Usually some of them have gone ahead and completed the figures in some way, either by actually drawing lines or imaginatively by thinking of ways to complete the figures. I then ask them to go ahead and complete the figures in some way that will be satisfying to them. There is usually almost no reluctance, even in the most staid audience. Rather, there is an obvious atmosphere of relief, increased liveliness, even smiles and laughter. There is also a spontaneous interest in communicating the results and seeing what everyone else has created.

If the thinking of the audience is bound to some specific curricular content, such as reading, art, science, or language arts, I try to show how the process operates with that specific curricular content. For example, let us take the problem of reading creatively. When anyone reads creatively, he must first of all become sensitive to the problems and possibilities involved in whatever he reads. He makes himself aware of the gaps in knowledge, unsolved problems, missing elements, and things that are incomplete or out of focus. To resolve this tension, the creative reader sees new relationships, creates new combinations, synthesizes relatively unrelated elements into coherent wholes, redefines or transforms certain pieces of information to discover new uses, and builds onto what is known. In this search, the creative reader produces a variety of possibilities, uses a great variety of approaches, looks at the available information in a variety of ways, breaks away from commonplace solutions into bold new ways, and develops his idea by filling in the details and making the idea attractive or exciting to others.

If at this point I want to communicate something about the qualities of the creative product, I ask my audience to discuss the qualities of the products which they have just produced. In addition to the divergent thinking qualities (fluency or number of ideas, flexibility or shifts in approaches, originality or statistical infrequency of the idea, and elaboration or the amount of detail or completeness manifested), we talk about such qualities as penetration or the mental leap from the stimulus to the response, the degree to which the idea communicates, and the like.

In order to communicate something of the importance of the press or environment, I have on several occasions conducted a tape-recorded exercise created by Cunnington and myself (1962), called "Sounds and Images." It has built into it several "presses," applications of research findings which have been discovered to facilitate originality of thinking. The tape recording consists of four different sound effects, ranging from an easily recognizable familiar one, having few "missing elements," to a strange one made up of six relatively unrelated sounds. This set of four sound effects is presented with a slight pause between each with instructions to the listener to write down a word picture of the image generated by the sound effect. The sound effects are then repeated with instructions to let the imagination roam more widely and depart from the most obvious images. After this, the sound effects are repeated a third time with instructions to let the imagination swing free. An attempt is made to free the audience from threats of evaluation and to encourage it to "have fun." An attempt is also made to break the "set" between each of the repetitions of the sound effects. Finally, the audience is asked to select its favorite image or word picture and translate it into a picture. I then ask the members of the audience to describe what they had experienced, trying to identify what features of the environment (the taped exercise, the situation, etc.) facilitated or inhibited their efforts to think of original images. They quickly identify such things as the warm-up process, going from the easy to the difficult, the legitimacy of thinking divergently, freedom from the threat of evaluation, and the like.

If I want to communicate something of the importance of the person, I identify built-in environmental features and then ask the audience to identify those forces in themselves which facilitated or inhibited them in making use of these built-in features. This usually results in a lengthy list of personality factors (most of which have been found to be related to creative behavior), and hopefully in an increased awareness by the audience of its own creative potential and an increased understanding of the forces in individual personalities which influence their creative functioning and those of their associates.

Why Is Creative Thinking Important?

Among educators, there are those who look upon creative thinking in the school as threatening and dangerous, while others see it as a powerful force for lifting man to higher levels of intellectual functioning, human dignity, and achievement. To some extent both groups are justified in their attitudes. Creative thinking is indeed a powerful force. It has given us the alphabet, printing, radio, television, computers, and spacecraft. It has given us our great art, architecture, music, and literature. It has given us our great advances in scientific discovery and medicine. It has also given us war, plunder, crime, and the smashed atom.

RELATEDNESS TO EDUCATIONAL GOALS

As we formulated plans for the experiments described in this report, it was our dream that by achieving a better understanding of the human mind and the conditions which facilitate its full functioning, we might provide some of the information needed to fashion a more humane kind of education which will give every child a better chance than he now has to achieve his potentialities.

As our research evidence continued to accumulate (Torrance, 1962a), it became clear that creative thinking is important in mental health, educational achievement, vocational success, and many other important areas in life. As we studied creative behavior among both children and adults, it became increasingly clear that perhaps nothing could contribute more to the general welfare of our nation and the satisfactions and mental health of its people than a general raising of the level of creative behavior. There is little doubt but that the prolonged and severe stifling of creative thinking cuts at the very roots of satisfaction in living. This must inevitably create overwhelming tension and break-down.

Of course, there are those who are quick to point out that creative thinking leads only to trouble in the classroom. They say that children are very imaginative and inventive in their lying, that they cheat and steal in very ingenious ways, and that they disturb classroom organization and procedures with their unusual ideas. They insist that all of these are signs of a mentally unhealthy person. Almost always, if they are honest, they will find that these socially disapproved manifestations of creative thinking ability are linked with a lack of guidance or with coercive and overly punitive discipline. This does not mean that lying, cheating, and other socially undesirable behavior must be permitted to flourish. We do need to recognize that these undesirable behaviors may indicate valuable potentialities, which, if properly guided and developed, may lead to socially valued achievements.

PSYCHOTHERAPEUTIC GOALS

A number of writers have called attention to the healing values of creative activities. Wilt (1959), for example, maintains that there is therapeutic value in permitting a child to tell his own story in his own way. She declares, "It may be a chimney to carry away the smoke, an escape valve for the pent-up steam" (1959, p. 2). Such creative activities, she believes, will provide children under stress a legitimate, socially acceptable way to reduce the pressure. Through the creative activities of the child, teachers can gain a better understanding of children, and children can gain increased insights into their own behavior. Through these activities, the child reveals himself to his peers, and they reveal themselves to him, helping him to develop realistic concepts of himself and others.

Kubie warns, however, that merely being creative is not enough to protect us from mental illness or to cure us. Nevertheless, he too insists that "under appropriately devised circumstances creative activities can be used as one ingredient in the therapeutic process" (1958, p. 2). In fact, it might be argued that the goal in almost all of the major schools of psychotherapy is to aid individuals to become more creative, so that they can cope more adequately with the stresses of their lives.

SOCIAL IMPORTANCE

Social

We have tried never to lose sight of the social importance of creative thinking. This concept deserves special consideration in a world of stepped-up cultural change, explosion of knowledge, population explosion, and the like. We must be warned continually that the world is changing so fast that past "truths" often mislead instead of help. No longer is it easy to apply past truths to the problems of the present and the future. Today's world "calls for new approaches to experience, both in acquiring it and in using what we already have" (Stevens, 1963, p. 56). It is obviously impossible to prepare today's school children to cope with all the demands they will encounter, for all the changes they will experience. The occupations in which many of them will earn their livelihood do not even exist today. It is foolish to believe that we can impart to children all the facts and skills they will need. One obvious solution is to give them the motivations, the basic foundation, and the skills for continuing to learn for the rest of their lives.

Why Is It Important
that Creative Thinking Be Rewarded?

Although there are still many people who believe it is unnecessary to reward creative talent, most reasonable people recognize, at least at a superficial level, the need for rewarding creative thinking. It is true that there are some children with vigorous creative imaginations who maintain their creativity in spite of rejection, ridicule, and coercion, but the early phases of our studies of creative thinking in children yielded many indications that this is a prodigiously wasteful philosophy. We saw many children who had given numerous evidences of a powerful creative talent one year, deliberately and obviously sacrificing and suppressing this talent the next year. As the evidence from longitudinal and cross-cultural developmental studies of the creative thinking abilities began to accumulate, it became clearer and clearer that creativity needs to be energized and guided almost from birth. If it is stifled early, apparently it will only become imitative if it survives at all. The vigorous creative imaginations which survive early stifling and opposition may become dangerous to society and civilization, if they learn only to act vigorously without guidance.

We soon discovered that we were not alone in our observations and conclusions concerning the need for rewarding creative thinking. Barkan (1960) came to such a conclusion through intensive observations and analyses of children's behavior in elementary school art ac-

ivities. He observed that children are attentive to the reactions of other
people. If their inventions and ideas are viewed with interest, children
are encouraged to create more ideas. If their efforts are unnoticed or
rejected, children lose confidence in their ability to create. They depend
upon the ideas of others. Pepinsky (1959) came to a somewhat similar
conclusion as a result of intensive studies in three natural organizations,
a college campus, a research organization, and a planned community.
She points out the need for patrons or sponsors who can protect the
creative person whose ideas are ignored or rejected until he can work
them out and make them productive. She also identified some of the
strategies of productive independence. Buhl (1961) in a study of
creative engineers found that their families encouraged them to discuss
ideas with parents and friends and permitted them to try out some of
their original ideas and to pursue independent interests.

We need to examine the reasons why it is important to reward
creative thinking, since many aspects of our educational and social
system actively discourage and inhibit such thinking. Many people feel
that education has become highly standardized and discourages uniqueness. The pervasiveness of the problem in education and society is suggested by Rousseau's analysis (1962) of the ways in which giftedness
is handled in Rhodesia and Nyasaland. He points out that alertness and
questioning may irritate teachers and that in some African languages a
"clever" child is one who is docile and conforms. He warned that the
teacher's docile pet seldom turns out to be the industrial tycoon.

A number of American educators for some years have been advocating evaluative procedures which would give greater rewards for
creative behavior. Handlin (1962) believes that current grading or
evaluation systems encourage memory, accuracy, neatness, and cau-
tiousness, but rarely call upon students to use their ability independently
or speculatively to deal with situations in which the answers are not
known but must be discovered. Because of the premiums placed upon
teachers' grades, Handlin states that only the reckless will dare not to
know the right answer as the grader expects them or dare allow questions to draw their thinking in unexpected directions. Many high school
and college students have put down on examinations answers which
they know to be incorrect, because they knew or thought that the
grader did not know the correct answer.

The Overstreets (1954) would see the rewarding of creative thinking as a counteractant to the forces which discourage self-initiated
learning. They observe that at the stage in life when we insist that a
child learn what we want him to learn, we discourage his learning what
he wants to learn by our ill-placed humor, irritation, or evasiveness. At
this stage some children give up trying to learn anything and begin to
fail in school. Ojemann (1961), on the basis of his distinguished work
in the field of mental health, believes that our difficulty in rewarding

creative thinking arises from a lack of the basic orientation needed to appreciate individual differences. He believes that creativity and mental health will become compatible and mutually reinforcing when a person develops a basic causal orientation to his social environment

One of the reasons why deliberate efforts to reward creative behavior may be necessary is that creativity is perceived as a threat especially to those in authority. Toynbee (1962) identifies two inimical forces to creativity: (a) an incorrect view of the function of democracy to neutralize outstanding ability and (b) vested interests. Pepinsky (1959), in her study of productive independence in three situations, found that an organization or a group will tolerate and even reward "a few, but not too many" individuals who do not conform to the established standards. The number tolerated or rewarded apparently depends upon the extent to which the creative minority constitutes a disturbing challenge to entrenched beliefs, vested interests, "duly constituted" authority, and the accepted "way of life."

Some educators would reward creative behavior because they see in it a powerful motivation for learning. A number of contemporary learning theories stress the point that young children derive a powerful impetus to learning from their tendency to explore unknown situations, seek challenges which make use of freshly won skills, and deliberately find problems at the edge of their capacities (Rubin, 1963). A considerable number of educational psychologists believe that these motivations can be kept alive throughout a person's life-time and continue to serve an important role in learning. Some, like Strang (1959), believe that one solution is to include in the examinations in all subjects problems that call for creative responses rather than mere feats of memory and reproduction of facts. Others believe that it is necessary for all educators from kindergarten through graduate school to be alert to new ideas and to encourage those who produce new ideas to make the most of their abilities. Obviously, however, there are some types of so-called creative thinking which should be regarded with alarm. This is the kind which is based on false premises, distorts the truth, and fails to test hypotheses.

Conclusion

In this chapter, an effort has been made to describe what is meant by creative thinking, why creative thinking is important, and why it is important that creative thinking be rewarded. It is against this background that we ask the reader to evaluate and to interpret the studies which will be described in the chapters to follow. In the next chapter, an effort will be made to sketch the structure within which these studies fit.

PLAN
FOR STUDYING
EVALUATION
AND
CREATIVE
THINKING

2

As we became immersed in data concerning the lives of eminent creative people and as we attempted to observe and study the creative behavior of children and graduate students, it seemed to us that there are three aspects to the role of evaluation that we must study:

1. The way the society or immediate environment values creative behavior
2. The evaluative behavior of one's teachers, parents, and peers
3. A person's evaluation of his own creative behavior

In adopting this strategy, we did not intend to deny the importance of genetic factors. In fact, we had been doing and have continued to do many of the things that the investigator committed to a genetic approach would do. A person's creative thinking ability obviously is going to be influenced by the fact that he inherits his sense organs, peripheral nervous system, and brains. A person's environment is such a powerful influence on his curiosity and creativity needs, however, that it may greatly diminish the influence of genetic factors. At least, it seemed justifiable to adopt an environmental emphasis for the present series of studies.

An emphasis upon environmental factors leads to studies in which an attempt is made to change creative behavior. Thus, in the studies reported in this volume we shall not be looking for enduring personality traits which characterize individuals. Instead, we shall be looking for environmental factors which affect creative performance within an individual, either negatively or positively.

In this chapter I shall try to present some background ideas about each of the three aspects of evaluation already mentioned and to sketch the questions which the present studies attempt to answer.

The Environment
Which Values Creative Behavior

THE INHIBITING ENVIRONMENT

It is an almost obvious fact that creative behavior is not likely to flourish in an environment which is hostile or indifferent to creative achievement. M. S. Allen (1962) offers, from his boyhood experiences, the interesting analogy of facing an icy blast as he stepped out of the kitchen door of his Massachusetts home on a winter morning. He says that his reaction was to cover up a little more completely. He then points out that an idea that meets an icy blast is likewise painful to the producer. He tends to cover up and to withhold excellent ideas as well as ideas that are different. A person soon learns that it is better not to express his most precious ideas in an unfriendly environment.

The slowness with which investigators have been willing to study creative behavior may be a reflection of the value that society has placed upon such behavior. Ribot called attention to the neglect of creative imagination as a subject of study in 1906. At that time he maintained that the study of "creative or constructive imagination" had been almost entirely neglected. The best, most complete, and most recent treatises on psychology at that time either failed to mention creativity or devoted scarcely a page or two to the topic. He reported that a few articles and a few brief, scarce monographs made up the sum of the past twenty-five years' work on the subject. In 1950, Guilford, as president of the American Psychological Association, called attention to education's neglect of creativity. He reported that up to 1950 only 0.2 per cent of the titles in the *Psychological Abstracts* were in any way concerned with creativity. Osborn in 1948 called attention to this neglect and has continued to do so through his more recent books (1957, 1963) and the activities of the Creative Education Foundation.

The unfriendliness of the environment to creative behavior seems to be manifested by a decrease in certain kinds of creative behaviors with increasing age. Art teachers commonly state that the art techniques of young children are more like those of professional artists than are those of older children. Some workers have observed that the poetry, songs, and stories composed by young children are more crea-ive than those of older children. Even the vocal behavior of young children is more like that of great vocal artists than is the vocal behavior of older children. If creative products are not received with appreciation and respect, creative talents do not develop.

Many investigators have tried to show that by making whole areas of experience taboo, a culture inhibits creative potential (Murphy, 1958; Rogers, 1954). They do not have in mind a life lacking in discipline and order. They have in mind the need for openness to experience, a willingness to entertain and to test new ideas, to permit one thing to lead to another in thinking. Mead (1959) believes that we are too dependent for our original thinking on persons who have been accidentally isolated. Such persons, she maintains, are rarely able to function in a team, and creative achievements in the future will become increasingly dependent upon team efforts. She insists that our present ways of rearing children prepare them for team work but not to do the individual work which makes a team worthwhile.

Many social institutions and practices have been singled out as contributors to an unfriendly environment for creative behavior. One of these is higher education and its admission and evaluation procedures. In 1960, Getzels charged that the usual criteria used in college admission (tests, recommendations, and rank in class) are biased in favor of the student with "convergent" intellectual ability and social interests. His contention was that students with superior "divergent" intellectual ability may in the long run prove to be more creative and that such students deserve a place in college along with the superior convergent student. In 1961, Mednick made a similar charge, maintaining that many of our most eminent creative people would never have been admitted to college if selection techniques had reached the current state of technology at the time they had applied for admission. He contended that by evolving a "race of grade getters we have bred some extremely desirable characteristics *out* of our college population" (1961, p. 86).

At about this same time, the National Merit Scholarship Corporation (Holland and Kent, 1960) began recognizing that many of their scholarships might be going to the wrong persons. Later, this organization established a program for giving scholarships to two categories of students who would not otherwise have been awarded such financial aid: (a) students with high creative promise and (b) students who are truly outstanding in some one field but less outstanding in others. Follow-up studies of these awards will test the wisdom of this practice.

Another way in which the environment has failed to reward creative behavior has been in assuming that creativeness is the sole prerogative of certain professionals—artists, musicians, scientists, and the like. Maslow (1962) describes how his own views changed on this point as he began to study what he calls self-actualizing people. He describes one woman—uneducated, poor, a full-time housewife and mother—who did none of the conventionally creative things. As cook, mother, wife, and homemaker she was original, novel, ingenious, unexpected, and inventive. Maslow said that he just had to call her creative and that he had learned a first-rate soup is more creative than a second-rate painting or poem.

Riessman (1962) has examined this problem from the perspective of the culturally deprived child. He believes that what the culturally deprived child needs and does not receive is respect. Too many people in society at large deprecate him and laugh at him. Thus, it may be that our deprecation of certain categories of people (such as women, Negroes, and culturally deprived children) may be causing us to lose much creative talent and to reduce the general level of creative behavior in our society. Such a clue comes from Wylie's study (1963) of the self-evaluative tendencies according to sex, race, and socio-economic status. She found that girls think less of their own mental ability than do boys, that Negro children underestimate their mental ability more than do white children, and that children of lower socio-economic levels think less of their ability than children of upper levels. Wylie's conclusions are based on comparisons of self-estimates with actual performances on tests of mental ability. Although there are many possible explanations of these findings, it is quite likely that the reason may be that society in general deprecates girls more than boys, Negroes more than whites, and children from lower socio-economic levels more than those from upper levels. In other words, society teaches certain types of children that they are not as good as other children and erroneously gives them more cause for feeling inferior and for failing to develop their talents.

QUESTIONS ABOUT EVALUATION
IN THE LARGER ENVIRONMENT

Of the many questions which we might have investigated concerning education's problem of creating an environment which places a high value on creative behavior, we chose the following, each of which will be discussed further in subsequent chapters:

1. To what extent do teachers reward or respect creative thinking in the classroom and what happens when they make a deliberate effort to do so?
2. In talking with children about their creative work, do teachers recognize and respect creative thinking?

3. Can teachers be trained to value creative thinking in the class-room so that their pupils will show greater growth in their ability to do creative thinking than will the pupils of their col-leagues not so trained?
4. Does the teacher's own creative attitude affect the creative growth of his pupils?
5. To what extent does official sanction by the school principal affect the initiation of creative activities and creative growth among pupils?
6. Does the initiation of creative activities, irrespective of other factors, produce growth in creative thinking?
7. In what ways is the creative thinking of boys and girls rewarded differently?

External Evaluation

POWER OF TEACHER EVALUATION

In dealing with external evaluation, we shall be concerned primarily about the evaluative behavior of the teacher and the evalua-tive climate fostered by the teacher. It is my impression that teachers generally underestimate the power of their evaluative behavior on the lives of their pupils. Teachers influence pupils through the kinds of tests they give, the way they react to the questions children ask and the ideas they produce, the grades they assign, the assignments they make, even their wording in making an assignment. In administering tests of creative thinking we have noticed how greatly slight differences in the wording of our instructions influence what the children will pro-duce. For example, in administering a test which involves making a picture using a colored triangle as a major part, about 90 per cent of the children in the first grade will ordinarily use the triangle as the roof of a house. If we ask them to think of a picture that they think no one else in the class will think of and assure them that if they use their own ideas that what they produce will quite likely be different from the drawings of the others, almost none of them will make the triangle a housetop.

Similar findings have been reported by other investigators. Hyman (1960), for example, found a significant increase in the number of unique responses when "be creative" instructions were given to engineers as compared to the ideas they produced under "be practical" instruc-tions. Datta (1963), using a somewhat similar procedure, found that performance on tests of creative thinking can be significantly influenced by instructions. Most interesting, however, she found that the neutral instructions usually given in administering tests of creative thinking may decrease the power of the tests to discriminate among more or less creative individuals. In other words, the more creative individuals more than the less creative individuals tend to inhibit their creative thinking, unless they feel confident that original ideas will be acceptable.

Since children apparently are influenced greatly by the evaluative behavior of teachers, incorrect evaluations can be as powerful as correct ones. Having erroneous evaluations causes teachers to behave toward children as though they have attitudes, abilities, and skills which they do not in fact have. I know of one student whose IQ and classroom number were transposed on his cumulative record card. As a result, his teachers and counselors treated him as though he were mentally retarded, although his IQ was actually 140. His teachers and counselors discouraged him from attempting learning tasks which interested him. As a result, the boy had to seek the guidance of a college professor in a nearby college in pursuing his interests in science. At the time the boy was in the seventh and eighth grade, the college professor said that he wished his undergraduate science majors knew as much science as this youngster who was being treated as a retardate by his teachers. Fortunately this boy was able to find positive evaluation outside of his school and continued to learn as shown by outstandingly high scores on the science and mathematics College Board Examinations and by eight major awards at a national, state, and regional level for creative achievement in science. His school grades continued to be poor, however, and his fellow students continued to regard him as a "dumbbell."

Lichter, Rapien, Seibert, and Sklansky (1962) have called attention, in their drop-out study, to the problem of altering the schools' attitudes towards the youngsters. They found that even though a youngster had changed through counseling and altered circumstances, teachers continued to perceive him as a troublemaker. They observed that the materials in cumulative record folders prejudiced the attitudes of new teachers and led them to discipline these youngsters far out of proportion to the offenses. In our longitudinal studies of the development of the creative thinking abilities, I have observed amazing changes in a child's behavior after the teacher had learned that the child had made a high score on the test of creative thinking. The child had been considered a kind of hopeless case and had been relegated to the little group placed in the rear of the classroom to keep them from interfering with the classroom organization and procedures. Somewhat skeptically but perhaps influenced by the "authority" of a score on a test of "creative thinking," the teacher began to ask the child questions which formerly he would not have thought of asking. As a result the teacher found that the child was learning more and was capable of a higher level of thinking than he had imagined.

Perhaps children would not be so greatly influenced by a single teacher's evaluative behavior but for the fact that the teacher's evaluation also colors the evaluations of peers. Friedenberg (1959) believes that it is the relentless criticism and mockery of the peer group stimulated by the teacher which stamps out the originality and feeling expressed in children's writing. Teachers encourage children to be "carping" critics of one another's work, but they do not have to encourage it so much. An example is given of one teacher who, perceiving an element of genuine literary merit in a child's writing, tried to arrest the flow of criticism and mockery long enough to point it out. But she was unable to do so. The evaluative behavior she had unleashed had gotten out of control.

Much of the evaluative behavior of teachers appears to be designed to enable the teacher to control or coerce conformity to behavioral norms. Such evaluative behavior is not likely to have a positive influence upon any kind of truly creative behavior. Some teachers, like Mearns (1941), have observed that it is only when the child is convinced you are not trying to reform him that he is able to open up and behave creatively. Mearns found that when children realized he was there to enjoy and to share their productions, "they opened up a surprise box of truthful observation and offered wise deductions that belied their years" (1941, p. 3). Much scattered evidence suggests that creative thinking flourishes most when students feel that the teacher is on their side. Handlin (1962) believes that having to give grades subjugates the teaching role to the grading role. He contends that it destroys the intimacy of the relationship between the teacher and student. The student becomes afraid to turn to the teacher, fearing that he will be evaluated in the process.

Generally it has been thought that teachers should provide a stimulating environment to elicit creative thinking. This concept is compatible with the stimulus-response theory of learning. Other writers, like Applegate (1949), maintain that children will often react more creatively to teachers who are receptive than to those who are continually stimulating.

EVALUATION AND THE RESPONSIVE ENVIRONMENT

There has been much misunderstanding about what is involved in creating a responsive environment for creative thinking. Some equate it with permissiveness. Others equate it with a *laissez-faire* approach. Actually, the creation of a responsive environment involves a great deal of guidance, as will be indicated by the following characteristics identified by Ferebee (1950, p. 78):

1. Building an atmosphere of receptive listening
2. Relieving the fears of the timid and the overtaught
3. Fending off negative criticism
4. Making children aware of what is good
5. Stirring the sluggish and deepening the shallow
6. Making sure that every sincere effort, however poorly executed, brings enough satisfaction to the child to enable him to want to try again
7. Heightening sensory awareness
8. Keeping alive zest in creative activity
9. Being wise enough to halt the activity temporarily when creativity runs thin

A basic problem in providing a responsive environment is that many teachers do not genuinely respect individual differences. Some well-meaning ones think that they are being respectful of differences when they are merely *tolerating* them. As Jefferson (1959) suggests, merely tolerating differences indicates that the differences are distasteful and that we have to put up with them. Respect cannot be shown until the teacher recognizes that each child is unique and is glad to have the daily opportunity of enjoying the expression and development of each child's uniqueness.

QUESTIONS ABOUT EXTERNAL EVALUATION

Out of this background of issues and problems, we selected for exploration and testing the following questions:

1. How does the nature of the adult's evaluative behavior given during a practice or exploratory period affect the quantity and quality of the productive thinking of children in subsequent and related activities?
2. Is an initial period of experimentation and testing of ideas without external evaluation more conducive than immediate external evaluation in the subsequent production of original ideas?
3. Is peer discussion of defects following a practice exercise more conducive than peer discussion concerning constructive possibilities to the subsequent production of original ideas?
4. Does competition stimulate creative thinking?
5. What strategies do members of small groups of children use

in controlling the production of their more creative members and what counterstrategies do creative persons employ in coping with the coercive strategies of the group?

6. How does homogeneous and heterogeneous grouping affect the strategies of small groups in controlling their most creative members?

7. What type of evaluative thinking characterizes the behavior of effective teachers, as assessed by pupil learning?

Evaluative Behavior of the Individual

NEGLECT IN DEVELOPMENT
OF SELF-EVALUATION SKILLS

In view of the value which society places upon self-confidence, it might be regarded as surprising that educational procedures give so little attention to pupils judging the value of their own work. Teachers usually do all of the evaluating and perhaps get more experience in evaluating the work of others than any person should have. Many students of human behavior (Rogers, 1951; Maslow, 1954; Murphy, 1961) have given a place of great importance to the self-concept as a determinant of behavior. Both as a condition for constructive creative behavior and for psychotherapy, the internal locus of evaluation has been emphasized by Rogers. He feels that the value of a product is established by the creative person himself. Boraas (1922) maintained that next to the ability to produce an idea or some other piece of work is the ability to estimate its worth. Murphy (1961) believes that to free children to achieve their potentialities, teachers must help them to believe in their own individuality and their capacity to learn.

In spite of this overwhelming sentiment among psychologists and educators concerning the importance of the self-concept in creative behavior, there is little empirical evidence outside the clinical field to indicate that there is a relationship between self-concept and creative functioning. An interesting study reported by Sears (1960) does supply some evidence for such a relationship among boys in the middle childhood years. Her data indicate that high self-concept boys, as compared with the low, made higher scores on several tests of creative thinking, scored higher on need achievement, showed a more favorable attitude toward school subjects and activities, and were rated higher by their teachers in intrinsic interest. They did not differ, however, on achievement test reading scores, being liked by others, and observed work habits. These results suggest that creative behavior may be more dependent than school learning upon the self-evaluative behavior of the individual.

SELF-CONCEPT AND CREATIVE BEHAVIOR

The development of the self-concept as it relates to one's creative powers is a continuous process and does not result from a single earth-shaking experience. Griffiths (1945), who studied the development of the imagination in early childhood, describes it as a process of continually measuring one's strength against external forces. She found that children experiment continually and learn by hard and bitter experience what they are capable of doing. A critical stage in this development is when the child for the first time begins to recognize his personal separateness. Before this, children presume that all people think and see alike, namely as they themselves do. Immature adults either maintain this viewpoint, believing that everyone thinks as they do, or reach a point when they are unable and unwilling to trust their own perceiving and thinking and depend completely upon someone else.

Many of those who work with college students and adults maintain that there are too many people who depend entirely upon authorities outside of themselves for all thinking. There are many clues that this difficulty springs from the many things in society and education which interfere with a child's struggle to build up a schematic view of his own. We are too unwilling to take risks with them, too unwilling to permit them to learn how to fail intelligently. An inventor may try and fail a thousand times, whereas the student who fails once is out. Apparently very young children can learn to evaluate their own work (A. Allen, 1963).

The handling of a number of socially disapproved kinds of behavior also seems to have a great deal to do with a child's self-concept of himself as a creative person. One such problem is that of copying from other children. Jefferson (1959) insists that when children are made to feel proud of their independence, they will not want to copy ideas from others. She also feels that the child has a right to protection against having his ideas used or copied by another. Lying is one type of creative—or at least imaginative—behavior which is socially criticized. Our social disapproval of such behavior may blind us to its true meaning to the child—a creative, though disapproved of, solution to a problem. Although a teacher may disapprove of such behavior, she might at least recognize in it the manifestation of an ability which, if properly guided and developed, might be quite useful.

The importance of having a strong self-concept is reflected in a number of the findings from studies of the personalities of highly creative people in various fields. MacKinnon (1961) found that the highly creative people he and his associates studied are characterized by an unwillingness to accept anything on the mere say-so of instructors. Nothing was to be accepted because it had the voice of authority behind it. MacKinnon also concluded that because the creative person is not preoccupied with the impression he makes on others and is not overly concerned with their opinion of him, he is freer to be himself than most people. He is not socially irresponsible, however, and is not deliberately nonconformist.

HELPING CHILDREN DEVELOP POSITIVE SELF-CONCEPTS

From the observations and studies of people who have worked with children in creative activities and have studied the lives of creative people, we also derive many clues about treating them so as to give them a better chance to develop self-evaluative attitudes more conducive to creative behavior. Most children like to talk about their creative activities, and it is difficult to prevent some of them from doing so. Through such talk they clarify and develop their self-concepts as they relate to their creative functioning. It is my own observation that all, or almost all, children really desire and need such opportunities. Those silent ones who say little about their creative activities may have difficulty in developing healthy attitudes concerning the value of their ideas. In listening to children, young people, adults, or old people, it is important to remember that the originator of a novel solution needs to make a good argument for it. After being made to look bad, the originator of the novel idea is likely to present more commonplace, less original solutions. Thus, one of the studies in this volume will deal with the problem of talking with children about their creative productions.

Sometimes we assume that the individual who is accepted by his group is freer to think creatively than is the person who is rejected. Research by Julian and Steiner (1961), however, suggests that much depends upon the manner in which the members of a group are interdependent. Their findings indicate that high acceptance by the group is associated with low conformity in groups where each member's success promotes the success of other members and in groups where each member's success decreases the likelihood that other members will also be successful. High acceptance tends to be related to high conformity, however, in groups where the success of one member is unrelated to the success of other members. These and other findings suggest the importance of studying social influences on creative thinking. Thus, in one study of the present series we shall seek to examine the ways in which groups influence the evaluative behavior of individuals

A number of studies have suggested that freedom to engage in self-initiated activities and learning are essential to creative achievement. The Goertzels (1962) cite evidence to indicate that their eminent subjects had greater freedom to engage in self-initiated projects than did more conventionally reared children in their own times. Buhl (1961) found that this was also true of the creative engineers he studied. He found, too, that his creative engineers were not so subject to constant evaluation as were their less creative colleagues. They were freer to make mistakes and to develop confidence in their own problem solving. Riessman (1962) and others remind us that society's worship of the well-rounded person may also do damage to the self-concept of the culturally deprived child who may manifest a single-minded kind of creative talent. He believes that although this form of creativity may be found in any social group, it has greater relevance in working with underprivileged children who have fewer opportunities to develop in a variety of ways.

Relevant to the discussion of well-roundedness and conformity in general is Thoreau's often quoted statement which comes very close to the central issue: "If a man does not keep pace with his companions, perhaps it is because he hears a different drummer. Let him step to the music which he hears, however measured or far away" (1942, p. 216).

QUESTIONS ABOUT SELF-EVALUATION AND CREATIVE BEHAVIOR

Of the many issues related to the evaluative behavior of the individual and his creative thinking, we decided to explore the following questions in the present studies:

1. In evoking original ideas and in developing them, is it more helpful to provide practice in suggesting improvements, making different interpretations, and the like, or practice in identifying defects?
2. Does encouraging children to form the habit of writing down their own ideas contribute to creative growth and an increase in the individual's evaluation of his creative achievement?

MEASUREMENT
OF
CREATIVE
BEHAVIOR

3

Since most of the instruments used in this study involve in some way the measurement of creative behavior, it seems desirable to discuss briefly the problems of measurement in this field. A more detailed treatment will be found in my book, *Guiding Creative Talent* (Torrance, 1962a), and in my chapter in *Creativity: Progress and Potential* (Taylor, 1963), so only enough information will be given in this chapter to provide perspective. Appendix A contains a rather detailed description of the instruments used in these studies, their rationale, scoring information, and reliability and validity data.

Attention has been given to the problems of measurement and instrumentation because I believe that an understanding of the ideas behind the instruments used is necessary for an understanding of the meaning of these studies and for an honest evaluation of them.

Historical Perspective

Even before the turn of the century, and again in the 1920's and 1930's, interesting and exciting attempts were made to develop tests for measuring the creative thinking abilities and identifying creative talent. It was clear from most of this work and the research which accompanied it that the measures which were devised tapped different aspects of mental functioning and identified different intellectual talents from those involved in traditional tests of intelligence or scholastic ability. These efforts attracted very little attention, however, and there were no sustained research and development efforts to make these

measures of much practical use either for research or operational programs.

Since most of the efforts of the past have been limited to a particular age or educational level, it seems necessary to review these
developments in terms of early childhood, the elementary school years,
the high school years, and adulthood.

THE EARLY CHILDHOOD YEARS

Many scholars have continued to deny the possibility that children can think, in many cases erroneously equating the terms "think"
and "reasoning." A great majority of the early studies of "creative imagination," "creativity," or "creative thinking" were limited to artistic manifestations of creativeness. All the early scholars limited their observations of creative behavior quite severely. Most of this early research
reflects little recognition of the fact that no single test or area of observations taps all the individual's resources for creative thinking and
that the same test or kinds of observations are not valid or adequate at
all age levels.

Among the methods which have been used in assessing the creative
functioning of children are the following:

1. Ink blots (Kirkpatrick, 1900; Whipple, 1915)
2. Drawings (McCarty, 1924)
3. Paintings and verbalizations while painting (Grippen, 1933)
4. Tachistoscopically presented tasks with instructions to form
   new products (transformations); observations of imitation, experimentation, transformation of objects, acts of sympathy,
   dramatizations, imaginary playmates, fanciful explanations, fantastic stories, new uses of stories, constructions, new games, ex-
   tensions of language, appropriate quotations, leadership with
   plans, and aesthetic appreciation (Andrews, 1930)
5. Observation of standardized situations, such as a housekeeping
   game, the fanciful naming of visual stimuli, leadership in imaginative games, and block building (Markey, 1935)

In all these early attempts to measure creative behavior, the correlation tends to be low between such measures and traditional measures of intelligence. Markey sought to explain away in various ways the
relatively low correlation between mental age and creative behavior.
Andrews recognized more clearly the difference between the two types
of measures and concluded that "very little relationship exists between
intelligence and the fantastic imagination of the young child" (p. 135).
One might wonder why Binet did not include measures of this type in

his battery of intelligence-test tasks. In his 1909 book on new ideas about children, he certainly emphasized the importance of creative behavior, imagination, inventiveness, and the like. In fact, many of the exercises which he called "mental orthopedics" and used with mentally retarded children resemble quite closely some of the current tests for assessing creative behavior. It is quite likely that he was blinded to the inclusion of measures of this type because he was committed to a mental-age concept of mental development and such measures have never fit very well the mental-age concept. Kirkpatrick (1900), for example, found a sharp drop between the third and fourth grades, and Andrews (1930) found a drop between ages four and one-half and five.

THE ELEMENTARY SCHOOL YEARS

Of the many manifestations of creative thinking among children during the elementary school period, greatest attention has been given to creative writing and art. Thus, investigators of creative behavior during the elementary years, like those who have investigated it in the earlier childhood years, have seriously limited the scope of their observations of the manifestations of creative thinking, thereby limiting the accumulation of knowledge about creative thinking in this period. Also, failure to accept certain types of socially undesirable behavior as indicative of creative potential has eliminated consideration of large areas of childhood behavior.

Although a variety of measures have been used in studying the creative behavior of elementary school children, no single investigator has applied a large range of measures with a single sample of subjects. Typical of early efforts was Kirkpatrick's (1900) with ink blots. Colvin (1902) used compositions, giving attention to such qualities as invention, sense of humor, imaginative power, and perceptive power. Simpson (1922) used fifty sets of four small dots, representing the four corners of squares, as the stimuli for constructions which were used to assess fluency, originality, and flexibility. The methods of McCarty, Abramson, and Grippen were used with both preprimary children and elementary school children. Harms (1939) employed, in grades one through twelve, a test requiring the representation of words (mostly various actions) by single lines. Stephenson (1949) reports the use of a poetry-writing test and an art-form test.

THE HIGH SCHOOL YEARS

Devices for assessing the creative thinking abilities of high school pupils have tended to be in the direction of group administered tests with verbal stimuli requiring verbal responses. Although some of the instruments originally developed for use with children have been extended into or through the high school years, most of the instruments used with high school students were initially developed for use with college students or adults.

Colvin (1902) also made use of his measures based on compositions with high school students. The Abramson, Harms, and Stephenson instruments, already mentioned, have been used with high school subjects. M. D. Vernon (1948) used her Imaginative Construction Test (stories based on four colored pictures) with high school students.

Most of the recent studies involving high school students have made use of adaptations of a few of Guilford's tests, primarily his tests of divergent production abilities. Getzels and Jackson (1962) used four adapted tasks (Word Associations, Uses for Things, Hidden Shapes, and Fables) and constructed one of their own (Make-up Problems). McGuire, Hindsman, King and Jennings (1961), and Piers, Daniels, and Quackenbush (1960) used selected tasks from Guilford's battery. Guilford, Merrifield, and Cox (1961) administered Guilford's extensive battery to ninth-grade students and found essentially the same factors as they had found previously with adults.

THE COLLEGE AND ADULT YEARS

Although there has been practically no experimentation by colleges with measures of creative thinking as a functional part of programs, a great variety of such measures have been applied in studies with college students.

In 1916, Chassell reported rather detailed data concerning the following battery of twelve tests of originality: Word Building, Picture Writing, Analogues, Original Analogies, Chain Puzzle, Triangle Puzzle, Royce's Ring, Completion Test, Economic Prophecies, Code Test, Invention for Sheet Music, and Novel Situations (Consequences). In his 1922 book, Boraas described and discussed the following eight types of tests of "imaginative thinking": Interpretation of Ink Blots, Word Building, Sentence Building, Making Metaphors or Similes (by combining any two of a series of words), Completion of Mutilated Sentences, Painted Cube Test, Imaginary Journey Test, and Production of Rhymes.

Hargreaves (1927) used twelve tasks which he scored for fluency and originality: Word Building and Composition, Ebbinghaus Test, Invention of Stories, Indeterminate Picture Completion, Unfinished Pictures, Ink Blots, Indeterminate Language Completion, Unfinished Stories, Writing Words, Probable Situations, and Imaginary Situations. Maier and his associates (McCloy and Maier, 1939) experimented with a variety of measures closely related to their interest in art education. They have included such tasks as Interpretative Titles to Pictures, Critical Appraisal and Interpretation of Completed Works of Art, Compositions, and Opinions and Interpretations of Paintings. Welch (1946) developed tasks which emphasize the perception of new combinations. His tasks include: Block Constructions (make as many pieces of furniture or home furnishings as possible from ten blocks), Sentence Construction (from ten words), Letter Construction (from three straight lines), and Short-story Construction.

Owens, Schumacher, and Clark (1957) developed a series of tasks to assess creativity in machine design. The test tasks include: Power Source Apparatus Test, Design-a-Machine Test, Three-dimensional Space Relations Test, and Figure Matrices Test. Harris (1960) has developed two forms of a twenty-item test of creativity in engineering which has been standardized on engineering students. The content is oriented to engineering and the tasks require subjects to list possible uses of various objects and to guess "What is it?" Buhl (1961) and others both in higher education and in industry have used the AC (Sparkplug) Test of Creative Thinking Ability among engineering students and various adult groups. This test includes problems calling for unusual uses of common objects, alternative explanations of conclusions, consequences of unusual occurrences, alternative solutions to problem situations, and the like (Harris and Simberg, 1959).

Barron (1958) and his associates at the University of California have developed a battery of tests for assessing originality, which includes Mosaic Constructions, Anagram Test, Drawing Completion (Franck), Figure Preference Test (Welsh), and Ink Blot Test (uncommon response). Other instruments which have been used with college students and other adults include: Flanagan's Ingenious Solutions to Problems (1963), one of the few attempts to assess creative thinking through multiple-choice items; Fredericksen's Formulating Hypotheses Test (1959), an attempt to elicit creative-type responses and transfer them to machine-scoreable answer sheets by having subjects code their own responses; Burkhart's Object Question Test (Burkhart, 1962; Burkhart and Bernheim, 1963), which requires subjects to ask divergent questions about a given object such as an apple or paper clips; and Mednick's Remote Associates Test (1962), which requires subjects to find a word which is an associative connective link between three disparate words.

Guilford's elaborate battery was originally devised for high level personnel. Thus, it has been used largely with college and professional personnel. Because of its length, most users have selected only a limited number of the test tasks. This work has been done within the framework of Guilford's "Structure of Intellect Model" (Guilford and Merrifield,

1960). The most recent conceptualization of the creative thinking abilities includes the following factors and there are several tasks to assess each: sensitivity to problems, flexibility (figural spontaneous, figural adaptive, and semantic spontaneous), fluency (word, expressional, and ideational), originality, elaboration, and redefinition (figural, symbolic, and semantic).

As with preschool, elementary school, and high school subjects, studies involving college and adult subjects have shown uniformly rather low relationships between measures of creative ability and measures of intelligence and scholastic aptitude. In general, the findings reported by Hargreaves in 1927 have continued to be supported. When he scored his tests of imagination for fluency of ideas, with emphasis on quantity rather than quality, he obtained fairly high correlation with intelligence tests. In addition to the appreciable amount of the general factor "g," he found a considerable group factor in common with other measures of imagination. The "speed" factor was also found to be important in fluency. When the same test responses were scored for originality, denoting novelty and uncommonness, Hargreaves found very little relationship. Barron (1957) reported a coefficient of correlation of .33 between his measure of originality and the Concept Mastery Test. Bentley (1961) obtained a coefficient of correlation of .11 between the Miller Analogies Test and a battery of the Minnesota Tests of Creative Thinking, and Palm (1959) found correlations of .10 with the Miller Analogies and −.02 with the Ohio State Psychological Examination and a battery of the Minnesota Tests of Creative Thinking among graduate students in education.

Early Development
of the Minnesota Tests of Creative Thinking

Early in 1958, Som Nath Ghei, Kenneth DeYoung, and I began simultaneously to survey what had been accomplished in the development of measures of creative thinking and to immerse ourselves in the lives and experiences of recognized creative persons through their autobiographies, biographies, and other writings. Approximately one and one-half years of developmental work preceded the studies which constitute this report and will be reviewed to help the reader understand the ideas behind the measurement instruments employed.

TEST OF IMAGINATION, FORMS A AND B

In trying to design measures of the creative thinking abilities, we felt that we needed a set of tasks which could be administered from kindergarten through graduate school—tasks which would challenge the graduate student and have a high ceiling and at the same time be easy enough to elicit creative responses from the kindergartener. Since we were at that time inexperienced with tests of creative thinking, we decided that our first attempts should be with materials about which something was already known and which had a sound theoretical rationale. Thus, we attempted first to adapt Guilford's materials (Guilford, Wilson, Christensen, and Lewis, 1951) with our objectives in mind. For example, we tried out several substitutes for "bricks" in Guilford's Unusual Uses Test—objects more common to the experiences of children. Our experimentation suggested that "tin cans" would be appropriate for our purposes.

Our first batteries consisted only of six tasks. Form A consisted of the following tasks: Unusual Uses of Tin Cans, Impossibilities (as many as you can think of), Consequences (if man could become invisible at will, if a hole could be bored through the earth, if birds and animals could be understood by man), Situations (handling a friend who kids others but cannot stand to be kidded, a charge of dishonesty in a club, and becoming educated if schools were abolished), Common Problems (taking a bath and doing school homework), and Improvements (bicycle, shoes, and children's clothes). Form B, designed as an alternate form, consisted of a parallel set of tasks.

We were pleased with the response to these tasks at the fifth-grade level and above. Some evidences of validity were found for them on the basis of their ability to differentiate those nominated by peers and teachers as having a "lot of good ideas" and other criteria of creative behavior from those not so nominated. Also, children identified as outstanding on these tests were found to differ in meaningful ways from their classmates of the same sex and equal mental age as measured by intelligence tests such as the Stanford-Binet, the Kuhlmann-Anderson Intelligence Test, the California Test of Mental Maturity, and the Otis Quick-scoring Mental Ability Test. The work of the highly creative children compared with their equally intelligent classmates (Torrance, 1962a, p. 78) is characterized by humor, playfulness, relative lack of rigidity, and relaxation. Products produced outside the test situation were rated as more original, more "off the beaten track." They also had reputations among their peers and teachers as having wild or silly ideas, especially the boys. Coefficients of correlation with traditional measures of intelligence were quite small, in most cases not statistically significant. Yet there were statistically significant relationships between these measures and standardized measures of achievement even after the effects of mental age had been discounted.

TEST OF IMAGINATION, FORM C

We were not satisfied with the responses obtained from these two batteries from children in the fourth grade and below. We decided to develop a different set of material for younger children which might possibly be useful with older subjects as well. We then started experimenting with two types of materials: the improvement of toys, and alternative solutions to some of the Mother Goose problem situations. We thought that the toys would challenge the ingenuity of children, give them some concrete object to work with, and elicit their personal involvement and interest. Subjects were asked to think of ideas for improving each toy so that it would be more "fun to play with." This invitation to regress (to have fun) was an important part of the instructions and represents an attempt to apply the concept of "regression in the service of the ego" as it relates to creative behavior. Responses provided quantifiable data for assessing several kinds of thinking ability. We found that flexibility can be reliably assessed by analyzing the responses in terms of the number of approaches used in modifying the toy. These include the well-known Osborn principles (1957) of addition, subtraction, multiplication, division, substitution, combination, magnification, rearrangement, reversal, sensory appeal (motion, sound, light, odor), and the like. Scores on inventive level, constructiveness, and, later, originality were developed.

THE ASK-AND-GUESS TEST

As we began administering the three test batteries just described, it struck me that none of the tasks really gave an opportunity for the subject to express his curiosity, reveal his sensitivity to defects or gaps in knowledge, or demonstrate his ability to formulate hypotheses about causation. Thus, I developed the idea of showing the subject a picture, having him first ask all the questions he could think of about the events depicted and then having him make guesses concerning causes and consequences.

It seemed to us that much of the essence of creative scientific thinking is captured in the processes of asking and guessing. Such a concept is in harmony with the definition of creative thinking offered in Chapter 1, as the process of sensing deficiencies, forming ideas or hypotheses, testing them, and communicating a result. Curiosity has long been accepted as an important aspect of creative behavior and is recognized as being reflected in the number and kinds of questions asked. Scientific thought has long divided the phenomena of nature into two series: causal conditions and the results or consequences.

About a dozen pictures were pretested before we finally settled upon a pair of appealing human interest pictures: Tom, the Piper's Son, stealing a pig and being chased by a farmer; and Ding Dong Bell, a picture of two boys and a girl putting a cat in a well. Other pictures have been used with special groups, but the above two pictures are the ones used in the present set of studies.

Subjects are told that this is a test of how curious they are about the world in which they live and of how good they are at guessing causes and results of consequences. In introducing the first part, the examiner states that the main way we show our curiosity and obtain information is by asking questions. They are then instructed to think of all the questions they can about what they see in the picture. They are encouraged to ask questions about any or all parts of the picture and of the event pictured but are cautioned to ask only questions which cannot be answered by looking at the picture. In the instructions for hypotheses concerning causes, subjects are told that they cannot always obtain the information they want by asking questions; there are times when they must make guesses and then test their guesses through further investigation. They are then instructed to make all the guesses they can concerning the possible causes of the events depicted. Similarly, for the third part, subjects are directed to give as many possible consequences as they can of the action shown in the picture.

This test was given orally in the first three grades and as a group test to older persons. A time limit of five minutes for each of the three parts has been used in the studies in the present series. We found significant differences between individual and group administrations in the fourth, fifth, and sixth grades. The mean number of responses on each part is significantly higher in the individual administration than in the group administration. We also found that some children profit more than others from one or the other types of administration. For example, the reliability coefficients for oral (individual) versus written (group) administration are .61, .46, and .54 for the fourth, fifth, and sixth grades, respectively. In other studies using alternate forms (different pictures) of the Ask-and-Guess Test, test-retest reliabilities of .76 (McGreevey, 1961), .79 (Torrance, 1960e), and .85 (Yamamoto, 1962) have been reported.

FIGURAL TESTS

At about this same time, a number of considerations made it highly desirable to develop figural or nonverbal measures of creative thinking. First, it seems quite likely that figural types of creative thinking are important for the same reason that other kinds of creative thinking are important. Second, the individual administration of an adequate battery of tests of creative thinking is tremendously time-consuming. Figural tests of creative thinking which could be administered in a group would contribute something to the solution of this problem. Third, some highly creative children appear to lag in their verbal development, while others are shy and fearful about voicing their ideas even in an individual testing situation with the best efforts to establish rapport. It was believed that figural tests as a supplement to verbal measures might compensate for some of this deficiency.

Although we have by now extended this exploration into a variety of areas, we had developed only two figural tasks at the time the present studies were undertaken. Two others were developed as a part of this project and will be described in Appendix A. The first is a measure involving the number of extra details or ideas put into drawings of a house, tree, and person. The other is the Circles Test and its alternate form, the Squares Test. Since the first is no longer of use, only the latter will be discussed in this chapter.

The original format for the Circles Test consisted of a page filled with forty-two circles, each one inch in diameter. Although a number of modifications have since been made both in the format and in the instructions, the subjects in the earlier studies were simply directed to "see how many objects they can sketch which have a circle as the main element in their design."

Initially, only three aspects of divergent production were assessed through this task: fluency, flexibility, and originality. Fluency was determined by counting the number of different ideas produced on a circle or circles without duplication. Flexibility was determined by counting the number of categories into which responses fell. Some of the more common categories include: human faces or heads, animal faces or heads, human figures, animal figures, coins, fruit, and the like. Originality included all responses not appearing in a list of highly frequent ones.

A much more detailed scoring guide has now been developed on the basis of tabulations of the frequency of responses in the records of several hundred subjects. Later, responses were evaluated in terms of several other criteria, such as communicativeness, complexity, elaboration, and the like. At the present time, elaboration is the only one of these which has been retained.

CONCEPT OF INVENTIVE LEVEL

Since the concept of inventive level as defined by the U.S. Patent Office enters into the evaluation of a number of the products which resulted from some of the experiments in the present series, mention should be made of our early work with this concept. We had thought that we could obtain a more powerful measure of creative behavior by scoring based on logically meaningful but complex sets of criteria. We believed that the practical criteria for "patentable" creativity might be adapted to a scoring measure of a task designed to stimulate creative thinking.

This scoring concept was applied first to the Product Improvement and Unusual Uses Tests involving the stuffed toy dog. After much discussion and trial-and-error, we decided upon six basic points with which to judge each response:

1. Newness and novelty
2. Usefulness
3. Productive and thought-provoking
4. Challenging ideas
5. Rarity
6. Quality of being well thought out

The use of definitions of these six characteristics did not result in satisfactory interscorer reliability. We then compiled a list of responses of some 200 records and scored each response by consensus of raters. By referring to this list we attained interscorer coefficients of reliability of .92. Because this procedure proved to be rather time-consuming, however, Necla Palamutlu worked out a simplification, trying to maintain as much as possible of the power of this complex scoring concept. She did this by grouping related responses into broader categories.

The Patent Office criteria of inventive level have also been applied to the new ideas produced by graduate students in a teaching experiment. After experimenting with various combinations of these criteria, we finally settled upon ten-point scales attempting to rate the following qualities of the products submitted:

1. How much creative strength or qualified intellectual energy was involved in solving the problem?
2. How useful would the idea be, if executed or found tenable?
3. Does the idea represent a step forward or advance over present knowledge, theory, or practice?
4. How much originality was used in overcoming a special difficulty? How close have others come to the same solution?
5. How surprising or remarkable is the solution suggested? How shocking is it?
6. How adequate is the statement of the idea and proposed plans for its development?

LIVES OF EMINENT CREATIVE PEOPLE AS DATA

As we have developed and experimented with dozens of other approaches for assessing creative behavior, we have at every turn endeavored to keep ourselves grounded in reality by checking our cues against the experiences of recognized creative people, living and dead. Kenneth DeYoung and I tried to apply our insights from data concerning eminent creative persons in constructing a life experience inventory which could be used in studying adolescents and young people. Circumstances have not permitted us to follow through with this proposed work. Having immersed ourselves in such data, the experience has served us well in generating ideas for test tasks, in refining them, and in selecting those which would be truest to the process as we are able to comprehend it from the experiences of eminent creative individuals. In addition to the biographies, autobiographies, and writings of these creative people, we have found such works as the following especially useful: Goertzel and Goertzel's *Cradles of Eminence* (1962); Rossman's *The Psychology of the Inventor* (1931); Schwartz and Bishop's two-volume work, *Moments of Discovery* (1958); and Taton's *Reason and Chance in Scientific Discovery* (1957).

 Summary of Approach in Instrument Development

In developing instruments to test hypotheses concerning the role of evaluation in creative thinking, we have tried to make the best possible use of what is known about creativity—the creative process, the creative person, the creative product, and the presses which facilitate creative functioning. We have relied upon the historical accounts of creative achievement, studies of the lives of creative persons, laboratory and field studies designed to affect creative functioning, studies involving the evaluation of creative products and processes, efforts to measure various aspects of man's mental functioning, and the like. We have used these sources in generating ideas and in testing them theoretically to make certain that the instruments developed would have as good face validity as possible.

We have also gone as far as time and resources will permit in demonstrating objectively that these instruments have validity and reliability. The charges of some critics that studies of creative behavior are being made with instruments which have validity only in the minds of their creators is not true. It may be correct that the criterion of creative behavior is a sticky one, but we decided at the outset to define creative thinking as adequately as we could and then to try to remain true to this definition. We believed that if we could do this, we could afford to ignore some of the hopeless bickering about the meaning of creative behavior. I had observed similar rather futile discussions about the meaning of personality over the past 25 years of my own life and knew how useless such discussions can be. I did not feel that we could afford to waste time on such matters.

In seeking to assemble objective evidence of the validity of the instruments which have been developed for the study of creative behavior, we have considered a wide range of indicators. In considering the matter of the creative thinking abilities, we have been concerned about the mental abilities which appear to be involved in the creative process and in producing creative ideas. For example, some of the ideas which we score in determining ideational fluency are certainly not very creative. We continue to derive a fluency score in this manner because we believe that the evidence indicates that the person who is able to produce a large number of ideas will be more likely to think creatively than the person who is unable to do so. Certainly, this ability to produce a large number of ideas has characterized many of our eminent creative persons. For example, one of Edison's staff members once remarked:

> Edison can think of more ways of doing a thing than any man I ever saw or heard of. He tries everything and never lets up, even though failure is apparently staring him in the face. He only stops when he simply can't go any further on that particular line (Meadowcroft, 1949, p. 219).

The above statement implies that Edison was also flexible, that he tried many approaches and abandoned an approach when it no longer seemed to offer promise. Thus, we have continued to obtain a flexibility score to show the number of different approaches or the variety of ideas produced. It is true that some of these approaches are not in themselves creative, but we believe that they indicate the presence of an ability which is important in creative functioning.

In a similar manner, we have continued to try to refine our measures of originality, believing that such a quality comes close to the essence of creative thinking. Certainly there is rather good agreement that creative behavior involves the production of something that is novel or at least statistically infrequent. Even in devising the scoring guide for determining originality scores, we have given recognition to the fact that more than statistical infrequency is necessary to make a response original. We have required that it be to some extent adaptive to reality. We have relied rather heavily upon empirical signs of novelty in terms of the statistical infrequency of the response among members of culturally relatively homogeneous groups. We believe that this is justified because it gives us, as Guilford (1962) maintains, a practical way of applying the criterion of unusualness. The index of unusualness can, therefore, be objective.

In the same way, the various indices of elaboration which we have developed are objective. Their determination involves only the counting of the number of different ideas used in elaborating a basic idea or plan. This does not mean that every idea counted in determining the elaboration index is creative or even original. In fact, some of our measures of originality on a particular test may have a negative correlation with the measure of elaboration on the same test. We believe that the ability to elaborate an idea is a valuable kind of creative ability. The successful creative person must sustain his original insight, elaborate upon it, and develop it to the full. Henry Ford is an excellent example of such a person in history. Thus, we believe that the person who is able to elaborate to a high degree the ideas he produces will have a better chance of making creative achievements than the person who is unable to do so.

One strategy that we have used constantly is to generate ideas for test tasks and for scoring them from descriptions of the creative process, the behavior of creative men and women in achieving their break-throughs, and the like. We then identify children as high or low in these measures and see if the same characteristics differentiate these persons as differentiate eminent creative persons and appropriate comparison groups of less creative persons. For example, MacKinnon (1962) reports that the creative persons studied by him and his associates have strong self-images or self-concepts, are both more sensitive and more inde-pendent than their peers, make more unconventional responses, have considerable senses of humor, and the like. Thus, it was not without significance when Weisberg and Springer (1961) found that fourth-grade children identified as highly creative by one of the instruments used in the present series of studies differed in similar ways from their less creative peers. Therefore, in searching to test the validity of in-struments, it is necessary to go back and forth between a variety of kinds of data. Certainly it is possible that we could be deceived by the presumed similarity between certain characteristics of the thinking of children and that of people who have made outstanding creative achieve-ments. We believe, however, that we can reduce the extent to which we deceive ourselves by this constant going back and forth from data to instrument and from instrument to data, checking and rechecking our "anchors in reality."

In Appendix A the key instruments used in the present series of studies are described. Where I have not already done so in this chapter, I have set forth the main ideas behind each instrument and present what I consider to be some of the more important objective evidences of reliability and validity.

APPLYING
PRINCIPLES
FOR
REWARDING
CREATIVE
THINKING

4

The purpose of this chapter is to describe from the viewpoint of teachers what happens when they try to reward creative thinking. I believe it will help identify not only some of the important values which come from rewarding classroom creativity, but also some of the difficulties and the problems a teacher encounters in rewarding creative behavior.

First, I shall try to communicate what rewarding creative thinking means to me. Usually, when we speak of rewarding behavior, we immediately think of money or status. Although we may work for money, none of us works for money alone. Some people work for status or power, but this does not seem to be the case with a highly creative person. In fact, we probably do a disservice to all concerned when we try to reward him by placing him in a position where he is boss. He would prefer to be in some other position. Yet this is a commonly used method for rewarding creative achievement. We find this phenomenon occurring as early as the fifth grade. I shall never forget my amazement at how it works in small groups of children. In one of our experiments designed to study the behavior of highly creative children in small

I was assisted in the preparation of this chapter by R. E. Myers, now on the faculty of the School of Education, University of Oregon, Eugene, Oregon.

groups of their less creative peers, one group of children said immediately, "Mark is our genius. I think he ought to be chairman and recorder." The task involved discovering many uses, both intended and unintended, of a box of science toys and explaining their principles of operation. As chairman and recorder, the group's most creative performer was unable even to play with these toys to find out what they could do. He was made an "authority" and loaded down with responsibility and paper work.

Thus, when we use the term "rewarding creative thinking," we are not thinking of the rewards of money or power, nor even of school grades. What we have in mind might more accurately be expressed as genuine respect for the child's creative needs and abilities—a recognition of their importance.

The problem of rewarding creative behavior is admittedly a difficult and complex one. Perhaps one of the most serious obstacles is that it is difficult for us to accept as creative anything which threatens to upset the very thin balance we have achieved in our lives. Mead (1962) points out that nowhere does this difficulty show up so clearly in our society as in the classroom. She maintains that the teacher "cannot risk bringing out gifts that may disrupt the precarious balance of her overcrowded classroom" (1962, p. 19). Imagination requires room and its free exercise may give a good deal of trouble. Young children are ardent researchers or investigators, but an investigator can be very troublesome in a classroom.

Many teachers also find threatening anything other than an authority relationship with a child. Some cannot tolerate an individual relationship with a child. The relationship must be kept on a safe, group basis. Mearns (1958) maintained that the "deeper rhythms of the child's mind" necessary in creative thinking were not to be disclosed except in very private interviews. Although children may chatter a great deal, they are remarkably reticent about revealing their genuine feelings. He found, however, that when he regarded the confidences of children as right and respectable, he learned much. Even then he rarely touched the serious stirrings of the heart and mind. He respected this side of their lives and did not probe.

We believe that there are some things which almost all teachers can do to facilitate the creative growth of their pupils. However, doubts have been expressed frequently as to whether teachers, even when fully informed of these principles, can put them into practice under the pressures of their day-by-day interaction with children. This study represents an attempt to cast some light upon the forces which are at play when teachers are asked to apply deliberately a few widely accepted educational principles in their classrooms.

Identifying Widely Accepted Principles
for Rewarding Creative Behavior

On the basis of earlier exploratory research and discussions with many groups of classroom teachers, we had identified five principles which seemed to be rather widely accepted at an intellectual level if not at an emotional one. Although many people have said that these principles are obvious—too obvious to mention—it was apparent to me that they were neither understood nor practiced by any large number of teachers. Thus, it seemed necessary to try to understand what happens when teachers do try to apply these principles.

The following five principles were identified as widely accepted and made the focus of our initial exploration:

1. Be respectful of unusual questions.
2. Be respectful of imaginative, unusual ideas.
3. Show your pupils that their ideas have value.
4. Occasionally have pupils do something "for practice" without the threat of evaluation.
5. Tie in evaluation with causes and consequences.

BE RESPECTFUL OF UNUSUAL QUESTIONS

Nothing is more rewarding to a child who asks questions than to find the answer to his questions and to have others take his questions seriously. Questions are a reflection of a "mind hunger" that must be satisfied lest the mind be starved. Although the need must be dealt with immediately, there is much that teachers can do to enrich the period between the question and the answer. It is a good rule to tell children only what they cannot learn for themselves. This means that we need to teach them the skills of inquiry, the skills of using questions to discover, to test, to reach conclusions. Children need to learn how to sustain a question, to play with it, toss it back and forth, refine it, and accept the questioning mood without the need for ready-made answers from the teacher or parent.

It is not easy for teachers to do what we generally agree that they should do. Teachers are expected to be able to give the answers immediately, and many will try to do so, even when they do not know the correct answer. Furthermore, it is tension-producing to delay giving the answer, and in the rush of a busy schedule, giving immediate answers or ignoring questions is the easiest course. The teacher who sets out to be respectful of the questions children ask must be prepared for shocks. Children will ask many questions which the teacher cannot answer. This should be accepted as normal and desirable, but it can be tremendously threatening to the insecure teacher. Children ask questions for which there are no known answers, so why should teachers feel threatened by such questions?

A number of observers of classroom behavior have noted that few children have the power to stand up against the irritation and evasiveness of their teachers. They give up and stop questioning altogether. They receive the impression that it is bad manners to ask questions and is a cause for disciplinary action. Only a few rare individuals such as Albert Einstein are willing to incur the risk of asking the questions which puzzle them. We are told that during his early school years, Einstein was frequently beaten for asking questions. Finally, before completing his course in the *gymnasium*, his science teacher asked him to withdraw from school because the questions he was asking were undermining the status of the teachers in the school. This teacher had apparently discussed the problem with the other teachers, and all, except for his mathematics teacher, apparently agreed that Einstein should be asked to withdraw. The science teacher had kept a record of some of the questions Einstein had been asking and pointed out that no one knew the answers to these questions. Einstein, of course, later found the answers to many of these questions himself.

Many writers (Patri, 1931; Mead, 1962) are sympathetic and understanding of the teacher's precarious position in this matter. Mead (1962) says that the teacher is unprepared to cope with the child who uses his creativity to defeat her, the child who poses unanswerable questions which will arouse his classmates to raucous laughter. The teacher, thus, comes to distrust the up-raised hand and the would-be questioner. Patri (1931) believes that the questioning child is irritating because he deters us in our smooth way, halts us, and makes us turn in our tracks and search in ways which are new to us. Questions stir up things that we would like to ignore or forget.

BE RESPECTFUL OF IMAGINATIVE, UNUSUAL IDEAS

Children who are stimulated by the creative approach will see many relationships and significances that their teachers miss. They will express ideas which will shock their teachers and which their teachers will not be able to evaluate. Thus, it is extremely difficult for the teacher to reward such thinking properly, and it is likely to be our more creatively gifted youngsters who suffer most from such unrewarded or even punished effort.

It is so obviously desirable that children's ideas be respected that many teachers have criticized the statement of this principle. They suggest that it should be changed to read, "Stimulate and encourage unusual or original ideas." Even after re-evaluation, it seems to me that the critical problem is not in stimulating unusual or original ideas but in learning how to respect them, how to use them when they are offered. In fact, it seems unkind to stimulate such thinking if we cannot be respectful of it. Certainly we shall not continue to elicit such thinking if we do not respect it. Teachers should recognize that using the ideas of children arouses interest, generates enthusiasm, and stimulates effort, but that it requires concentration and thoughtfulness to attend to and evaluate the contributions of others. Children's ideas also provide understanding of their needs and can be used in determining how to guide their learnings. A child's whole attitude may change when he finds that the teacher feels he has good ideas and the ability to express them. He relaxes, and his mind functions better. He is able to think.

SHOW CHILDREN THAT THEIR IDEAS HAVE VALUE

A major difficulty in applying the principle of showing children that their ideas have value is that many people do not honestly believe that children are capable of producing ideas that have value. Such teachers obviously will not be able to reward creative classroom behavior. They might even be able to say all the right words, but children can see through this. Children will know that you do not honestly value their ideas. I would only suggest that such a person be on the alert for a while to recognize new ideas among children and to search for ways of using them and giving them value.

Patrick (1955) points out that all the great thinkers of the world had to have confidence that their own ideas were more valuable than those they copied, or else they would not have spent their lives working out their great contributions. At the other end of the continuum from our renowned thinkers, Barkan (1960) points out that kindergarteners need from their teachers signs of assurance which convey the feeling that their ideas are valued and respected.

PROVIDE FOR PERIODS OF NONEVALUATED PRACTICE

It is difficult for many teachers to realize that it is not necessary to evaluate everything that a child does. Some even feel that they must correct and grade everything that a child does. Some kindergarten teachers correct and grade the drawings that their pupils produce. One mother wrote me of her son's experiences under such a teacher. The child had been generally recognized as being unusually bright before he entered kindergarten. His mother soon noted, however, that many of his kindergarten drawings were graded as failing because he would add cowboy boots or hats to his teacher's dittoed drawing, or he might even change the dittoed drawing. Crushed by constant failure for such behavior, he apparently stopped trying to learn and is now suspected of being mentally retarded.

There is a need for periods when a person can learn without threats of immediate evaluation. This would appear to be especially true in regard to the learning of new skills and in creative activities. External evaluation is always a threat and creates a need for defensiveness. As Rogers (1954) points out, this makes some portion of a person's experiencing or sensing denied to awareness. Thus, there is lacking the openness so necessary in creative thinking.

There is more behind this principle, however, than the reduction of defensiveness. Man has a deep need to establish anchors, to maintain contact with his environment. He must determine the limits of his abilities, the materials with which he works, and the situation. In creative activities, he must test the medium—whatever it is—to discover its limits, its possibilities. The personal experiences of others are insufficient.

TIE IN EVALUATION WITH CAUSES AND CONSEQUENCES

In asking teachers to apply the principle of tying in evaluation with causes and consequences, we suggested that in criticizing defects in ideas or in punishing naughty or dangerous behavior, they do so in a way that would foster ability to see causes and consequences of behavior. Special emphasis was placed upon the consideration of multiple possible consequences whenever appropriate. We especially cautioned against the overuse of such remarks as, "This is good" or "This is bad." Instead, it was suggested that they use such approaches as "I like this because . . ." or "This could be improved by . . ." and the like.

This principle was included in the present list as a kind of safeguard against a dangerous type of so-called creative thinking. The divergent thinking associated with creativity can be dangerous as well as beneficial and needs direction and guidance. Thus, it is important that we cultivate the habit of looking for causes and consequences, refrain from jumping to final conclusions without examining evidence, and learn to examine the validity of different kinds of evidence. This kind of causal thinking does not exclude the encouragement of open-mindedness, tolerance of the opinions of others, and the critical evaluation of one's own thinking. If the teacher himself does causal thinking, it will be easier to encourage children to think in terms of causes and consequences. It will be only natural for him to ask children the basis for their assertions and to think of the possible consequences of their actions.

There is fairly general agreement concerning the value of causal thinking as an educational objective, in spite of apparently limited application in practice. Ojemann (1961) has been especially insistent over a number of years concerning the importance of causal thinking. He maintains that creativity and mental health will become both compatible and mutually reinforcing if people develop a basic causal orientation to their social environment. According to him, the development of the skills of thinking in terms of causes and consequences is at the very base of creative behavior.

Procedures of the Study

In the fall of 1959, the staff of the Bureau of Educational Research with the assistance of four experienced elementary teachers (Joseph Buzzelli, Warren Peterson, Lucille Teppen, and Viola Svensson) developed a manual entitled *Rewarding Creative Thinking* for use in the study presented in the next chapter. Somehow there developed a rather widespread demand for this manual. Within less than six months, approximately 750 copies had been distributed.

During the following winter, questionnaires were mailed to approximately 150 of the earliest requesters of the manual. Recipients were asked to "seek systematically and consciously to apply in a reasonable way" the five principles which have just been reviewed. We told them we realized that all teachers to some extent apply these principles in the classrooms. We urged them, however, to experiment with deliberate applications of the principles. We cautioned that all these principles must be applied within the limitations of the age group being taught. It was emphasized that applications should be continued and consistent rather than just "one-shot treatments." After a period of experimentation, it was requested that each recipient write a description of some specific experience in which he had tried to apply one or more of these principles and to answer certain questions about each experience described. A separate mimeographed sheet was supplied for each of the five principles.

The following questions were used in obtaining the data:

Being respectful of questions

1. What was the question? Who asked it? What were the general conditions under which it was asked?
2. What was *your* immediate reaction?

3. What was the immediate reaction of the class, if observable?
4. In what way was respect shown for the question?
5. What, if any, were the observable effects (immediate and/or long-range)?

Being respectful of imaginative ideas

1. What was the idea? Who expressed it? What were the general conditions under which the idea was offered?
2. What was *your* immediate reaction to the idea?
3. What was the immediate reaction of the class, if observable?
4. In what way was respect shown for the idea?
5. What, if any, were the observable effects (immediate and/or long-range)?

Showing pupils that their ideas have value

1. What was the occasion which provided the opportunity to show a pupil that his ideas are valuable? Who was the child? What did he do? How did he seem to feel about his idea(s)?
2. What did you do to try to show him that his ideas are of value?
3. How did he react to what you did (immediate and/or long-range)?
4. What was the reaction of the class, if observable?

Providing for unevaluated practice

1. Describe the initial assignment and the general situation in which provision was made for unevaluated practice.
2. How did you communicate to your pupils that they were free to experiment, that "it didn't count on the record?"
3. What happened during the practice period?
4. What was the nature of the similar task given "for the record"?
5. How was it rewarded, if rewarded?

Tying evaluation to cause and effect

1. What was the nature of the behavior to be evaluated? Who was involved?
2. What was your personal evaluation of the behavior?
3. How did you or the class show the relationship of the behavior to cause and/or consequence?
4. What were the effects, if observable (immediate and/or long-range)?

During the first three months of 1960, 114 teachers in thirteen different states and the District of Columbia completed questionnaires and returned them. They were rather evenly distributed from kindergarten through the eighth grade. Some respondents submitted descriptions of ncidents related to each of the five principles. Others submitted descriptions of applications related to as few as one principle.

Results

HOW WELL TEACHERS APPLY PRINCIPLES OF REWARDING CREATIVE BEHAVIOR

Many of the teachers responding to the request for descriptions of actual experiences in which they believed that they had rewarded creative behavior showed a thorough understanding of the principles by the manner in which they reported anecdotes illustrating the application of principles. The response of the pupils to their teachers' attitudes of respect and encouragement was enthusiastic and apparently rewarding to the teachers.

On the other hand, quite a few teachers demonstrated by their descriptions an inability either to interpret the meaning of the principles correctly or to cite an appropriate instance of its use. Many of their reports were puzzling. In relating incidents where they were supposed to have shown respect for children's questions or ideas, teachers told of their own plainly evasive, rejecting, or derisive behavior. Asked when they had been reassuring and accepting, they recited occasions when they had actually rebuffed their pupils. It is unlikely, however, that any of the teachers wanted consciously to refute the principles which they had been urged consciously to apply in their classrooms. A discouragingly large number simply were unable to incorporate the principles into their teaching.

I judged each incident submitted in terms of whether or not the teacher did, in fact, manifest respect for or reward the creative thinking of their pupils. The results obtained in this way are presented in Table 4.1. It will be noted that only a slight majority of the respondents were judged to have shown respect for the unusual questions and ideas of their pupils. Over 90 per cent were judged to have been successful in rewarding creative thinking both when they attempted to show pupils that their ideas had value and when they provided for unevaluated practice. Only two thirds of them were judged to have been successful in doing so when they tried to relate evaluation to causes and consequences.

It was noted that in some cases the teacher succeeded in respecting a question or idea but that the class as a whole did not register a similar degree of acceptance. In other cases, the teacher tended to be derisive only to find that her pupils held a more respectful attitude. In some cases, this seems to have altered the teacher's behavior. In others, no

TABLE 4.1 Manifestation of Respect or Reward for Creative Thinking of Pupils in Apply ing Five Different Principles for Rewarding Creative Thinking

Principle	Respect/Reward		Lack of Respect		Mixed/Indeterminat	
	Number	Per Cent	Number	Per Cent	Number	Per Cent
Respect for questions	36	58.0	18	29.4	8	12.6
Respect for unusual ideas	29	51.8	15	26.8	12	21.4
Showing ideas have value	57	91.9	2	3.2	3	4.9
Unevaluated practice	54	96.4	0	0.0	2	3.6
Cause-and-effect relation	34	68.0	7	14.0	9	18.0

such evidences could be noted from the responses submitted. Table 4.2 presents the results of the degree of respect manifested by the classroom group as a whole, as described by the teacher. In general, the results follow rather closely those reported by the teachers of their own behavior. The greatest difficulties occur in showing respect for unusual questions, showing respect for imaginative or unusual ideas, and relating evaluation to causes and consequences.

TABLE 4.2 Manifestation of Respect or Reward for Creative Thinking of Pupils by Class mates When Teachers Applied Five Different Principles for Rewarding Creative Thinking

Principle	Respect/Reward		Lack of Respect		Mixed/Indeterminate	
	Number	Per Cent	Number	Per Cent	Number	Per Cent
Respect for questions	30	48.4	21	33.9	11	17.7
Respect for unusual ideas	29	44.7	18	32.1	13	23.2
Showing ideas have value	46	74.2	8	12.9	8	12.9
Unevaluated practice	49	87.5	0	0.0	7	12.5
Cause-and-effect relation	26	52.0	8	16.0	16	32.0

It should be remembered that of the innumerable interactions which took place between the responding teachers and their pupils during the two or three months that they were asked to be alert to opportunities to apply the principles, the incidents chosen must have been either memorable or convenient. Almost all the reports appeared to be quite candid and free from embellishment. Accordingly, the incidents cited were in some way reflective of the teachers' values and attitudes. If a teacher does not prize creative thinking, it is difficult for him to cite examples of his encouraging children to behave in creative ways. Some of the teachers who do not value creative behavior may have been trying to tell us that the principles "won't work." It was clear, however, that some teachers honestly tried at an intellectual level to reward crea-

tive behavior, but their deeper feelings "showed through" this intellectual veneer.

WHAT HAPPENED WHEN TEACHERS
TRIED TO RESPECT UNUSUAL QUESTIONS

Many of the pupils' questions reported by teachers constituted a
rigorous test of a teacher's ability to be respectful of unusual questions.
The following is a sample of those reported:

1. How do we stay on the earth?
2. Do rocks grow?
3. Could our club have a code?
4. What becomes of men salmon when females go upstream to
   spawn?
5. Why isn't the plural of cat written as kittens—because if you
   have more than one cat, you would have kittens, wouldn't you?
6. Does a baby have a smaller number of bones than we do?
7. Why didn't I get paid for how good I was? (In a variety show)
8. Where does the water on the blackboard go?
9. Why don't people like Negroes?
10. How far does space go and what comes after space?

In about 54 per cent of the reports, the questioner was identified
as a boy, and in 11 per cent, as a girl. In the remainder of the cases,
the sex of the questioner was not specified. In a few cases, the questioner
was identified as dull or as of average intelligence, but never as bright
or gifted.

The most frequently mentioned immediate teacher reaction was
puzzlement (22 per cent of the respondents). Other frequently registered reactions are:

	Per Cent
Irritation and annoyance	17
Avoidance, making light of question	17
Desire to answer question immediately	13
Surprise or shock	13
Amusement, laughter	11
Admiration, sympathy	7
Interest in finding out himself	6

The most frequently reported classroom reactions are:

	Per Cent
Interest, acceptance, excitement	46
Amusement, laughter, giggles	39

	Per Cent
Puzzlement, curiosity	15
Anxiety, tension	7
Irritation, disgust	6
Surprise, shock	6
Disinterest, scowls	6

The most frequently mentioned way of showing respect for questions is "answering the question directly," a response reported by 44 per cent of the teachers who reported an incident related to the application of the principle of respecting unusual questions. Other frequently mentioned ways of manifesting respect for questions are:

	Per Cent
Letting the class answer or discuss the question	22
Helping class answer question by discussing	13
Praise, recognition	11
Helping pupil find answer to question	9
Helping class answer question by reading, testing	9
Stopping laughter	7

Satisfaction on the part of the pupil was reported by 37 per cent of the respondents and increased interest by 32 per cent as the immediate effects of the reported attempt to apply the principle of being respectful of unusual questions. Fifteen per cent reported that their pupils developed new insights, and 7 per cent noted a lack of satisfaction and continued undesirable behavior.

The most frequently reported long-range effects are continued or increased motivation and improved insight or judgment, each given by 22 per cent of the respondents. One third reported no long-range effect. Seven per cent of the teachers observed an increased respect among their students for the questions of others, and the same percentages noted continued curiosity regarding the subject of the question and decreased fear of asking questions among pupils.

The total report was considered in making a determination as to whether or not the teacher did, in fact, show respect for the unusual question reported. Reported immediate reactions such as anger, desire "to kick him in the pants," unpleasant sensations, and the like by themselves were not sufficient evidence for a judgment of lack of respect. Such indications might become a part of a pattern of signs which were accepted as indicating a lack of respect for unusual questions. Usually, however, giving an evasive or false answer, failing to deal with the question, scolding the questioner, and admitted pretense were considered sufficient evidence for such a judgment. Laughter or shocked silence and laughter were not regarded as sufficient evidence. If laughter on the part of the teacher was accompanied by such an immediate or long-range effect as reluctance by pupils to ask questions thereafter, such a judgment seemed justified.

A few reports might profitably be examined in detail. For example, it is questionable whether the fourth-grade teacher who gave the following report was aware that she had missed an excellent opportunity to apply the principle of treating pupils' questions with respect. She may have actually felt, as she reported, that by labelling the questions as unanswerable, she was complying with the spirit of the principle. It may have been, on the other hand, that this report could be the result of some belated prodding from her conscience.

1. *What was the question, who asked it, and what were the general conditions under which it was asked?*

The question asked dealt with sex; we had a rabbit in our room and discussion was centered around it. All of the class was very much interested in the discussion; a boy asked, "Why do you need two rabbits to have little rabbits?" Everyone joined in and wanted to know.

2. *What was your immediate reaction?*

My immediate thought was: "Can't teach sex in school." My action was to laugh and casually change the subject.

3. *What was the immediate reaction of the class, if observable?*

There was keen interest in the question. I observed that a couple of pupils drew a little color.

4. *In what way was respect shown for the question?*

I told the class that many questions that are asked are good, but too hard to answer without going into research.

5. *What, if any, were the observable effects (immediate and/or long-range)?*

Everyone sort of shrugged it off with teacher-doesn't-know-anything attitude.

A majority of the reports dealt with orthodox interpretations of the principle. The attitude of one first-grade teacher, as revealed in the remarks which follow, contrasts sharply with the manner in which the teacher just cited reported that he showed respect for his pupils' questions.

1. *What was the question, who asked it, and what were the general conditions under which it was asked?*

Where does the water on the blackboard go? This was asked when the board was being washed. The teacher then asked the question of the class. One child thought it soaked into the blackboard.

2. *What was your immediate reaction?*

Return the question to the class. Get their opinions.

3. *What was the immediate reaction of the class, if observable?*
Many children said, "Oh, no—it goes into the air." The boy who answered the question looked embarrassed.

4. *In what way was respect shown for the question?*
I said that it did look as though water seemed to soak into the board and thought we would find out what did happen.

5. *What, if any, were the observable effects (immediate and/or long-range)?*
Discussion of evaporation. Experiments on causes of evaporation—heat, air, etc. We fanned a wet blackboard and saw evaporation take place more rapidly. This all led to a study of water, clouds, rain, fog, etc.

Some of the reports suggest that one of the most genuine ways of showing respect for the unusual questions of children is to become genuinely interested in exploring the question. Children's questions, however, may stir up things which the teacher would prefer to forget or to ignore. The following report is an example of this type of threatening question and a brief description of the way in which a sixth-grade teacher coped with it.

1. *What was the question, who asked it, and what were the general conditions under which it was asked?*
Question: Mr. Nelson, would you turn Communist if the Russians captured America?
Asked by: Robert Koski.
Conditions: During social studies period, while discussing living conditions of the Russian people. We were studying the unit on the Soviet Union.

2. *What was your immediate reaction?*
Does he feel we eventually will be attacked by the Russians? Why?

3. *What was the immediate reaction of the class, if observable?*
General reaction: What would happen if America were attacked and captured?

4. *In what way was respect shown for the question?*
The children really seriously considered or thought about the question.

5. *What, if any, were the observable effects (immediate and/or long-range)?*
General conclusion was that even though the question provoked a bit of insecurity, by being good American citizens and upholding our national traditions, we would not be conquered by Communism. The spirit of freedom *must continue* to prevail.

It is interesting to note that the teacher reported that the children thought seriously about the question, but he never indicates that he himself thought seriously about the question. The original question was a personal one: "Mr. Nelson, would you turn Communist if the Russians captured America?" Admitting that the question would be threatening to almost any American citizen, it seems to us that Mr. Nelson was evasive and could not consider the question asked.

Since it has often been asserted that children lose much of their curiosity by the time they reach the fourth grade, a comparison was made of the judged respect manifested by primary teachers and intermediate grade teachers. The results indicate a statistically significant trend in favor of primary teachers. Seventy-two per cent of the reports of primary teachers compared to 43 per cent of those of intermediate grade teachers were judged to manifest respect for unusual questions. Similarly, 40 per cent of the intermediate grade teachers compared with 19 per cent of the primary grade teachers were judged to have manifested a lack of respect for the unusual questions of their pupils.

BEING RESPECTFUL OF IMAGINATIVE OR UNUSUAL IDEAS

The second of the recommended principles, "Be respectful of imaginative or unusual ideas," is sometimes difficult to apply in the elementary grades because a part of the teacher's job is to disentangle fact from fantasy with young children and to move them from fantasy to a sounder type of creative thinking. However, it seems essential that fantasy be kept alive until a child's mental development is such that he can move to this sounder type of creative thinking.

Suggestions for demonstrations or experiments and naive concepts are the two types of ideas most frequently reported by the respondents (about 20 per cent in each category). The following types of ideas were also mentioned:

	Per Cent
Idea for an assembly program or other special event	13
Fantasy behavior, story of imaginary person	11
Idea for a drawing, painting	9
Invention, innovation	7
New classroom procedure	5

About two thirds of the initiators of the imaginative or unusual ideas were identified as boys, and only 18 per cent were identified as girls. The sex of the other initiators of ideas was not identified. In about 15 per cent of the cases, the initiator was identified as "lonely" or "isolated."

The single most frequently reported (34 per cent of the incidents reported) teacher reaction was pleasure or approval. Other frequently reported reactions include:

	Per Cent
Silly, immature, unreasonable, wild, fantastic	20
Surprise, shock, skepticism	18
Disapproval, attempt to dissuade	18
Compassion, pity, sympathy	9
Recognition of idea as original, thoughtful	9

The most common classroom reaction reported by teachers in response to imaginative or unusual ideas was "interest, excitement, and approval" (39 per cent). Other common classroom reactions are:

	Per Cent
Laughter, amusement, giggling	21
Puzzlement, surprise, doubt	13
Failure of teacher to observe or recall pupil reaction	13
Disapproving, restraining	9

The following are the most frequently reported ways by which respect was shown for imaginative or unusual ideas:

	Per Cent
Discussed, explained, considered	39
Approval of class	21
Experiment conducted, idea tested	14
Idea, contribution, accepted or used	14
Some other activity substituted, idea evaded	11
Stimulated other activity	9

The most commonly reported immediate effects are:

	Per Cent
Satisfaction, pleasure	39
Interest, motivation aroused	35
Sustained effort	18
Continued curiosity, questioning	7

The most frequently mentioned long-range effects are:

	Per Cent
Satisfaction, sustained interest	23
Change in attitude, behavior	23
New pupil insight	11
Stimulus for other original ideas	9
Execution of experiment at home, discussion at home	5
Not satisfied, rejection of idea	5

It will be observed that the reports of the teachers reflect a great deal of scoffing at imaginative or unusual ideas. The dividends in pupil growth are usually great when the teacher is willing to give pupils an opportunity to communicate the results of their experiments and self-initiated learning. The following incident reported by a first-grade teacher is an example of what frequently happens when this is done.

1. *What was the idea, who expressed it, and what were the general conditions under which the idea was suggested?*

The idea was a science experiment to be set up by a boy who had tried it at home, following several class discussions. He mentioned several experiments about floating and magnets and suggested demonstrating each. Conditions were a normal class discussion about floating and nonfloating objects, but the boy who contributed had always seemed to have a passive attitude.

2. *What was your immediate reaction to the idea?*

I was thrilled to think we had finally hit upon a subject of interest to him.

3. *What was the immediate reaction of the class, if observable?*

Quite excited and eager to see the experiments carried out.

4. *In what way was respect shown for the idea?*

The boy was asked to bring the needed items and was allowed to show what he had discovered on his own time.

5. *What, if any, were the observable effects (immediate and/or long-range)?*

Every child seemed to be interested enough to carry out some experimenting at home, and several brought their experiments and conclusions to share with the class. The passive interest of the boy became very active, not only in the area of science, but also in all other subjects. His attitude changed almost completely from not caring to high interest.

As in this case, it is interesting to note from the data already presented that in 39 per cent of the reports submitted the classroom reaction was one of "interest, excitement, and approval." Such a response naturally makes it easier for the teacher to provide the kind of opportunity for experimentation described above. It is a different matter when the immediate response of the class is one of rejection. It is difficult to support and protect a minority of one, as we see in the following report.

1. *What was the idea, who expressed it, and what were the general conditions under which the idea was suggested?*

The idea was to pretend that everyone was a different animal and how it felt to be this animal. One of the girls in my top reading group expressed the idea. We were studying the settlement of the West, and different animals were mentioned (fourth grade).

2. *What was your immediate reaction to the idea?*

My reaction was that it had possibilities if motivation could be brought up.

3. *What was the immediate reaction of the class, if observable?*
The class thought that it was sort of childish.

4. *In what way was respect shown for the idea?*
We discussed the idea and different possibilities were brought up—things that could be brought in.

5. *What, if any, were the observable effects (immediate and/or long-range)?*
The class carried through with the project, making it into a play. Everyone took the role of a different animal. Research was done on each animal, his habits, home, and eating, and a play was produced out of our findings.

Another teacher reported a project in which pupils had written stories about such topics as "My Life as a Paper Sack," "My Life as a Sweater," and the like. They drew pictures of themselves in these roles and wrote interesting stories of their adventures. Some teachers feel themselves that such activities are silly. Teachers who hold this view might find it useful to read Gordon's *Synectics* (1961), which contains many examples of how such imaginative activities have been used deliberately by scientists and inventors in making discoveries and inventions of great social importance.

SHOWING CHILDREN THAT THEIR IDEAS HAVE VALUE

Wilt (1959) counsels teachers to exploit carefully and subtly any hint of creativity which reveals itself in the classroom. One of the best ways to make certain that creativity is not frightened away is to show children that their ideas have value. This principle seems to be one of the fundamental tenets in the teaching philosophy of those teachers who offered the most clear-cut evidence in their reports of the importance of showing children that their ideas have value.

An analysis of the kinds of signs reported by teachers to indicate that they had respected the ideas of their pupils by showing them that their ideas have value are as follows:

	Per Cent
Uses of applied idea, material contributed	58
Provided time to implement idea, changed schedule	34
Demonstrated idea was true or permitted pupil to do so	33
Permitted or encouraged further inquiry	21
Listened or watched with interest	19
Agreed with, approved, or praised idea	16
Provided materials or other resources to implement idea	15
Gave credit or recognition for authorship of idea	11

A similar analysis of pupil responses when teachers made efforts to show children that their ideas have value revealed the following to be the most frequently reported reactions:

	Per Cent
Expressed pleasure, smiled, brightened	44
Expressed approval of classmate's idea	37
Followed through with idea, imitated	32
Became enthusiastically absorbed with idea	29
Acceptance of originator as a person increased	24
Interest in learning increased	24
Confidence increased in other areas of work	16

The following report by a first-grade teacher illustrates why it is important to show children that their ideas have value.

1. *What was the occasion which provided the opportunity to show a pupil that his ideas are valuable? Who was the child? What did he do? How did he seem to feel about his idea(s)?*

The class was writing a poem to set to music. We were discussing snow and its qualities, trying to discover rhyming words. Jess is bashful and hesitates to contribute although he has a vivid imagination. He mumbled something about snow looking like jewels. He seemed embarrassed that snow looked like jewels to him.

2. *What did you do to try to show him that his ideas are of value?*

I was very pleased that he could see such beautiful things as jewels in the snow, and I encouraged him to tell us why snow made him think of jewels and what kind of jewels he thought of.

3. *How did he react to what you did (immediate and/or long-range)?*

He sensed the approval of the class and their approving of "snow looking like jewels." He said that snow seemed to look like diamonds. When asked why he thought so, he said that it sparkles. We were able to use his idea in our song. "It sparkled like a diamond bright." This led Jess to have more self-confidence, and he expresses himself more freely. The class benefits by this, since he has an exceptionally large vocabulary plus a vivid imagination.

4. *What was the reaction of the class, if observable?*

The children were delighted with his choice of words, for it sparked their imaginations as well as contributed to the song we were writing.

This teacher perhaps unknowingly reinforced what appears to be an exceptionally important kind of creative behavior—the use of analogy. Young children and outstanding creative people seem to have a natural tendency to analogize, but some observers have noted that this ability seems to fade out as children proceed through school. Perhaps it is because children are embarrassed that they think in terms of analogy because it isn't really like that. In other words, the child knows that snow is not really a diamond, and he is embarrassed that he sees snow in this unreal way. Perhaps this teacher has taken an important step in keeping alive this boy's apparently excellent ability to analogize.

Many of the teachers showed through their reports that they understood and could apply the principle of showing children that their ideas have value. The skill with which many of them handled their pupils' venturesome ideas was heartening. For example, a second-grade teacher related how she was able to utilize a boy's imaginative idea in a stimulating lesson for everyone in the class.

1. *What was the occasion which provided the opportunity to show a pupil that his ideas are valuable? Who was the child? What did he do? How did he seem to feel about his idea(s)?*

Science incident: Studying about the sun and how it affects the earth.

Student's idea: Some people must sleep while we are awake. He examined the globe which was at his disposal to see which countries were actually having day. A large flashlight was also used to give half of the earth a shadow. This child went on with his intense interest to make a picture of the solar system to show the relation of the sun to the earth and the other planets.

2. *What did you do to try to show him that his ideas are of value?*

Set up a display letting him help to show the entire class how he had arrived at his conclusion. Then a bulletin board was made with a huge sun and earth made by the class committees which were chosen. People (paper dolls) who were awake were made and cut out, then placed on the board.

3. *How did he react to what you did (immediate and/or long-range)?*

Created a more intense interest toward the study of heavenly bodies and how they are affected by the sun. Are now more aware of how space can affect us.

4. *What was the reaction of the class, if observable?*

Enthusiasm and a very intense interest in what was being studied. Some were even beginning to display some small ideas which they wanted to develop further. A mural was also drawn as a result of this type of study in science.

Clark (1951) has hypothesized that a teacher's response to pupil behavior is a function of her personality. If such is the case (his hypothesis was only partially confirmed by his own experiment), the fifth-grade teacher who submitted the following report has several of those personality characteristics which are essential for a teacher who wishes to show her pupils that their ideas have value.

1. *What was the occasion which provided the opportunity to show a pupil that his ideas are valuable? Who was the child? What did he do? How did he seem to feel about his idea?*

Our class had been going through the morning routine of taking lunch money, attendance, giving news, giving the pledge, and singing the anthem under my direction. One morning a girl, Sue—a bright child with many new ideas—told me she thought it would be a good idea if the president of the class took charge at this time and they called this a class meeting. She felt quite strongly about her suggestion and asked me what we had a president for if he didn't do anything. (We had in reality been having a meeting, but it wasn't their meeting, and she thought it might be useful to use the time in this way.)

2. *What did you do to try to show her that her ideas are of value?*

I simply told her that it might be worthwhile to try it and see how it worked. I told her that the officers of the class might get together each day and plan this meeting and could take care of discussing any class problems at this time.

3. *How did she react to what you did (immediate and/or long-range)?*

She was very pleased that I would try her idea and simply told me, "Thank you!"

4. *What was the reaction of the class, if observable?*

The class liked this idea very much, and when it was tried, they got more out of this period than they ever had under my supervision. They showed much respect for their president and carried on very mature discussions during this time. The period had become more meaningful for them. Many of the children looked to Susan as a person with a great idea and wondered why no one had thought of it before.

In contrast to the preceding anecdote is the following report by a third-grade teacher who was evidently unable to support the idea of one of her pupils.

1. *What was the occasion which provided the opportunity to show a pupil that his ideas are valuable? Who was the child? What did he do? How did he seem to feel about his idea(s)?*

We were putting to music a song we wrote, as well as making up individual songs. This one little girl got up and started to sing a song she had composed, and everybody laughed at her.

2. *What did you do to try to show her that her ideas are of value?*

The song she sang was good and had a lot of truth in it, even though some of the words were funny.

3. *How did she react to what you did (immediate and/or long-range)?*

She felt hurt that the class had laughed at her contribution.

4. *What was the reaction of the class, if observable?*

(No reply).

Apparently this third-grade teacher was sensitive enough to recognize that the child's song had a message, a truth, and that the child was hurt by her classmates' laughter and ridicule. Yet she was evidently helpless to do anything about it. She evaded stating what she (the teacher) did to show the child that her ideas had value by acknowledging (apparently to herself) that the child's song was good and had a lot of truth in it. It is interesting that this teacher was impelled to select this incident from the many others she might possibly have given.

Some of the respondents in their reports manifested a keen sensitivity which enabled them to forestall incidents such as the above or to make such painful experiences into constructive ones. One second-grade teacher reported, "At first I had a feeling that some children were about to laugh at the suggestion, but because I quickly acknowledged the contribution, no embarrassing laughter took place." Another wrote, "I showed respect for his idea by my interest, surprise, and delight." It is in such an evaluative condition as these attitudes provide that the following behavior of a first-grader could occur: "He seemed to feel positive about what he said and did not look at the other children to see their approval or disapproval. . . ."

UNEVALUATED PRACTICE

Although we realized that the principle of unevaluated practice would perhaps be unfamiliar to some teachers, we had not expected so much distortion of the principle and lack of genuine understanding as the reports reflected. In spite of this, however, it is interesting to note that forty-six (82 per cent) of the fifty-six incidents submitted were described as successful. Eight of the ten unsuccessful experiences reported were in the intermediate grades. It was observed that almost all the failures occurred in the practice of skills or already learned tasks rather than in creative activities or new tasks or content.

The following is a summary of the most frequently reported signs that creative thinking was respected when the principle of unevaluated practice was applied:

	Per Cent
Later performance evaluated, produced publicly	47
Conducted interesting and exciting activity	29
Showed personal pride in performance of pupils	29
Recognized subsequent achievement	21
Accepted contribution, made no remark	21
Emphasized enjoyment, doing for fun	9
Gave pupils responsibility for activity	9

The following is a summary of the pupil responses reported by teachers:

	Per Cent
Manifested enjoyment, relaxation	42
Deep involvement and absorption in tasks	35
Performance in subsequent situations showed improvement	29
Increased motivation shown	21
Reported to class on self-initiated learning	13
Wanted to see or read productions of others	9

The fact that there is no evaluation of the practice performance does not mean that pupils have no need for reaction from teachers. The aim, however, is to learn, discover, or develop skills, rather than to earn a grade. The need actually seems to be one of communicating what one had discovered or produced. The intense need for this is illustrated by the following report of a teacher of a combined fifth-and-sixth-grade class.

1. *Describe the initial assignment and the general situation in which it was given.*

We were just finishing a unit on the Southern states in fifth-grade social studies. Several different students volunteered to find out more about some of the important crops of the Southern states and some of their unusual uses.

2. *How did you communicate to them that they were free to experiment, that it didn't count "on the record"?*

I told the students that this assignment was for their own benefit so that they as individuals might know more about the subjects given. I told them that they would not be expected to report their information to either the class or to me.

3. *What happened during the "practice" period?*

During the practice period the children could be observed using the encyclopedia and other reference books in the room and the library to gather information on the subject. Some children brought books from home for others to use.

4. *What happened immediately after the practice period?*

After finishing their reading, they seemed anxious to tell me and the students some of the things they had learned. I, therefore, allowed time for those who wanted to report their findings to the class.

5. *What was the nature of the similar task given for "the record"?*

Later, in a unit on the Central states, boys and girls volunteered to look up information of a similar kind, and they were asked to give an oral report to the class on their subjects.

6. *How was it rewarded, if rewarded?*

This task was rewarded by their receiving an "extra-credit" grade in social studies.

It was clear from a number of the reports that the respondents believe that anything a child does in school is wasted unless it counts on the record. It is quite possible that it is this kind of attitude that conditions high school, college, and even graduate students to be interested in learning only those things which will appear on examinations or count directly in determining their grades.

Even the reports submitted by teachers in the present study indicate that young people *can* learn and gain confidence in their abilities when they are not being evaluated. Among the reports submitted by classroom teachers regarding their application of the practice-for-fun principle is the following account by a sixth-grade teacher.

1. *Describe the initial assignment and the general situation in which it was given.*

I asked three boys to try filtering dirty water. They were told that paper toweling or a cloth inside a funnel could serve as a filter.

2. *How did you communicate to them that they were free to experiment, that it didn't count on the record?*

I told them that it had been a long time since I had done the same and could no longer remember how I obtained the best filtering. I told them to work up a good demonstration for the class.

3. *What happened during the "practice" period?*

They first used one towel filter in one funnel—they poured the filtered water through again but used a clean filter. They repeated this seven or eight times to get clear water. Another start was made using a double-towel filter. Found it saved time so they hooked up another funnel and filter above the other. Quicker and cleaner.

4. *What happened immediately after the practice period?*

Materials were put away. The boys were anxious to demonstrate to the class. Very happy with "their new" fast method.

5. *What was the nature of the similar task given for "the record"?*

The demonstration for the class. Objective: obtain clear water in fifteen minutes. The boys used two funnels triple-toweled with a piece of sheet (cloth) between the two funnels.

6. *How was it rewarded, if rewarded?*

Through the praise, amazement, and "Thank you's" from the class.

Several teachers reported that evaluation made their pupils tense. A second-grade teacher remarked, "Tension was increased (when a task was evaluated), and some students who knew their facts well made many mistakes. This was especially evident in very young children." Performance is reduced when tension is increased. To be realistic, we must recognize that ultimate evaluation is inescapable and that children do need to learn how to work adequately under stressful conditions. If stress is too great, however, children are unable to learn and to think. It becomes necessary to reduce stress in order for them to perform adequately. After skills have been attained, this kind of freedom from stress becomes less important. The following account illustrates how one fourth-grade teacher used her understanding of these facts.

1. *Describe the initial assignment and the general situation in which it was given.*

Handwriting has received much more emphasis in our curriculum this year. At fourth-grade level, the big experience is that of using pens for the first time. When the pens were shown for the first time, a general hand-clapping swept through the room, and faces immediately lighted up. My comment: "We have all worked so hard to improve our writing that I think we have now earned the right to try our new pens."

2. *How did you communicate to them that they were free to experiment, that it didn't count on the record?*

I told the children, directly, that their first work with pens would in no way affect grades. I assured them that all of us had to practice so that we would know how to handle the pen, how much pressure should be used on the point, and even how to "think" with a pen in hand. The sigh of relief was quite audible.

3. *What happened during the "practice" period?*

The "practice" period was a great success. I feel that I could safely say that I had never seen such a concerted effort on the part of every child in the room. The effort and concentration was fun to observe. Their evident pride and satisfaction in what they were doing was also rewarding.

4. *What happened immediately after the practice period?*

When I told the class that we had worked long enough for the first time, they set up an immediate clamor: "Don't make us stop now!" "Can't we work just a little longer?" "May we do this again tomorrow?" The enthusiasm was still at a very high level.

5. *What was the nature of the similar task given for the record?*

After about two weeks of daily practice, I had the children write a little note to take home. In the note they stated that they wanted their parents to see how well they could write with an ink pen. I was well aware that my marks were a little on the "high side," but I would not have done anything to dampen that eagerness and enthusiasm for the new experience.

6. *How was it rewarded, if rewarded?*

I feel that the children created their own reward. On Friday morning, when the weekly spelling test is given, they begged to be allowed to use their pens. My personal feeling was that all were not ready for this experience. But the demand was so insistent throughout the room that it didn't take me long to give my consent. Again, came the general clapping and "Oh, boy's!" I did assure the children that, in all fairness, I would give them the benefit of the doubt when there would be a question in my mind as to just which letter was meant. This relieved them of any feeling of strain or tension, and they happily wrote their test with pens. I might add that we still have "practice sessions."

There is in this collection of reports a strong indication that the attitudes and values of the teacher are the major determinants of success in applying the principle of unevaluated practice.

RELATING EVALUATION TO CAUSES AND CONSEQUENCES

When reporting incidents in which evaluation was related to causes and consequences, the teachers who participated in this study most often cited cases of misconduct. Perhaps nothing concerns the average classroom teacher more than discipline. Since the kind of learning which the school emphasizes does not take place without the presence of some minimal degree of discipline, their concern is justifiable. Children learn constructive things in a reasonably orderly, purposeful classroom; they usually learn the wrong things in a disorderly, disorganized, purposeless classroom. The following report from a fourth-grade teacher is illustrative of the concern for discipline which most of the teachers revealed.

1. *What was the nature of the behavior to be evaluated? Who was involved?*

We were taking a field trip, and just before we went we had a fire drill. The children were disturbed and ran out of the room yelling.

2. *What was your personal evaluation of the behavior?*

I was just plain mad, mad, mad.

3. *How did you or the class show the relationship of the behavior to cause and consequence?*

We really had it out and talked about it. I used the wrong type of discipline. . . . I told them that they were not going on their field trip.

4. *What were the effects, if observable (immediate and/or long-range)?*

Sadness and a feeling of guilt and shame. We did get to go on the field trip, and I think they did learn their lesson, even if the wrong way.

The above report is particularly interesting for its manifestation of conflict between the teacher's desire for order and her feelings about the very way order should be achieved. The methods most frequently reported for achieving order and for showing the relationship of evaluation to causes and consequences are as follows:

	Per Cent
Used group discussion to show relationships	38
Used actual consequences (illness, injury) to show relationship usually between some nonconforming behavior and unfavorable consequence	22

Per Cent

Explained dangers of a certain kind of behavior	12
Scolded	12
Rewarded changed or improved behavior	8
Showed relationship between idea and success of project	8
Isolated offending member from group	8

Forty per cent of the reports mentioned some kind of improved pupil or class behavior resulting from applying the principle of showing causal relationships. Other reports named such outcomes as: cessation of offending behavior, improved group functioning, spontaneous creative behavior, increased problem-solving behavior, and a few negative behaviors. These data suggest that teachers do believe in this principle and perceive positive outcomes from efforts to show relationships between cause and effect.

Not all the incidents submitted describe success stories, however. Some of the reports indicate that there was apparently no resolution of conflicts between desires for order and the means of obtaining it. The one which follows, written by a first-grade teacher, is somewhat depressing.

1. *What was the nature of the behavior to be evaluated? Who was involved?*
A child broke a milk bottle and, when corrected, became most disturbed and began a little "tantrum."

2. *What was your personal evaluation of the behavior?*
I tried to help him but finally had to use force.

3. *How did you or the class show the relationship of the behavior to cause and/or consequence?*
Didn't have time.

4. *What were the effects, if observable (immediate and/or long-range)?*
Very poor on all.

We cannot be certain what this teacher is trying to say by submitting this report. My guess is that she is trying to say that there are occasions when behavior is so serious there is no time to show relationships to causes and consequences. All that the teacher can do is to punish or to use force. After all, she had tried to "correct" him after he had broken the bottle.

Some of the reports provide excellent examples of how the application of this principle can be used in helping pupils to accept their own divergency or individuality. The following example is concerned with the somewhat divergent physical characteristic of left-handedness, but the general approach might be applied to many other types of divergency.

1. *What was the nature of the behavior to be evaluated? Who was involved?*

Pupil showed great reluctance to attempt to learn cursive writing.

2. *What was your personal evaluation of the behavior?*

Child, though larger and heavier than most children in the class, was immature, and his coordination was not normal. He was left-handed and told me his previous teacher insisted that he use his right hand when writing. He was not enjoying success in his endeavors.

3. *How did you or the class show the relationship of the behavior to cause and/or consequence?*

I told the child that there were several other left-handed children in the class and pointed them out to him. It was emphasized to all that no attempt would be made to change writing hands. The boy was shown an example of one of the left-handed writer's work and was encouraged. All his early efforts were praised, regardless of the poor quality (how much better he was doing than he had been doing). After confidence was gained, refinements were made. At no time did the class ridicule his early attempts. In fact, more rapid learners offered assistance.

4. *What were the effects, if observable (immediate and/or long-range)?*

Marked improvement in writing, spelling, and reading.

It is also encouraging to note that some of the teachers reporting incidents had been able to identify in undesirable behavior a manifestation of strong human needs in the process of going wrong and to transform these into positive, creative behavior. The following account by a second-grade teacher is just such a case.

1. *What was the nature of the behavior to be evaluated? Who was involved?*

A boy had been collecting pencils unofficially. In other words, he was "lifting" other children's pencils during the noon hour. A parent sent me a note about her child's missing pencils.

2. *What was your personal evaluation of the behavior?*

This was a simple form of stealing, but it is tied in some way to a child's wish to collect. Aha! We need a collecting project and a hobby show! We need to stress mutual aid with permission.

3. *How did you or the class show the relationship of the behavior to cause and/or consequence?*

We talked about the inconveniences of not finding one's pencil when it is needed. We talked about how good it is to help one another with permission and planned to help one another with hobby collections.

4. *What were the effects, if observable (immediate and/or long-range)?*

We had a hobby show in the making. I sent out a three-page letter to parents with the request that hobbies be started for an April hobby show. I included some explanatory paragraphs about children's desires for collecting sometimes running rampant and the need for channeling these. I asked for mutual aid with permission. The mother who sent the note was contacted by telephone, and she agreed to make bags for collecting for all the boys to use. I obtained pieces of cloth free-of-charge from a local store (odds and ends), and the mother made the collection bags for the boys. Other cloth pieces and pages from pattern books were given the girls for making and dressing paper dolls or for use in any other hobby.

A hobby show is planned in April. Children already have some good hobbies under way, such as key collections, car pictures, railroad trains, model ships, and submarines. The mother who wrote the note is delighted with the way the problem was handled. Children are helping one another with their hobbies. They talk about their hobbies and continue to find out things related to them.

Although some educators may not agree with this teacher's interpretation of a child's stealing pencils as a frustrated need to collect, it must be admitted that this teacher was apparently able to transform socially undesirable behavior into positive, creative behavior. Furthermore, he was apparently able to make use of the children's altruistic motivations and use them to enrich the experience for all. This is a far cry from the usual punitive, retributive approach commonly applied in the case of socially disapproved behavior.

The reports concerning the principle of relating evaluation to cause and consequence exposed another common concern of teachers: whether pupils are paying attention to them. Because they do a great deal of talking (directing, admonishing, explaining, reading), teachers are often worried that their pupils may not be listening to them. Their fear that many youngsters in close physical proximity have "tuned them out" is well-founded. It *is* true that children do not hear their teachers at various times during the school day, especially teachers who spend a great deal of their time warning, scolding, and exhorting their pupils.

Not all the reports submitted concerning applications of the relating-evaluation-to-cause-and-consequence principle dealt with discipline and attention, however. Among the many "faithful" interpretations of the spirit of the principle was this one by a sixth-grade teacher in Utah.

1. *What was the nature of the behavior to be evaluated? Who was involved?*
   Student made response in class discussion that was not entirely in keeping with the subject under discussion.

2. *What was your personal evaluation of the behavior?*

Child's desire to be recognized by peers for having contributed something of value to discussion caused him to chance a comment even though he wasn't sure of the subject.

3. *How did you or the class show the relationship of the behavior to cause and/or consequence?*

Changed discussion trend slightly to make student's remarks be seen as relevant. Amplified and clarified his remarks to make them more important and applicable to situation.

4. *What were the effects, if observable (immediate and/or long-range)?*

Student continues to participate. Not deterred by what might have been a failure in contributing something of value. He maintains an interest in discussion. Earnestly tried to reach solutions in problem-centered discussion.

An incident such as the one just described can often do a great deal to make a child feel he is making a contribution. In such incidents it is frequently difficult to make use of the divergent thinker's contributions because he sees relationships which his teacher and classmates miss. Lacking in articulateness, he is sometimes unable to make others see these unusual relationships. This case is an interesting example of a teacher who met the challenge by extending himself to see relationships and to give relevance and salience to the divergent thinker's contribution.

Discussion of Results

LIMITATIONS OF THE STUDY

Although the sample of teacher behavior obtained from the reports might be regarded as fairly representative—reports were received from 114 teachers of children at every grade level from kindergarten through ninth grade in 35 public and private schools in 13 states and the District of Columbia—it is obviously dangerous to infer too much about the teachers from their questionnaires. No attempt is being made here to equate effective teachers with those who can accept and apply the five principles of rewarding creative thinking (although that is admittedly the bias of the writer). Similarly, there is no reason to conclude that teachers who are unable to interpret one or more of the principles correctly are inferior to those who can understand them. The extent to which the respondents had been exposed to these ideas prior to their reporting would greatly influence their ability to interpret the meanings of the five principles. The picture painted of the rejecting teacher is

significant primarily because it exposes the values and teacher characteristics which are antagonistic to divergent thinking in children.

At least three points need to be noted when it comes to determining teacher values:

1. Teachers are subject to the same sort of frailties, foibles, and
   fantasies to which other humans are subject.
2. Teachers, like other occupational groups, are conditioned by
   their work, developing certain predispositions or sets.
3. Teachers share a third characteristic with their nonteaching
   brethren—those who enjoy their work do a better job than
   those who do not.

Let's consider what significance these generalizations have for an
investigation of teacher values.

Judging from the responses of the persons who participated in
this study, teachers are much like other people. There are several personality traits, however, which are apparently discernible in teachers
to a marked degree. These characteristics may be pronounced in teachers because of the physical and psychological circumstances of their
employment. For instance, the time factor bulks large in the thinking
of many teachers. If time is not the same force for a teacher as it is for
a clerk, stationmaster, or farmer, if it does not hold the same fears for
the teacher as it does for a professional athlete, time does dominate
the thinking of many teachers. Innumerable classrooms are run on a
rigidly kept timetable, and any serious deviation in the daily schedule
is upsetting to the teachers who govern the activities in these rooms.

The explanation for this preoccupation with time can be found—
at least in part—in the nature of our educational system. In most elementary schools the teacher has nine months to work with his pupils;
in most high schools he is limited to a period of about forty-five minutes out of the day's schedule. The actual amount of teaching time is
further reduced by extracurricular encroachments of various kinds,
interruptions, announcements, roll-calling, and other procedural matters.
Because their time with young people is limited in these and other
ways, teachers become extremely conscious of the time factor in the
educational process. In addition, they themselves are always faced with
the threat of implicit or explicit evaluation. If they are formally evaluated
by supervisors or administrators, teachers assume that their evaluation
will involve measures of pupil growth in respect to the acquisition of
certain skills and abilities. Even when they are not evaluated formally,
there is always the tacit evaluation of the next teacher who is to
instruct their former pupils, not to mention the considerable effect

which the community's judgment of their professional competence has upon them. Naturally these threats are very real to the teacher, and he often finds himself quite anxious.

Another important trait which seems to be fostered by the circumstances of teaching is the much publicized tendency to conform. Educational institutions are perceived essentially as transmitters of the culture of a society to its youth. Accordingly, it is not too surprising that the individuals upon whom rests most of the responsibility for putting over society's wisdom and ways are either conservative to begin with or soon become so because of their roles. It is said that teachers are fearful they will be criticized by administrators and parents, and therefore they act in ways which will spare them censure. This anxiety curtails a significant amount of experimentation and innovation in the public schools. Even when research studies have shown certain techniques to be far superior to traditional ones and teachers are informed of these findings, teachers are often reluctant to adopt the new ways until they become much less than new. If teachers are in fact anxious about their jobs or emotionally sensitive to criticism, it is understandable if they tend to be conforming.

From the reports, ten personality factors seem to have contributed to a rejection of the five principles. The teachers who were unable to apply the principles were *authoritarian* (Ridiculous for children in second grade; Children who lost their place were not allowed to read when their turn came); *defensive* (I was disturbed and felt my students were not involved; Everyone sort of shrugged it off—with teacher doesn't know anything attitude); *dominated by time* (Our schedule is so full already); *insensitive to their pupils' intellectual and emotional needs* (She's just a problem child and no matter what you do it doesn't help); *intellectually inert* (see some of the misinterpretations above); *lacking in intellectual energy* (At this time of day I was ready to slug him [for suggesting that the room be painted]); *preoccupied with information-giving functions* (Evaluation of behavior: he did not listen to directions or follow through); *disinterested in promoting intellectual curiosity in their pupils* (My action was to laugh and casually change the subject); *preoccupied with disciplinary matters* (I was horrified at his actions); and *unwilling to give much of themselves in the teaching-learning compact* (I was quite put out with the girl and at first thought I would not answer such an obvious and silly question).

The reports also revealed that as a group the teachers who could not accept the principles which were advocated placed a high value on the following concepts: *time* (but not timeliness), *orderliness* (but not necessarily logical thinking), *respect for authority* (but not respect for the potentialities of the individual), *the child's responsibility to the group* (but not especially the teacher's responsibility to the child nor he group's responsibility to the child), *the preservation of their self-images* (but not the enhancement of their pupils' self-images), and *he importance of information* (but not the importance of information-getting skills).

"Resistance to change" is not listed among the personality characteristics of the rejecting teachers because it was not evident from he reports that they were any more opposed to change than the teachers who apparently accepted the principles. However, it seems logical o suppose that they were in fact more conservative than the accepting teachers. The kind of teacher who welcomes unusual questions or imaginative ideas is probably more receptive to new ways of teaching han the type of teacher who rejects this kind of behavior—although ^o basis for this assumption has been made in this study.

Despite their esteem for orderliness, the rejecting teachers were narkedly inaccurate in their spelling, slipshod in their punctuation, and disrespectful of the ordinary rules of grammar. The excerpts which have been presented in this chapter have undergone considerable correction in spelling, punctuation, capitalization, and grammar to improve readability and comprehension.

Although the great majority of the teachers who participated in he study gave excellent examples, the characteristics and values of he teachers who gave inappropriate responses presents a picture of several types of teachers. This is significant for a number of reasons. First, no one disputes the world's desperate need for creative people. However, helping young people realize their talents is no easy matter, and it is especially difficult for teachers who have been oblivious to the dividends which accrue from encouraging children to develop their powers of self-expression.

Second, since the teachers who cooperated in the study were instructed by means of the instruction sheet or supervisors and principals as to how they could cultivate creativity in their classrooms, the ones who were unable to apply the principles could not accept them *in spite of the forces which had been exerted to alter their attitudes and values.* More than literature or lectures is required.

Third, a considerable amount of research has been conducted regarding teacher attitudes and values, and most of the ten characteristics which were found in the rejecting teachers have been found again and again in other groups of teachers. Although the rejecting teachers were decidedly in the minority in this study, it may possibly be that they would be representative of American teachers in general.

Although the values and traits of the teachers who participated in this study could not be determined with any degree of certainty from their reports, it was possible to detect in the words of a great many of the teachers an enthusiasm for teaching.

Conclusion

What is the answer, then? How can we help teachers acquire values which have been demonstrated to be basic to the promotion of intellectual growth when these values are outside their experience? The only way for a teacher to value principles such as those advanced here is to make them a part of his experience. When an individual has known nothing of the relaxation provided by a massage, he will have no disposition to go to a masseur to find relief from tension. Similarly, if a teacher has never allowed his pupils to probe, to challenge, to test, it is foolish to expect him to encourage his pupils to think critically and creatively—even though he is told how to do it. He does not really understand what is involved in putting into practice such principles as "Show your pupils that their ideas have value" or "Treat imaginative ideas with respect." These principles are really the manifestations of an attitude he does not possess. The solution lies somehow in providing the teacher with experiences wherein he can see the advantages— or disadvantages—of such techniques. (We must always admit the possibility that even if the teacher does try out the principles of rewarding creative behavior, he may find them unsatisfactory in his scheme of teaching; we must allow *him* the right to be different also!)

There are at least three procedures which can be taken to help teachers who have had no background in promoting creative thinking gain in this experience. One excellent way to encourage teachers to value unusual or original ideas is to provide them with materials which are easily administered and which lead naturally into creative performance. Such instructional aids as tapes, films, workbooks, and manipulative materials can be used by relatively inexperienced teachers to foster creative activity. Once these devices have been used, the teachers will have more confidence in their ability to bring creative thinking and doing into being.

Actually, the message which comes in loud and clear from these reports of incidents of rewarding creative thinking is that when we ask teachers to behave in certain ways, we must take their values into consideration.

CREATIVE
AND
CRITICAL
EVALUATIVE
ATTITUDES
OF TEACHERS

5

A consideration of the creative and critical evaluative attitudes of teachers in relation to the creative growth of children was suggested by the outcomes of two relatively unsuccessful in-service education experiments. Such a consideration is also suggested by the data presented in Chapter 4.

The first in-service education experiment involved all the regular classes from kindergarten through grade six in a large suburban elementary school. Ten of the teachers were assigned through random procedures to participate in the in-service education sessions, and the other ten were encouraged to proceed as they normally would. All pupils were administered a battery of creative thinking tests (Picture Construction, Incomplete Figures, Circles-Squares, Ask-and-Guess, Product Improvement, and Unusual Uses) in January at the beginning of the program and again in May at the end of the program. The in-service program consisted of a discussion of a manual entitled *Rewarding Creative Thinking*, developed specifically for this purpose. The ten experimental teachers were also supplied a variety of aids for encouraging creative thinking through the language arts (see Appendix B), ideas for teaching elementary school science creatively, and materials on creative methods of teaching mathematics to children.

The results of this in-service experiment were inconclusive and inconsistent. In nineteen of forty-four pre- and post-test comparisons, the experimental classes actually registered losses between January and

May on the measures of creative thinking ability. This is of special interest, since the pre- and post-tests actually consisted of the same tasks, using different stimulus materials. The control groups showed losses in twenty-five of the forty-four comparisons. When the post-test scores were corrected for differences in pre-test scores, there were twelve significant differences in favor of the experimentals and five in favor of the controls.

In a second in-service education experiment, the results were no more encouraging. In this case, the experimental teachers were eleven fourth-, fifth-, and sixth-grade teachers who had participated in a city-wide workshop on creativity in language arts. They were encouraged to participate in the experiment by the central administrative staff in charge of the workshop conducted by the author. There was no pressure upon them to participate, however; in fact, twenty-two other teachers participating in the workshop did not volunteer to participate. The building principals were not involved with the workshop nor with the arrangements for the data collection. The pupils of the experimental teachers and their controls (other teachers in similar schools at the same grade levels who had not been enrolled in the workshop) were asked to write imaginative stories at the beginning of the experiment in February and again at the end in May. The teachers were asked to indicate on a checklist which of the specific activities (suggested by the author for developing creative thinking through the language arts) they had actually carried out. The imaginative stories were analyzed for originality, interest, and the composite index of creativity described in Appendix A.

The teachers who had participated in the workshop and had been given specific suggestions and ideas for creative activities in the language arts did not use any more of the suggested activities than did the teachers who had not participated in the workshop and had not been given these experimental materials. In fact, the control teachers actually used a slightly larger number of these activities than did the experimental teachers. Furthermore, the pupils of the experimental teachers failed to show creative growth on either of the three measures used. In another school system, however, an elementary school principal introduced the collection of suggested ideas to his teachers and conducted the same tests as in this experiment. The results showed that the teachers in this school used a larger number of the suggested activities for promoting creative growth in language arts than the controls, and their pupils showed significant growth on the three measures used.

Out of these relatively discouraging experiences, I began wondering if the evaluative attitudes of the teachers might be more powerful in determining the creative growth of children than the kinds of in-

ervice education which seem to be available. It was possible to administer the Personal-Social Motivation Inventory described in the
Appendix A to most of the teachers involved in these studies. Since this
inventory provides measures of Creative and Critical Evaluative Attitudes or Motivation, this gave me an opportunity to explore the possible influence of teachers' evaluative attitudes on the creative growth
of pupils.

Before describing the analysis of the data and presenting the
results, I shall review some of what we know already about the influence of teacher attitudes on intellectual growth, especially creative
growth.

Other Studies
of Teacher Attitude and Pupil Growth

There has long been a feeling among some educators that the
motivations and attitudes of teachers have an important influence
upon the mental and emotional growth of pupils. There have been
few studies, however, that have given much dependable information
about what kinds of motivations and attitudes of teachers affect what
kinds of growth. The research problem is a complex and difficult one.
Those who have made honest attempts to conduct such studies are
usually overwhelmed by the complexity of the problem. The few carefully conducted studies which have been reported, however, have been
quite encouraging.

An example of one of the more carefully conducted studies related
to achievement is one by McCardle (1959) which uses the Minnesota
Teacher Attitude Inventory, a measure of teachers' attitudes toward
children. McCardle's study involved 29 teachers and 1643 pupils in first-
year algebra. Teachers having the most favorable attitudes towards
children, as measured by the Minnesota Teacher Attitude Inventory,
achieved significantly higher gains on quantitative thinking and functional competence in mathematics. There were no statistically significant differences in pupil means on the mechanics of elementary
algebra. The teachers high on the MTAI were apparently not so
"textbook bound" as the teachers falling into the low and middle groups
on this measure. In other words, the pupils of the high MTAI teachers
were better able to use what they had learned in the solution of
problems.

The complexity of the problem is reflected in a set of clues I
derived from data collected by Yamamoto (1962). The nineteen fifth-
grade teachers in this study were administered a battery of the Min-

nesota Tests of Creative Thinking (Form D) and the Californi,
measures of Tolerance for Complexity and Theoretical Orientation. Th
pupils were administered the same test of creative thinking, befor
and after administrations of the Iowa Tests of Educational Develop
ment, and the Lorge-Thorndike measure of intelligence, among othe
measures. It was thus possible to estimate over- and underachievemen
both in terms of expected level and expected growth as predicted b
mental age. Pupils within a single school had been divided randoml
among the fifth-grade teachers of that school. In analyzing the data
Yamamoto had divided the pupils in the nineteen classes roughly int
thirds on the basis of their total scores on the battery of creative think
ing tests. It is thus interesting to analyze the patterns of under- anc
overachievement under different teachers for different types of pupils
such as the highly creative and the least creative.

One teacher in a particular school had the lowest score of any o
the nineteen teachers on the measures of theoretical orientation anc
tolerance for complexity. Her score on the test of creative thinking wa
also among the lowest of the group. Of the seven highly creative chil
dren in her class, five could be classed definitely as underachievers o
the basis of their level of achievement, and six of them could be clas
sified as underachievers on the basis of gains in achievement during
the five-month period of the study. All twelve of the children in thi
class having low scores on the creative thinking test overachieved o
the basis of level of achievement, and eleven of them overachieved i
terms of gains during the five-month period of the study.

Another teacher in this same school ranked very near the top o
this group of nineteen teachers on theoretical orientation, toleranc
for complexity, and creative thinking. By contrast, all four of the highl
creative children in this teacher's classroom could be classified as over
achievers. In other words, their educational quotients were highe
than their IQ's. However, ten of her twelve low creatives could als
be classified as overachievers. My guess would be that this teache
with her tolerance for complexity, theoretical orientation, and creativ
thinking ability was able to assist both the highly creative child and th
relatively uncreative child to grow mentally. The other teacher, lackin
all three of these characteristics, was unable to help the highly creativ
children in her classroom to achieve their potentialities.

Although I have been unable to locate any carefully conductec
empirical studies of teacher motivations and attitudes and the creativ
growth of children, many observers have maintained that there ar
important relationships between these two sets of variables. Barka
(1960), who studied intensively creative art activities in selected ele
mentary school classrooms, likewise emphasizes this searching, inquirin
attitude on the part of the teacher—an attitude which apparently result

1 or is at least accompanied by freedom, courage, independent think-
1g, and discipline on the part of pupils. For example, he describes an
1cident in which the teacher was talking with some girls working on
mural. It was clear that the teacher respected the girls' feelings, and
hey knew she did. At the beginning of the discussion, the girls and
he teacher clearly disagreed. They wanted to scrap their first attempt,
nd the teacher tried to convince them otherwise. She told them what
he thought and listened to what they had to say. Barkan reports that
heir reasons and feelings were sufficiently strong for the teacher to
ome to agree with them. In other words, she was willing to join with
he girls in an inquiry which led to a change in her opinion.

A study by Wodtke (1963) further underlines the importance of
he teacher's need or motivation to control children. Through observation
echniques, Wodtke identified elementary teachers as high controlling
r low controlling. He then compared the creative thinking test gains
f pupils of high controlling teachers to those of pupils of low controlling
eachers. He found that the pupils of low controlling teachers achieved
igher gains on verbal creativity and the pupils of the high controlling
eachers achieved higher gains on nonverbal elaboration. Wodtke con-
luded that a high controlling teacher discourages self-initiated pupil
alk, verbal creativity, and verbal flexibility, but tends to encourage
ncreased detail, at least in drawings.

These observations and research findings are especially relevant
o the study to be reported in this chapter, since many of the elements
nvolved in the McCardle, Yamamoto, Barkan, and Wodtke studies are
ncluded in the rationale of the Personal-Social Motivation Inventory
ised as the measure of creative teacher motivation. The creative motiva-
ion scale includes items which reflect an inquiring, searching, reaching-
ut, and courageous attitude. The critical motivation scale, on the
ther hand, reflects a controlling, censoring, and inhibiting attitude. The
ower motivation scale, the other measure used in the present study,
lso reflects a controlling attitude. Experience has shown that there is
lmost a zero correlation between the scores on creative and critical
notivations and a negative relationship between the scores on creative
nd power motivations. In a factor analysis involving a variety of other
ersonality variables, the creative motivation score loaded heavily in
 factor including variables which represent a need to manipulate ob-
ects or artifacts through empirical analysis, reflection, and discussion;
 striving to overcome experienced frustration, failure, and humiliation;
n intense, vigorous effort as contrasted to sluggish inertia; the giving
f support to others by providing love, assistance, and protection; an
nterest in intellectual activity and problem solving; and an introspec-
ive preoccupation with private psychological, spiritual, aesthetic, or
netaphysical experiences.

Procedures

Data from two different studies are involved in this investigation of the role of the teacher's creative motivations in bringing about creative growth in pupils. In the studies described in the introduction of this chapter, the participating teachers were administered the Personal Social Motivations Inventory from which we derived a measure of creative motivation. This enabled us to study the relationship between the teachers' creative motivations and growth in general creative thinking ability over a period of approximately five months and in creative writing over a four-month period.

GROWTH IN GENERAL CREATIVE THINKING ABILITY

All pupils in the twenty regular classes of a single elementary school were administered a test of creative thinking ability early in January and an alternate form of the test about the middle of May as described earlier. The present analyses are made without reference to experimental or control condition. This seems justified, since the effects of the experimental treatment were not especially strong and since the experimental and control teachers are about equally divided between the two criterion groups selected for this study.

One of the criterion groups might be called the creative motivation group and the other the critical-power motivation group. The index used in assigning teachers to these two groups was obtained by subtracting the Creative Motivation Score from the Critical Motivation and Power Motivation scores combined. The data for the primary grade teachers (first, second, and third grades) are analyzed separately from those for the intermediate grade teachers (fourth, fifth, and sixth grades). In addition, we have also analyzed the data for four kindergarten classes.

GROWTH IN CREATIVE WRITING

In the study designed to assess the relationship of the teacher creative motivation to growth in creative writing, pupils were asked to write an imaginative story first in February and then in May. In each case, they were offered a list of suggested titles involving an animal or a person with some divergent characteristic. They could choose from hese titles or create a similar one of their own. The teachers participating in this study had been members of the in-service education group described earlier in this chapter.

On the basis of the Personal-Social Motivation Inventory, six teachers were identified as expressing strong creative motivations, and six were identified as expressing weak creative motivations or strong critical and control motivations. This represented the total number of participants who completed the Personal-Social Motivation Inventory.

Results

GROWTH IN GENERAL CREATIVE THINKING ABILITY

A picture of creative growth as shown by the pre- and post-tests of general creative thinking ability can be obtained in a number of ways. A rough picture of this growth can be obtained by comparing the proportion of children who achieved gains as measured by the alternate forms described in Appendix A. These comparisons are presented in Table 5.1 separately for the kindergarten, primary, and intermediate

TABLE 5.1   Comparison of Proportions of Pupils Showing Gains in General Creative Thinking Ability Under Teachers with High and Low Creative Motivations

Grade Level	High Motivation Teachers			Low Motivation Teachers			
	Total Number	Number Gained	Per Cent Gained	Total Number	Number Gained	Per Cent Gained	Chi-square
Kindergarten	58	39	67.0	58	18	31.0	16.85*
Primary	89	59	66.3	87	35	40.2	12.98*
Intermediate	93	74	79.5	110	95	86.4	1.66

° Significant at 1 per cent level

evels. It will be noted that in the kindergarten classes and in the primary grades, a significantly greater proportion of the pupils taught by teachers with creative motivations made gains in their total creative thinking scores than did their peers taught by teachers who expressed weak creative motivations or stronger motivations to control and to correct. In the kindergarten classes the proportion is more than twice as great under the teacher with a strong creative motivation than under the teacher with a strong motivation to control and correct. The differences are not statistically different at the intermediate grade level, however. It should be recognized that the kindergarteners and primary pupils are subjected to a more difficult test than are the intermediate level pupils. This greater difficulty arose from the fact that the kindergarteners and primary pupils were administered the easier Circles Tes as a part of the pre-test and the more difficult Square Test as a part c the post-test. The reverse was true in the fourth, fifth, and sixth grade Thus, it was easier for pupils in these grades to make gains. Neverthe less, the results are still strong enough to suggest that the creativ motivation of the teacher may be more important in supporting creativ growth in the kindergarten and primary grades than in the intermediat grades.

Growth in general creative thinking ability can also be studie by comparing mean pre- and post-test scores and mean gain score The method of covariance was employed for this purpose in order t correct for any initial differences in scores. The results of these analyse are presented separately for the kindergarten, primary, and inte mediate grades in Table 5.2. It will be noted that there is a consisten

TABLE 5.2 Covariance Analysis of Pre- and Post-test Means and Mean Gains in Gener Creative Thinking Ability Under Teachers with High and Low Creative Motivations

Grade Level	High Motivation				Low Motivation				
	Number	Pre-	Post-	Gain	Number	Pre-	Post-	Gain	F-ratic
Kindergarten	58	33.1	40.3	7.2	58	36.9	29.0	-7.9	25.090
Primary	89	86.4	94.0	7.6	87	110.4	106.2	-4.2	0.092
Intermediate	93	106.9	138.3	31.4	110	112.5	137.7	21.2	1.310

° Significant at .1 per cent level

tendency for the pupils of the creatively motivated teachers to sho\ greater gains than the pupils of the teachers not motivated creativel In fact, in the kindergarten and primary levels, the pupils of th creatively motivated teachers showed over-all gains while their peer taught by the less creatively motivated teachers actually showed sligh losses. Except at the kindergarten level, all of these differences fa short of significance when covariance is applied and adjustments ar made for pre-test differences.

GROWTH IN CREATIVE WRITING

Growth in creative writing was assessed by means of the con posite creative writing score developed by Yamamoto. This score take into consideration such elements as organization, sensitivity, originality imagination, psychological insight, and richness. The comparative dat concerning the creative writing performances of the pupils whose si teachers express strong creative motivations and those of the pupil whose six teachers express weak creative motivation are presented i

Table 5.3. It will be noted that the initial difference in means is not statistically significant. The pupils of the high motivation teachers made statistically significant gains, while those of the low motivation teachers made slight, though insignificant, losses.

TABLE 5.3 Comparison of Composite Creative Writing Scores of Pupils of Teachers Expressing High Creative Motivation with Those of Teachers Expressing Low Creative Motivation

Comparison	Number	Mean	t-ratio	Level of Significance
High motivation, pre-test	122	14.34	-0.1183	Not significant
Low motivation, pre-test	134	15.23		
High motivation, pre-test	122	14.34	2.1339	Less than 5 per cent
High motivation, post-test	122	16.02		
Low motivation, pre-test	134	15.23	-0.1863	Not significant
Low motivation, post-test	134	15.07		

Discussion

Admitting that the problem of studying the effects of teacher motivation on creative growth is a complex one and fraught with the hazards of many contaminating variables, these data appear to be strong enough to indicate that this variable has enough power to merit consideration and further study. Although some of the more rigorous statistical tests indicate that some of the observed effects may have been due to chance factors, much of the raw evidence is impressive. For example, when one goes through the tabulated scores pupil by pupil in the kindergarten classes, one feels very strongly the impact of the difference, since under the teacher whose creative motivation is weaker than his critical and control motivation, child after child shows clear losses. The impact is still stronger if one examines the actual productions of the children. The loss in creativity can be sensed by almost any perceptive person. One does not experience this feeling in examining the pre- and post-test productions of the pupils of the teacher who expressed a strong creative motivation. It is interesting to note that this teacher was assigned to the control group in the basic study. We observed much outstanding creative learning in her classroom. By comparison, we had the feeling that the pupils in the classroom of the less creatively motivated teacher were subjected to a kind of sensory deprivation.

It is also perhaps not without significance that after six years of administering tests of creative thinking to elementary school children, some of the research team's most memorable experiences occurred in the classroom of the kindergarten teacher who expressed strong creative motivation. Not one such memorable experience occurred in the room of the other teacher. Who could forget the little girl who, when told that there was only two more minutes for the Circles Test, drew a girl blowing soap bubbles? The unused circles all became soap bubbles. Then there was the thoughtful little boy who used fully four of his ten minutes on the Picture Construction Test to think before drawing a single line. I had shown how the gummed triangle could be used as the roof of a bird house with considerable elaboration. I then said, "Now, don't draw a bird house like I did. This was just to show you one thing you can make." All these kindergartners except two began immediately to put their ideas on paper. One began working after about a minute's delay. The other sat in absorbed thought for at least four minutes. During this time I was anxious and only with difficulty restrained myself from encouraging him to get to work, to see if he understood what I wanted him to do, or otherwise find out what was wrong. Finally, a big smile came on his face, and he went to work with great vigor. He had been thinking how a bird house would look on the inside and then attempted to draw what he had visualized. The teacher was absent on the day of the pre-test and was greeted the next morning by, "Gee, you ought to have been here yesterday. That man sure did work us hard, but it was fun."

Perhaps another indicator of the differences between the two classes is to be found in the experiences of the photographer who was instructed to photograph behavior in all four classes which would illustrate creative ways of learning. He had no difficulty obtaining pictures in the classroom of the creatively motivated teacher, but he was barely able to take any photographs which would illustrate creative ways of learning in the two groups taught by the other teacher.

Similarly, we cannot pass off too lightly the fact that, in most of the statistical analyses, the pupils of the creatively motivated teachers showed significant growth, while those of the less creatively motivated teachers actually showed decrements, although certainly not statistically significant ones. At any rate, it seems rather clear that little creative growth occurred during the period of these studies (approximately five months in one case and four months in the other) under those teachers who expressed comparatively more motivation to control and correct than to inquire and create, at least insofar as we were able to measure creative growth in this study.

CREATIVE
ACTIVITIES
AS REWARDS
FOR
CREATIVE
THINKING

6

Educators have long puzzled over the problem of whether mental abilities are developed by exercising them through appropriate activities. Binet (1909), for example, made "mental orthopedics" an important part of his educational program for mentally retarded children. In days past, the inclusion of certain courses in the curriculum was justified on the basis that the mastery of these courses was good mental discipline. Mental abilities developed through such discipline could then be expected to function more effectively in solving difficult problems in "real life." Later, there developed a reaction against the mental discipline school of thought.

In recent concern about the development of the creative thinking abilities, many people have assumed that these abilities are developed through activities which provide opportunities for the development of these abilities. In the light of the concerns of the present series of studies, we wondered if the power of a total environment which values creative behavior might not be greater than the power of creative activities themselves. We recognized, of course, that the provision of creative activities carries with it some implicit positive evaluation of creative achievement. Yet, we knew that the attitudes of the teacher often communicated something that was quite different.

Let us review briefly some of the opinions and assumptions of some educators who have been concerned about this problem. Payne (1958), in discussing the teaching of mathematics to bright pupils, maintains that the ability to do creative work and creative thinking is dependent largely on the pupil's opportunities for creative work. He apparently includes also the environment which values creative achievement when he states, "A little encouragement by an inspiring teacher often helps a bright pupil to exhibit his potentiality for creativity" (1958, p. 98). D. Flanagan (1959) maintains that the more creative acts we experience, whether they are our own or those of others, the better are the chances that we will behave creatively. He argues that perceptive poetry may stimulate the scientist and that a keen scientific insight into nature stimulates the poet. One of the early studies of the Union College Character Education Project (O'Brien, Elder, Putnam, and Sewell, 1954) involving two- and three-year-olds showed that there was a significant relationship between an increase in the number of possessions available for dramatic and pretend play and an increase in creative activities of this type. Children who were provided a larger number of media for imaginative play developed a greater enjoyment of creative imagination. It can, of course, be argued that parents who provide materials for creative play probably place a greater value on creative behavior than do parents who do not make such provisions for their children.

Also of importance in assessing the value of creative activities in developing the creative thinking abilities is the role of guidance. Markey (1935), who has studied extensively the imaginative behavior of preschool children, leans toward the view that more adult-directed imaginative activities and supervised creative activities might foster better the development of creative imagination than undirected freedom of action.

Although it has not been possible within the limitations of the power and financial resources available to this investigator to investigate directly the issues which have just been raised, three different situations with relatively high degrees of pertinence have been studied. It is believed that these three situations yield some useful clues for understanding the roles of creative activities and an environment which values creative behavior.

Study 1:
Creative Language Arts Activities

THE RESEARCH SITUATION

The research situation is the same as the creative writing study described in Chapter 5. It will be recalled that the pupils of teachers having strong creative motivations showed statistically significant creative growth in their imaginative writing, whereas the pupils of teachers having weak creative motivations showed small, but not statistically significant, losses in creative writing over a period of approximately four months. It was also found that teachers having strong creative motivations also reported having conducted a significantly larger number of creative language arts activities than their less creatively motivated peers. Our question now becomes, "Given the significant relationship between creative motivations and the provision for creative activities, do we still find a significant relationship between the provision of a large number of creative language arts activities and growth in creative writing?" Thus, a further analysis of the data described in Chapter 5 was made in terms of the number of different creative activities reported by the teacher during the creative writing project.

The pupils of those teachers whose number of different creative language arts activities placed them in the upper half of the distribution were called the High Creative Activity Group, while those in the lower half were called the Low Creative Activity Group. Eight teachers and 188 pupils constituted the High Creative Activity Group, and nine teachers and 234 pupils made up the Low Creative Activity Group. In a few cases, it did not seem reasonable to make one or more of the evaluations under consideration so there are slight variations in the number of cases reported from evaluation to evaluation.

INSTRUMENTS

The instrument used in assessing creative growth was the Imaginative Stories Test described in Appendix A. The instrument used to assess the extent to which teachers had conducted creative language arts activities and had applied the ideas suggested in the monograph was the "Things Done: Language Arts Checklist." This checklist includes the activities suggested and described in the author's monograph as ways of developing the creative thinking abilities. The items in the checklist as presented below will give the reader some idea of the contents of the monograph and of the extent to which teachers used each activity. The percentage figures are based on the responses of fifty fourth-, fifth-, and sixth-grade teachers in the Twin Cities area.

	Per Cent
"Brainstorming" as a technique for stimulating ideas, developing fluency of ideas	38
"Props" and "starters" such as a set of general questions to generate ideas or solutions	88
Some specific set of questions to generate ideas	72
Practice in playing word games	64

Per Cent

Pupil invention of new words	32
Stories from varied arrangements of pictures	42
Pupil dictation of stories, ideas on a tape recorder or other electrical recording device	30
Competition to stimulate fluency of ideas	58
Stories based on two or more objects, concepts	44
Regular role playing to stimulate spontaneity and naturalness of expression	38
"Competitive Team Role Playing" to stimulate fluency of ideas	12
Introduction to Roget's *Thesaurus,* some book of synonyms, or other word reference in addition to dictionary	22
Exercises in recognizing word relationships, words of similar meaning, words of opposite meaning	98
Exercises in thinking of new uses for some device or product	44
Practice in thinking of many alternative solutions to a problem	86
Exercise in writing the same message or story in several forms, for different audiences, for different effects	18
Exercise in rewriting story or other composition to have opposite ending	30
Practice in rewriting story or other composition in a different setting, with different characters	20
Practice in writing unusual titles or captions for cartoons, pictures, news items	52
Unusual natural events to stimulate ideas for creative writing	46
Creation of unusual events or situations to stimulate writing	42
Book reports in an original manner	70
Practice in writing humorous stories, anecdotes	72
Exercise in writing limericks, humorous verses	58
Study of writings by humorists to learn basis of humor	10
Film, picture, radio broadcast, TV program, or similar medium to stimulate original writing	52
Critical reading of comic books and suggestions for changes	10
Reading of stories and poems and suggestions of changes to make them more realistic, accurate, etc.	34
Specific practice to develop keener observation through senses	56

	Per Cent
Practice in creative listening, thinking how the speaker really feels about what he says	54
Expression of ideas and feelings stimulated by music	72
Expression of ideas and feelings stimulated by art experiences	72
Practice in drawing conclusions based on facts from several sources	48
Assignments to write original plays	34
Sessions recording pupils' discussion or other oral work on tape recorder and playing it back	36
Assignments to find errors in facts, grammar in newspapers and similar sources	34
Puppet or marionette show	20
Illustration of stories or other writings with drawings	86
Assignment in writing a book or carrying out some other sustained writing project	12
Pupils worked out their ideas in some concrete, polished product (letter to be mailed, articles to be printed)	88
Pupils told entire stories through pictures, cartoons, photographs, drawings	42
Exercises to improve ability to ask good questions	60
Exercises to improve ability to make guesses from limited clues	42
Assignment of reading to stimulate curiosity, question asking	62
Encouragement of "idea-trap" habit for creative writings	0
Suggestions that children keep a folder of their creative writings	50
Instruction to evolve and test rules of grammar from readings	24
Assignment of unusually difficult or even impossible problems to stimulate imagination	28
Practice exercises or periods which "don't count" on grades	64
"Writer's Corner," a quiet retreat where pupils can go to think and work out ideas	10
Special times occasionally for pupils to think	50
Time for self-initiated learning	66
Credit for self-initiated learning	56
Definite tasks for identifying pupils with special talent in creative writing	38

Per Cent

Special encouragement and guidance to pupils
gifted in creative writing 66
Special tasks for identifying pupils gifted in creative dramatics 28
Special encouragement and guidance to pupils
gifted in creative dramatics 26
Other creative activities in language arts 28

RESULTS

The data derived from the composite creativity score developed
by Yamamoto and described in Appendix A are presented in Table 6.1.

TABLE 6.1 Comparison of Mean Pre- and Post-test Composite Creativity Scores of Pupils
Under High and Low Creative Activity Conditions

Condition	Number	Mean Pre-	Mean Post-	Gain	t-ratio	Level of Significance
High creative activity in language arts	184	14.68	15.21	0.53	1.422	Not significant
Low creative activity in language arts	233	14.11	14.94	0.83	2.239	Less than 5 per cent

Note: Difference in mean gains not statistically significant (Cochran-Cox Test
$t = 0.040$)

It will be noted that the slight gain registered by the pupils of the
teachers who reported the larger variety of creative language arts activities is not statistically significant at the 5 per cent level of confidence,
while that registered by their peers who presumably engaged in a
smaller variety of creative language arts achieved a statistically significant gain. When the Cochran-Cox Test is applied to test the significance of the difference in mean gains, however, the t-ratio obtained
is not significant at the 5 per cent level.

The number of words in each story were counted, and the resulting comparisons are shown in Table 6.2. It will be noted that there are
statistically significant gains in the number of words written by the
pupils in both the high and low creative activity conditions. The analysis
of the difference in mean gains, however, indicates that the pupils
under the high activity condition achieved greater gains in number
of words written than did those under low activity conditions.

Comparisons on the originality score developed by Torrance and
described in Appendix A are presented in Table 6.3. Again, it will be
observed that pupils under both high and low activity conditions made

TABLE 6.2 Comparison of Mean Pre- and Post-test Number of Words on Imaginative Stories of Pupils Under High and Low Creative Activity Conditions

Condition	Number	Mean Pre-	Post-	Gain	t-ratio	Level of Significance
High creative activity in language arts	188	130.7	162.1	31.4	7.4301	Less than .1 per cent
Low creative activity in language arts	226	142.8	159.8	17.0	4.3941	Less than .1 per cent

Note: Difference in mean gains significant at 1 per cent level (Cochran-Cox Test $t = 3.7425$)

TABLE 6.3 Comparison of Mean Pre- and Post-test Originality Scores on Imaginative Stories of Pupils Under High and Low Creative Activity Conditions

Condition	Number	Mean Pre-	Post-	Gain	t-ratio	Level of Significance
High creative activity in language arts	188	3.53	4.65	1.12	6.9829	Less than .1 per cent
Low creative activity in language arts	227	4.15	4.81	0.66	5.3097	Less than .1 per cent

Note: Difference in mean gains not statistically significant (Cochran-Cox Test $t = 0.1634$)

statistically significant gains. The difference in mean gains, however, is not statistically significant.

Comparisons based on the interest score developed by Torrance and described in Appendix A are included in Table 6.4. It will be noted

TABLE 6.4 Comparison of Mean Pre- and Post-test Interest Scores on Imaginative Stories of Pupils Under High and Low Creative Activity Conditions

Condition	Number	Mean Pre-	Post-	Gain	t-ratio	Level of Significance
High creative activity in language arts	188	3.77	4.71	0.94	5.5647	Less than .1 per cent
Low creative activity in language arts	227	4.53	5.11	0.58	3.1921	Less than 1 per cent

Note: Difference in mean gains not statistically significant (Cochran-Cox Test $t = 0.1035$)

that the results are strikingly similar to those obtained for originality: both groups made significant gains, but the difference in gains is not statistically significant.

In summary, it might be concluded that engaging in a larger variety of creative activities may result in greater word fluency (as seen in the increased length of imaginative stories written), but that this does not guarantee an improvement in the creative quality of productions (as seen in such measures as the composite creativity score, the originality score, and the interest score of the imaginative stories).

Study 2:
Creative Activities from
"An Experimental Training Program in Creative Thinking"

In Study 1, I had wondered if the failure of teachers to conduct a large number of the suggested creative activities might not have been due to the fact that so much was left to the initiative of the teacher. In our in-service education experiments, a number of teachers had asked, "Why don't you give us some specific activities to carry out, some things that we can do and then check off?" Although we believed that genuine creative growth was likely to take place only when the environment rewards creative behavior and that it is important for teachers to manifest consistently positive attitudes towards creative behavior, we decided that something of positive value might be achieved by giving teachers more specific exercises in a workbook format. We recognized at the outset that we would not be able to "can" creative teaching. We hoped, however, that if we gave teachers materials which would give them support and enable them to begin conducting activities involving creative thinking, they would then be better able to think up activities of their own.

R. E. Myers, at that time a teacher in the University of Minnesota Laboratory School and now a member of the College of Education faculty at the University of Oregon, had developed a number of exercises which he and other teachers had tested with excellent results. These exercises were combined into a teacher's guide with additional suggestions for using them in meaningful ways under the title, "An Experimental Training Program in Creative Thinking." These training exercises included materials for activities which involved combining ideas and elements, exploring a variety of possibilities, seeing relationships, analyzing ideas, elaborating ideas, and becoming more sensitive and aware of the environment.

Although these and similar materials have been used since that time in varied kinds of experiments whose results varied, too, depending on the ways they were used, the idea in the study described herein was simply to determine what success fourth-, fifth-, and sixth-grade teachers would have in using this experimental training program to bring about creative growth in writing imaginative stories.

PROCEDURE

The elementary supervisors in two suburban school systems expressed an interest in testing the materials in their school systems and agreed to carry out the study. In System A, all teachers were asked to participate and agreed to do so. None of the teachers actually carried out enough of the activities to lead us to expect that any creative growth could have taken place as a result of the use of experimental materials. Thus, the pre- and post-tests and the pre- and post-imaginative stories were not analyzed. In System B, teachers were given the opportunity to volunteer their participation, and an unexpectedly large number did so. In contrast to the teachers in System A, almost all the teachers in System B conducted enough activities to expect that creative growth might have taken place. Rather disappointingly, however, few of the teachers went beyond the bare exercises given in the teacher's guide and gave little or no evidence of letting one thing lead to another as we had suggested and had hoped they would. (This led us to devise a different kind of format arranged in stages so that pupils produce ideas and then do something with these ideas. This has proved to be more successful in encouraging creative development.) For the analyses reported herein, 199 sample stories, drawn randomly from the total number of stories submitted by System B, were scored.

In the introduction to the manual, we indicated that we did not know whether such exercises could be used successfully in developing creative potentialities, as follows:

We don't know for sure that individuals can become more creative as a result of being involved in experiences designed to make them so. That is why you are being asked to help us conduct an experiment which may give some indication as to whether an individual's creative abilities can be enhanced through training.

We tried to stress the importance of the teacher's role in the following words:

As is always true in the classroom, the materials to be used in this experiment are no better than the teacher using them. However, it is earnestly believed that the exercises which were developed for this study are in no way the equal of an alert, imaginative teacher. The lessons really represent an attitude more than anything else—an attitude that children should be encouraged to use their imaginations fully in exploring the wonders of human existence. For the desired results, this attitude must be shared by those using these materials.

In brief, the following study procedure was established for participating teachers:

1. Administer Form A of the Imaginative Stories Test using a twenty-minute time limit.
2. During the next six-week period try out at least ten of the twenty exercises given in the manual or guide, "An Experimental Training Program in Creative Thinking."
3. After six weeks, administer Form B of the Imaginative Stories Test, again using the twenty-minute time limit.

It was explained to the teachers that they should feel free to select only those exercises which they felt would be most effective in *their* classrooms. No schedule of lessons was suggested, we explained, because we believe that the teacher can determine which exercises will fit in best with the activities and interests of his pupils and proceed according to the most promising plan. It was also explained that each lesson was designed as a springboard for further creative thinking, but that the amount of time which any of the exercises should consume must be left to the individual teacher. As it worked out in this study, however, a period of about twenty minutes was allotted to each exercise, and there was apparently little or no opportunity for the exercises to lead to other creative activities and explorations, at least not in the classroom.

CRITERION MEASURE

Since the key purpose of the study was to help children write with greater originality and to get away from the obvious and commonplace, an attempt was made to develop and apply what might be a more discriminating and inclusive measure of originality. This was done primarily by adding other elements to the originality scale described in Appendix A. The rater was given a list of twenty-three characteristics to be judged on what amounts to a three-point scale, with the following guide (a more elaborate guide has been prepared and was used by scorers):

If the writing manifests none of the quality under consideration, the judge assigns a value of "0." If the writing definitely and clearly manifests the quality being judged, he assigns a value of "2." If the quality under consideration comes through very weakly, is of poor quality, or is contaminated by the obvious and banal, he assigns a value of "1." The following qualities are included:

1. Unusual title (catchy, unusual twist, surprising, reasonable synthesis of the contents)

2. Picturesque speech (suggests a picture, is colorful, is strikingly graphic, is objectively descriptive, makes you see a picture, generates a definite image)
3. Vivid (liveliness, intenseness, stirs emotionally, vigorous, strong, fresh, spirited)
4. Flavor (has a noticeable, characteristic element or taste, appeals to sense of taste or smell)
5. Personal element (author involves self, expresses personal feelings or opinions)
6. Original solution or ending, surprising (usually has a punch line, but need not be funny; must be unexpected, unusual, surprising)
7. Original setting or plot
8. Humor (portrays the comical, funny, amusing, brings together incongruities)
9. Invention of words, names
10. Individuality of style
11. Becomingness (choice of words or expressions uniquely appropriate to characters and situations, fit as though author identified with characters, animals)
12. Imagination (fantasy, written as though the author is some character in history, literature)
13. Emotions or feeling (writing itself expresses emotion)
14. Abstractive element consisting of finding the essence (skims off unessential words and ideas, selects the most appropriate ones)
15. Immediacy of experience (direct relationship or closeness of writer to experience)
16. Curiosity (open awareness to world; searching, inquiring quality)
17. Reservoir of experiential data (draws upon personal experiences)
18. Perceptive sensitivity (shows sensitivity to people and to environment; uses analogy, metaphor)
19. Flexibility or versatility (versatility of style and word usage, abandonment of cliché and worn-out simile)
20. Symbolism (uses symbols in a new, refreshing way)
21. Coherent unity (refers to the structural or formative quality, synthesizes and brings into harmony diverse elements)
22. Expressive-communicative element (causes a mood, feeling)
23. Unique punctuation, capitalization (punctuation or capitalization used in unusual way to communicate idea, feeling)

RESULTS

By applying the foregoing scoring system, a mean of 9.49 was obtained for the pre-test stories and one of 9.06 for the post-test stories. This slight decrease of .43 was found to be statistically not significant ($t = -0.956$). Thus, under the conditions described in the foregoing sections, engaging in creative activities or exercises was not accompanied by growth in the originality of the writing of the subjects.

It might be added parenthetically that these exercises have been revised and used in other experiments with positive results. In each case, however, the positive results can be explained on the basis of the way in which the exercises were used. It seems clear, however, that exercises alone do not guarantee creative growth. In the study described herein, it was apparent that the exercises were placed in the class schedule as "twenty minutes of creativity," just as there was already "twenty minutes of arithmetic," "twenty minutes of geography," and the like. In the successful experiments which will be reported elsewhere, teachers permitted the creative exercises or activities to lead to other activities, related them to the rest of the curriculum, and the like.

Study 3:
An Environment Which Values Creativity

Since the creation of a larger environment which values creativity is such a complex matter and involves such a complex of family, social, and community values, this investigator has searched in vain for a situation appropriate for study. At the time the project was initiated, negotiations were begun with a system of private schools boasting a long and interesting history of dedication to the development of creativity in children. At first, leaders in this system were reluctant to participate in a study, feeling that the introduction of measurement would do violence to the objectives which they sought to achieve or would certainly not do them justice. About two years later, however, these leaders volunteered the cooperation of some of their schools for study. At that time, there was no support available to conduct such a study.

Soon after the project was initiated and again two years later, it became possible to study creative growth in a situation which combined many of the features which the investigator considered essential to a larger environment which values creativity. It combined an expression of creative values on the part of the families and schools of the participants and a variety of community resources. The research situation was provided by a seminar for senior high school students on "Man, Nature, and the Arts" and co-sponsored by the Walker Art Center and the Center Arts Council, Minneapolis, Minnesota.

THE RESEARCH SITUATION

The "Man, Nature, and the Arts" seminar was an experimental program relating the arts and sciences for high school students in grades ten through twelve. The first of these seminars was begun in the fall of 1959 and continued through April of 1960. The second began in January 1962 and lasted through April of that year.

The stated objective of the series of seminars was to increase the students' perception and understanding of the natural and man-made worlds. The series was opened with sessions on the mechanics of vision and visual perception, one conducted by an outstanding ophthalmologist and the other by an outstanding psychologist. Other sessions involved such topics as:

Selective Seeing—Design in the Film
Other Ways of Perceiving and Communicating: Music, Dance, Writing
Man (Physiologically)
Man, Sea, and the Air
Men and Societies
History of Architecture—A Synopsis
Objects for Man's Use—A History of Industrial Design
The Artist and Society
Art and the Consumer of Art
Economic Factors Shaping Culture and Environment
Minneapolis, Architecture, and City Planning
Design for the Individual and the Family
Planning the City and Region: Design for Society

Awareness and perception were consistent points of emphasis throughout the series. Most of the lecturers or session leaders are rather eminent in their own fields and were drawn from the University of Minnesota, the art and cultural institutions of the Twin Cities, and from the Minneapolis City Planning Commission.

The initial series was limited to a small, highly selected group. Participants were nominated by the schools in the Twin Cities area, and final selections were made by the Children's and Education Committee of the Center Arts Council. The second series was less restricted in membership but certainly attracted highly creative youngsters. Small tuition fees were charged but a small number of scholarships or part-scholarships were available. Sessions began on Saturday mornings at 9:30 A.M. and continued until noon.

It was believed that this situation combined many of the features of a larger environment which values creativity: nomination by the school implies creative values on the part of the school, especially on the part of the teachers who nominated students or called the seminar to the attention of students; parental values were usually expressed by providing tuition fees, transportation to the Center, and willingness to permit or encourage youngsters to use their Saturday mornings in this way; community values were reflected in the enthusiastic efforts of the outstanding lecturers who conducted the sessions; and the lectures and discussions also highlighted the fact that societies also place a high value on creative achievements.

It was believed that an appropriate control group was not essential to the conduct of this study since the same test tasks had already been administered to a number of groups of high school students of similar status. For example, it had been found that under ordinary circumstances the experiences of one year of schooling do not result in an increase in measured creative thinking abilities at the senior high school level (Torrance, 1962a; Yamamoto, 1960). Thus, it did not seem too unreasonable to assume that significant growth in the measured creative thinking abilities of participants in the Man, Nature, and the Arts seminar would be due to a complex of factors which might be labeled "a larger environment which values creativity."

PROCEDURES

Soon after the beginning of each series of sessions, a battery of creative thinking tests was administered to all participants present. Alternate forms were administered at the last session of the series in April. Participants in the first series were administered the Product Improvement Test, the Unusual Uses Test, the Circles Test, and the Ask-and-Guess Test. Participants in the second series were administered the Product Improvement Test, the Incomplete Figures Test, and the Sounds and Images Test of Originality. Twenty-four students were administered the pre-test in the first series, but only eight were available for the post-test. Thirty-five were tested at the beginning of the second series, and seventeen were available for the post-test. Unfortunately, the schedule of the post-tests conflicted with various nationwide testing programs for scholarships, college admission, and the like, and it was not possible to arrange for the testing of all participants.

RESULTS

As a group, the participants in both series of seminars achieved higher scores on the tests of creative thinking than any other educational groups which have been tested with these particular measures. The pre- and post-test means of the eight participants for whom we have complete data in the first series are presented in Table 6.5 together with tests of statistical significance. It will be noted that these participants achieved rather large gains on all the measures. All the sub-

TABLE 6.5 Mean Pre- and Post-test Scores on a Battery of Creative Thinking Tests of Eight High School Students Completing Walker Art Center Seminar

| Measure | Mean | | | t-ratio | Level of Significance |
	Pre-	Post-	Gain		
Ideational fluency	75.00	91.25	16.25	3.00	Less than 5 per cent
Flexibility	30.00	42.88	12.88	5.59	Less than 1 per cent
Originality	14.12	25.00	10.88	6.62	Less than 1 per cent
Elaboration	13.38	18.25	4.87	3.43	Less than 5 per cent
Inventive level	48.63	64.50	15.87	2.42	Less than 5 per cent
Ask-and-Guess Test	20.88	29.62	8.74	3.41	Less than 5 per cent
Composite creativity score	202.00	271.50	69.50	5.77	Less than 1 per cent

jects except one, in fact, gained on each of the subscores. This subject dropped sixteen points on ideational fluency, but in spite of this disadvantage he achieved substantial gains in the quality of his thinking flexibility, originality, elaboration, inventiveness, and the like).

The results obtained from an analysis of the performance of the seventeen students who completed the second series of sessions are shown in Table 6.6. It will be noted that only the gains for originality,

TABLE 6.6 Mean Pre- and Post-test Scores on Figure Completion and Product Improvement Tests of Seventeen High School Students Completing Walker Art Center Seminar

| Measure | Mean | | | t-ratio | Level of Significance |
	Pre-	Post-	Gain		
Ideational fluency	20.29	21.41	1.12	1.26	Not significant
Flexibility	12.47	12.00	0.47	0.48	Not significant
Originality	44.06	48.29	4.23	2.00	Less than 5 per cent
Elaboration	26.18	29.29	3.11	3.17	Less than 1 per cent
Sounds and images	30.30	41.10	10.80	7.48	Less than .1 per cent

elaboration, and the Sounds and Images Test are statistically significant. From this, we would infer that participation in this set of educational and cultural experiences did not make these youngsters more facile but that it gave them greater penetration and depth, as reflected in their significantly higher scores on originality and elaboration.

Conclusion

The situations investigated in this study were not ideal for providing firm information concerning the issues raised at the beginning of this
chapter. Thus, conclusions reached must be accepted with reservations.
In my opinion, however, the results lend support to the idea that although creative activities or exercises may at times lead to creative
growth, the provision of such exercises or activities does not guarantee
creative growth. Other factors must apparently be present for such
growth to take place. It is quite likely that one important condition is a
"larger environment which values creativity."

DIFFERENTIAL
REWARDS
FOR
BOYS
AND
GIRLS

7

Educational research has shown repeatedly that people tend to earn and develop along whatever lines they find rewarding. Thus, it is reasonable to expect that sex differences in creative development and achievement can be explained in part by the differential rewards given boys and girls for specific kinds of behavior. While different concepts such as "same-sex identification," "conformity to same-sex norms," and the like have been employed to explain sex differences in mental functioning, the role of differential rewards can be inferred from most explanations.

Mussen and Conger (1956) chose the differential reward explanation in their textbook on child development and personality. They point out that boys are more likely to be highly rewarded for motor activities and as a consequence devote greater attention to manipulative and motor tasks than to language. Girls, they contend, are more likely to be rewarded for verbal accomplishments and thus make more progress in language development than boys.

A number of investigators (Sigel, 1962; Oetzel, 1962; Bosselman, 1953) have given attention to the difficulties involved in explaining observed sex differences and in determining the relative importance of biological and social factors. Bosselman (1953) argues that the boy by virtue of his usually stronger muscular endowment and his more active sexual role seems predisposed to more aggressive characteristics. The girl is similarly predisposed to passivity. At the same time, Bosselman

points out that from the earliest months of life the male child is pres
sured to become a typical boy, the female child a typical girl. Oetze
(1962) compiled a review of the literature on sex differences whic
shows that many of the assumed or claimed sex differences in menta
functioning are not consistent from study to study. Of twenty-seve
studies on vocabulary differences, sixteen reported no differences, fou
reported boys superior, and seven reported girls superior. In spelling
however, girls were superior in all of the reported studies. Of the reporte
studies in numerical reasoning, boys were better in ten, girls in only one
and no differences in seven. Sigel (1962) has discussed the difficulty i
interpreting these studies and suggests that we examine the difference
in the routes through which boys and girls attain a certain level of de
velopment, even though there may be no differences. He caution
against combining male and female samples, even when there are n
statistically significant differences between them.

Sex Differences in Intellectual Development

A number of thought-provoking findings concerning differences i
the ways boys and girls learn and think can be found in the researc
literature. One interesting clue concerning the advantage usually attrib
uted to girls in vocabulary development is found in a study by Rober
Dykstra (1959) of beginning second-grade pupils. He found that b
most measures girls outdistance boys in reading skill after only one yea
of reading instruction. Girls, however, did not surpass boys in identify
ing "untaught" words. These findings fit a general theory which hold
that girls tend to learn better than boys when the learning is deliberat
or by authoritative identification rather than by more spontaneous o
creative ways of learning or learning on one's own.

Many of the studies of problem solving have shown male su
periority, even on "intuitive" problem solving. One example of such
study was reported by Crutchfield (1960). In this study, two group
(179 experimental subjects and 199 controls) were tested on thre
puzzles requiring spatial reorganization. Immediately beforehand, th
experimental subjects worked on three tasks involving spatial cue
relevant to the puzzle solutions. The control subjects worked on simila
tasks not involving such cues. The experimental subjects excelled th
control subjects in percentage of solutions, and this occurred withou
awareness of the relevance of the cues. This "intuitive" use of cue
however, was found in males only. Experimental and control female
did not differ in the degree of success achieved in problem solving, bu
the experimental males markedly surpassed male controls (e.g., 57 pe
cent solutions versus 37 per cent). A study by Hoffman and Maie

1961) yielded results favoring male superiority in problem solving.
ver twice the percentage of men, compared to women, solved the
perimental problem correctly. Furthermore, after discussion in groups
four, a significantly larger percentage of males than females changed
om an incorrect to a correct solution.

Proposals for Educational Change
for Boys and Girls

Our culture has differential expectations for boys and girls and
wards them differentially for specific kinds of behavior. Yet we gen-
ally insist upon equality of boys and girls in education and evaluate
th sexes on the same kinds of achievement. Generally, we have been
nhappy because boys lag in ability to read, spell, write, and the like,
d because girls are not interested in mathematics and science and are
t so original as boys. A variety of proposals has been made for remedy-
g this unsatisfactory state of affairs.

A number of educators, such as Maxwell (1960), have advocated
at boys be kept out of school a year or two longer than girls. They
te evidence that girls are superior to boys in practically every area of
evelopment until they are well in their teens, specifically mentioning
ndwriting, verbal expression, vocabulary, muscular control, reading,
d written composition. A number of other educators (Ginn, 1962),
wever, insist that the real difficulty arises from the fact that elemen-
ry education is designed for girls and that boys do not have a fair
ance to learn in today's schools. They have recommended that boys
d girls be separated for a part or all of the school day. An increasing
mber of experiments involving such separation are in progress in Vir-
nia, Maryland, Florida, and other states. Actually, separate classes for
oys and girls have been common for generations in some European
untries, have continued to prevail in some cities in the deep South,
d are common among private schools in the United States. This segre-
ation, however, has usually occurred because the sexes were being
ducated for different purposes or because one sex was thought to be
istracting to the other. The segregation has rarely been designed de-
berately to take advantage of developmental differences and differ-
ces in preferred ways of learning.

Concerns Regarding Education for Potential

It seems apparent that by our differential rewards for boys and
irls we make taboo entire areas of experiencing. In so doing, we reduce

these pupils' potentialities as human beings. We reduce their openne
to experience and their contacts with their environments. Then, in spi
of the fact that the culture makes taboo certain areas of experience f
boys and certain other areas of experience for girls, the school expec
and grades them on the same kinds of achievement.

In our exploratory investigations it seemed to me that we have son
serious blind spots in our thinking insofar as education for potenti
is concerned. Almost everyone had conceded that boys in the secor
and third grades are inferior to girls in the second and third grades
practically every kind of intellectual performance and on many kinds
physical performance. However, in even our earliest testing of the
children with tasks designed to elicit divergent thinking, this contentic
was not supported.

From first through third grade, we found that boys become i
creasingly superior on most tests of creative thinking. By the fourt
grade, however, we found that boys began losing their battle again
conformity to behavioral norms and showed a sharp measured decreme
in most of these abilities, especially if the test task required that the su
ject express his ideas in words.

Among second- and third-grade children (Torrance, 1963a), v
found that the differences in favor of boys emerge even when stimu
used are inappropriate to the sex role of boys. For example, in one e
periment three toys were used: a nurse's kit, a fire truck, and a dog.
the first-grade level, girls produced more ideas than boys for improvir
the nurse's kit so that it would be "more fun to play with." Some of tl
boys stubbornly refused to think of ideas for improving the nurse's k
while others first changed it to a doctor's kit and then suggested ir
provements. Boys produced more ideas than girls for improving the fi
truck, and there were scant differences between boys and girls on tl
stuffed toy dog task. By the third grade, however, boys were clear
superior to girls on this task, both in the quantity and quality (flexibilit
originality) of their ideas for improving all the toys, including tl
nurse's kit.

The superiority of boys over girls in creative thinking was al
shown in a group task involving experimentation with science toys (To
rance, 1963a). Each group, composed of five members (two boys ar
three girls or three boys and two girls), was confronted with the task
discovering in the first thirty minutes how many things these toys cou
be made to do (both intended and unintended). In a second thirt
minute period, group members were given a chance to demonstra
what could be done with the toys and to explain their discoveries.
almost every level from second through sixth, boys demonstrated ar
explained more principles than girls. In the fifth grade, girls initiated

many ideas as boys in the initial period but demonstrated and explained fewer principles than the boys.

At the same time that boys are becoming increasingly more inventive and curious between the first and third grades, peer pressures against boys with clever and original ideas are apparently increasing. Girls appear to learn earlier than boys how to gain peer acceptance of their ideas and to avoid being labeled as having "silly" or "crazy" ideas. For example, we found in our exploratory studies that highly creative boys (as identified by tests) received about four times as many peer nominations as girls on such criteria as "Who in your class has the silliest or wildest ideas?" or "Who in your class has the most ideas for being naughty?" Highly creative boys also tend to have a reputation among their teachers for having "a lot of wild ideas," but highly creative girls do not gain such a reputation. This state of affairs may stem from the fact that highly creative boys exhibit more uniqueness, inventiveness, and originality in their drawings and other productions than do highly creative girls. Highly creative boys in comparison with highly creative girls also tend to be less accessible psychologically and to have more internal tension.

It is the purpose of this chapter to examine evidence from several different studies in an effort to add to our understanding of how differential rewards for boys and girls operate insofar as their influence on creative behavior and growth are concerned. None of the studies cited may be regarded as a definitive attempt to solve the problems which have been posed here. It is hoped that, taken together, these various pieces of evidence may push forward our understanding of differential rewards for boys and girls.

Who Is Rewarded
When Teachers "Reward Creative Thinking"?

THE PROBLEM

In Chapter 4, we examined what happens when teachers are asked deliberately to reward creative behavior in the classroom. At that time, we did not examine the differential way in which teachers rewarded boys and girls under such conditions. In this section, the data will be reexamined from this viewpoint. In general, evidence from many other studies indicates that girls excel boys on almost all the kinds of behaviors which are rewarded by the school. If we ask teachers to reward creative thinking, does this help to balance somewhat the rewards given by the school? If so, it would then be appropriate to determine

whether or not this motivates boys to achieve more of the conformin
skills which the school already rewards. This question, however, mus
be left for further study.

PROCEDURES

Teachers were asked to describe incidents in which they believe
that they had rewarded creative behavior in the classroom. They wer
provided with a description of the following five principles or attitude
for rewarding creative thinking:

1. Be respectful of the unusual questions of children.
2. Be respectful of the unusual ideas of children.
3. Show children that their ideas have value.
4. Provide for periods of nonevaluated practice.
5. Help children see the consequences of their ideas and tie i
   cause and effect.

In their descriptions of the rewarded incidents, teachers were asked t
tell who initiated the behavior that was rewarded. In some cases, how
ever, the sex of the initiator was not identified, and the rewarded be
havior was group rather than individual.

RESULTS

The results of the analyses of the data described above are pre
sented in Table 7.1. From a comparison of the total number of report
and the number of reports where the sex of the originator of the creativ

TABLE 7.1 Comparison of Frequency with Which Boys and Girls Are Named as Initiato
of Creative Behavior in Reports by Teachers of Rewarded Creative Behavior

Principle	Total Reports	Reports Identifying Sex	Per Cent Rewarded Boys	Per Cent Rewarded Girls	Chi-square
Respectful of unusual questions	62	47	74	26	11.26*
Respectful of unusual ideas	56	46	76	24	12.52*
Unevaluated practice	56	49	61	39	2.47
Ideas have consequences	50	36	83	17	16.00*
Total	224	178	74	27	39.92*

* Indicates difference in proportion of boys and girls significant at less than .
per cent level

ehavior was indicated, it was possible to identify the sex in about 75
er cent of the reports, except in the case of the third principle. There
, a clear and consistent tendency for teachers to cite boys more fre-
uently than girls. The over-all difference is highly significant statisti-
ally, as are, too, the differences for principles one, two, and four.

The writer makes no assumption that these reports represent an
dequate sampling of the rewarding behavior of the reporting teachers.
he teachers chose the incidents they described from all the possible
nes which they had experienced. Thus, we may assume that the inci-
ents described represented some kind of salience to the teachers re-
orting them. These findings are offered only as an indication that when
achers are asked deliberately to reward creative classroom behavior,
ey mention boys more frequently than girls in describing incidents in
hich they have tried to reward such behavior. Thus, it is reasonable
infer that to some degree rewarding creative classroom behavior may
alance somewhat the rewards which go to boys and girls.

Differential Evaluation
of Science Ideas by Peers

THE PROBLEM

From exploratory studies conducted during the 1958–59 term, it
ecame obvious that boys and girls themselves differentially valued the
leas of boys and girls, especially in the area of science. It seemed from
ese exploratory experiences that in the early school years girls were
eveloping attitudes, interests, and disabilities which would make it
ifficult for them to make a healthy adjustment to a scientific world,
uch less become scientific discoverers. They were so reluctant to
andle the science toys used in the laboratory type experiment we were
sing that one would suspect they considered much of their world
trange, incomprehensible, and unfriendly.

In this experiment involving science toys, many girls in the fourth
rough sixth grades shrunk from participation, saying, "I'm a girl. I'm
ot supposed to know anything about science." As a consequence, the
oys' performances were significantly superior to the girls' on this task
nd the boys' ideas were valued more highly by both the boys and girls
an were those of girls.

Thirteen months after the original study, the experiment was repli-
ated in the fourth, fifth, and sixth grades with an alternate set of
cience materials. During the conduct of the experiment it became ob-
ious that a marked change had taken place among the girls in their
esponse to the science toys. It is the purpose of the study described

herein to compare the performance of boys and girls in a single scho
at two different points in time to determine whether the observed diffe
ences in attitudes are accompanied by improved contributions fro
girls and by a change in the differential evaluation of the boys' ar
girls' ideas about science phenomena.

PROCEDURES

Subjects

The subjects of the study were the pupils enrolled in the fourt
fifth, and sixth grades of a university elementary school during tw
school years, 1958–59 and 1959–60. Twenty-five children were enroll
in each grade and were divided into five groups of five each. In a fe
groups one member was absent at the time of the experiment, but r
group consisted of less than four members. In both years, the study w
conducted near the end of the school year (April 1959 and May 1960

In 1959, thirty-four boys and thirty-six girls participated; in 196
there were thirty-two boys and thirty-eight girls. The proportion of bo
and girls was about the same in all classes, and an effort was made
keep the ratio 2:3 or 3:2 in each group. Although there is a wide ran
of ability among the children enrolled in this school, there is a dispr
portionately large number of high ability children and children fro
professional families.

Experimental Procedures

In each class, all five groups were tested simultaneously, each in
different room under a trained experimenter. In an attempt to maximi
motivation, prizes of interesting science books were offered for the be
group or team performance. In the orientation, the terms "group" ar
"team" were emphasized. To simplify the recording of observations an
the reporting of results, each subject was given a colored arm band an
observations recorded according to arm-band color.

Each group was provided a box of science toys and toy parts.
1959, Science Toy Collection Number 2 of the Library of Science (
Fourth Ave., New York 3, N. Y.) was used. This collection includes
sparkler, finger trap, pin trick, four-ball puzzle, topsy-turvy top, jum
ing top, blow ball, flying saucer, and nutty putty. To this collection w
added a magnifying glass, magnet, and whistle. In 1960, Science T
Collection Number 3 was used. This collection includes a bang gu
string telephone, siren, busy bee, calliope whistle, cat cry, tower
Hanoi puzzle, secret, Nim, square puzzle, something-for-nothing puzz
and tetrahedron puzzle. In addition, a magnet and magnifying gla
were included.

Each group was given twenty-five minutes in which to explore d experiment to discover what could be done with the toys and why ey function as they do. It was emphasized that in addition to figuring t what each toy was intended to do, they should try to think of intended uses. Five minutes were then allotted for planning and or- nizing the demonstrations and explanations. The group then demon- ated and explained the principles which they had figured out. The ne limit was twenty-five minutes. Finally, each subject was asked to nk each member of his group according to the value of his contribu- n to the group's success. In addition, in 1960, subjects were asked how ll they enjoyed the activity.

The experimenters tabulated on a specially prepared record sheet e number of ideas initiated by each subject during the exploratory ase and recorded all of the ideas demonstrated and explained during e subsequent phase. In addition, observations were made concerning w the group organized itself and got under way, how the members ouped themselves during the exploratory period, the general activity el, the roles developed by specific members, how the group planned e demonstrations, and the like.

RESULTS

In 1959, boys were far ahead of girls on ideas demonstrated and ientific principles explained, averaging 6.18 and 4.65, respectively, mpared with 3.06 and 1.78 for girls. In 1960, the means for boys and rls were almost identical: 4.47 and 2.33 for boys and 4.34 and 2.11 for rls. This comparison is shown in Figure 7.1.

The observed differences were tested by means of analysis of vari- ice. In both "ideas demonstrated" and "principles explained" there ere no differences from year to year, but there were significant sex fferences and interactions between sex and year. The differences were en tested separately for each of the two years, and it was found that in 59 boys demonstrated significantly more ideas and explained more inciples than did girls. In 1960, however, the performance of girls as not significantly different from that of boys.

Since girls contributed as much to the scores of their groups as did ys, it is of interest to know whether or not their contributions to the ccess of their groups were valued to the same extent as that of boys. mposite ranks were determined by adding the individual rankings d then ranking the totals. Figure 7.2 presents a comparison of the mposite rankings of girls and boys for each of the two years. It will seen that in *both years* the contribution of boys are more highly lued than those of girls.

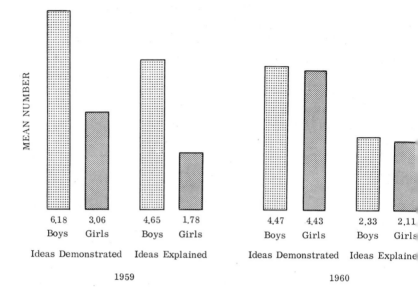

6,18   3,06   4,65   1,78   4,47   4,43   2,33   2,11

Boys   Girls   Boys   Girls   Boys   Girls   Boys   Girls

Ideas Demonstrated   Ideas Explained   Ideas Demonstrated   Ideas Explained

1959   1960

FIGURE 7.1 *Comparison of Boys and Girls on Mean Number of Ideas Demonstrated a Mean Number of Principles Explained in 1959 and 1960*

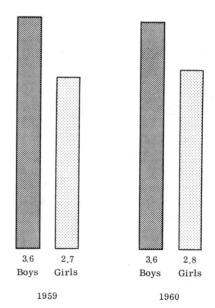

3,6   2,7   3,6   2,8

Boys   Girls   Boys   Girls

1959   1960

FIGURE 7.2 *Comparison of Boys and Girls on Mean Ranking of Importance of Contri tion by Peers in 1959 and 1960*

In 1959, it was apparent that many girls did not enjoy the experi-
ent, stating that it was not an appropriate activity for girls. In 1960,
ch subject was asked to indicate how much he enjoyed or disliked par-
ipation in the experiment. Responses were made on a five-point scale,
t only one subject (a boy) used the dislike end of the scale. It was
und that girls reported as much enjoyment of the activity as did boys.
fact, what little difference there is favors girls.

It is also important to know how boys and girls value their own
ntribution. The rankings made in both 1959 and 1960 required sub-
ts to include themselves. It was found that there is a consistent but
t quite statistically significant tendency (10 per cent level of con-
lence) over the two years for boys to value their contribution to their
oup's success more highly than girls value theirs.

DISCUSSION

From the data it seems clear that the reactions of fourth-, fifth,-
d sixth-grade girls in the elementary school studied changed in sig-
ficant and important ways during the period between April 1959 and
ay 1960. In 1959, boys demonstrated more ideas and explained more
ientific principles than did girls. In 1960 in the same school, girls
monstrated as many ideas and explained as many principles as did
ys. In 1959, many girls expressed obvious dislike for the science toy
sk and tended to withdraw from active participation in it. In 1960,
ne of this expressed dislike was observed. In fact, girls reported as
uch enjoyment of the task as boys did.

One aspect of the situation, however, had not changed. The con-
ibution of boys to the success of the group continues to be evaluated
ore highly than that of girls. In other words, cultural and/or subcul-
ral changes seem to be making it more permissible for girls to par-
ipate in and enjoy tasks requiring creative scientific thinking, but the
ntributions of boys are still more highly valued by peers than are those
girls.

In trying to understand the reasons for the changes which have
en described herein, several facts should be mentioned. During the
riod the data were collected, national interest was focused on the
ed for identifying and developing creative scientific talent. There
little doubt in my mind that attitudes in general have become more
vorable toward science and scientists. It should also be reported that
discussed with the teachers and parents of the subjects some of the
sults of earlier studies concerning sex differences in creative thinking.
these discussions, I assumed the position that there is misplaced em-

phasis on sex roles during the early school years and that this interfe▨
with the development of potentialities.

It seems clear that cultural emphasis on sex roles is a source
many conflicts for highly creative individuals and actually interfe▨
with school learning and the full development of children's creati▨
potential. The high degree of sensitivity involved in creative thinki▨
has a distinctly feminine character in our society; the independence ▨
quired has a distinctly masculine character. Thus, the highly creati▨
boy is likely to appear more effeminate than other boys his age, and t▨
highly creative girl is likely to appear more masculine than other gi▨
her age. Pressures against such development may cause many childr▨
to sacrifice their creativity at an early age.

In talks with parents, I maintained that even though they mig▨
not want their girls to have careers in invention and scientific discove▨
girls will still need to know much about the physical world. Thus, b▨
boys and girls should be encouraged to talk, ask questions, seek answe▨
and experiment. There should be no discrimination between boys a▨
girls in the explanations given about how things work. Girls should
taught to be as accurate and keen in their observations as boys. Th▨
questions should be taken as seriously as those asked by their brothe▨
It is not necessary that this in any way interfere with the boy's learni▨
to be a man and the girl's learning to be a woman.

Areas of Experiencing Off Limits
for Boys and Girls

THE PROBLEM

If our culture rewards differentially specific kinds of behavior,
is to be expected that this will tend to place certain areas of creati▨
experiencing virtually off limits for boys and certain others off limits f▨
girls. It is to be expected that this process will influence the kinds
creative activities in which boys and girls will engage on their ow▨
with or without the encouragement of parents and teachers. It is t▨
purpose of the section which follows to provide specific informati▨
about differences in the creative experiencing of boys and girls, as ▨
flected by their self-reports of "things done on their own."

PROCEDURES

The subjects of the study were the third-, fourth-, and fifth-gra▨
pupils of a rather heterogeneous suburban school in the Twin Cities are▨

ata were available for 94 boys and 117 girls in the third grade, 93 boys
d 90 girls in the fourth grade, and 93 boys and 99 girls in the fifth
ade. These three grades were chosen because it was believed that
ildren at these educational levels are subjected to rather strong social
essures to conform to sex norms and the differential rewards are rather
werful. It was also observed that children at these educational levels
e usually given some degree of freedom in choosing what they do on
eir own.

In May 1960, the subjects were asked to respond to a 100-item
ecklist of creative activities compiled by the author. The checklist
cluded a variety of creative writing and speaking activities, dramatics,
mes, dances, scientific reading and experimentation or exploration,
ts and crafts, social studies, and household activities. Subjects were
ven the following instructions in responding to the checklist:

You have been given a list of activities boys and girls sometimes do on
eir own. Indicate which ones you have done during this school term by
ecking the blank at the left. Include only the things you have done on
ur own, not the things you have been assigned or made to do.

RESULTS

The percentage of boys and the percentage of girls checking each
the 100 activities listed in the checklist are shown separately for each
ade in Table 7.2. An asterisk (°) is used to indicate those activities
ecked by a significantly different percentage of boys and girls at about
e 5 per cent level or better.

It will be observed that, in the third grade, thirty-two of the differ-
ces are significant at about the 5 per cent level or better. Fifty of the
tivities show such differences at the fourth-grade level, and thirty-five
them show significant differences at the fifth-grade level. The pro-
ortion of the activities showing statistically significant differences is
eater at the fourth-grade level than at either the third- or fifth-grade
vel. This would suggest that the differential rewards for various kinds
f creative behavior reach a peak between the third and fourth grades
d that the number of forbidden areas of experiencing is great.

At the third-grade level boys appear to be more inhibited than
rls in writing poems and plays, making up original dances, and de-
gning greeting cards. Girls appear to be more inhibited than boys in
ploring caves, reading science books, making firecrackers, making
lectric motors, dissecting animals, grafting or rooting plants, distilling
ater, starting a fire with a lens, collecting insects, using a chemistry set,
roducing static electricity, constructing a model airplane, designing a

TABLE 7.2 Comparison of Percentages of Responses of Boys and Girls on "Things Do on Your Own" Checklist in Third, Fourth, and Fifth Grades

Creative Activity	Third Grade		Fourth Grade		Fifth Grade	
	Boys (N=94)	Girls (N=117)	Boys (N=93)	Girls (N=90)	Boys (N=93)	Girls (N=99)
Wrote poem	45	64*	56	69*	34	54*
Wrote story	64	69	80	71	41	57*
Wrote play	22	28*	20	36*	22	25
Kept collection of writings	52	52	58	50	33	38
Wrote song, jingle	46	47	32	41	24	36
Produced puppet show	34	34	40	33	32	36
Kept diary one month	16	18	16	29*	19	33*
Played word games	85	80	82	83	69	82
Used Thesaurus or similar	33	37	22	17	17	19
Recorded reading	39	33	31	28	37	26*
Found errors in print	32	31	57	38*	54	48
Acted in play, skit	65	67	94	79*	58	64
Organized play, skit	27	30	40	36	31	41
Made up and sang song	50	58	44	54	34	54*
Made up musical composition	28	27	19	27	19	27
Made up and taught game	69	67	83	74	59	69
Pantomimed some story	32	27	46	48	32	38
Acted out story	56	56	75	70	41	55
Wrote letter to family member	81	82	99	86*	66	92*
Made up original dance	22	48*	13	37*	13	41*
Played charades	31	31	53	50	50	51
Visited zoo	83	80	81	73	61	54
Explored cave	38	21*	48	21*	53	15*
Read science magazine	61	50	77	49*	69	47*
Read science book	79	63*	99	68*	69	49*
Mixed colors	86	77	91	81*	74	79

° Difference between boys and girls significant at 5 per cent level

TABLE 7.2 (Cont.)

| Creative Activity | Third Grade | | Fourth Grade | | Fifth Grade | |
	Boys (N=94)	Girls (N=117)	Boys (N=93)	Girls (N=90)	Boys (N=93)	Girls (N=99)
Made firecracker	29	6*	26	4*	32	6*
Printed photographs	8	15	18	9*	8	10
Grew crystals	19	10	38	20*	19	9*
Made leaf collection	39	49	53	49	46	41
Made wild flower collection	23	25	30	38	9	15
Made electric motor	14	1*	8	0*	27	3*
Made musical instrument	31	25	51	23*	24	19
Planned experiment	53	49	72	39*	64	45*
Dissected animal	36	21*	30	9*	23	11*
Grafted plant, rooted	30	18*	31	23	22	19
Distilled water	24	7*	22	14	7	5
Used magnifying glass	66	57	90	71*	76	67
Made ink	18	16	26	12*	32	15*
Made leaf prints	36	38	43	42	27	41*
Started fire with lens	28	5*	46	11*	44	24*
Used magnet	83	74	86	78	83	83
Raised rats, mice	39	28	42	28*	42	25*
Collected insects	46	23*	45	24*	37	18*
Collected rocks	81	78	97	81*	68	75
Kept weather record	11	12	22	10*	13	5
Was bird watcher	43	34	41	44	26	31
Kept science notebook	16	14	22	11*	10	11
Kept science scrapbook	24	22	33	14*	18	6*
Attended science fair	22	18	41	40	42	36
Used chemistry set	54	19*	54	21*	66	23*
Produced static electricity	30	17*	43	20*	52	33*
Constructed model airplane	61	10*	90	11*	79	20*

* Difference between boys and girls significant at 5 per cent level

TABLE 7.2 (Cont.)

Creative Activity	Third Grade Boys (N=94)	Third Grade Girls (N=117)	Fourth Grade Boys (N=93)	Fourth Grade Girls (N=90)	Fifth Grade Boys (N=93)	Fifth Grade Girls (N=99)
Designed model airplane	46	8*	45	3*	49	11*
Counted annual log rings	21	15	47	32*	36	22*
Made stamp collection	36	35	49	33*	47	36
Made collection of postmarks	17	8*	13	10	10	6
Organized club	55	46	67	57	69	70
Was officer in club	32	36	57	48	56	63
Improved game	46	38	57	51	29	41
Improved something (home)	43	40	61	56	41	48
Improved something (school)	38	27	44	33	13	17
Improved something (club)	40	26*	49	36	39	34
Solved parental problem	35	42	57	41*	30	38
Solved peer problem	59	62	57	58	32	54*
Acted out historical event	21	14	28	16*	24	13*
Found out about local history	38	21*	53	24*	34	27
Found out about government	23	11*	38	23*	30	22
Wrote letter to foreign country	33	24	35	49*	33	45
Wrote letter to another state	41	39	61	68	51	69*
Made map of community	26	8*	48	41	26	19
Made decision on money	54	41	71	63	76	62*
Asked questions on business	42	37	52	41	44	42
Made poster	43	38	53	43	51	47
Organized sale, drive	17	17	40	21*	26	18

* Difference between boys and girls significant at 5 per cent level

TABLE 7.2 (Cont.)

Creative Activity	Third Grade		Fourth Grade		Fifth Grade	
	Boys (N=94)	Girls (N=117)	Boys (N=93)	Girls (N=90)	Boys (N=93)	Girls (N=99)
Sketched landscape	33	22*	35	41	31	31
Designed stage setting	23	25	22	22	23	29
Designed jewelry	20	15	18	15	4	14*
Designed cloth	19	15	24	16	13	22
Illustrated story	48	39	48	32*	27	33
Took color photographs	31	28	40	23*	41	29
Took black and white photographs	44	44	80	54*	67	74
Made illustrated map	12	8	19	16	12	5
Made plaster molds	32	25	43	41	30	20
Drew cartoons	51	33*	73	42*	72	57*
Designed greeting cards	50	64*	65	70	56	60
Made linoleum cuts	19	7*	23	11*	10	7
Made block prints	20	9*	28	11*	14	15
Made water-color painting	36	38	51	52	38	42
Made oil-color painting	33	32	43	48	38	49
Made paper animals	34	15*	40	40	33	32
Made toy for child	46	38*	59	42*	50	45
Built scale model	21	12*	12	13	17	12
Made wood carving	62	16*	76	22*	53	27*
Made soap carving	44	32*	58	48	58	63
Made ornamental basket	28	28	30	25	24	16
Made plans for invention	15	10	25	11*	26	8*
Made model of invention	14	0*	23	4*	29	4*
Made food recipe	32	35	26	42*	24	31
Made drink recipe	46	38	53	44	48	36

° Difference between boys and girls significant at 5 per cent level

model airplane, making a collection of postmarks, improving something in a club or organization outside the home or school, finding out about local history, finding out about the way government operates, making a map of the community, sketching a landscape, drawing cartoons, making linoleum cuts and block prints, making papier mâché animals, making toys, building scale models, making wood and soap carvings, and making models of inventions. Although the checklist makes no pretense of presenting a random sample of all possible creative activities children do on their own, an attempt was made to design a checklist which would be reasonably representative. Thus, we can place some degree of confidence in the finding that a larger number of activities seem to be somewhat off limits for girls than for boys in the third grade.

Fourth-grade boys appear to be more reluctant than fourth-grade girls to write poems and plays, keep diaries, make up original dances, write letters to someone in a foreign country, and make up original food recipes. The girls are more restricted than the boys in finding errors in print, acting in plays and skits, writing letters to family members, exploring caves, reading science magazines and books, mixing colors, making firecrackers, printing photographs, growing crystals, making electric motors, making musical instruments, planning experiments, dissecting animals, using a magnifying glass, making ink, starting a fire with a lens, raising rats and mice, collecting insects, collecting rocks, keeping weather records, keeping science notebooks and scrapbooks, using chemistry sets, producing static electricity, constructing and designing model airplanes, counting annual rings on logs, making a stamp collection, solving an interpersonal relations problem with parents, acting out historical events, finding out about local history and government, organizing a sale or drive, illustrating a story, taking color and black and white photographs, drawing cartoons, making linoleum cuts and block prints, making toys, making wood carvings, planning an invention, and making a model of an invention. It is also observed that more areas of experiencing also tend to be off limits for girls in the fourth grade than for boys. This raises some questions about the tendency for girls to forge ahead of boys on tests of creative thinking in the fourth grade. It will be recalled, however, that almost all these differences occur in verbal tasks in group administered tests where subjects must write out their answers. It does not occur with tasks such as the science toy test and individually administered oral tests.

In the fifth grade, boys appear to be more resistant than girls to writing poems and stories, keeping a diary, making up and singing songs, writing letters to family members away from home, making up original dances, solving problems with peers, making leaf prints, writing letters to someone in another state, and designing jewelry. Girls in the fifth grade are more likely than boys to block out such areas of experience as making a recording, exploring caves, reading science magazines and books, making firecrackers, growing crystals, making electric motors, planning experiments, dissecting animals, making ink, starting fires with a lens, raising rats and mice, collecting insects, keeping a science scrapbook, using chemistry sets, producing static electricity, constructing and designing model airplanes, counting annual rings on logs, acting out historical events, making decisions on money, drawing cartoons, making wood carvings, and making models of inventions. In some cases, third-grade children are more likely to engage in an activity which tends to be off limits for their sex than are older children. For example, third-grade girls are more likely to dissect an animal than their older sisters, while a third-grade boy is more likely to make up an original dance than are his older brothers.

In summary, it seems that certain areas of creative experiencing tend to be off limits for girls while others tend to be off limits for boys. In general, creative experiencing through writing is more open to girls than to boys, but certain kinds of creative writing experiences are more open to boys than to girls. Similarly, there is a general tendency for creative experiencing through nature and science to be less open to girls than to boys, but certain areas of experiencing in nature and science are more open to girls than are other areas.

Although the differences found in this study may not hold in all cultures, it is believed that these data supply useful cues to parents and teachers in keeping open to both boys and girls a larger number of areas of creative experiencing.

Occupations Off Limits for Sexes

THE PROBLEM

If boys find that there are social pressures which tend to place certain childhood creative experiences off limits for them and if girls find that these pressures tend to place certain other activities off limits for them, it is reasonable to expect that both sexes will perceive certain occupational goals as off limits for them. During the past few years the National Science Foundation and other similar organizations have been concerned that so few women choose science careers. Generally, their investigations have led to the conclusions that women shun science careers because American society regards science work as traditionally male. The roots of the problem have been traced to the high schools and the colleges where girls are discouraged from taking science courses. It has been pointed out that many women's colleges do not even offer adequate science courses. Seldom, however, has anything been said about the earlier roots of sex differences in vocational choice.

The purpose of this section is to present data from a larger exploratory study of children's vocational choices, which might throw some light upon the problems created by placing certain experiences and certain occupations off limits for one sex rather than another.

PROCEDURES

As a part of the administration of tests of creative thinking, information has been obtained concerning the vocational choices of children and young people from kindergarten through college. Attention will be given here only to the data for the fourth through ninth grades, the years critical to our concern at this point. In all cases, total grade or school populations have been included. The samples have been drawn from Minnesota, Michigan, North Dakota, California, Illinois, South Carolina, North Carolina, and New York. In the fourth grade, data were obtained from 1228 children (643 boys and 585 girls); in the fifth grade, 749 children (375 boys and 374 girls); in the sixth grade, 2225 (1146 boys and 1079 girls); in the seventh grade, 473 subjects (221 boys and 252 girls); in the eighth grade, 514 subjects (250 boys and 264 girls); in the ninth grade, 636 subjects (304 boys and 332 girls).

RESULTS

Table 7.3 reports the respective percentages of boys and girls choosing each of the twenty-three most popular occupations for subjects from the fourth through the ninth grades. In several occupational areas, it is rather obvious that children accept the "off limits" signs for their sex. Engineering, professional athletics, carpentry, law, mechanics, military occupations, operation of trucks and heavy equipment, piloting and space travel, and police detective work are almost excluded by girls in their choice of occupational goals. Similarly, boys almost totally exclude consideration of such occupations as nursing, air hostess or steward, barber or hair stylist, and secretarial work. The differences are rather sharp (in most cases, significant at better than the 5 per cent level of confidence), but not so extreme in boys' rejection of teaching and girls' rejection of science, medicine, and farming. It is interesting to note that young girls find acceptable goals for science and medical interests in veterinary medicine, but the older girls reject choices in this area. This may result from society's approval of girls having and caring for pets.

TABLE 7.3 Most Popular Occupational Goals Expressed by Boys and Girls in Grades Four to Nine

Occupational Goals	Fourth Grade Boys (N=643)	Fourth Grade Girls (N=585)	Fifth Grade Boys (N=375)	Fifth Grade Girls (N=374)	Sixth Grade Boys (N=1146)	Sixth Grade Girls (N=1079)	Seventh Grade Boys (N=221)	Seventh Grade Girls (N=252)	Eighth Grade Boys (N=250)	Eighth Grade Girls (N=264)	Ninth Grade Boys (N=304)	Ninth Grade Girls (N=332)
Actor, actress	0.5	1.4	0.5	2.1	0.3	1.9	0.9	0.8	0.0	0.0	0.3	3.3
Air hostess	0.0	4.6	0.0	4.5	0.0	2.3	0.0	3.6	0.0	5.7	0.0	6.4
Artist (cartoon)	2.0	2.7	2.4	1.1	2.1	2.8	1.4	3.6	3.2	3.0	3.9	0.9
Athlete (pro)	12.9	0.2	8.3	0.0	9.1	0.3	8.1	0.0	2.8	0.0	2.3	0.0
Barber, beautician	0.3	1.2	0.0	0.5	0.2	3.0	0.0	3.0	0.2	4.8	0.0	7.2
Carpenter	2.3	0.0	2.1	0.0	2.1	0.0	2.3	0.0	2.4	0.0	4.6	0.6
Engineer	5.9	0.0	6.7	0.0	7.8	0.1	10.0	0.8	13.2	0.0	5.6	0.3
Farmer, rancher	3.7	1.2	9.1	1.9	4.8	1.3	6.8	2.0	2.4	0.0	2.3	0.9
Housewife, husband	0.0	8.5	0.1	6.7	0.1	7.1	0.0	5.6	0.0	8.3	0.0	1.5
Lawyer	3.3	0.3	2.7	0.0	4.8	1.6	3.6	0.8	4.0	0.4	2.3	1.8
Mechanic	3.0	0.0	1.9	0.0	3.2	0.0	4.1	0.0	5.6	0.0	6.9	0.0
Medical doctor	6.1	1.0	10.1	3.2	11.3	4.9	8.6	3.6	4.0	4.2	2.6	1.8
Military	7.2	0.0	6.7	0.0	4.4	0.4	4.5	0.8	4.4	0.4	3.9	0.3
Minister, priest	1.6	2.1	2.1	4.0	1.5	2.0	2.3	2.8	1.6	1.6	1.6	1.8
Musician	0.8	0.9	0.3	2.4	1.0	1.4	1.8	1.6	0.4	1.1	0.7	0.6
Nurse	0.2	29.6	0.0	27.5	0.1	22.1	0.0	21.0	0.0	19.3	0.0	8.4
Operator (truck)	3.1	0.2	3.2	0.0	2.2	0.0	2.7	0.0	3.6	0.0	3.0	0.0
Pilot, astronaut	6.7	0.0	5.3	0.0	3.8	0.1	3.6	0.0	4.4	0.0	2.3	0.3
Police detective	3.3	0.3	5.1	0.3	3.1	0.5	2.4	0.4	1.8	0.8	3.7	0.6
Scientist	9.3	2.1	9.1	3.2	6.0	2.3	9.0	2.4	8.4	3.4	5.6	0.3
Secretary	0.0	4.1	0.0	8.3	0.0	8.2	0.0	12.3	0.4	10.2	0.0	21.4
Teacher	2.3	31.5	1.0	32.1	3.2	27.5	2.3	27.4	4.0	25.8	3.0	18.4
Undecided	10.3	6.8	10.1	6.1	10.6	5.9	22.6	8.3	23.2	20.8	35.9	22.0
Veterinarian	2.6	3.8	2.4	1.3	2.9	2.3	2.7	2.4	0.8	4.5	0.3	0.0
Other occupations	56.0	26.0	31.0	14.0	53.0	36.0	30.0	23.0	30.0	28.0	46.0	21.0

Although there is a general rejection of what are recognized as some of the more creative occupations, sex differences do not appear to be great. Girls tend, however, to choose more frequently than boys such occupational goals as acting, the visual arts, fashion designing, religious occupations, interior decorating, music, linguistics, library work, dancing, and writing. Boys appear to hope for creative outlets through some of the more adventurous occupations such as exploring, clowning, hunting, archaeology, cartography, inventing, skin diving, diplomacy, racing, and the like. A few girls, however, expressed interest in such adventurous occupations as espionage, archaeology, animal training, criminology, and the like.

In summary, it seems clear that at least by the time children reach the fourth grade, and perhaps earlier, they have come to perceive certain occupational goals as being off limits for them because of their sex. It seems likely, for example, that if we want girls to be open to the consideration of science careers, this type of vocational guidance must be initiated before the high school years.

Differential Rewards
and Manipulative and Reading Activities of Children

THE PROBLEM

There are doubtless many areas of motor, mental, emotional, and spiritual experiencing that are affected by the differential rewards given boys and girls for specific behavior. Manipulative and reading activities have been chosen as examples of kinds of experiencing which may be expected to affect creative achievement.

Investigators in the field of creativity have long given attention to the role of manipulativeness in invention, scientific discovery, and the like. Rossman (1931), in his study of the psychology of inventors, assigned an important role to manipulative tendencies in inventiveness but offered little or no empirical data in support of his contention. He maintained that an irresistible tendency of manipulation and exploration of objects begins at an early stage and is probably the basis of curiosity and playfulness. He thus argued that manipulation supplies much of the necessary experience for the development of creative imagination. The studies of Barron (1958), Rossman (1931), and others also support this contention.

In one of my own studies (Torrance, 1963a), it was also shown that children who do the most manipulation of objects while trying to produce ideas for improving those objects succeed in producing a larger number of ideas and a higher quality of original ideas than those who do little or no manipulation. Data will now be presented relative to male-female differences from this study.

PROCEDURE IN MANIPULATION STUDY

The subjects of the manipulation study were first-, second-, and third-grade pupils enrolled in two elementary schools. Systematic recording of observations concerning the behavior of sixty-eight first-graders, sixty-two second-graders, and eighty-two third-graders was made.

Observations were made during the individual administration of the Product Improvement Test, involving three different toys (nurse's kit, fire truck, and stuffed toy dog). Three categories were used in classifying the degree of manipulation. Those who did not handle the toys at all were placed in the "Low" category. Those who handled one or more of the toys to some degree, but not to a high degree, were placed in the "Moderate" class; and those whose manipulation of the toys was described by the examiner as "considerable," "extreme," "excessive," "high degree," and the like were rated in the "High" category.

RESULTS OF THE MANIPULATION STUDY

To study any differential behavior of boys and girls, the number of boys and girls engaging in each of the three degrees of manipulation at each grade level are shown in Table 7.4. It will be seen that differences

TABLE 7.4 Number of First-, Second-, and Third-graders Engaging in Varying Degrees of Manipulation for Boys and for Girls and Chi-squares

Degree of Manipulation	Boys				Girls			
	First Grade	Second Grade	Third Grade	Total	First Grade	Second Grade	Third Grade	Total
High	5	11	11	27	4	6	5	15
Medium	16	16	24	56	17	16	20	53
Low	12	2	1	15	14	11	21	46
Total	33	29	36	98	35	33	46	114

Note: Chi-square (Boys) $= 18.7208$; $df = 4$; p significant at less than .1 per cent level
Chi-square (Girls) $= 1.7698$; $df = 4$; p not significant
Chi-square (Over-all) $= 20.4906$; $df = 8$; p significant at less than 1 per cent level

in the first grade are not statistically significant. By the second grade, greater manipulative tendencies are found among boys than among girls. By the third grade, these differences have become quite marked. Thus, the tendency ·for boys to become more manipulative in the test situation increases steadily and significantly from grade to grade from the first through the third grade. No such tendency exists among girls. Thus, it appears that manipulation of objects is an area of experiencing which tends to become more limited among girls than among boys as they go through the second and third grades.

READING EXPERIENCES

Since it takes a prepared mind to think creatively and since the reading and information gathering habits of the more productive creative scientists are different from those of their less productive peers, the reading experiences of children are of special interest in any consideration of the conditions necessary for fostering creative potential. In this section, I shall present data from a modest study conducted by Punsalan (1961) under my direction. Other studies have shown that girls generally excel boys in various reading skills, but little has been reported concerning differences in the reading habits and attitudes of boys and girls—matters which make a difference in how what has been read influences thinking.

The data were obtained through questionnaires administered to eighty-six boys and eighty-five girls in the sixth grade at three different schools.

RESULTS

Contrary to popular beliefs, the proportion of boys and girls who like to read is about the same. Almost all the subjects in this study stated that they like to read and were able to give reasons why they like to read. Boys and girls in this study did differ, however, in what they would sacrifice or not sacrifice in order to read. Boys would be more likely than girls to give up going to a party in order to have time to read (31 per cent of boys and 18 per cent of girls, significant at 1 per cent level of confidence). Girls, however, would be more likely than boys to sacrifice play activities, skating, and the like for reading (34 per cent of girls and 19 per cent of boys, significant at the 1 per cent level of confidence).

A majority of both boys and girls reported that they spend from four to seven hours a week in leisure reading, in addition to the reading they do for their school assignments. Boys, however, are less likely than girls to go to the library for the purpose of checking out books for home reading (89 per cent of girls and 70 per cent of boys, significant at the 1 per cent level of confidence). Girls also obtain more enjoyment than boys from giving oral book reports before the class (46 per cent of the girls and 23 per cent of the boys, significant at the 1 per cent level).

There are interesting sex differences in the kinds of books which boys and girls like to read. Boys express a greater preference than girls for books dealing with sports, science, and hobbies. Girls, however, express greater preference than boys for fiction, animal stories, fairy tales, classical novels, career stories, drama, poetry, and religion. These differences suggest rather clearly that girls have a stronger preference than boys at the sixth-grade level for imaginative materials.

In spite of the fact that there is no difference in the expressed liking of boys and girls in this study for reading, girls report having read a larger number of books per month than boys. The mean number of books read per month is 7.5 for girls and 4.9 for boys (significant at the 5 per cent level of confidence). Boys, however, report ownership of more books than do girls (significant at the 5 per cent level of confidence). Twenty-seven per cent of the boys own fifty or more books compared with 14 per cent of the girls owning this number.

Girls more frequently than boys report that they ask for suggestions about what to read (50 per cent and 36 per cent, respectively). Next to browsing through library shelves, girls choose to read what is recommended by friends their own age. They also obtain books from their peers through mutual exchanges. About three fourths of the boys reported that they make most of their choices of reading matter by browsing through the library. Though peers influence their choices more than teachers and librarians, boys seem to be rather independent in selecting their reading material.

A majority of both boys and girls report that they sometimes become so absorbed in what they are reading they are unable to think of anything else. A greater proportion of girls than boys report that this happens to them (83 per cent of the girls and 55 per cent of the boys). Both boys and girls, in about the same proportions, enjoy guessing what is going to happen next when they are reading something exciting (86 per cent of the girls and 82 per cent of the boys). Boys are more likely than girls to check on the accuracy of a statement which they do not believe (63 per cent of the boys and 45 per cent of the girls, significant at the 5 per cent level of confidence). Girls, however, tend to be more likely than boys to find errors in spelling and grammar during their reading, but the difference is not statistically significant (72 per cent of the girls and 62 per cent of the boys).

A greater proportion of girls than boys reported that they become so interested in their reading that there are times when they do not do other things that they should (74 per cent of the girls and 51 per cent of the boys) and that they are inclined to become "lost to the world" when they begin to read (82 per cent of the girls and 51 per cent of the boys). Both boys and girls, in about the same proportions, enjoy telling others about what they read (82 per cent of the boys and 84 per cent of the girls).

In general, then, both boys and girls report that they like to read. Girls read more books than boys, but boys own more books than girls. Boys are more willing than girls to forego a party in order to read, but girls are more willing than boys to forego skating or other games for this purpose. Both boys and girls feel they are fairly independent in choosing what they shall read, but boys appear to be somewhat more independent than girls in this respect. Girls express greater pleasure than boys about giving oral book reports before the class. Boys, however, appear to be just as eager as girls to tell others about what they read. Apparently they prefer not to talk about their reading to a class, but rather with special friends, family members, or others who have similar interests. Boys and girls differ fairly markedly in the kinds of books they enjoy reading, and this is probably related to differences in expectations for boys and girls. Although girls appear more likely to become completely absorbed in their reading, boys are apparently more likely to stop and check the accuracy of some statement which they do not believe. Thus, we have further clues concerning the ways in which differential rewards to boys and girls affect their experiencing.

Differential Rewards and Thinking Abilities

THE PROBLEM

From the data which have already been presented, it would be reasonable to expect that the differential rewards to boys and girls and the differences in their experiences have consequences insofar as the development of the creative thinking abilities are concerned.

One of the rare studies which gives consideration to the differential development of the thinking of boys and girls is one by Pitcher and Prelinger (1963). In this study, fathers and mothers, when questioned, agreed that women are more indirect, illogical, and circuitous in their thinking than men. Men's thinking was considered to be more analytical, definite, precise, abstract, and direct. Through the use of drawings, stories, and other data, Pitcher and Prelinger (1963) found many interesting differences in the thinking of children from a very early age. They found that girls very early focus their interest on persons and boys on things and processes. Girls are more aware of themselves as persons than are boys. Girls very early show a greater interest in details than do boys. Boys, on the other hand, show greater interest in aggressive activities and independence and less interest in pleasing others. These investigators concluded that boys and girls are from an early age subjected to influences that develop different thinking characteristics. The parents interviewed by them, however, were apparently unaware that they were doing or saying anything directly to cause these differences.

As one might hypothesize from the findings thus far presented, the matter of sex differences in creative thinking abilities is a complex one. The superiority of one sex over the other, as one might suspect, depends upon the age or educational level of the subjects and the nature of the task and kind of thinking involved. The adequate treatment of this problem would require a lengthy report. This chapter would not be complete, however, without some examination of sex differences on tests of creative thinking ability. Thus, we shall present only a few representative sets of data.

THE ASK-AND-GUESS TEST (Sensing Problems)

Yamamoto (1962) has presented a fairly extensive set of data picturing sex differences on the Ask-and-Guess Test. Figure 7.3 presents

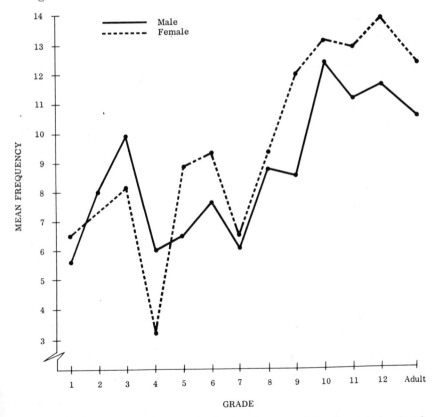

FIGURE 7.3 Developmental Curve for the Mean Frequency of Questions Asked on Part 1, Ask, of Ask-and-Guess Test

data on the question asking (sensing problems) part of this test for males and females separately for grades one through twelve, and for a group of adults (graduate students in Educational Psychology). The subjects include the entire enrollment of an elementary school in a small Minnesota town, a Minneapolis high school, and a graduate class in educational psychology.

From Figure 7.3 it will be observed that, as a general tendency, the number of questions produced in the Ask-and-Guess Test increases with grade. It reaches a maximum at about the end of the high school period and then appears to decrease slightly. It also shows decreases at the fourth- and seventh-grade levels. The difference in the means at the seventh-grade level is significant at the 2 per cent level of confidence. Except for the second, third, and fourth grades, the female subjects ask more questions than the male subjects. The largest difference occurs at the fourth-grade level.

DIFFERENCES AMONG GIFTED SIXTH-GRADERS AND JUNIOR HIGH STUDENTS

It is of special interest to know how boys and girls who have been identified as intellectually gifted differ in their thinking abilities. Data will be presented for an upper elementary and a junior high school group carefully identified as high achievers and as highly intelligent (minimum Stanford-Binet IQ, 135) and placed in special programs to enhance their giftedness.

The junior high school group consists of seventy-five seventh- and eighth-grade students (thirty-five boys and forty girls). The means and tests of significance for this group are presented in Table 7.5. It will be noted that the boys excelled the girls on all the scores derived from the nonverbal or figural tests and on both scores of the Consequences Test. The girls, however, showed superiority on both of the make-up problems tests. They have a slight but nonsignificant edge on the boys on the Product Improvement, Ask-and-Guess, and Unusual Uses Tests.

The elementary school group consisted of fifty high achieving sixth-grade pupils (twenty-four boys and twenty-six girls). The results of the Parallel Lines Test and the Ask-and-Guess Test are shown in Table 7.6. In this table it will be observed that on the nonverbal or figural task, the boys excelled the girls on originality, but the girls turned the tables on the boys on the elaboration score of this same task. The girls outdistanced the boys on two of the three subtasks of the Ask-and-Guess Test.

TABLE 7.5 Comparison of Means of Gifted Junior High School Boys and Girls on Measures of Creative Thinking

Measure	Mean Male (N=35)	Female (N=40)	t-ratio	Level of Significance
Nonverbal fluency	8.22	6.62	2.729	Less than .5 per cent
Nonverbal originality	22.17	15.49	3.564	Less than .5 per cent
Nonverbal penetration	34.00	28.37	2.160	Less than 2.5 per cent
Consequences: fluency	9.19	8.16	1.518	Less than 10 per cent
Consequences: flexibility	7.64	6.58	2.074	Less than 2.5 per cent
Make-up arithmetic problems	4.25	5.26	1.580	Less than 10 per cent
Make-up social studies problems	4.22	7.51	3.640	Less than .5 per cent
Product Improvement: fluency	10.64	10.67	-----	Not significant
Product Improvement: flexibility	5.47	6.05	-----	Not significant
Product Improvement: originality	26.31	27.79	-----	Not significant
Asking questions	12.36	12.79	-----	Not significant
Causal hypotheses	8.33	7.68	-----	Not significant
Consequential hypotheses	9.36	10.05	-----	Not significant
Unusual Uses: fluency	7.97	8.86	-----	Not significant
Unusual Uses: originality	21.64	23.93	-----	Not significant

TABLE 7.6 Comparison of Means of Gifted Elementary Boys and Girls on Measures of Creative Thinking

Measure	Mean Male (N=24)	Female (N=26)	t-ratio	Level of Significance
Nonverbal fluency	12.19	10.61	1.23	Not significant
Nonverbal flexibility	9.38	7.83	1.12	Not significant
Nonverbal originality	7.96	5.65	2.12	2.5 per cent
Nonverbal elaboration	25.96	37.09	2.71	1 per cent
Asking questions	9.43	12.17	2.32	2.5 per cent
Causal hypotheses	7.43	9.39	2.09	2.5 per cent
Consequential hypotheses	11.57	13.39	1.39	Not significant

Summary

In this chapter, a variety of evidence relevant to the problems created by differential rewards to boys and girls for specific kinds of creative behavior has been presented. The evidence suggests that differential rewards make off limits for both boys and girls whole areas of experiencing, perhaps needlessly, and that this takes a heavy toll upon the potentialities of both boys and girls. When teachers are asked deliberately to reward creative behavior, they describe incidents in which boys have been rewarded. This may mean that this emphasis brings about a better equalization of rewards for boys. It may also mean that teachers reward the creative behavior of boys more frequently than they reward the creative behavior of girls. It may also mean that boys behave more creatively in the classroom, but even this may mean that girls are rewarded for conforming behavior and are satisfied with this reward.

In an experimental situation, it was found that regarding science matters children tend to place more value on boys' ideas than on girls'. Over a period of one year (1958–59 to 1959–60) some kind of social-cultural change took place for the subjects of this study which apparently made it acceptable for girls to participate in science activities and to enjoy them. This change was not accompanied by a change in the value placed on girls' ideas concerning the science toys used in this study. A study of the creative activities done on their own reported by children shows that there are many areas of childhood creative experiencing which seem to be off limits for boys and girls apparently because of their sex. Similar phenomena are found in regard to the occupational goals or choices reported by children and young people. These differential rewards were also shown to be accompanied by differences in such experiencing as manipulation of objects and reading, kinds of experiencing which are likely to be related to creative achievement. Finally, it was shown that the influence of these differential rewards on the development of the creative thinking abilities is complex, but that there are nevertheless differences which can be associated logically with the nature of the differential rewards and their influence on the kinds of experiencing open to boys and to girls.

HOW
DIFFERENTIAL
REWARDS
INFLUENCE
ORIGINALITY

8

Since educational research had repeatedly and consistently shown that people tend to learn and develop along whatever lines they find rewarding, I was willing to assume that in order to encourage originality and other types of creative thinking, it is necessary to find ways of rewarding these kinds of achievements. With my own eyes, I had seen children do excitingly original thinking when the conditions had rewarded such achievement. I had also seen an almost total lack of originality of thinking when the conditions punished or did not reward this kind of achievement. Yet as I began to discuss the results of the experiments which will be described in the next four chapters, I was continually challenged on my basic assumption. I was told repeatedly that I had no basis on which to make such an assumption. It might be true, my critics said, that educational research has repeatedly shown that people tend to remember those things which they know that they will be graded on or to learn motor skills which they find rewarding, but this does not mean that rewarding creative thinking will improve the quality of creative thinking. It is for this reason that we conducted the simple studies described in this chapter.

It is the purpose of the two modest experimental studies described herein to determine whether or not simple instructions in setting up the reward system for a creative activity can affect the differential nature of the thinking which results. Every effort was exerted to follow as rigorous procedures as possible.

The author was assisted in the conduct of these studies by R. E. Myers.

Before describing these two small studies, however, I would li
to ask the reader to follow me imaginatively through one of my obse
vational experiences. It was through such observational experiences th
I formulated the designs of the studies described herein.

First, come with me to a first-grade class. These children range
IQ's from about 80 to 180, as determined by one of our better indivi
ually administered tests of intelligence, the Stanford-Binet. They cor
from a variety of backgrounds. They are the children of doctors, lawye
college professors, engineers, milkmen, plumbers, mechanics, and fa
tory workers. In some cases, the father is unemployed and on reli
Some of these children are clean and well-dressed; others are dirty a
unkempt. They are indeed different. Let us see, however, how they b
have when I administer the test. First, I shall administer the Pictu
Construction Test, using a colored triangle which is gummed on o
side. Let us ask them to think of a picture which they can make, usi
the colored triangle as one of the main parts and see what happens. C
you guess what they will do? Will their pictures be as different as th
are? Let us look.

Here is quick little Mary. She is using the triangle as the roof
a house. Let's see what Mark is doing. Yes, he is drawing a house to
and so is Tom who is sitting behind him. Surely the children in t
back row must be drawing something else. Let us see what Ann is dra
ing. Yes, she is drawing a house also. As we go around the classroom, v
find that 24 of the 25 children have drawn houses. Only unruly, ene
getic, nonconforming Madeline over in the "isolation corner" has dar
draw anything different. She used her triangle as a diaper on a bab
You will say, "Well, there is not much creativity here. All except Mad
line produced the most obvious object possible, and all were along t
same pattern, just as similar as the houses in the housing developme
in which many of them live."

Let us go now into another first-grade class in the same scho
Classes in this school are not grouped according to ability. Childre
enrolled in the first grade are divided randomly among three teache
Thus, we find the same range in IQ, socio-economic status, and the li
that we found in the first class. Again, we shall administer the Pictu
Construction Test, only this time we shall make the instructions a litt
different. We shall do more this time to try to free them to express the
own ideas, to be creative. After distributing the materials, let us gi
them these instructions:

You have been given a blank sheet of paper and a triangular-shap
piece of paper. Think of a picture or an object in which this triangle will l
an important part. Then lick the triangle on the gummed side just like y
would a postage stamp and stick it wherever you want it on the page. Th
add lines with your pencil or crayon to make your picture.

Try to think of a picture that no one else will think of. If you draw
a picture that *you* think of, it probably *will be* different from anyone else's.
ep adding new ideas to your first idea to make it tell an interesting and
citing story.

Let us see what happens now! Here is Sally. She is using her tri-
gle as the top of an umbrella being carried by a girl leading a pig
wn the street. Bill is using his triangle as a Christmas tree and is
corating it with all the presents he wants for Christmas. Helen is
ing hers as the skirt on a girl jumping the rope. Mike is using his as an
row point whizzing through the air at a deer. Tom's is a high mountain
a busy camp scene. Jim's triangle becomes a part of a rocket and Sue's
a sail on a boat skimming on Lake Nokomis. No two are alike. They
e as different as the boys and girls who drew them. They have gotten
way from the obvious, the safe, the reproductive and dared to express
eir own individual thoughts.

We have thus seen one example of how slight changes in the way
e reward original thinking can free the creative thinking abilities and
ve the rich diversity which goes with the achievement of potentialities.
e noticed that in the first class there was little excitement. No one was
erested in looking at what anyone else had drawn. In the second
ss, the reaction to one another's work was entirely different. Every-
e was bubbling over with excitement to see what stories the others
d told through their drawings. Whenever there is creative thinking in
classroom, we have almost always seen this excitement. Everybody is
xious to show each other what they have done or tell them their
ory.

The methodological principle is a very simple one. In the first
ss, nothing was done to make it legitimate for each child to produce
s idea. Each child had the usual expectation that there was one "right"
sponse, the one that the teacher wanted. The teacher had made a tri-
gular roof on the house she had them draw yesterday. Obviously, the
ght" response (the response which would be rewarded) must be a
use. In the second class, definite steps were taken to free each child
produce whatever picture occurred to him. It was legitimate for him
produce rather than *reproduce* something. The instructions for the
tivity had assured the children that originality would be rewarded,
d they felt free to express their own ideas.

The Imaginative Story-writing Study

Authorities in the language arts field hold a diversity of points of
ew regarding what should be rewarded in children's writings. Most
the teachers with whom I have talked personally believe that the

teacher should correct everything that the child writes from kind·
garten on up. Many teachers become acutely uncomfortable when th·
pupils are asked to participate in experiments which urge them to p
their mental energies into the production of an interesting, excitir
original story without worrying about errors. The emphasis upon c(
rectness has been so thoroughly taught that some children will bu:
into tears if they are not given an opportunity to copy meticulously th·
stories so that there will be no errors in them. Some authorities in t
field, like Applegate (1949), urge that some things be written only to
read and enjoyed and that others be written to be corrected. Some, li
Ferebee (1950), maintain that correct form can be learned throu;
creative expression in a setting where children write stories freely a·
happily with an opportunity to share their stories with their fellov
Others recommend that two different grades be assigned to the creati
writings of children—one for correctness and another for creative qua
ties or content.

It is the purpose of the simple study described herein to investiga
the differential effects of differential rewards on the creative writing
sixth-grade children.

PROCEDURE

Four sixth-grade classes in one school were placed randomly in
two experimental conditions. Pupils assigned to Condition A were giv·
the following instructions by their teachers:

> During this period we are going to participate in an impromptu sto:
> writing contest. You will have your choice of the ten titles on the bookl·
> which have been passed out.
> You will have twenty minutes in which to write your story. A prize
> two dollars will be awarded to the pupil in your grade who writes the b·
> story. Stories will be judged on correctness of spelling, punctuation, gramm
> and sentence structure; neatness and correctness of margins and indentatic
> and handwriting. You will want to make your stories interesting and origin·
> too, but the important thing is to avoid making errors.
> All right! Go ahead and write your stories in the booklets which y
> have been given. Write on both sides of the paper if you need to do so.

Pupils assigned to Condition B were given the following instru
tions by their teachers:

> During this period we are going to participate in an impromptu sto:
> writing contest. You will have your choice of the ten titles listed on the book
> which has been passed out.

You will have twenty minutes in which to write your story. A prize of
o dollars will be awarded to the pupil in your grade who writes the best
ory. Stories will be judged on the basis of how interesting, exciting, unusual,
d original they are. You will want to write legibly and correctly, but the
ing that really counts is interest and originality.

All right! Go ahead and write your stories in the booklets which you
ve been given. Write on both sides of the paper if you need to do so.

Both groups were given the Imaginative Stories Test described in
ppendix A.

Stories were obtained from fifty pupils under Condition A and
ty-three pupils under Condition B. Each story was scored for Orig-
ality and Interest according to the guide prepared previously by Tor-
nce and described in Appendix A. Scorers did not know to which con-
tion the writers had been assigned. To obtain objectivity in scoring
r correctness, Myers developed the following checklist involving skills
hich might reasonably be expected of sixth-grade pupils:

nctuation

1. *Omission of period* at the end of a sentence, after an abbreviation,
   after initials, to indicate dollars and cents.
2. *Omission of comma* after the various parts of an address, after the
   parts of a date, to set off a noun in direct address, to separate city
   and state, to separate the day of the month from the year, to separate a direct quotation from the words quoted, and to separate the
   two parts of a compound sentence when they are joined by a con-
   junction if the sentence is so constructed that the pupil would see a
   need for a pause. In most cases, no penalty should be given for unnecessary commas.
3. *Omission of a question mark* at the end of an interrogatory sentence.
4. *Omission of an exclamation mark* after sentences which contain strong
   elements of emotion.
5. *Omission of an apostrophe* where one is needed to show possession
   or contraction.
6. *Omission of a hyphen* when a word is divided at the end of a line.
7. *Omission of a colon* when writing time or the substitution of a semi-
   colon for a colon in such a case.
8. *Omission of quotation marks* to indicate the speaker's exact words.

pelling and capitalization

1. *Misspelling of a word.* If the pupil spells a word incorrectly more
   than once, do not score for errors after the first misspelling.
2. *Lack of capitalization.*

rammar

1. *Incorrect use of a verb:* where a verb does not agree with its noun
   subject in number; where an incorrect form is used (He *give* me a

dime, Our teacher *learns* us arithmetic); where an incorrect form
used with a helping verb (Jerry has *went* home, I have *writ* so mu
my hand is tired); where an unacceptable form is employed (T
ain't my brother, His little sister almost *drownded* in the lake l
summer).

2. *Incorrect use of a pronoun:* where an objective pronoun is used
place of a nominative pronoun (*Him* and me are good friend
where a nominative pronoun is used in place of an objective p
noun (The dog chased Jim and *I*, The Jensens always invite
Smiths to their summer cottage); where a pronoun does not have
antecedent or where it is especially confusing as to which noun
the antecedent; where a pronoun is used unnecessarily with a no
(My father *he* is a great fisherman, Mr. and Mrs. Jones *they* ha
a farm).

3. *Incorrect use of an adjective:* where the article "a" is used before
word beginning with a vowel or a vowel sound (Mother gave me
egg and some cereal for breakfast, Receiving the award was *a* hor
he wouldn't forget); where "them" is used in place of "those" (G
me *them* books!); where the comparative or superlative forms a
incorrect (Jane is *more* better than Jill in spelling, Harry is t
bestest of all); where an adjective is used in place of an adve
(Terry plays tennis *good*, Ann really sings *poor*).

4. *Incorrect use of an adverb:* where two negative words are used in
sentence but only one is necessary (This coat *isn't nothing* like mir
You *don't hardly* look the same in your new suit).

5. *Incorrect use of a preposition:* where "of" is used with "off" (He g
off *of* that horse in a hurry!); where it is not necessary to use
preposition (Where does she stay *at* when she is in Chicag
Where were you going *to*?).

Sentence sense

1. *Incomplete sentences or fragments* (However he wanted to trav
because of the girl's unhappiness).

2. *Run-together sentences* (Harry ran from the house, when he got
the road he stopped abruptly; Gary and his friends were always
trouble one day they got into trouble because they were throwi
tomatoes which were not too fresh at the girls). Although fragmer
and run-together sentences involve errors of punctuation and cap
talization as well as of sentence structure, the judge should sco
a maximum of two errors when the pupil is guilty of this type
mistake.

Penmanship and neatness

1. *Crossed-out words and phrases.*
2. *Ugly erasure or smudges.*
3. *Illegible words.*

anuscript form

1. *Insufficient left-hand margin.*
2. *Insufficient right-hand margin.*
   A maximum of two errors should be given for improper margins, even though the pupil uses two or more sides of a piece of paper.
3. *Lack of indentation at the beginning of a paragraph.* Because the use of direct quotations poses so many serious problems of form for an elementary pupil, the scorer should *not* expect the pupil to start a new paragraph for each change of speaker.

iscellaneous

1. *Omission of words* where such omission causes confusion.

It is apparent whenever compositions are evaluated for accuracy form that the pupil whose composition is lengthy runs the risk of ving more errors than the pupil whose work is brief. Accordingly, a ir measure of technical proficiency should make some allowance for e length of the composition. The index used in this study attempts to ke this factor into account by using the total number of words written well as the errors which have been noted by the scorer. Thus, the dex is the relationship of the number of errors to the length of the mposition. For example, a pupil whose paper contained 32 errors and 7 words would earn a rating of .782 (32/147 = .218 deficiency or .782 oficiency).

RESULTS

The results of the foregoing analyses are presented in Table 8.1. will be noted that the primary reward for originality apparently re-lted in a higher level of originality and interest and that the primary

TABLE 8.1 Comparison of Performances of Subjects Under Conditions A and B on iginality, Interest, Number of Errors, Proficiency Index, and Total Number of Words

Measure	Condition A (N=50)		Condition B (N=53)		t-ratio	Level of Confidence
	Mean	St. Dev.	Mean	St. Dev.		
iginality	4.60	1.47	5.83	1.30	4.49	Less than 1 per cent
erest	4.58	1.58	5.57	1.42	3.33	Less than 1 per cent
mber of errors	9.92	6.23	25.83	16.41	6.63	Less than 1 per cent
oficiency index	.93	0.01	.84	0.03	7.59	Less than 1 per cent
mber of words	161.16	4.95	165.19	5.49	0.39	Not significant

reward for correctness resulted in fewer errors and a higher proficien
index of correctness. There was a nonsignificant tendency for tho
working under the reward for originality to write longer stories th
those working under the correctness reward.

Thus, the results of this simple study support the contention th
children tend to achieve along whatever lines they are rewarded wh
originality of thinking is concerned.

Originality of Ideas of Gifted Children

The author has on a number of occasions been presented with t
argument that it is not necessary to reward gifted children for creati
thinking. Gifted or high achieving children, it is maintained, are not i
fluenced by such rewards and produce original ideas without bei
encouraged to do so. The present small experiment with two classes
carefully selected, high achieving sixth-grade pupils was designed
explore some of the problems posed by those who present argumen
of this nature and to explore further the original hypothesis that creati
thinking is influenced by differential rewards.

PROCEDURES

The two classes of high achieving pupils were each divided ra
domly into Groups A and B. This was done by having each pupil dra
an assignment card from a stack which had been carefully and obvious
shuffled. All members of Group A assembled in one of the classroon
and all of the B's in the other. Twenty-three subjects were placed
Condition A, and twenty-two in Condition B.

Group A was given the following instructions:

Your task is to think of ideas for improving this stuffed toy dog so th
it will be more fun for a child to play with. Try to think of just as many ide
as you can. Don't worry about how good your ideas are or how much it wou
cost to carry them out. A prize of two dollars will be awarded to the o
who thinks of the greatest number of ideas, regardless of how clever
original they are. Of course you want to think of clever and original ideas,
we shall give a prize of twenty-five cents to the one who thinks of the greate
number of unusual or original ideas. You will have only ten minutes, so y
will want to make good use of your time.

Group B was shown identically the same stuffed toy dog and give
the following instructions:

Your task is to think of ideas for improving this stuffed toy dog so that will be more fun for a child to play with. Try to think of as clever, unusual, d original ideas as you can. Don't worry about how much it would cost to ry them out. A prize of two dollars will be awarded to the one who thinks the greatest number of clever, unusual, or original ideas. A prize of twenty-e cents will be awarded to the one who thinks of the greatest number of as, whether they are original or not. You will have only ten minutes, so u will want to make good use of your time.

Responses were scored for Fluency, Flexibility, and Originality. iency was determined by counting the number of relevant ideas ven. Ideas not related to the improvement of the toy as something to iy with were eliminated as not relevant. Flexibility was determined by unting the number of different approaches used in making the im- ovements. The categories used are as follows:

1. Adaptation
2. Addition
3. Change color
4. Change shape
5. Combination
6. Division
7. Magnification
8. Minification
9. Motion
10. Multiplication
11. Position
12. Quality of material
13. Rearrangement
14. Reversal
15. Sensory appeal (ear)
16. Sensory appeal (eye)
17. Sensory appeal (nose)
18. Sensory appeal (touch)
19. Substitution
20. Subtraction

iese categories are described and illustrated more fully in *Guiding eative Talent* (Torrance, 1962a). A response was scored as original it had been given by fewer than 5 per cent of the subjects in a norm pulation of 594 subjects and if it showed creative strength.

RESULTS

The means, standard deviations, and *t*-ratios of the subjects on ency, flexibility, and originality for the subjects in Conditions A and are presented in Table 8.2. It will be noted that the differential in- uctions with the accompanying differential rewards apparently influ- ce significantly the originality of the thinking of gifted sixth-grade pils with relatively little difference in fluency and no difference in xibility. In fact, the subjects rewarded for originality of thinking pro- ced about twice as many original responses as did their peers who re being rewarded for sheer number of responses. (It should be inted out that irrelevant, "wild" responses were eliminated and are

TABLE 8.2 Comparison of Performances of Subjects Under Conditions A and B
Fluency, Flexibility, and Originality Scores of Product Improvement Test

Measure	Condition A (N=23)		Condition B (N=22)		t-ratio	Level of Confidence
	Mean	St. Dev.	Mean	St. Dev.		
Fluency	23.0	7.95	20.4	6.73	1.19	Less than 25 per c
Flexibility	8.5	2.43	8.5	1.84	----	Not significant
Originality	6.2	3.60	12.2	6.12	4.00	Less than 1 per c

not counted in the above results. It should also be pointed out that t
subjects rewarded for original responses did produce a larger numl
of such responses than their peers.)

Conclusions

The evidence obtained from the two simple studies described
this chapter support strongly the conclusion that differential rewa
influence originality of thinking. Giving instructions in terms of rewa
for correctness or for quantity with secondary attention to original
appears to work against the production of original ideas.

COMPETITION
AS
EXTERNAL
EVALUATION

9

Since our society is a competitive one and gives many of its re-
rds on the basis of open competition, children are conditioned early
excel in activities which are rewarded through competition. Thus,
study of the role of evaluation in the development of creative think-
requires research on the effects of competition upon creative be-
vior. The study described in this chapter does not do justice to the
ue and even runs the danger of being misunderstood. If interpreted
the light of the problem which it investigates, however, it does give
dence of both some of the advantages and limitations of competition
evoking creative behavior. It does not tell us anything about the cu-
lative effects of competition on creative behavior.

In an earlier study (Torrance, 1961c) involving grades one through
ee, it was found that children under competitive conditions achieved
her fluency and flexibility scores on the Product Improvement Task
n under noncompetitive conditions. In fact, the competitive condi-
ns produced about twice as many responses at each grade level as the
ncompetitive conditions. In this earlier study, the children in the
ncompetitive conditions had not been given any specific "warm-up" or
ctice for this particular task. Thus, some have suggested that what
s really lacking in the noncompetitive condition was a "warm-up ex-
rience" and that such an experience without competition would have
duced just as good performance. The study described in this chapter
an exploratory one to test the hypothesis implied in this suggestion.

There is a recurrent note concerning competition in the literature

about adult creativity. It pervades the literature concerning inventi
scientific discovery, industrial product improvement, and even the a
Present-day educators writing about conditions necessary for the devel
ment of creative thinking and the expression of creativity have be
strangely silent on the issue of competition. Art educators have perh;
been more articulate than others on this issue. Lowenfeld (1952),
example, rather consistently argued against the use of competition
cept with oneself. He maintained that the family and the natural cla
room condition will confront the child with enough competitive ex]
riences and that the child is unable to see the achievement of oth
beyond his own level. Benson (1958) argues against evaluation of cr
tive products and competition in creative activities on the basis of (
lack of satisfactory criteria in making judgments and maintains th
those who excel are least in need of encouragement.

Since competition implies external evaluation, however, one m
assume that many current writers would oppose the use of competit
with regard to creativity. The elimination of external evaluation
promoting creativity holds a major place in the theories of Rogers (195
Stein (1958), and Osborn (1957). Although the attack on competition
education has continued to arise for many decades (LaPiere, 1959).
has been especially active in the United States since 1930. First,
attack was made on competitive grading. As a result, some schools ab
ished examinations and grades altogether. Others shifted to some ty
of evaluation presumed to be "noncompetitive." Perhaps the most favo
of these practices has been comparison or competition with one's o'
performance, or evaluation in terms of the extent to which one v
"over- or underachieving"—usually in terms of the IQ. Next, accordi
to LaPiere (1959), there was an attempt to eliminate competition in a
form from the classroom. Advocates of this noncompetitive society argu
that it was necessary to eliminate competition from education and
develop a generation of noncompetitive adults in order to bring ab
"the good society." Thus, the current relative silence concerning comp
tion is of interest in itself.

Procedures

Data concerning the competitive (not practiced) condition in t
earlier study were re-analyzed in the present study. Children assign
to this condition served as a control group in the earlier study, and c
half of the pupils enrolled in each class were assigned randomly to t
condition. After being given the general orientation concerning t
activity and assigned to this group, these subjects went directly to t
testing situation. Their task was to think of as many ideas as they co

improving a stuffed toy dog so that it would be more fun as a play
. In the first three grades, subjects were tested individually and orally
l the examiner wrote down their responses. In the upper three grades,
ojects were tested in a group and were required to write their ideas.
all cases, the time limit was eight minutes.

In another school where the average IQ is almost identical to that
ind in the school in the first study, the practiced (not competitive)
idition was conducted. As a part of the orientation, the entire class in
grades was asked to think of ideas for improving a toy fire truck so
t it would be "more fun for children to play with." Testing procedures
re the same as in the other condition.

A total of 199 subjects were involved in the competitive (not
cticed) condition, and 356 in the practiced (not competitive) condi-
n. The tests under competitive conditions were administered in Decem-
and in the other condition in February.

Responses to the test task were scored for the number of ideas
uency), the number of principles or approaches used (flexibility) in
proving the toy, and the number of uncommon (original) responses.
lowing a previously developed scoring manual, an interscorer relia-
ity of .93 was obtained between the two judges.

Results

The mean fluency scores on the Product Improvement Task under
competitive (not practiced) and the practiced (not competitive)
idition are presented in Table 9.1 by grade and sex. It will be noted
m this table that there is a general tendency for subjects in the com-
titive condition to give more responses than those in the other condi-
n. This tendency is consistent except for girls in the second grade and
ys in the fifth and sixth grades. A number of sex differences are also
served and there are also some indications that boys and girls at dif-
ent grade levels may respond differently to competition and practice
used in this study.

The effects observed in Table 9.1 were tested for significance by
alysis of variance. It was found that the effects due to competition are
nificant in the first, third, and fourth grades, but not in the second,
h, and sixth grades. The sex differences are significant in the third
d fifth grades with boys excelling girls in the third and the reverse
curring in the fifth. The interaction effects are not statistically sig-
icant.

The mean flexibility scores by condition, grade, and sex are shown
Table 9.2. Again it will be observed that there is a general trend for

TABLE 9.1 Mean Fluency Scores on Product Improvement Task Under Competitive Practiced) and Practiced (Not Competitive) Conditions by Grade and Sex

Grade	Condition	Number			Mean		
		Boys	Girls	Total	Boys	Girls	Total
1	Competitive (NP)	19	16	35	10.95	11.50	11.20
	Practiced (NC)	30	26	56	8.37	6.27	7.39
2	Competitive (NP)	22	20	42	11.50	8.45	10.05
	Practiced (NC)	38	16	54	9.84	9.00	9.59
3	Competitive (NP)	17	15	32	17.65	13.67	15.78
	Practiced (NC)	22	21	43	11.41	8.67	10.07
4	Competitive (NP)	20	11	31	9.50	8.46	9.13
	Practiced (NC)	39	35	74	6.46	7.31	6.86
5	Competitive (NP)	21	15	36	7.76	11.40	9.28
	Practiced (NC)	32	24	56	10.66	11.29	10.93
6	Competitive (NP)	15	21	36	8.67	13.13	10.22
	Practiced (NC)	27	46	73	10.48	10.96	10.78

TABLE 9.2 Mean Flexibility Scores on Product Improvement Task Under Competitive Practiced) and Practiced (Not Competitive) Conditions by Grade and Sex

Grade	Condition	Number			Mean		
		Boys	Girls	Total	Boys	Girls	Total
1	Competitive (NP)	19	16	35	4.32	4.63	4.46
	Practiced (NC)	30	26	56	4.23	3.46	3.88
2	Competitive (NP)	22	20	42	5.18	4.45	4.93
	Practiced (NC)	38	16	54	3.86	3.69	3.79
3	Competitive (NP)	17	15	32	5.59	5.53	5.56
	Practiced (NC)	22	21	43	4.73	4.90	4.81
4	Competitive (NP)	20	11	31	4.90	4.91	4.90
	Practiced (NC)	39	35	74	3.26	4.14	3.68
5	Competitive (NP)	21	15	36	4.38	6.07	5.08
	Practiced (NC)	32	24	56	4.38	4.79	4.55
6	Competitive (NP)	15	21	36	5.07	6.00	5.39
	Practiced (NC)	27	46	73	4.96	5.67	5.42

ᵥjects under the competitive conditions to excel those in the other
ᵢdition. The analysis of variance to test the significance of the ob-
ᵥed effects of conditions and sex shows that the competitive condition
duced superior flexibility scores only in the second and fourth grades.
. differences are statistically significant only in the fifth grade, with
ᵢs scoring higher than boys. (The 5 per cent level of confidence was
ᵢblished as the accepted level of significance.)

Since the originality score is frequently influenced strongly by the
ᵢncy score, the index of originality chosen for use in this study is the
centage of original or uncommon responses given by a subject. As
the study described in Chapter 8, a response was considered original
t was given by less than 5 per cent of the norm population of ap-
ᵥximately 600 subjects from grades one through twelve.

The percentages of original responses given by the subjects at each
ᵢde level are presented in Figure 9.1 separately for the competitive,

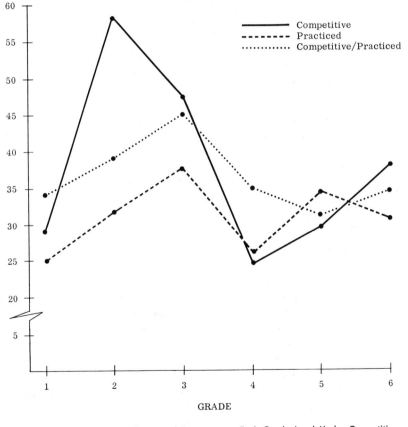

FIGURE 9.1 *Percentages of Original Responses at Each Grade Level Under Competitive,*
cticed, and Competitive/Practiced Conditions

practiced, and competitive/practiced conditions. The data for the cc petitive/practiced condition were taken from a previously reported stu (Torrance, 1963a). Considering first the differences between the cc petitive (not practiced) and practiced (not competitive) conditions, differences are statistically significant at the 5 per cent level or bet for the second, third, and sixth grades in favor of competitive conditio The combined competitive and practiced condition gives superiority o in the first and fourth grades, while the purely competitive condit gives superiority over the competitive/practiced condition in the seco grade.

It is also interesting to note that the percentage of original sponses tends to reach a peak in the second and third grades un the competitive condition, reaching a low point in the fourth grade a rising somewhat thereafter. Under practiced (but not competitive) c ditions the rise in percentage of original responses does not really co until the third grade, but is followed by a decrease in the fourth gra It is of further interest to note that the combined competitive/practic condition is not sufficient to overcome the apparent drop at the four grade level.

A breakdown of the results according to sex reveals a number sex differences which might be noted. Under competitive (not practice conditions, boys show superiority over girls in the second (62 per c versus 53 per cent), third (52 per cent versus 41 per cent), and si grades (45 per cent versus 25 per cent). Under practiced (not co petitive) conditions, there are no sex differences at the 5 per cent le of significance or better. Under competitive/practiced conditions, b show superiority only in the third grade (49 per cent versus 40 cent) at the 5 per cent level or better, although boys have a slight ed at all other grade levels except the fourth grade.

Discussion

The results presented herein concerning the relative effectiven of competition without practice and practice without competition not conclusive. Since there is a fairly general tendency for almost groups under competitive conditions to achieve somewhat higher sco than the other groups, and since the time lag between the administr tion of the tests to the two groups favored the practice condition, c must admit that the argument in favor of competition is fairly stro When these results are compared with those found in the earlier stu it is clear that the practice (or the "warm-up" resulting from practi does much to compensate for the difference between performance und competitive and noncompetitive conditions. It should be emphasiz hat this study makes no attempt to tell anything about the cumulative ffects of competition on creative behavior.

It is unfortunate that there was a two-month lag between the col-ection of the data under the two conditions. Such data collection equires a great deal of manpower since children in the first three grades must be tested individually and arrangements for such studies re rather time-consuming and complex. Since growth of the abilities measured by this task are far from linear, it would be risky to attempt) correct for this lag. In fact, there is no measureable growth between grades at some levels. It is not believed that this time lag affected the results very much.

Summary

A previous study indicated that the use of competition in the orm of prizes resulted in a much larger number and greater flexibility f responses on the Product Improvement Task than conditions identical xcept for the absence of competition. The present study was conducted) determine whether or not the learning and/or "warm-up" effects esulting from a brief practice session would "make up" for this dif-erence which seems to result from the introduction of competition. One undred and ninety-nine children from first through sixth grades were nvolved in the competitive (but not practiced) conditions, and 356 n the practiced (but not competitive) conditions.

There was a fairly consistent tendency for children under com-etitive conditions to excel those under the other condition. On the measure of fluency the results are statistically significant only in the rst, third, and fourth grades. On the measure of flexibility, the results re statistically significant in the second and fourth grades. On per-entage of original or uncommon responses, the results are statistically gnificant in the second, third, and sixth grades. Thus, it was con-luded that the practice and "warm-up" did not completely compensate or the stimulating effects of competition, but that it did a great deal) reduce the difference between the results under competitive and oncompetitive conditions found in the earlier study.

UNEVALUATED PRACTICE AND CREATIVE BEHAVIOR

10

In most school situations that I have observed, children are seldom free—even for a moment—from evaluation. Adults and/or peers constantly and unrelentingly watch and correct children's every error as they attempt to learn and think. In many instances, children are prevented from making any but the tiniest leaps in thinking, producing the most obvious, safest, and surest responses. It is my fear that such conditioning binds a child in this thinking and makes him afraid to experiment, guess, or learn how to identify and correct his own errors. My hypothesis is that children need periods during which they can experiment, make mistakes, and test various approaches without fear of evaluation and the failure that making a mistake implies.

In the classroom and in textbooks for teachers we find a wide range of attitudes concerning the freedom allowed children in determining what they shall do, especially in the realm of creative activities as in the visual arts. Some teachers prescribe and evaluate every move the child makes. Others go to the opposite extreme of leaving the child free to do whatever he likes and merely encourage him to "express himself."

Most recent writers in the field of art education have deplored those methods which require the teacher to correct and evaluate all the art work done by a child; and also those which permit children to do whatever they want to do and merely encourage them to express themselves. Gibbs (1958) expressed this view in criticizing the extreme

Dr. Dietmar P. Schenitzski assisted in the preparation of this chapter.

freedom approach, such as leaving children to flounder without help or criticism. She admits that freedom to paint what the child wants to paint provides a great outlet for the primary child, but that, without direction and constructive criticism from the teacher, the average child will cease to develop and will become discouraged.

A number of apparently successful teachers have attempted to describe their own strategies and techniques for maintaining this balance between rigid and dictated methods on the one hand and undirected freedom on the other. One of the techniques described by Cole is to reinforce individuality of style. She would say, "Make your pictures your own way, Theresa. Don't ever try to paint like anyone else. We want to be able to look at your picture and say, 'That's Theresa's picture'" (1940, p. 7). She believes that the teacher should go about lifting one picture after another, giving some appreciation. She cautions that the other children may not lift their eyes from their own paintings but that this will make them strive to do as much or better.

H. H. Anderson (1960) believes that external evaluation by the teacher becomes damaging to creative growth because the teacher exercises power or control over the child. Grades, rewards, punishments, praise, and reproof are some of the ways in which external evaluation and *power over* are combined. This makes it difficult for children to learn to think for themselves and makes them content with rewards and approval as substitutes for the satisfactions of intrinsic and meaningful originality. Children, Anderson argues, are also taught to avoid punishment and reproof and this must often be done by sham, pretense, falseness, and a stifling kind of conformity.

In one study conducted by the author and his associates (Torrance, 1964b), it was found that too frequent evaluation of creative activities during the practice stage, regardless of its nature, seemed to interfere with creative exploration and the initiation of ideas. This experiment was set up to test the hypotheses that "creative productivity" of small groups of elementary school children is influenced by the type of evaluative practice applied during a practice session. Groups were randomly selected and the three forms of experimental manipulation applied randomly to them. The experimental conditions were "criticism and correction," "suggestion of other possibilities," and a combination of these two. The practice and test tasks required the subjects to demonstrate and explain the scientific principles underlying the operations of sets of science toys.

The analyses revealed no statistically significant differences between the performances of the groups. Significant differences were found when data were divided according to "frequency of application" of the treatment. This difference was in favor of the group to which the experimental treatment was least frequently applied, and as a result, it is suggested that the treatment acts as an "interference mechanism" and when frequently applied tends to "inhibit" productivity of the group

In the study described in this chapter, an effort has been made to extend the above finding one step further by freeing children entirely from evaluation during the practice period. In the other condition, an effort was made to offer the most intelligent kind of evaluation we were capable of giving, not intervening too frequently but giving directions and suggestions as they seemed appropriate. We believed that this would enable us to assess whether children who have experienced a period of no evaluation but encouragement for free experimentation and exploration will do better creative work on a set of tasks than children who have experienced a period of constructive, positive evaluation.

Procedures

GENERAL

This classroom experiment was conducted in a Minneapolis public elementary school and involved the total enrollment of the school from grades one through six. In an introductory period prior to the experiment, procedures and instructions were introduced which attempted to provide a brief orientation to the children concerning what they would be expected to do and to arouse their motivation. They were told that we would like to have their help in learning how people develop interesting, unusual, original, and well-worked-out ideas. They were told that a prize would be awarded to each of the three pupils who produced the most interesting and unusual ideas in the tasks which they would be given.

The experimenters explained that there would be two different tasks and that before each task they would be given a practice task during which they would have a chance to learn how to produce interesting, unusual, and well-developed ideas. Following these orientation procedures and the more specific instructions which varied with the two experimental treatments, the materials for the first five-minute practice task were distributed. After the practice task involving the experimental manipulations described below, the children began the main task. The second task was administered in the same manner.

EXPERIMENTAL TASKS

The Incomplete Figures Tasks, Forms A and B

The material for the first practice task consisted of six incomplete figures on a single sheet of paper. This sheet was divided into six squares, each 2 × 2 inches. For the test task, an alternate set of incomplete figures was used. These figures were adapted from those developed by Kate Franck and described by Barron (1958) and Torrance (1962a).

Subjects were told that it was their task to think of pictures or objects they could make from these incomplete figures, as follows:

By adding lines to the six figures on your sheet, sketch some object or picture. Try to think of some object or picture that no one else in the class will think of. Try to put as many ideas as you can into your drawings, and make them tell as interesting and as complete a picture as you can. In other words, do not stop with your first idea for completing the figure; keep building on to it.

At the beginning of the practice session, the experimenter placed on the blackboard three examples for the first figure (a ladder, an apartment house, and an object suggested by someone in the class).

Picture Construction or Shape Task
(Triangle and Curved-Shape)

The materials for the second test task consisted of three sheets of paper about 6 × 9 inches, three differently colored curved-shape (jelly bean) pieces of paper, and a bottle of glue for each subject. For the practice session, subjects were given a single sheet of paper, a small triangle, and a bottle of glue. Subjects were instructed to think of a picture or object with the colored piece of paper as a main part. They were instructed to paste the shape wherever they wanted it on the sheet of paper to make the picture they had in mind. They were told to complete the picture by adding lines. As in the Incomplete Figures Task, they were told to think of a picture that no one else in the room would think of and to keep adding ideas to the picture, making it tell as interesting and as complete a story as possible. They were authorized to use pencil, crayons, or whatever other materials they had available to make their pictures.

MANIPULATION OF EXPERIMENTAL VARIABLES

Condition A (Unevaluated Practice Accompanied
by Encouragement of Experimentation)

Under Condition A, the subjects were told to experiment freely with different ideas and not be afraid to spoil or "mess up" their drawings because the practice session did not count toward winning the prize. Questions by the children were answered as sensitively as possible, giving only the direction requested by individuals. At the end of the time limit of five minutes, the children were permitted to hold up their drawings and show them to one another. This was done with much eagerness and enthusiasm.

Condition B (Constructive, Positive Evaluation)

Under Condition B, the subjects were told during the practice session to think of more uncommon things, to put in more ideas, to elaborate their ideas and to make their pictures tell a more exciting or complete story. Nothing specific was said to the effect that work during this practice session did not count toward winning the prize. A deliberate effort was made to avoid too frequent evaluation and to communicate the ideas of originality and elaboration (something no one else will think of and make the picture tell a story).

Each of the practice sessions lasted ten minutes and each of the test sessions lasted ten minutes. The entire session, including orientation, instructions, evaluation, and the practice and test sessions lasted about sixty minutes. To sustain interest throughout this rather extended experiment, a brief candy break was given between the first test task and the second practice task. Subjects were assigned randomly to the two conditions. In each case, the Principal Investigator served as the experimenter.

DATA ANALYSIS

The productions of the subjects on both the Picture Construction and Incomplete Figures Tasks were each evaluated according to a number of different dimensions regarded as important aspects of creative thinking. Detailed scoring guides were prepared for each dimension and for each task. Scorers were put through a thorough training program and were required to achieve an interscorer reliability of .90 or higher with the scoring of the designers of the scoring procedures.

Scoring of the Picture Construction Task

Responses to the Picture Construction or Shape Task were assessed for originality, elaboration or complexity, sensitivity, communication, activity, and productivity. The *originality* score was obtained by applying a five-point scale based on the statistical infrequency of the responses of 223 elementary school pupils to the task. *Elaboration or complexity* was also assessed by means of a five-point scale, the greater the number of ideas used to construct a picture, the higher the elaboration score. Scores on *sensitivity* represent an attempt to assess the subect's ability to overcome the limitations of the immediate stimulus situation and use the stimulus in an unusual and novel way. Ratings are made on a five-point scale. *Communication* scores represent an estimate of the subject's ability to communicate his ideas by sketching the object or picture. Ratings are made on a five-point scale. *Flexibility* refers to he subject's tendency to produce responses belonging to different classes or categories. *Activity* was assessed by means of a three-point scale rating the degree of movement or activity shown in the drawing. The *productivity* score refers to the number of pictures attempted by an individual.

Scoring of the Incomplete Figures Task

Productions made on the Incomplete Figures Task were scored for originality, elaboration or complexity, penetration or closure, and productivity. *Originality* is determined by a five-point scale based on a frequency analysis of the responses of a sample of 217 elementary pupils to the incomplete figures. *Elaboration or complexity* is assessed by a seven-point scale which attempts to represent the individual's ability to implement, build on to the basic idea, and make it tell a story. *Penetration or closure* is assessed by a seven-point scale designed to measure the subject's tendency to close the incomplete figure. The higher a subject's score the greater is his assumed resistance to close the incomplete figure in the simplest way possible and to make the kind of mental leap which seems to occur in original or penetrating thinking. *Productivity* refers to the number of incomplete figures attempted by a subject.

Results

PICTURE CONSTRUCTION TEST

Since the purpose of the experiment described herein was to determine which of the two evaluative conditions under study produces the more creative behavior following practice, the criterion measures used in the evaluation are the raw scores resulting from the scoring of the test tasks without reference to any pre-test or practice scores. It did not seem fair to use the practice scores as pre-test scores, since the evaluative condition involved what might be considered a type of coaching of a fairly direct nature.

The means of the total scores derived from the Picture Construction Test by sex and grade are presented in Figure 10.1. It will be noted

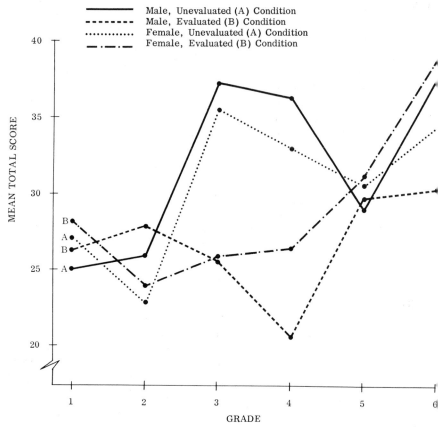

FIGURE 10.1 *Means of Total Scores on Picture Construction Test by Sex and Grade Under Unevaluated (A) and Evaluated (B) Conditions*

that both boys and girls in grades three and four under the unevaluated condition excel their same sex peers under the evaluated condition. The results at other grade levels, however, are less consistent. Under the unevaluated condition, there are slight advantages for first-grade girls and sixth-grade girls. Under evaluated conditions, there are similar advantages for first-grade boys, second-grade boys and girls, fifth-grade girls and boys, and sixth-grade girls. It will be noted that the unevaluated condition tends to produce greater variability than the evaluated condition in the first and second grades, but that the reverse occurs in the third, fourth, and fifth grades.

The analysis of variance data for testing the significance of the differences in mean total scores on the Picture Construction Test show that the differences due to experimental condition are significant at the 1 per cent level of confidence in both the third and fourth grades.

avoring the unevaluated condition. Differences due to sex are significant
n the first grade in favor of girls and in the fourth grade in favor of
)oys. In both cases, however, the interaction between sex and condi-
ions is statistically significant, with first-grade girls tending to do pro-
)ortionately better under unevaluated conditions and fourth-grade girls
ending to do proportionately better under evaluated conditions. Sixth-
;rade girls also tend to do proportionately better under evaluated than
nder unevaluated conditions.

Means and standard deviations of the originality scores on the
'icture Construction Test are presented in Table 10.1. It will be noted

TABLE 10.1 Means and Standard Deviations of Originality Scores on Picture Construc-
ion Test by Sex and Grade Under Unevaluated (A) and Evaluated (B) Conditions

| Grade | Condition | Number | | Boys | | Girls | |
		Boys	Girls	Mean	St. Dev.	Mean	St. Dev.
1	A	13	15	2.62	1.44	3.93	2.30
	B	14	15	4.07	2.37	4.93	1.64
2	A	15	14	3.67	2.52	4.57	3.36
	B	14	16	5.07	2.02	4.94	2.52
3	A	12	9	7.25	2.68	1.89	0.87
	B	15	18	4.07	2.60	4.28	2.19
4	A	7	11	6.57	2.99	5.91	2.30
	B	16	22	4.31	3.05	4.32	2.40
5	A	12	15	6.17	2.26	5.00	3.27
	B	11	8	3.82	2.60	5.50	2.62
6	A	16	19	4.38	3.33	3.32	1.83
	B	6	7	5.17	1.72	5.29	1.93

hat fourth-grade boys tend to produce more original ideas under un-
:valuated than under evaluated conditions. In the first, second, and
;ixth grades, both sexes tend to produce more original ideas under
:valuated than under unevaluated conditions. In the third and fifth
;rades, boys tend to be more original under unevaluated conditions,
ind there is a tendency for the reverse to occur for third- and fifth-grade
;irls. Thus, in five of six cases girls tend to perform better under
:valuated than under unevaluated conditions, while this occurs for
)oys in only three of six cases.

The only clearly significant difference due to experimental condi-
ions revealed by analysis of variance occurs in the fourth grade in
:avor of the unevaluated condition. The differences in the first and

sixth grades approach statistical significance and are both in favo
of the evaluated condition. Significant differences due to sex occur i
the first and third grades, favoring girls in the first grade and boys i
the third grade. Interaction is significant only in the third grade, wit
boys performing better under unevaluated conditions, and girls unde
evaluated conditions.

The means and standard deviations for the elaboration scores o
the Picture Construction Test are presented in Table 10.2. Here, i

TABLE 10.2 Means and Standard Deviations of Elaboration Scores of Picture Constru
tion Test by Sex and Grade Under Unevaluated (A) and Evaluated (B) Conditions

Grade	Condition	Number		Boys		Girls	
		Boys	Girls	Mean	St. Dev.	Mean	St. Dev.
1	A	13	15	5.31	1.85	6.00	1.79
	B	14	15	4.50	1.70	4.33	2.10
2	A	15	14	5.07	2.64	4.64	1.96
	B	14	16	4.71	1.59	3.62	1.78
3	A	12	9	6.83	2.28	8.56	1.22
	B	15	18	3.80	2.31	4.72	1.93
4	A	7	11	6.86	1.57	6.09	2.07
	B	16	22	3.06	1.88	4.41	2.08
5	A	12	15	4.17	1.81	6.80	2.14
	B	11	8	6.45	1.86	4.38	1.33
6	A	16	19	6.19	2.32	6.00	1.78
	B	6	7	5.83	1.83	8.43	2.14

will be noted that there is a consistent tendency in the first four grade
for both boys and girls to show greater elaboration under unevaluate
conditions than under evaluated conditions. Fifth-grade girls also ten
to show greater elaboration under unevaluated conditions, but fifth
grade boys and sixth-grade boys and girls show a reversal of this trend
The analysis of variance indicates that the observed differences due t
experimental conditions are significant at the 1 per cent level in th
first, third, and fourth grades. Only in the third grade are the dif
ferences due to sex significant, in this case in favor of girls. This latte
result is of special interest since third-grade boys excelled third-grad
girls on originality in this same task. Interaction between sex and cond
tion is statistically significant in the first, fifth, and sixth grades, an
approaches significance in the fourth grade. The unevaluated condi

tions appear to favor disproportionately first-grade girls, fourth-grade boys, fifth-grade girls, and sixth-grade boys.

INCOMPLETE FIGURES TEST

Means on the Incomplete Figures Test are presented in Figure 10.2 by sex, grade, and experimental condition. In the first four grades, both boys and girls tend to perform more creatively on the Incomplete Figures Test under unevaluated than under evaluated conditions. This is also true of fifth-grade girls and sixth-grade boys.

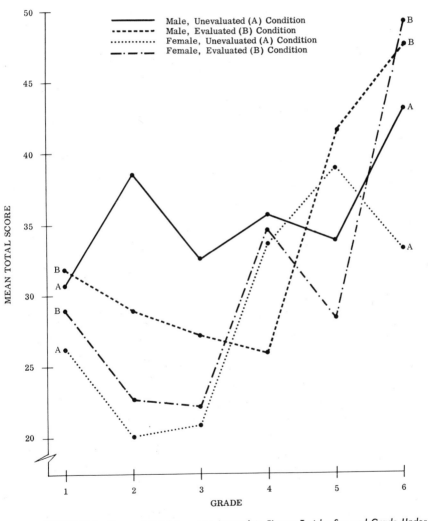

FIGURE 10.2 Means of Total Scores on Incomplete Figures Test by Sex and Grade Under Unevaluated (A) and Evaluated (B) Conditions

The analysis of variance indicates that the differences in means observed in Figure 10.2 due to experimental conditions are significant at the 1 per cent level in the second and third grades, but do not reach the 5 per cent level of confidence in the other grades. Only in the sixth grade are differences due to sex significant, in this case in favor of boys. Interaction is statistically significant in both the fifth and sixth grades, with fifth- and sixth-grade girls enjoying disproportionate advantages from the unevaluated conditions.

Mean and standard deviation data relative to the originality scores of the Incomplete Figures Test are contained in Table 10.3. Both boys

TABLE 10.3 Means and Standard Deviations of Originality Scores on Incomplete Figures Test by Sex and Grade Under Unevaluated (A) and Evaluated (B) Conditions

Grade	Condition	Number		Boys		Girls	
		Boys	Girls	Mean	St. Dev.	Mean	St. Dev.
1	A	13	14	2.08	3.35	3.29	3.10
	B	14	15	5.71	2.43	6.07	3.49
2	A	14	15	7.93	5.51	5.73	3.06
	B	13	16	3.08	2.90	4.44	2.85
3	A	12	9	6.75	4.05	7.22	3.77
	B	15	16	4.07	2.81	4.56	3.10
4	A	7	11	7.29	2.87	9.55	6.12
	B	16	22	7.88	2.85	7.41	3.70
5	A	12	19	7.42	4.14	10.16	5.10
	B	11	8	8.45	3.88	6.38	4.41
6	A	16	19	6.69	4.61	7.47	4.39
	B	6	7	5.33	2.16	10.14	5.27

and girls in the second and third grades tend to produce more original ideas under unevaluated than under evaluated conditions with the reverse being true in the first and sixth grades. The unevaluated conditions also seem to favor fourth- and fifth-grade boys.

The analysis of variance data on originality of the Incomplete Figures Test indicate that the experimental conditions appear to produce statistically significant differences in originality in the first and second grades. Only in the third grade is there a statistically significant sex difference, this time in favor of girls.

Means and standard deviations of the elaboration scores are shown in Table 10.4. In the second, third, fourth, and sixth grades,

TABLE 10.4 Means and Standard Deviations of Elaboration Scores on Incomplete Figures Test by Sex and Grade Under Unevaluated (A) and Evaluated (B) Conditions

		Number		Boys		Girls	
Grade	Condition	Boys	Girls	Mean	St. Dev.	Mean	St. Dev.
1	A	13	14	3.69	4.53	2.64	2.98
	B	14	15	5.07	2.49	5.07	2.94
2	A	14	15	8.00	7.95	3.87	3.42
	B	13	16	3.54	2.47	4.12	2.25
3	A	12	9	5.33	3.17	3.22	2.33
	B	15	16	4.27	2.43	4.79	1.64
4	A	7	11	6.43	4.20	6.64	6.25
	B	16	22	5.62	2.00	6.77	2.00
5	A	12	19	6.25	1.96	8.58	1.54
	B	11	8	9.09	4.16	7.25	4.80
6	A	16	19	8.94	4.68	11.26	5.18
	B	6	7	8.00	0.89	11.43	1.99

boys show greater elaboration under unevaluated than under evaluated conditions. Only in the fifth grade, do girls tend to show greater elaboration under unevaluated than under evaluated conditions.

Analysis of variance data to test the differences in means observed in Table 10.4 indicate that only in the first grade are the differences due to experimental conditions significant at the 5 per cent level of confidence or better. A sex difference in favor of girls is found in the sixth grade, and a significant interaction is found in the fifth grade, with girls profiting disproportionately from the unevaluated conditions.

The means and standard deviations of the closure scores of the Incomplete Figures Test are contained in Table 10.5. In eleven of the twelve differences, it will be observed that subjects working under unevaluated conditions are able to delay closure better than those working under evaluated conditions. It will also be observed that there is a rather general tendency for the unevaluated conditions to produce greater variability than the evaluated conditions.

The analysis of variance data indicate that the differences in favor of the unevaluated condition are significant at the 1 per cent level of confidence or better in the first, second, third, and sixth grades. There are no significant differences due to sex, but interaction is significant in the third and sixth grades, with boys profiting most by the unevaluated condition in both cases.

TABLE 10.5 Means and Standard Deviations of Closure Scores on Incomplete Figures Test by Sex and Grade Under Unevaluated (A) and Evaluated (B) Conditions

Grade	Condition	Number Boys	Number Girls	Boys Mean	Boys St. Dev.	Girls Mean	Girls St. Dev.
1	A	13	14	19.31	6.77	20.07	4.48
	B	14	15	10.79	3.53	12.80	3.95
2	A	14	15	23.57	14.78	17.53	6.90
	B	13	16	9.54	5.97	10.88	4.65
3	A	12	9	14.92	3.87	11.00	2.92
	B	15	16	9.13	4.03	9.81	2.93
4	A	7	11	16.57	2.44	16.64	6.36
	B	11	8	15.06	2.32	14.77	3.29
5	A	12	19	4.92	2.78	16.79	3.08
	B	11	8	16.55	4.76	14.25	4.43
6	A	16	19	22.19	5.46	22.89	3.74
	B	6	7	15.00	4.15	22.00	2.52

Discussion

The central hypothesis examined in the classroom experiments described in this chapter is that individuals having experienced a period of unevaluated practice coupled with encouragement for free experimentation will produce ideas which will be judged to have a higher degree of various creative qualities than ideas of individuals who have experienced a period of constructive, positive evaluation. In executing the experiment, a careful attempt was made to conduct both the unevaluated and the evaluated practice sessions in as intelligent and as expert a manner as possible. Thus, there was some direction in the unevaluated sessions and a great deal of freedom and permissiveness in the evaluated session. In some ways, this probably weakened the experimental treatments by making them less distinct from one another than they might have been. We believed, however, that this was the reasonable and fair test that we wanted to make.

Although far from conclusive, the results obtained from these experiments are generally consistent with the hypothesis. Fifty-three of the eighty-four differences are in favor of the unevaluated condition. It is fairly clear that the third- and fourth-grade subjects under unevaluated conditions perform significantly better than similar subjects under valuated practice. The differences in means for these grades are rather consistently in favor of the unevaluated condition but do not always each statistical significance. The results pertaining to the first and second grades also lend support to the hypothesis.

The results for the fifth and sixth grades are more complicated than those for the first four grades. Most of the differences are very small and nonsignificant, but a few of them are statistically significant in the opposite direction. In general, it is perhaps fair to say that children in the first four grades tend to respond more favorably to unevaluated than to evaluated practice but that this is not true of children in the fifth and sixth grades. They appear to be either relatively unaffected by the differences in practice conditions or to respond better to the evaluated practice condition. Apparently children of this age group, more than younger children, are made more dependent upon external evaluation because of their school experiences. It would probably require a number of experiences under unevaluated conditions before children at this age would be able to respond to the freedom of this condition with an increase in the level of their creative behavior.

Summary and Conclusions

Discussions of the teacher's evaluative practices and issues concerning external evaluation in general led us to formulate the hypothesis that individuals working under unevaluated practice and with encouragement to experiment freely would produce better creative work on subsequent occasions than individuals working under conditions of evaluated practice.

To test this hypothesis a classroom experiment was conducted in grades one through six in a public elementary school. The results indicate that younger children (grades one through four) are apparently affected more strongly by adult evaluation than are the older children (grades five and six). For the former an unevaluated period free from the fear of making mistakes seems to be somewhat more conducive to creative work in general than for older children. It seems quite likely that younger children behave more creatively under unevaluated practice conditions than under the best constructive evaluation conditions. There are indications, however, that evaluation differentially affects some of the dimensions thought to be important in creative work.

CRITICAL AND CREATIVE PEER- EVALUATED PRACTICE

11

In Chapter 10, we were concerned about the influence of the teacher as a source of external evaluation upon the creative behavior of children. In this chapter, we shall be concerned about the peer group as a source of external evaluation. Some teachers make rather extensive use of peer evaluation in the classroom, maintaining that "such a practice develops critical thinking and contributes to the development of the judgmental abilities." Some teachers also justify the use of peer evaluation because it is more powerful than teacher evaluation in bringing about proper (conforming) behavior. In the study described in this chapter we shall be interested in finding out how two different types of peer evaluation influence the creative behavior of children from kindergarten through sixth grade. We shall be especially concerned about originality and elaboration.

Henry (1963), in the following description of a classroom incident, highlights a common complaint about peer evaluation of creative work in the classroom.

Carping criticism, painfully evident in almost any American classroom, is viciously destructive of the early tillage of those creative impulses we say we cherish.

Listen to a fifth-grade class: The children are taking turns reading stories they have made up. Charlie's is called *The Unknown Guest*.

One dark, dreary night, on a hill a house stood. This house was forbidden territory for Bill and Joe, but they were going in anyway. The door creaked, squealed, slammed. A voice warned them to go home. They went upstairs. A stair cracked. They entered a room. A voice said that they might as well stay and find out now; and their father came out. He laughed and they laughed, but they never forgot their adventure together.

TEACHER:
Are there any words that give you the mood of the story?

LUCY:
He could have made the sentences a little better. . . .

TEACHER:
Let's come back to Lucy's comment. What about the sentences?

GERT:
They were too short. (Charlie and Jeanne have a discussion about the position of the word "stood" in the first sentence.)

TEACHER:
Wait a minute; some people are forgetting their manners. . . .

JEFF:
About the room: the boys went up the stairs and one "cracked," when they were in the room. Did they fall through the stairs, or what? The teacher suggests Charlie make that a little clearer. . . .

TEACHER:
We still haven't decided about the short sentences. Perhaps they make the story more spooky and mysterious.

GWYNNE:
I wish he had read with more expression instead of all at one time.

RACHEL:
Not enough expression.

TEACHER:
Charlie, they want a little more expression from you. I guess we've given you enough suggestions for one time. (Charlie does not raise his head, which is bent over his desk as if studying a paper.) Charlie! I guess we've given you enough suggestions for one time, Charlie, haven't we? (Henry, 1963, p. 28).*

Friedenberg (1959) and other observers of the classroom process, especially in the adolescent years, report that peer evaluation gets out of control and teachers find themselves practically helpless even to acknowledge something truly excellent about the creative production of a pupil.

From our knowledge of developmental psychology, we know that we can expect a great deal of disparaging peer evaluation among children during what Sullivan (1953) calls the Juvenile Era (usually occurring during the primary school years). During this period children

---

learn the techniques and strategies of ostracizing group members, segregating into groups, stereotyping, and disparagement. We know that children may find life during this period very stressful if there develops in their peer group an atmosphere of overcompetition and if the stereotyping, ostracizing, and disparaging are severe. Since disparagement is presumed to have developmental aspects, we shall be interested in the present investigation to notice grade-level differences in reactions to the two different kinds of peer evaluation studied.

Procedures

This field experiment was conducted in a public, metropolitan elementary school and involved the total enrollment of the school from kindergarten through sixth grade. The experiment and its objectives were discussed with the entire faculty of the school one week in advance of the conduct of the study. I served as the experimenter in all cases and an assistant recorded almost verbatim the verbal interaction between me and the children. In each classroom, I explained the purpose and procedures of the experiment to the subjects. An attempt was made to heighten interest and motivation. As in the experiment reported in the previous chapter, prizes were offered for outstanding performances in the test task. I tried to make it clear that the practice performance did not count towards winning the prize but was to permit experimentation with different ideas.

I told the children that I wanted their help in learning how pupils think of original, i.e., unusual and interesting, ideas. Originality and elaboration were emphasized in the instructions. Following the motivation instructions, the experimental procedure was outlined briefly. After this brief orientation, materials for the first practice task were distributed.

TASKS AND INSTRUCTIONS

The two tasks used in the study described in Chapter 10 were used in the present study (Picture Construction and Incomplete Figures).

Under Condition A (Critical Peer Evaluation), subjects were encouraged at the end of each practice session to evaluate critically one another's productions. They were asked specifically to point out things which could be corrected, "things that were wrong with it," and the like. (Children in the kindergarten and early primary grades, however, were rather reluctant to criticize the work of their peers.)

Under Condition B (Creative Peer Evaluation), subjects were

ncouraged at the end of each practice session to suggest other pos-
ibilities for making the pictures more unusual and interesting, possible
additions which would have made the pictures tell a more complete or
elaborate story.

In other words, Condition A emphasized deficiencies, and Condi-
ion B stressed other possibilities.

Scoring of the productions was the same as those already described
or the Picture Construction and Incomplete Figures Tests. Since the
actual practice session in this experiment was not itself affected by the
differences in experimental manipulations, we were able to work with
gain or improvement scores, whereas this was not possible in the study
described in Chapter 10.

Results

PICTURE CONSTRUCTION OR SHAPE TEST

The means of the total gain scores on the Picture Construction
Test are shown in Figure 11.1 for kindergarten through sixth grade. It
will be noted that under Condition A (Critical Evaluation), the mean
gains rise from kindergarten through the third grade, but the fourth-
grade mean drops below the level of the second-grade mean. Under
Condition B (Creative Evaluation), however, a peak is reached in the
fourth grade followed by only slight drops in the fifth and sixth grades.
t will also be noted that the differences are relatively small and are in
favor of the Critical Evaluation Condition in the kindergarten through
third grade. The reverse is true in the fourth, fifth, and sixth grades, and
he observed differences are more impressive than in the lower grades.

The analysis of variance data for testing the significance of the
differences observed in Figure 11.1 indicate that the differences in
kindergarten and the first, second, and third grades are not statistically
significant. The differences in both the fourth and fifth grades are
statistically significant at better than the 5 per cent level, but the difference in the sixth grade falls slightly short of statistical significance.

The mean difference or improvement scores for elaboration and
originality on the Picture Construction Test are contained in Table 11.1.
In general the trends noted for total scores hold also for elaboration and
originality. Under both conditions there is a drop in elaboration in the
fourth grade.

The analysis of variance data for testing the significance of the
differences in means indicate that although four of the differences in
elaboration tend to favor the Creative Evaluation Condition, none of

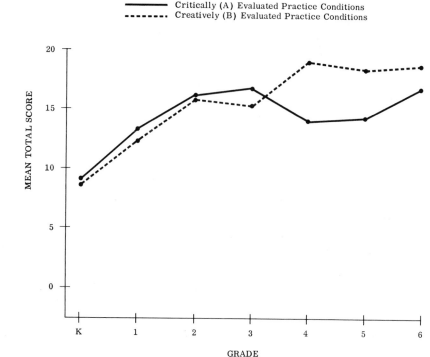

FIGURE 11.1   Means of the Total Creativity Difference Scores (Post-test Means—Pre-tes Means) on the Picture Construction or Shape Task Under Critically (A) and Creatively (B) Evalu ated Practice Conditions

them is significant at the 5 per cent level. The differences in originality are significant at the 10 per cent level of confidence in the second and fourth grades.

The mean improvement scores for the dimensions of sensitivity and communication on the Picture Construction Test are presented in Table 11.2. The differences in sensitivity are rather consistently in favor of the creatively evaluated condition, whereas communication scores show the same general tendency as the total scores.

On sensitivity, we find from the analysis of variance that the differences are statistically significant only in the upper grades (fourth fifth, and sixth grades). All are in favor of the creatively evaluated condition. High levels of significance are also noted in the same direction for the communication dimension in these same grades. The difference in the first grade is significant at the 5 per cent level on communication, but the difference is in favor of the critically evaluated condition.

TABLE 11.1 Means and Standard Deviations of Difference Scores (Post-test Means—Pre-test Means) for Elaboration (or Complexity) and Originality on the Picture Construction Task Under Critically (A) and Creatively (B) Evaluated Practice Conditions for Grades Kindergarten Through Six

Grade	Condition	Number	Elaboration		Originality	
			Mean	St. Dev.	Mean	St. Dev.
K	A	53	2.85	2.21	2.40	2.97
	B	62	2.87	2.37	1.73	2.57
1	A	43	3.28	2.30	3.16	2.79
	B	19	4.21	1.70	1.95	2.09
2	A	26	4.15	1.55	4.85	3.18
	B	56	4.38	1.82	3.80	3.23
3	A	32	4.94	1.95	4.91	3.06
	B	28	4.71	2.94	4.07	3.30
4	A	38	4.08	1.78	3.55	2.84
	B	16	4.19	1.72	5.31	3.55
5	A	34	4.32	2.29	4.47	3.49
	B	27	5.22	2.61	3.56	2.75
6	A	30	5.80	2.20	3.30	3.13
	B	21	4.95	2.29	3.76	2.98

TABLE 11.2 Means and Standard Deviations of Difference Scores (Post-test Means—Pre-Test Means) for Dimensions of Sensitivity and Communication on the Picture Construction Test Under Critically (A) and Creatively (B) Evaluated Practice Conditions for Grades Kindergarten Through Six

Grade	Condition	Number	Sensitivity		Communication	
			Mean	St. Dev.	Mean	St. Dev.
K	A	53	1.49	1.80	1.40	2.50
	B	62	1.58	2.08	1.65	1.98
1	A	43	2.00	1.59	3.37	2.04
	B	19	2.11	1.41	2.00	2.21
2	A	26	2.15	1.24	3.50	1.38
	B	56	2.18	1.73	4.11	1.88
3	A	32	2.69	1.52	2.75	1.57
	B	28	2.57	1.95	2.39	1.93
4	A	38	2.29	1.90	2.87	1.75
	B	16	3.81	2.37	4.94	2.20
5	A	34	2.15	1.40	2.76	2.17
	B	27	3.30	2.16	4.67	1.92
6	A	30	1.97	1.63	3.07	1.67
	B	21	3.24	1.81	5.14	2.33

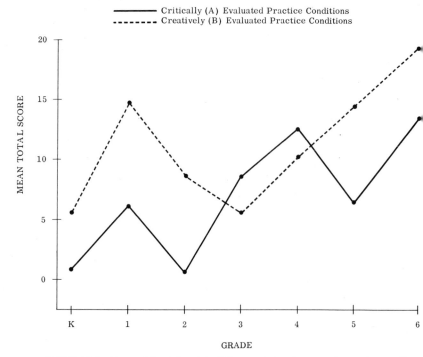

FIGURE 11.2 *Means of Total Creativity Difference Scores (Post-test Means—Pre-test Mean on the Incomplete Figures Test Under Critically (A) and Creatively (B) Evaluated Practice Conditions*

INCOMPLETE FIGURES TEST

The means of the total improvement scores on the Incomplete Figures Test are shown in Figure 11.2. It will be noted that the differences are in favor of creatively evaluated conditions in the kindergarten and the first, second, fifth, and sixth grades.

The analysis of variance data for testing the significance of these observed differences indicate that all four of the differences in favor of the creatively evaluated condition are statistically significant at least at the 10 per cent level, where neither of the other two differences even approaches statistical significance.

The mean difference scores for originality, elaboration, and closure on the Incomplete Figures Test are shown in Table 11.3. We see here what is essentially a repetition of the pattern observed for total scores. The differences favor the creatively evaluated condition except in the third and fourth grades.

The analysis of variance data indicate that the differences in

TABLE 11.3 Means and Standard Deviations of Difference Scores (Post-test Means—Pretest Means) for Originality, Closure, and Elaboration on the Incomplete Figures Test Under Critically (A) and Creatively (B) Evaluated Practice Conditions for Grades Kindergarten Through Six

Grade	Condition	Number	Originality Mean	St. Dev.	Elaboration Mean	St. Dev.	Closure Mean	St. Dev.
K	A	20	- .95	3.32	- .45	2.25	2.50	5.03
	B	57	1.09	3.83	.26	2.36	4.00	7.84
1	A	41	2.05	4.65	.85	4.27	5.32	6.07
	B	20	4.15	4.06	1.05	3.75	9.45	6.35
2	A	25	.44	5.10	-1.40	5.63	1.60	4.56
	B	59	.85	4.40	3.37	5.78	4.15	6.16
3	A	31	2.74	5.44	1.65	4.92	4.03	5.62
	B	31	.65	4.69	2.77	5.96	2.06	5.81
4	A	40	3.82	6.04	3.32	6.03	5.20	5.95
	B	16	3.06	6.21	2.56	5.06	3.94	6.04
5	A	33	1.24	4.96	1.42	5.49	3.61	7.46
	B	27	3.22	5.67	4.22	5.77	5.67	7.08
6	A	31	1.61	5.03	5.29	4.12	6.39	4.83
	B	21	4.48	4.74	4.95	6.52	9.00	7.32

originality scores in favor of the creatively evaluated condition are statistically significant in the kindergarten, first grade, and sixth grade, and approach significance in the fifth grade. On elaboration, the differences in favor of the creatively evaluated condition are statistically significant in the second and fifth grades. On closure, we find statistically significant differences only in the first and second grades, although the difference in the sixth grade approaches statistical significance. All three of these differences are in favor of the creatively evaluated condition.

SUMMARY

Nineteen of the thirty-two differences examined in the kindergarten through third grade are in favor of the creative evaluation condition. Ten of these differences are statistically significant at the 10 per cent level or better, but only one of the reversals is statistically significant at this level. In the fourth, fifth, and sixth grades, nineteen of the twenty-four differences studied are in favor of the creatively evaluated condition. Thirteen of these differences are statistically significant at the 10 per cent level or better, and none of the reversals is statistically significant. Thus, although the results are not highly conclusive, the weight of the evidence definitely leans on the side of the creative rather than of the critical peer evaluated condition. The evidence in the fourth, fifth, and sixth grades is especially strong.

Discussion

We pointed out earlier that teachers often employ peer evaluation with the expectation that this technique might successfully facilitate the learning process. The hypothesis was proposed that creative peer evaluation is more conducive to creative thinking than critical peer evaluation. This expectation is at least partially confirmed by our data.

Considering the trends for the total scores first, we find significant differences between the conditions in favor of the creative peer evaluation treatment for the upper three grades on the first task, the Picture Construction Test. The data for the lower four grades, however, do not support the hypothesis. There are in fact no statistically significant differences between the conditions. The failure to obtain differential effects in the kindergarten and primary grades may be due to several factors. First, it is possible that the experimental manipulations were not effective. There are some incidental observations to the effect that the pupils in these grades were rather reluctant to evaluate critically their peers' productions. Second, it is possible that critical peer evaluation in the lower grades is as effective as creative peer evaluation; or third, that it actually makes no difference to younger children what their peers think of their productions. However, we find differential effects in the predicted direction in the upper two as well as in the lower three grades on the Incomplete Figures Task. These results suggest that task differences are probably at least partially responsible for the differential effects of the treatment. Or, it might be that the cumulative effects of peer criticism may become inhibiting, whereas the initial critical session did not have this effect.

Two of the dimensions, namely complexity (or elaboration) and originality, are common to both the Incomplete Figures Task and the Picture Construction Task. The data on complexity or elaboration indicate that the creative peer evaluation condition is more effective in stimulating creative work than the critical peer evaluation condition regardless of the task. On the Picture Construction Test, the net means for elaboration are higher in the creative peer evaluation condition

han in the critical peer evaluation condition in kindergarten, the lower
hree grades, and the fourth and fifth grades. The data on the Incom-
)lete Figures Test are in favor of the creative peer evaluation in the
ower four grades and the fifth grade.

The data on originality, however, suggest that the effectiveness of
he treatments may depend on the nature of the task. On the Picture
Construction Test, only two differences concerning originality occur
n favor of the creative peer evaluation (fourth and fifth grades). On
he Incomplete Figures Test, all but two originality net means (those
n the third and fourth grades) are in favor of the creative peer evalua-
ion condition. This may mean that the treatments affect originality dif-
erently depending on the nature of the task; or that the originality di-
nension in the Picture Construction Test is different from the originality
limension in the Incomplete Figures Test. However, in both cases the
ssessment of originality is based on infrequency of response. Therefore,
t seems unlikely that the differences between the tasks on originality are
ttributable to differences in methods of assessment.

The other dimensions of the two tasks are unique to each task.
)n sensitivity, on the Picture Construction Test, the upper grades show
 higher scores in the creative evaluation condition than in the critical
)eer evaluation condition. The same results are obtained on the scores
f the Picture Construction Test on communication. There occur no
lifferential effects (with the exception in the first grade) in the lower
,rades on communication. In regard to the Incomplete Figures Test,
here is less of a tendency in the lower three and the upper two grades
) close the figures in a simple way under the creative peer evaluation
han under the critical peer evaluation.

Across the tasks and, irrespective of the different dimensions we
onsistently find that the students in the third grade tend to do better
reative work under the critical peer evaluation than under the creative
eer evaluation. This is also true for the fourth grade on the Incom-
)lete Figures Task. However, these differences are not statistically
ignificant.

It must be remembered that the subjects of this experiment were
hildren from kindergarten through sixth grade and that there are dif-
erences in the reactions of children at different age-grade levels. Thus,
: is not possible to say from these results how adolescent and adult
,roups would react to the two types of peer evaluation studied in this
xperiment. An interesting study involving college-age women from
ighteen to twenty-four years has been reported by Parloff and Handlon
1963). This experiment studied different levels of criticalness in two-
)erson groups engaged in what might be called creative problem solv-
ng. Rather consistently Parloff and Handlon found that the low critical

situation produced more "good" solutions than the high critical. The
found, however, that increasing the number of ideas did not itself in
crease the number of "good" ideas. Parloff and Handlon thus argu
that the efficacy of "brainstorming" is a function of lowering the evalua
tive standards, thereby permitting the reporting of ideas that woul
otherwise be dismissed. Thus, even though Parloff and Handlon wer
working with young adult females in two-person groups, their result
are in harmony with the results reported herein for pre-adolescent chil
dren.

Summary

The classroom experiment reported herein was undertaken t
examine the effect of critical and creative peer evaluation upon creativ
work and thinking. We hypothesized that creative peer evaluation i
more conducive to creative thinking than critical peer evaluation. Thi
hypothesis is based on the assumption that critical evaluation of an
type is less promotive of creative work than positive or no evaluation
This assumption is made by a number of researchers and has also som
empirical support.

To test this hypothesis, a classroom experiment was carried ou
in a metropolitan public elementary school. The classes at each grad
level were assigned randomly to the experimental conditions of creativ
and critical peer evaluation. The two tasks were the Picture Construc
tion and the Incomplete Figures Tasks. First, the students worked fo
five minutes on the practice task. Before they were administered th
test task, the experimenter manipulated the evaluation variable.

The results on the Picture Construction Task indicate that th
students in the upper grades do better creative work under the creativ
peer evaluation than under critical peer evaluation. To the younge
children, differences in the types of evaluation appear to make no dif
ferences. The results on the Incomplete Figures Test show, howeve
that younger as well as older children do better creative thinking unde
the creative peer evaluation than under critical peer evaluation. Stu
dents in the intermediate grades are not differentially affected by th
different types of peer evaluations. Factors likely to be responsible fo
these differences were discussed. Controlled studies that systematicall
attempt to disentangle factors related to task differences, the natur
and intensity of the evaluation, and the cumulative effects of th
treatments are needed.

EVALUATIVE
DISCUSSIONS
ABOUT
CREATIVE
PRODUCTIONS

12

In Chapters 10 and 11, we were concerned about the evaluative behavior of the teacher when all members of a class experience essentially the same evaluative approach. It was obvious from the data presented that some children responded positively and others negatively to each of the conditions created. Again, this observation reminds us of the importance of individualizing instruction. An important aspect of individualization of instruction relative to creative work is the way in which teachers talk with individual pupils about their productions. The study described in this chapter represents an attempt to find out how teachers and student teachers talk with children about their creative writing, or at least how they think they should talk with pupils about their creative work.

Problems in Correcting Creative Writing

There has been much discussion among experts devoted to the problem of correcting or evaluating the creative writings of children. A few of these opinions and research results will be reviewed in order to identify the issues involved in the present exploratory investigation.

Hourd and Cooper (1959), two British authorities on creative writing among children, lament that in correcting written compositions teachers are often too bent on assessment to hear what a child is try-

---

I was assisted in the preparation of this chapter by R. E. Myers.

ing to convey on deeper levels simultaneously with the manifest dri
of the narrative" (p. 153). They believe that teachers rarely have th
time to grasp the fullness of children's creative writings and descrik
some of their own experiences in savoring the heroic spirit of childre
as manifested in their original writings.

Ashton-Warner, a New Zealand teacher, takes an even strong
stand against correcting the writings of children. She writes:

> You never want to say that it's good or bad. . . . You've got no rig
> at all to criticize the content of another's mind. A child doesn't make his ow
> mind. It's just there. . . . I never mark their books in any way; never cro
> out anything beyond helping them to rub out a mistake, never put a tic
> or stamp on it and never complain of bad writing. . . . (1963, p. 57).

Most United States experts on creative writing recognize th
complexity of the problem of evaluating the productions of childrei
Almost none of them is willing to abandon the correction of children
writings to the extent advocated by Ashton-Warner. In general, the
maintain that a child writing for others must write his thoughts co
rectly. Some place their emphasis on the prevention and elimination o
errors. They maintain that this can be accomplished by orderliness, in
tensive planning, the development of good work habits, emphasis o
accuracy, and the like. They recommend that errors in writing b
prevented by postponing writing until children are older, requirin
children to write very little, or having children dictate their storie
These efforts are to avoid the dangers of practicing errors.

Guided Self-evaluation

Some writers, like Marshall (1960), believe that the greatest pe
sonal growth and development in creative writing results from learnin
to evaluate one's own work. Marshall has described how she used th
approach with seventh-graders. Her pupils kept their weekly theme
filed in chronological order. Each theme was graded and commente
upon by the teacher. Themes were sometimes read aloud in class an
criticized by the group. Later the students were asked to look ove
the themes they had written, list their grades, reread the comments, an
decide upon a mark which would fairly express what they had don
Marshall reported that themes showed continuous improvement througl
out the year.

A number of United States writers recommend that children k
instructed to concentrate first upon the expression of their ideas witl
out concern about correctness and then to work over what they hav

ritten several times until it is polished. Others oppose even this
omentary respite from concern about correctness because it involves
racticing errors. They insist that all errors be corrected in written
ork, while others argue that the correction of all errors in creative
riting leaves the teacher with no time to do anything else and tends
▸ bewilder rather than help the child. They maintain that when chil-
ren find some strong purpose for writing correctly and neatly, they
ill be motivated to do so. Illustrative of this point of view is the fol-
wing example described by Dinkmeyer and Dreikurs:

> Tim does well in creative work but is apt to be in such a hurry that his
> riting is messy. For an American history assignment, he wrote a poem about
> aptain John Smith which was so good that each of the other fifth-grade
> asses wanted a copy. Thrilled by this recognition, Tim made three very
> ▸at copies for them. (1963, p. 65).

Dinkmeyer and Dreikurs make the point that correctness and
▸atness took on new significance when there was a real purpose for
riting to be legible. They point out that the teacher focused on an
▸set, the creative work, and used the opportunity to let the child
▸cognize for himself the value of neat work.

The Theme-a-week Practice

The research related to the effects of requiring a theme a week
ıd/or correcting creative writing has been rather consistent. Un-
▸rtunately much of this research has not been reported. Both the
ıblished and unpublished studies indicate that the theme-a-week re-
ıirement tends to defeat its purpose of promoting either correct writ-
g or creative writing. Two studies reported by Heys (1962) are ap-
ırently rather typical. The first involved only two eleventh-grade
ısses. One of them wrote the equivalent of a theme a week, and the
▸cond was excused from practically all composition work for the
ıtire year. Instead, this latter class did a greater amount of reading
▸th inside and outside class. The results at the end of the year showed
ıat both groups had improved in their ability to write, both groups
ıd improved about the same amount, and the slight differences ob-
ined were in favor of the group that had done little or no writing.

Eight classes, two in each grade and taught by the same teacher,
ırticipated in the second study. One class at each grade level was
▸signated as the "writing class" and the other as the "reading class."
he writing class wrote the equivalent of a theme a week, and the
▸ading class wrote a theme every third week and spent the rest of the

time reading. In all other respects all classes followed the curriculur appropriate for their grades. The evaluation involved the administra- tion of the STEP Writing Test, Form 2A, in the fall and the STE Writing Test, Form 2B, in the spring. All students also wrote two te compositions, one in the fall and the other in the spring. These wer read and evaluated by three experienced readers of the College Board English Achievement Test. Except for some seniors (but not all), son low groups (but not all), and the area of content and organization (bi not always), Heys obtained consistently better results from students : the reading classes than in the writing classes. He concluded that th way to learn to write is not substantiated by the experiment, and neith is the claim that ability to write well is related to the amount of wri ing done. He also concluded that for many students reading is a positiv influence on writing ability.

A Study of Three Methods of Evaluation

An experiment reported by Darnell (1962) involving three di ferent methods of evaluating writings upon creativity in writing al indicates that no advantages result from emphases upon correctir errors. Darnell's methods of evaluation were labeled accepting, critic and stoical. In the *accepting approach,* creative productions were a ceptable as they were. Children were encouraged to share their writte products by reading them to their classmates and teacher. The produc were neither graded nor corrected, but were placed into individu folders for each child. In the *critical approach,* the written products we not acceptable as they were turned in unless they were perfect. Produc were graded and corrected and then returned to pupils for proofrea ing and recopying. The papers were then collected again and place in individual folders. Under the *stoical approach,* no value was place on the products. Responses were simply collected and placed into i dividual folders. The experiment lasted for ten weeks.

The method of product evaluation did not influence the quality the creative expression. A number of qualities of writing, however, we influenced differentially at certain grade levels (fourth, fifth, and six grades). The *accepting approach* produced more total products tha either of the other two methods, fewer errors in spelling for the fif grades than under the other two methods of evaluating products, ar fewer punctuation errors for fourth, fifth, and sixth grades at the nin week than at the first or fifth week. The *critical approach* produced mo different types of writing and more spelling errors than the acceptir approach. The *stoical approach* produced more total products than th

ritical approach and fewer spelling errors for the fourth grades than
he accepting approach.

Procedure

SUBJECTS

Data were obtained from three groups of subjects. The first group
ncluded 128 students enrolled in undergraduate language arts courses
t the University of Minnesota. Ninety-five had had no teaching expe-
ience, and the remaining thirty-three had either had some teaching experience or were at the time of the study engaged in their student-teach-
ng experience.

The second group consisted of thirty-four experienced teachers
not enrolled at the University. They were volunteers who had par-
icipated in language arts workshops or lectures conducted by the
uthor and had responded to the announcement of a contest to deter-
nine who could devise the best strategy for dealing with the problem
f talking with two children who had submitted the sample stories.
The subjects were given these sample stories as a basis for talking with
he pupils.)

The third group included ninety graduate students, most of whom
vere experienced teachers, enrolled in a course in personality develop-
nent and mental health. All subjects were given a relatively unlimited
ime in which to prepare their responses.

Almost all of the subjects took the task seriously, and many prepared very elaborate proposals. Some subjects were extremely con-
cientious in relating, step-by-step, how they would attempt to help
he two young authors. A few refused to try to devise a strategy, report-
ng their inability to cope with such "impossible cases." All of these,
however, were the student teachers or undergraduates.

THE TEST TASK

Subjects were asked to sketch the strategies they would use in
alking to two elementary pupils who had written the following stories:

Story 1

This story is neatly written; each letter is formed almost perfectly;
and the margin is straight.

The Cat That Does Not Scratch

If a cat were to scratch me I would scratch it back. I do not lik
to be scratched by a cat. If a cat were to scratch me, I would try t
make friends with the cat. If he likes me, I will feed him.

Story 2

The following story is rather untidy; the margin is uneven; an
the writing is irregular and smudged.

The Cat That Coundn't Scratch

What a cold and dark night it was! Chester my cat was awfu
lonsum and tird. That was the nite he went to the hot hous and sav
alot of Fire Flies. He asked them if they wud make frens because h
was so lonly. But do you know what happend! They thot he was a Fir
Flie too. You see his eyes glowed. So they sat on him and wouldn't g
off.

So the next mornin, Chester went into the house and he couldn
scrach, or else he wud have a hot foot.

Results

In order to begin formulating a picture of the way teachers an
student teachers believe they should talk with children about thei
creative writing, an analysis was made first of the thematic content b
groups (undergraduates, teachers in service, and graduate students
and then according to the educational level of the teaching experienc
(primary grades, intermediate grades, and high school and higher
Tabulations were made for each of the plans for the two pupils fo
each subject for each reference to criticism (about mechanics, conten
or adjustment), praise (about mechanics, content, and adjustment
creative aspects of the productions, the use of a nonevaluative approacl
the use of self-evaluation, a remedial or first-aid plan (relative to me
chanics, content, and adjustment), and a developmental plan (relative t
mechanics, content, and adjustment). The results expressed in percent
ages are presented in Table 12.1 for the three basic groups of subjects. I
will be noted that there are large differences due to the nature of the crea
tive production. Accordingly, many of the subjects would criticize th
mechanics of the second story and the content of the first story, praise th
mechanics of the first story and the content of the second, comment upo
the creative aspects of the second story but not the lack of creativity c
imagination of the first. A considerable number would pursue remedia
plans related to mechanics with the author of the second story and de

TABLE 12.1   Results of Thematic Analysis of Treatment Plans for Talking with Two Children Concerning Their Creative Writing by Undergraduates, Experienced Teachers, and Graduate Students in Education

Category	Undergraduates (N=95)		Teachers (N=34)		Graduate Students (N=90)	
	Story 1	Story 2	Story 1	Story 2	Story 1	Story 2
Criticism						
About mechanics	3.2	32.6	5.9	14.7	0.0	21.1
About content	31.6	1.1	11.8	0.0	27.8	12.2
About adjustment	10.5	1.1	11.8	5.9	5.6	4.4
Praise						
About mechanics	61.0	0.0	52.9	0.0	34.4	1.1
About content	7.4	70.5	2.9	70.6	5.6	50.0
About adjustment	1.1	3.2	0.0	0.0	1.1	0.0
Creative aspects	7.4	34.7	5.9	41.2	11.1	36.7
Nonevaluation	26.3	14.7	29.4	26.5	10.0	11.1
Self-evaluation	12.6	15.8	35.3	14.7	10.0	6.7
Remedial Plan						
About mechanics	1.1	58.9	2.9	55.9	3.3	31.1
About content	52.6	1.1	44.1	2.9	30.0	6.7
About adjustment	15.8	1.1	29.4	20.6	52.2	52.2
Development Plan						
About mechanics	0.0	14.7	0.0	20.6	1.1	4.4
About content	3.2	4.2	8.8	8.8	8.9	3.3
About adjustment	0.0	2.1	2.9	2.9	16.7	30.0

sign remedial action relative to content with the author of the first story.

A number of interesting differences among the three groups were observed and were tested for statistical significance by use of chi-square analysis. The differences among groups on criticism of the mechanics of the second story is significant at about the 5 per cent level of confidence. The undergraduates are the most critical, and the experienced teachers not enrolled at the University are the least critical of the mechanics of the second story. In fact, the undergraduates are freest with criticism on all categories, while the experienced teachers not enrolled in the University are least critical.

Praise related to the mechanics of the first story also varies significantly among the three groups, significant at the 1 per cent level of confidence. Here the undergraduates are freest with praise, while the educators enrolled in the mental health course are least free with praise. Praise related to the content of the second story also differs significantly among the groups, significant at the 1 per cent level of confidence. The undergraduates and the experienced teachers are equally free with praise, while the educators in the mental health course are less free.

Significant differences occur in relation to the use of nonevaluative approaches (significant at the 1 per cent level of confidence). The experienced teachers not enrolled at the University include some kind of nonevaluative approach in their plans, while the mental health students make least use of this approach. The findings concerning the use of self-evaluative approaches show the same pattern (significant at the 1 per cent level of confidence).

The undergraduates and the volunteer teachers are more likely than the mental health students to include remedial plans relative to the mechanics of the second story and the content of the first story (both significant at the 1 per cent level of confidence). The mental health students far more frequently propose remedial plans relative to the adjustment of the author of the second story than the other two groups (significant at the 1 per cent level of confidence). A similar finding is noted concerning the author of the first story as well. In other words, the mental health students are more highly sensitized than the other subjects to the possibility that the impoverished content of the first story and the erratic writing and mechanics of the second story may be related to anxieties, tensions, and accompanying problems of mental functioning. Quite interestingly, the experienced volunteer teachers not enrolled in the University occupy a position midway between the other two groups in their sensitivity to the mental health needs of the writers.

The findings relative to developmental plans parallel those for remedial plans, although fewer subjects propose long-range developmental plans than propose remedial or first-aid plans. The differences relevant to the mechanics of the author of the second story are significant at between the 1 and 2 per cent levels of confidence. Differences relevant to the adjustment of the author of both stories are significant at the 1 per cent level. Actually *few of the subjects outside the mental health class make any reference to the possible need for long-range plans directed at improved emotional adjustment.*

The results according to the educational level at which the teachers are working are presented in Table 12.2. Again, attention will be given only to major differences among the three educational levels (primary, intermediate, and high school or above).

The primary and intermediate grade teachers tend to be generally less critical than the high school teachers. The difference is not statistically significant for the mechanics of the second story but is significant at the 1 per cent level for the content of the first story.

The differences relative to praise are less striking than those for criticism. All three groups, however, are freer with praise than with criticism. Differences relative to praise of the mechanics of the first

TABLE 12.2   Results of Thematic Analysis of Treatment Plans for Talking with Two Children Concerning Their Creative Writing by Primary, Intermediate, and High School Teachers

Category	Primary (N=38)		Intermediate (N=26)		High School (N=60)	
	Story 1	Story 2	Story 1	Story 2	Story 1	Story 2
Criticism						
About mechanics	0.0	10.5	0.0	19.2	0.0	25.0
About content	10.5	0.0	11.5	0.0	36.7	18.3
About adjustment	10.5	5.3	3.8	3.8	6.7	5.0
Praise						
About mechanics	47.4	0.0	53.8	0.0	30.0	1.7
About content	5.3	60.5	0.0	57.7	6.7	51.6
About adjustment	2.6	0.0	0.0	0.0	0.0	0.0
Creative aspects	10.5	23.7	23.1	38.5	3.3	46.6
Nonevaluation	18.4	18.4	30.8	15.4	6.7	11.7
Self-evaluation	34.2	10.5	30.8	19.2	0.0	3.3
Remedial Plan						
About mechanics	2.6	44.7	3.8	57.7	1.7	25.0
About content	31.6	5.3	50.0	7.7	28.3	5.0
About adjustment	44.7	42.1	50.0	46.2	45.0	45.0
Development Plan						
About mechanics	0.0	18.4	0.0	15.4	1.7	5.0
About content	15.8	10.5	7.7	0.0	5.0	3.3
About adjustment	5.3	15.8	7.7	11.5	20.0	31.7

story are at between the 5 and 10 per cent levels of confidence. The elementary teachers appear to be freer with praise than the high school ones.

The three groups according to educational level differ at the 1 per cent level on the matter of using self-evaluative approaches. The high school teachers make far less use of self-evaluation than do the elementary teachers.

There is a tendency for the intermediate teachers to be most concerned about remedial programs for both mechanics and content and for high school teachers to be least concerned (significant at the 1 and 10 per cent levels of confidence, respectively).

The differences relative to remedial plans for adjustment are not statistically significant, but the differences relative to long-range plans for adjustment are statistically significant (significant at between the 5 and 10 per cent levels of confidence for the first story and at the same level for the second story). Quite interestingly, the high school and college teachers more frequently recognize the role of adjustive factors than the primary and intermediate teachers.

STRATEGIES FOR TALKING WITH CHILDREN

Myers identified four different strategies or orientations in the approaches suggested by the subjects: creative, critical, implicit (example), and remedial. Examples will be quoted to illustrate each of these strategies. The creative strategy is illustrative of the approach which attempts to involve the pupil in *ideas*. The following strategy was designed to help the author of the first story:

> I would begin by showing the child that I am genuinely interested in his writing, and would try to enlist his interest in our cooperative effort to find out how his writing might be made more interesting. I would talk about ways of adding on to his thought, about ways of building images—pictures—in the mind and then getting them down on paper. I would discuss with him not so much techniques of writing as ways of thinking about a thing; I would encourage him to suggest as many different ways as he can of talking about a cat that does not scratch, asking him to consider how the cat looks, where it lives, how it feels, and what else it does. Then I would try to get him to generalize about this way of writing, showing him that any subject can be made more interesting by thinking of it in different ways. I would encourage him to be bold—even "crazy"—in his thinking.

The following critical strategy is faithful to the attitude of the respondents who were disturbed by the inconsistencies found in the first story:

> The sentences seem to oppose each other. The first two sentences display revenge. The third and fourth sentences express kindness. I would ask the author just what he would do—either express kindness or hostility. The title also is not indicative of the lines that follow. I would ask the author his reasons for using such a title and then to explain if he felt he carried out these reasons.

Interestingly enough, the respondent whose strategy so aptly typifies the critical approach to creative writing also exemplifies quite well the remedial approach in her remarks to the author of the second story:

> I would work on correct spelling, capitalization, and punctuation. I would ask the child what he meant by the hot house and what the last sentence means in relation to the first paragraph. The child also needs help with paragraph structure and handwriting.

Many of the respondents whose strategies involved teaching by example offered the first author models in the form of books, as this respondent did:

First, I would praise the author for the mechanical part of his story, which he has done very well. Then I would have available some well-written, short stories which contain a simple plot or idea and ones which make good use of descriptive adjectives. I would suggest we read these together, and decide why they are good stories. Next I would suggest we make a comparison of these stories with his story and judge it by the criteria we had set up together. By making this comparison, the child would then be able to observe how he might make improvements in his story and stories he would be writing.

Most of the strategies which were analyzed were not so easily classified as those just given, although it is evident that these too contain elements which are not entirely consistent with the central theme. Many of the respondents incorporated all four approaches into their strategies. From a practical viewpoint, this eclecticism is often effective. It tends to reduce the analyst's confidence in his taxonomy, however. There were some solutions which suggested other classifications.

The primary teachers often attempted to get the pupils more deeply involved in their stories, but it was less evident how deeply involved many of them become with their pupils, except in the case of this second-grade teacher:

After receiving these stories and others which were written by the group members, I probably would not say anything to the individuals. I, however, would share with them some added information about cats. I would show them a live cat which I had put inside the surprise box preceding the creative story motivation. We would take the time to appreciate it together and talk about it in our own way. In a few minutes' time, I would ask them, "What are the most interesting parts of a cat, and why are those parts interesting?" As we would be watching the cat together and experiencing the presence of a favorite pet, the following responses might be heard:

His tail because it looks like the top of a furry question mark.
His glowing eyes because they match the night time stars.
His back because it looks like an arch in an outdoor croquet game.
His whiskers because they look like the bristle stick ups on a hair brush.

When someone mentions his scratchers, we will discuss how the cat uses that part of his body. We will discover together that he has the privilege to use his scratching feet in his own way, just as we can use our hands to help protect us in our daily living.

We could talk with and listen to each other tell of "places where cats could have their scratching lessons." We might hear things like this:

On a swaying down apple tree.
On a white wooden guard fence around the yard.
On children's necks and noses.

We could compare our hands to the cat paws and discuss "things that hands can do that paws can't do." Some children might respond in these ways:

My hands can help me turn upside down somersaults.

My hands can go inside puppets and make them do their work.

My hands can go in a pie and pull out a plum.

Upon concluding these talking topics, the entire group will have received a better understanding of how people and animals react in different ways to the world around them. This discussion might be especially worked in for the author of story number one who thinks cat-scratching lessons are not fun for people to receive. It would be a just-right time to have Wanda Gag's book *Millions of Cats* available for extra reading. I hope that the author of the first story is the lucky child to take this book. It would help him understand how wonderful cats really are.

When these children leave school, I would enjoy finding the time to relax and read the stories which came from the hearts of my friends. I will not have said anything to the individual authors about their stories, because it is their privilege to write as they feel, and to be free at all times to say as they please without wondering if Teacher will like it.

After reading each story in my own curious way, I would write a personal note to each child on his story paper as I do in my own day-to-day teaching.

On Story 1 I would write:

> Dear _____, I am glad that you decided to feed your cat and be so kind to him. I think any cat would like to be your pet. I wish I were as kind and as good as you are. Your friend, Miss G.

I will note from this story that _____ lacks organization in planning his ideas. In days to come I would see a need to work closer with him in the arranging of thought sequences. I would listen more carefully to him during talking times to see if he gets the order of events properly, and if he often changes his mind.

On Story 2 I would write this note:

> Dear _____, I'd like to go out prowling with Chester Cat and meet all the lighted fireflies. I've always wanted to touch one and see how they make their magic night-time lights come on. I think that would be the biggest adventure in the whole wide world for me. Your friend, Miss G.

I would secretly know that this child is very creative and uses his imagination well. I would know that he needs a great deal of extra help in spelling. (But he'd never guess that by my note to him.)

The individual help for spelling time would not come when he is doing his creative writing. (At that time it is the word thought and the expression of ideas which we are seeking. He is never worried about how words are spelled in his original child-made stories. It is then when he is free to say the very special things that he feels inside.)

This child will have guided help with spelling in his free time. His misspelled words might help me in my selection of spelling words for him. It seems that since there is a need to write words in story form, this is the time for him to learn them in his spelling. They are his words. He is ready now. It's my job to help him. As his spelling improves, his neatness in work will also come easier, because erasers will need a vacation time.

As I'd finish reading the stories created by each child and after adding personal notes on the ungraded papers, I would know that I had just finished talking with each of my children in a more personal way than making oral conversations with them which the other children could also hear—conversations which could cause embarrassment and take spark out of future creative thinking. At this time I would also know that I was holding in my hands the inside word pockets of their minds which came from within during an atmosphere of freedom "to say it their own way." I'd know that I was holding hints which will guide me to their individual needs.

I'd be certain that when they would come into our room the following morning, every child would know, by the personal notes which they can read and keep forever, that I appreciated their individual stories.

They won't know that I have learned a few new secrets about them which will help them on this day and in days to come.

They will know that when they say, "Good Morning, Teacher," I'll be glad that we can be together for another happy day when we are free to be ourselves, just the way we are.

The values of the teacher who wrote the words above were brought out in sharp relief when she responded to the request to offer a solution to the problem. What may have been brought out also is the tendency of many students to "pad" their answers or to give unrealistic answers. Notwithstanding the artifices and delusions of the respondents, however, their values do shine through. If someone devotes a reasonable amount of thought to problems such as those posed in the questionnaire, he is bound to reveal something of his attitudes.

Discussion

As has already been mentioned, the subjects in this study were probably acting on their "best behavior" in terms of what they consider ideal practices. The volunteer, experienced teacher group had attended workshops or lectures conducted by the author on encouraging creative development and were competing to offer solutions which would promote creative growth. The graduate students and experienced educators, enrolled in a course on personality development and mental health, had been given considerable orientation concerning conditions conducive to mental health and creative growth. They were also working for grades. The undergraduates were assured that their responses would not count on their grades, but they too had received considerable orientation concerning teaching for growth in creative writing. In spite of all these factors which might have influenced the subjects to offer "ideal" solutions, responses involve plans which are far from ideal in the light of what we know about conditions for fostering creative growth. Many of the plans offered reflect again man's strong needs to punish and to pity. Criticism and praise are among the favorite weapons and defenses of the respondents. Appeals to the child's own creative problem skills, the use of self-evaluative approaches, and the like are rarely used. Outside of the mental health students, few of the respondents recognize that the mental health of the children who wrote the stories may be interfering with their performance and that these children may not do either more creative or more correct writing until they are better able to cope with problems of adjustment.

As we examined the responses submitted by subjects, the idea occurred repeatedly that teachers apparently lack the concepts and/or vocabulary with which to communicate with children about their creative writing. It occurred to us that teachers might gain these concepts and become skilled in their use by evaluating their students' creative productions according to the procedures described in earlier chapters of this volume for assessing the originality and the interest of imaginative stories.

PEER PRESSURES IN HOMOGENEOUS AND HETEROGENEOUS GROUPS

13

Research in social psychology has shown repeatedly that the evaluative behavior of one's peers in small groups is a powerful inhibitor of original ideas. Studies of adult groups (Pepinsky and Pepinsky, 1958) indicate, however, that those individuals who produce original ideas in groups have developed identifiable strategies which enable them to counteract these inhibiting forces to a considerable extent. Pepinsky (1960) has identified seven strategies of what she has termed "productive nonconformity." The productive nonconformist, according to Pepinsky, translates his own ideas into the language of the other members of his group so that they can see his contribution as instrumental to their own needs, or at least not in conflict with them. He states his criticism in a positive and constructive way and makes it evident that basically he stands for something that commands the respect of others in the group. He minimizes personal threat by listening to others and according them respect and dignity. He establishes a kind of "credit rating" and "buys" increased freedom over a period of time by initial service in terms of existing demands and requirements. He emphasizes the job to be done, rather than "personalities" and "status." He is good at timing his ideas and is able to delay responses as well as act upon them.

I was assisted in the preparation of this chapter by Dr. Kevser Arsan, University of Istanbul, Turkey. A portion of this chapter has appeared in W. W. Charters, Jr. and N. L. Gage, eds., *Readings in the Social Psychology of Education* (Boston: Allyn and Bacon, Inc., 1963), pp. 133-140.

It is the thesis of this chapter that by the time children reach the intermediate grades, they have developed some rather well-defined small-group strategies for controlling their more creative members and that highly creative children have in turn developed some rather well-defined counterstrategies for maintaining the productive nonconformity or creativity. It was further hypothesized that these strategies are different in homogeneous and heterogeneous grouping, whether the grouping be based on a measure of creative thinking ability or upon some other measure of intellectual talent such as mental age or IQ.

Classroom Grouping and Creative Activities

When assigning creative tasks in elementary school classes, it is frequently necessary to divide pupils into small groups. If each group is to undertake a different task, the basis for the grouping is usually some kind of homogeneity of interest. If all groups are assigned the same task as a common educational experience, the problem is different. There are many possibilities. Strevell and Oliver (1957), for example, have identified twenty-four types of classroom grouping practices. If the task to be assigned requires creative thinking, one logical basis for grouping would be some kind of score on tests of creative thinking ability. The question then becomes, "Should the groups be homogeneous or heterogeneous?"

In grouping pupils for tasks requiring creative thinking, one must consider a number of special problems. The groupings should help to create conditions which will free each child to think, to express his thoughts, and to have them considered honestly. Disruptive social stress should be reduced as much as possible, and positive, productive interaction should be fostered.

There is a considerable body of literature concerning homogeneous and heterogeneous grouping in reading, mathematics, and other subjects. Using scores on tests of reading achievement as the basis of homogeneity and heterogeneity, research workers have generally given the nod to homogeneous grouping (Barbe and Waterhouse, 1956; Heyl, 1955). Some, however, stress flexibility in grouping (Bremer, 1958; Canfield, 1957; Heyl, 1955).

Almost no attention has been given, however, to the special problems of grouping for tasks requiring creative thinking. One exploratory experiment with young adults as subjects in laboratory tasks requiring group creativity has been reported by Fiedler, Meuwese, and Oonk (1960). Homogeneity and heterogeneity were based on religious and collegiate affiliations. The subject were students in Calvinist and Catholic colleges in Amsterdam, Holland. The same subjects took part in both homogeneous and heterogeneous groups under both formal and informal organizations. Under both forms of organization, the heterogeneous groups showed much social strain and communication difficulty. The homogeneous groups showed little social strain and had few problems of communication.

Some of the findings from Drews' studies (1961a) of homogeneous and heterogeneous ability groupings in ninth-grade English classes provide clues concerning what we may expect in creative activities. Her results indicate that slow students read more, recited more, were more confident, liked school better, and were more accepted socially and intellectually in the homogeneous groups. Superior students wrote many more compositions, did more research, discussed at a more mature level, used more difficult words, expressed more complex and abstract thoughts, and were more interested in learning in homogeneous than in heterogeneous groups. They were also much more modest in their ratings of self in relationship to others.

Procedures

SUBJECTS

The subjects of the study were fourth-, fifth-, and sixth-grade pupils in three Minneapolis elementary schools. School A is a private school which limits its enrollment to twenty-five pupils per class. Schools B and C are metropolitan public schools, each having two classes at each grade level.

In 1959, the pupils in each class of School A were divided heterogeneously into groups of five on the basis of Form A, Test of Imagination. In 1960, each class was divided homogeneously on the basis of Form DX, Test of Imagination. (See full description of tests in Appendix A.)

In School B, one class in each grade was grouped homogeneously and the other heterogeneously on the basis of intelligence quotients as determined by the California Test of Mental Maturity. In this school, twenty-three groups were included in the study.

In School C, one class in each grade was grouped homogeneously and the other heterogeneously on the basis of IQ's as determined by the California Test of Mental Maturity. In this school, twenty-three groups were included in the study.

Homogeneous groups were formed by ranking all pupils in a class on the measure (IQ or creativity score) used as the basis for grouping and placing the first five pupils in one group, the next five in a second, and so on. In forming heterogeneous groups, one of the top ranking pupils was placed in each group, followed by one of the next highest ranking pupils, and so on. Subjects were not informed of the basis used in forming the groups. Each of the five-person groups were about equally divided insofar as sex is concerned.

EXPERIMENTAL PROCEDURES

In each class, all groups were tested simultaneously, each in a different room under a trained experimenter who made detailed observations of the interaction. Tabulations were made for ideas or actions initiated, uses discovered, explanations advanced, and reasons suggested during the exploratory period. In addition, the experimenters described how the group got organized and underway with the task, how the members grouped themselves, the general activity level of the exploratory period, the special roles of members, how the demonstrations were planned, special roles in planning and demonstrating, and the like.

To set the task, after the homogeneous or heterogeneous groups had been formed, each group was provided a box of science toys and toy parts obtainable from Science Materials Center, The Library of Science, 59 Fourth Avenue, New York 3, New York. Each toy illustrates at least one basic principle of science. Science Toy Collection Number 2 was used in the 1959 administration in School A. This collection includes a sparkler, finger trap, pin trick, four-ball puzzle, topsy-turvy top, blow ball, flying saucer, and nutty putty. To this collection was added a magnifying glass, magnet, and whistle. Science Toy Collection Number 3 was used in all other administrations and includes a bang gun, string telephone, siren, busy bee, calliope whistle, cat cry, Tower of Hanoi puzzle, tetrahedron puzzle, and other puzzles. A magnet and magnifying glass were added to this collection.

Before a class was divided into groups, the author gave the entire class the following orientation:

I would like to ask you to help us find out more about the ways people learn how to think of new ideas. During this next hour we have arranged what is a kind of test of how inventive you can be about science things and how well you can develop ideas as groups. We will divide you into groups of five, and each group will work in a separate place with a different observer. Each group will be given a box of science toys. Your job will be to find out as many things as you can that these toys can do or be used for. Some of you will recognize the scientific principles that these toys were made to illustrate. But we want you to be concerned about *any* possible uses of these toys, not just the ones they were made for.

For twenty-five minutes, you may experiment with these toys and try to find out as many things as you can that you can do with them. Then we will give you another twenty-five-minute period in which to demonstrate what these toys can do and explain the principles behind them.

The object is to see how many science principles you can demonstrate and explain. We are not interested in individual performance but in how well the group does. One of my helpers will be with each group and will take down your ideas and record some things about the way you do your job. In addition to seeing how you can use and figure out scientific principles, we want to see how you work as a group on problems like this.

To make this more interesting, we shall award a prize to each member of the group who demonstrates and explains the largest number of science principles.

The membership and places of meeting for each group were then announced. When the five-person groups had assembled, the experimenter gave each person a colored arm band, according to a predetermined code. He then gave the following instructions for the exploratory phase:

Here is a box of science toys. All of them were made to illustrate some scientific principle. I am sure that you can think of many uses other than the ones originally intended. Your job is to find out as many things as you can that these toys can do and explain them. Don't give up when you have discovered one use; there are several possible uses for each toy. You can combine them in different ways. You will have twenty-five minutes to do this.

At the end of this phase, the following instructions were given:

Now, I would like you to demonstrate these toys to me just as though I were a class that you are trying to teach what these toys can do and why they do it. You will have only twenty-five minutes to do this. Remember that group performance is what counts. First, demonstrate what the toy can do. Second, explain the principle or reason why it does what it does. All right, go ahead.

At the end of the experiment, each subject was asked to rank each member of his group, including himself, according to the value of his contribution to the success of the group. In all the 1960 administrations, subjects were also asked to indicate how well they had enjoyed the activity and how they thought their own group had performed in comparison with the others in the class.

Upon completion of the experiment, the observers prepared their records which consisted of the tabulations and descriptions for the exploratory and planning phases, accounts of the demonstrations and explanations, and other observations of interaction during the ratings and demonstrations. Except for checks on reliability of observers, each group was observed by only one experimenter. The same persons observed both homogeneous and heterogeneous groups on various occasions.

ANALYSIS OF DATA

Using categories developed in a pilot study, a careful analysis was made of the records of interaction between the group and the most outstanding member on whatever measure was used as the basis for the grouping, whether homogeneous or heterogeneous. This means, of course, that there was relatively little difference between the most outstanding member of the homogeneous groups and the other members of a given group.

A score was obtained for each individual on number of ideas initiated, number of ideas demonstrated and explained, reported enjoyment of the activity, self-ranking of performance, and rating of own group. At each of the five ability levels, comparisons were made between the homogeneous and heterogeneous groups—separately for each school.

The record of each group was then analyzed for positive and negative signs. This was done by first drawing up lists of words which would be accepted as indicators of social stress and of positive, productive interaction. A high degree of agreement ($r = .95$) was achieved by raters in scoring records according to these lists.

The following terms appearing in the records were classified as indications of disruptive social stress or tension:

Bickering	Reprimanding
Fighting	Loss of temper
Squabbling	Apathy or passivity
Uncontrolled behavior	Refusal to cooperate
Disorder	Loss of interest
Disorganization	Sarcasm
Dominating	Disruptive talking
Squelching	Joking

The following terms were classified as signs of positive, productive interaction or tension-reducing behaviors:

Cooperating	Considering others' ideas
Helping	Trying out others' ideas
Working together	Communicating ideas
Organizing	Consulting with one another
Absorption in task	Congenial
Praising one another	Interested
Respecting others' ideas	Questioning
Listening	Curious

A tabulation of both positive and negative signs was made for each group. Homogeneous and heterogeneous groups in each of the three schools were compared by means of chi-square analysis.

Results

STRATEGIES OF GROUP CONTROL

Table 13.1 contains the results of the analysis of the observed strategies of group control of the most outstanding group member (most

TABLE 13.1 Observed Strategies of Group Control of Most Outstanding Group Member with Heterogeneous and Homogeneous Grouping According to Scores on a Creative Thinking Test and According to IQ's

Type of Pressure or Strategy of Control	Creative Hetero. (N=26)	Creative Homo. (N=24)	IQ Hetero. (N=11)	IQ Homo. (N=12)
Open aggression and hostility	19	4	0	0
Criticism, ridicule	19	0	0	8
Ignoring, rejection, unresponsive	31	13	18	8
Use of organizational machinery	12	4	9	0
Assignment of organizational responsibility	19	4	73	17
Lack of structure	19	17	0	83
No pressure observed	19	71	18	58
High IQ member pressured to produce ideas	4	13	64	0

creative or most intelligent as the case might be). Several observations appear to be important.

First, high ability members are more likely to experience group pressures in heterogeneous than in homogeneous groups, regardless of the basis of the grouping. In the creatively homogeneous groups 71 per cent experienced freedom from pressure, and in the homogeneous groups based on IQ, 58 per cent enjoyed such freedom, compared with 19 and 18 per cents in the heterogeneously formed groups. This difference is significant at the 1 per cent level of confidence.

Second, high IQ members experience a different kind of pressure from that experienced by highly creative members. This is especially clear in the heterogeneous groups based on IQ where 64 per cent of the groups exercised rather obvious pressures on the high IQ member to produce ideas. Even in the groups formed on the basis of measures of creative thinking, some of the high IQ members experienced such pressures. In a considerable number of cases, the high IQ member was unable to meet this expectation to produce ideas with the result that both he and the group were disappointed in his performance. For example, one observer recorded the following comment about the group which contained the boy who had the highest IQ of the class:

> Blue (lowest IQ) was really the "hero" of the group and was its spark plug. The group openly expressed the feeling of being let down by White (highest IQ) when he was unable to respond to their urging to supply ideas. He recognized that this was expected of him but seemed to be unable to "get going" and expressed disgust concerning his performance.

Group members identified as outstanding on the basis of their creative thinking ability generally experienced quite a different kind of pressure. Instead of urging highly creative members to produce ideas, groups exercised pressures to reduce their production of ideas by open aggression and hostility, criticism and ridicule, ignoring and rejecting, restraining by organizational machinery, or saddling them with organizational responsibility. This is rather ironic, since the highly creative members may be better able to produce ideas to help the group than highly intelligent members could. It is understandable, however, since the highly intelligent youngster is likely to have a reputation for having the "right" answer rather consistently. The highly creative youngster, however, is not likely to have such a reputation. Most groups thus appeared to feel that "the rules of the game had been switched on them," so to speak.

It is interesting to note that the homogeneous groups based on IQ tended to experience the pressure of lack of structure more frequently than any other type of group. Apparently the heterogeneous groups acted upon the structure built into the groups by different levels of ability (creativity or intelligence). What is most interesting, however, is the fact that the homogeneous groups based on creative thinking ability tended not to experience this difficulty.

High IQ members in heterogeneous groups are more likely to be given organizational responsibility than highly creative members in heterogeneous groups (73 per cent and 19 per cent, respectively, significant at the 1 per cent level of confidence). A closer analysis of the records shows that in the few cases where highly creative subjects were given organizational responsibility, they were also in the high group on the intelligence test measure.

COUNTERACTION STRATEGIES

The data derived from the analysis of the observed counteraction
rategies of the most outstanding group member (as determined by
·eativity score or IQ as the case might be) are presented in Table
3.2. Again, only the most remarkable observations will be mentioned.
Perhaps the most remarkable observation to be noted in Table 13.2

TABLE 13.2   Observed Counteraction Strategies of Most Outstanding Group Member with
eterogeneous and Homogeneous Grouping According to Scores on Creative Thinking Tests and
ccording to IQ's

Type of Reaction or Counteraction Strategy	Creative Hetero. (N=26)	Creative Homo. (N=24)	IQ Hetero. (N=11)	IQ Homo. (N=12)
Compliance	19	8	18	42
Counteraggressiveness	15	0	9	0
Persistence or calm resistance	37	13	0	0
Apparently ignoring criticism or attack	15	0	0	0
Clowning, giggling, humor	12	0	0	0
Silence, preoccupation, leaving field	27	17	0	17
Inconsistent performance	15	4	4	0
Solitary activity, working alone	27	33	18	17
Filling in gaps, but not structuring	42	13	18	42
Initiating structure, leading, coordinating	46	33	73	33

; the fact that only in the creatively heterogeneous groups do we find
1any counteraction strategies. These are rather evenly distributed
mong compliance, counteraggressiveness, persistence or calm resist-
1ce, the apparent ignoring of criticism, clowning and giggling, silence
1d preoccupation, inconsistent performance, and solitary activity. Al-
1ost one half of them, however, resorted to the strategy of filling in the
aps when other members bogged down or when other members of the
roup were unable to produce ideas. Again, these phenomena are easy
) understand, since it is only in the creatively heterogeneous groups

that there were very many restraining pressures against the most ab
member (as identified by creativity and IQ). These pressures in th
heterogeneous groups formed on the basis of IQ were in the directic
of increased production.

Another notable observation in Table 13.2 is that the most ab
members of heterogeneous groups are more likely to initiate structu
than are the most able members of homogeneous groups. Quite interes
ingly, however, the highly creative youngster seems to be somewh;
more reluctant to initiate structure than the high IQ youngster in heter
geneous groups. He seems instead to fill in the gaps when others a
unable to supply the answers or ideas needed.

NUMBER OF IDEAS INITIATED

The mean number of ideas initiated by subjects in each of the fi
ability levels in homogeneous and heterogeneous groups in each of th
three schools studied is shown in Figures 13.1, 13.2, and 13.3. In Scho

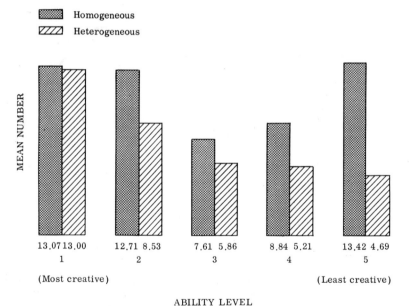

Homogeneous

Heterogeneous

MEAN NUMBER

| 13.07 13.00 | 12.71 8.53 | 7.61 5.86 | 8.84 5.21 | 13.42 4.69 |
| 1 | 2 | 3 | 4 | 5 |

(Most creative)   (Least creative)

ABILITY LEVEL

*FIGURE 13.1   Mean Numbers of Ideas Initiated by Pupils of Five Ability Levels of Cre
tive Thinking in Homogeneous and Heterogeneous Groups in School A*

A, in the homogeneous groups, those at the second, fourth, and fift
ability levels initiated significantly more ideas than did their counte
parts in the heterogeneous groups. In the heterogeneous groups, ther
is a tendency toward a linear relationship between ability level an

ean number of ideas initiated. This tendency does not prevail under
ᵒmogeneous conditions; those in the fourth and fifth ability levels di-
ᵣge from the linear tendency.

In School B, there are no statistically significant differences at any

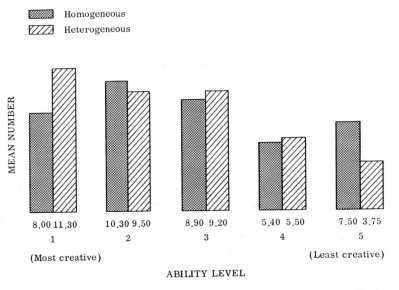

FIGURE 13.2 *Mean Numbers of Ideas Initiated by Pupils of Five Ability Levels of Crea-*
ᵉ Thinking in Homogeneous and Heterogeneous Groups in School B

ᵇility level under the two conditions. The trends noted in School B,
ᵣr subjects at the second and fifth levels of ability to initiate more ideas
ᵢ homogeneous than in heterogeneous groups, were not statistically
ᵍnificant. Those at the highest ability level, however, tended to initiate
ᵒre ideas in heterogeneous than in homogeneous groups. Again the
ᵢᵣnear trend between ability level and mean number of ideas initiated
ᵒpears in the heterogeneous but not in the homogeneous groups, the
ᵉcond and fifth ability levels diverging most sharply from the linear
ᵗend.

In School C, where IQ was the basis for grouping, those in the
ᵢghest ability level in heterogeneous groups excel their counterparts in
ᵗe homogeneous groups, while the reverse is true for those at the fourth
ᵇility level. Contrary to what was found in Schools A and B, where
ᵣeativity scores were used as a basis for grouping, there is no linear
ᵗend under any condition between IQ level and mean number of ideas
ᵢnitiated. The linear trend in the heterogeneous groups was upset by
ᵗose in the lowest ability level who excelled their peers at the second,
ᵗird, and fourth ability levels. In the homogeneous groups, there is al-

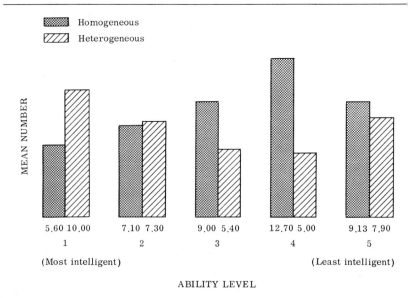

FIGURE 13.3   Mean Numbers of Ideas Initiated by Pupils of Five Ability Levels of Intel
gence in Homogeneous and Heterogeneous Groups in School C

most a linear trend in reverse. The lowest mean was achieved by grou
composed of children with the highest IQ's, the highest by those at t
fourth and fifth levels.

IDEAS DEMONSTRATED AND EXPLAINED

Figures 13.4, 13.5, and 13.6 show the mean number of ideas demo
strated and explained by subjects in the five ability levels in homog
neous and heterogeneous groups in each of the three schools. None
the differences is statistically significant in School A. The linear tre
between ability level (quintiles) and mean number of ideas demo
strated and explained is spoiled somewhat by those in the lowest grou
In the homogeneous groups, those at the lowest ability level (quintile
actually achieved the highest mean of any ability level.

In School B those at the third and fourth ability levels (third an
fourth quintiles) demonstrated and explained significantly more ide
in heterogeneous groups than in homogeneous groups. The reverse
true, however, for those in the lowest ability level. As in School A, tho
in the lowest ability level turned in the best performance of any abili
level.

In School C, the linear trend in the heterogeneous condition is di

rbed by the fourth and fifth ability levels. Again, subjects in the high-
t ability level turn in a rather mediocre performance under homoge-
ous condition.

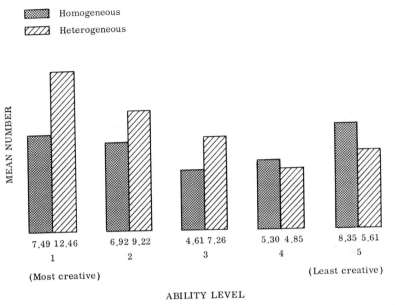

FIGURE 13.4 Mean Numbers of Ideas Demonstrated and Explained by Pupils of Five
bility Levels of Creative Thinking in Homogeneous and Heterogeneous Groups in School A

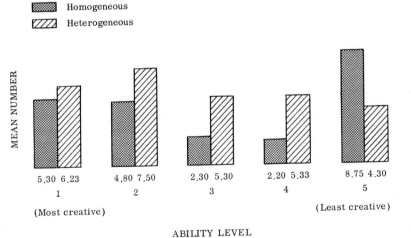

FIGURE 13.5 Mean Numbers of Ideas Demonstrated and Explained by Pupils of Five
Ability Levels of Creative Thinking in Homogeneous and Heterogeneous Groups in School B

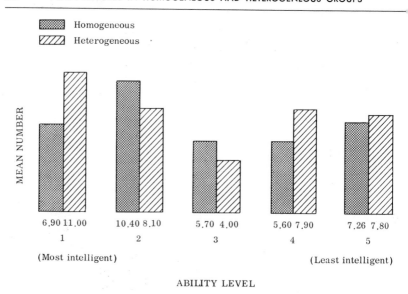

FIGURE 13.6 *Mean Numbers of Ideas Demonstrated and Explained by Pupils of Fi Ability Levels of Intelligence in Homogeneous and Heterogeneous Groups in School C*

ENJOYMENT OF TASK

Complete data concerning enjoyment of task were available on] for Schools B and C. In these two schools there was a consistent tenc ency for pupils under homogeneous conditions to report greater enjoy ment than those under heterogeneous conditions. The difference statistically significant only at the second ability level, however, and th occurs in both schools. When tabulations are made of the number choo ing each category for the entire school, the chi-square is significant fc School C but not for School B. In School C, 81 per cent of those in th homogeneous groups reported that they enjoyed the activity "ver much" compared with 67 per cent in the heterogeneous groups.

SELF-RANKINGS

There was a general tendency for the more able subjects in bot schools to be more modest or self-depreciating and for the less able one to be less modest or less self-depreciating under homogeneous condi tions than under heterogeneous conditions. In School B, subjects at th top ability level are extremely self-depreciating in homogeneous group: Their mean self-ranking is fourth, where the lowest ranking is five. The are significantly more self-depreciating than their counterparts unde heterogeneous conditions (1 per cent level).

RATING OF GROUP PERFORMANCE

Only at the top level (quintile) of ability are there statistically
gnificant differences between subjects in the two conditions in their
tings of their own group's performance. When creative thinking is the
asis for the grouping, the top ability subjects rate their group's per-
ormance less favorably under homogeneous than under heterogeneous
onditions. The reverse is true when IQ is used as the basis for grouping.

SOCIAL STRESS

Comparisons of the homogeneous and heterogeneous groups in
ach of the three schools on the number of signs of disruptive social
ress and positive interaction are presented in Table 13.3. The results

TABLE 13.3 Number of Positive and Negative Interactions in Homogeneous and Hetero-
neous Groups During Science-toy Task

| | Homogeneous | | | | Heterogeneous | | |
	Number of Groups	Number of Pupils	Interactions Positive	Negative	Number of Groups	Number of Pupils	Interactions Positive	Negative
ol	15	70	136	53	15	70	36	77
	8	39	53	32	12	63	52	73
	12	63	107	37	11	55	63	53

Note: X^2 (School A) $= 46.3873$; $df = 1$; p significant at less than .1 per cent level
      X^2 (School B) $= 8.6940$; $df = 1$; p significant at less than 1 per cent level
      X^2 (School C) $= 11.3360$; $df = 1$; p significant at less than 1 per cent level

re consistent from school to school, and in all cases the differences are
ignificant at better than the 1 per cent level of confidence. There were
ewer signs of social stress in the homogeneous than in the heteroge-
eous groups. This result holds when the same classes constitute the
omogeneous and heterogeneous groups about a year apart, when one
lass at each grade level is divided heterogeneously, when pupils are
rouped according to measures of creativity, and when they are grouped
ccording to IQ.

Discussion

From the data presented it seems reasonably clear that we may
xpect greater disruptive social stress when we divide classroom groups

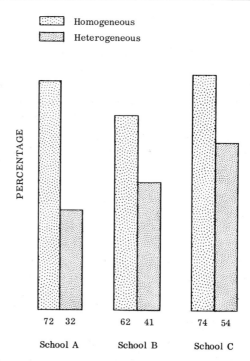

FIGURE 13.7 *Percentages of Positive Interactions in Homogeneous and Heterogeneoɑ Groups in Three Schools*

heterogeneously than when we divide them homogeneously for creɑ tive activities. These results seem to hold both when the groupings aɩ based on IQ's and when they are based on measures of creative thinᴋ ing. There did seem to be one major difference in the heterogeneoᴜ groups based on IQ and .those based on creativity. There seemed to ᴌ far less effort to "unseat" the high IQ member than the highly creatiᴠ member. The status of the child with the high IQ seemed far moɩ secure than that of the highly creative child. In fact, some groups seeɩ either to demand or plead for the high IQ member to produce, whereɑ there was a tendency to restrain, reduce, or control the productivity ɵ the highly creative child.

These results should not be interpreted to mean that teacheɩ should always form homogeneous groups for creative tasks. There aɩ signs that some homogeneous groups tend to be dull, uninteresting, anɩ unproductive when new ideas are required. There seem to be timᴇ when it is advantageous to increase social stress. On the basis of rᴇ search (Torrance, 1958) on the effects of varying intensity of stresɩ creative thinking is likely to be stimulated by increasing social stress ᴛ a point, after which thinking is disrupted, and productivity diminisheᴅ

ιus, it would seem that a classroom teacher may within limits control
ρ degree of social stress in work groups by choosing varying bases of
ρuping. Of course, still other methods of grouping need to be investi-
ted, and effects of groupings other than social stress need to be
ιdied.

Although the findings concerning individual behavior are not
ιarly as impressive as those relevant to social stress, several rather
·ong tendencies are worth noting. One of these is the fairly consistent
d frequently dramatic "all-out" performance of the low ability groups
ιder homogeneous conditions. The consistent linear trend in the heter-
eneous group provides some rather convincing evidence concerning
ρ validity of the tests of creative thinking used in forming the groups.
ιose who produced the most ideas on the written tests administered
veral months earlier also produced the most ideas in this task. The
ilure of this linear trend to hold under homogeneous conditions sug-
sts that many of our ability measures, including the IQ, might lose
ιne of their predictive value under conditions of homogeneous group-
ς, when the performance of one individual is not experimentally inde-
·ndent of that of his fellow group members.

The findings concerning enjoyment of the activity and self-rank-
ςs support those of Drews (1961a). They tend to contradict popular
·liefs that homogeneous grouping will make children unhappy, espe-
ιlly the low ability ones, and that high ability pupils will become con-
ited and low ability ones overwhelmed by their feelings of inferiority.
both studies, the very reverse seems to be true.

Finally, it should be pointed out that although in nature and
ciety there is more stress in heterogeneous than in homogeneous
ρups, it does not mean that nothing can be done to reduce the stress
the heterogeneous groups. Similarly, the fact that there are no clear-
t differences in the production of ideas in homogeneous and heteroge-
ous groups does not mean, for example, that heterogeneous groups
ιnnot become more productive than homogeneous ones. In fact, a study
· Triandis, Bass, Ewen, and Mikesell (1962) indicates that in heteroge-
ous groups guidance can be given which will reduce stress and
ιmmunication difficulties and create mutual trust and interpersonal
ιtraction. When this was done, it was found that groups heterogeneous
attitudes produced more creative ideas than groups homogeneous in
titudes. In "nature," however, they found the reverse to be true. In
ιer words, when nothing was done to help groups reduce stress and
ιmmunication difficulties, heterogeneous groups were less creative than
ιmogeneous ones. The subjects of the study reported by Triandis and
ς associates, however, were adults, and it remains to be seen whether
ιildren can be taught procedures whereby the stresses resulting in lack

of productivity can be reduced. The procedure of studying one anothe
semantic differentials employed by Triandis and his associates might n
be appropriate for children, but there is no reason to believe that ch
dren cannot be taught some means for reducing these stresses and achie
ing greater creative production in heterogeneous groups than w
observed in the study described in this chapter.

POSITIVE,

NEGATIVE,

AND

TROUBLE-SHOOTING

EVALUATION

14

Much of the research on the evaluative behavior of the teacher has en concerned with the relative merits of praise, or positive evaluation, d criticism, or negative evaluation. Although the evidence has con-ued through the ages to be overwhelmingly in favor of praise, or sitive evaluation, this accumulated evidence has somehow been un-tisfactory. It has not given teachers the guidance they need in making cisions about their evaluative behavior. Even though praise has rather nerally produced better results than punishment or criticism, there s still been something rather unpredictable about the effects of praise, d some observers have noted detrimental aftereffects, even when the aise has been honest. This seems to be especially true in trying to evoke eative behavior among children. Even in administering tests, we noted at children would reduce their productivity or produce only very vious and commonplace ideas, if we praised them. If we simply ac-pted and recorded their ideas, they seemed to increase their produc-n of ideas and to produce ideas that are more original.

In earlier chapters, some of the major points of view concerning gative and positive evaluation in creative problem solving have been scussed. Osborn (1957, 1963) and others have gone to great lengths taboo negative evaluation or criticism in encouraging groups to think new ideas. Clark (1958) has taken the same approach in training indi-

I am indebted to Dr. Paul C. Rosenbloom of the Minnemath Center, Univer-y of Minnesota, for interesting me in the study of the evaluative thinking of mathe-itics teachers and for making available the data used in preparing this chapter.

viduals to think creatively. Stein (1958) has maintained that an enviro
ment conducive to creativity must be free of hostility, criticism, a
evaluation. Rogers (1951) has contended that external evaluati
should be absent if creativity is to flourish. According to him, exter
evaluation is always a threat, elicits defensiveness, and results in der
ing the awareness of some area of experience.

Although the trend toward the abandonment of evaluation has
least shaken us out of the praise-blame, positive-negative, reward-pu
ishment dichotomies, it too has been unsatisfying. These new concep
have not given teachers the practical guidance they require in develo
ing the various thinking skills. Teachers simply cannot escape the
evaluative roles; evaluation pervades almost all of their classroom b
havior. Some researchers have pursued a more direct approach to t
actual classroom teaching situation. McKeachie (1958), for example,
the basis of learning studies in college classes, sees evaluation as a po
erful force in stimulating learning and thinking. The accumulated e
dence along this line tells teachers to model their evaluation procedur
to harmonize with their objectives. If teachers want students to thi
creatively about course materials or to evaluate course materials in ma
ing decisions, they must construct tests and assessment devices whi
will evaluate these kinds of achievements. This still does not tell t
teacher *how* to fulfill his evaluative role.

McDonald's (1959) concept of teaching as hypothesis making a
hypothesis testing offers a possible escape from the dilemmas of negati
vs. positive evaluation, evaluation vs. no evaluation, and the like. Th
would make the process of evaluation, as it is used to guide the learni
and thinking processes, one of hypothesis making and testing. M
Donald sees the teacher as engaged in an uninterrupted cycle
evaluation, generating and testing hypotheses about more adequate pr
cedures, always tentative in his conclusions.

In this chapter I have made a groping attempt to analyze t
nature of the evaluative behavior of mathematics teachers participati
in the Minnesota National Laboratory for the Improvement of Se
ondary Mathematics under the direction of Professor Paul C. Rose
bloom. This excursion began when Professor Rosenbloom handed r
two sets of logs of teacher and pupil activities, each consisting of t
reports of five seventh-, eighth-, and ninth-grade mathematics teache
One set of logs had been submitted by the five most effective teache
participating in the 1958–59 study, as determined by the regressi
coefficient of the post-test achievement scores of their pupils on the pr
test achievement and aptitude scores. The other set had been submitt
by the five least effective teachers on this criterion. Without indicati
which was the effective and which was the ineffective group, Rose
bloom challenged me to devise some way of analyzing the thinking

ese two groups of teachers in such a way as to differentiate between em. It seems appropriate to report this exploratory work as a study of e role of evaluation and creative thinking, since the experimental athematics materials place a great deal of emphasis upon learning by scovery, creative thinking, and the like, and since the analysis of the ta came to center upon the teacher's evaluative thinking.

The Minnesota National Laboratory

The Minnesota National Laboratory for the Improvement of Secondary Mathematics was established in 1958 to provide facilities for atewide testing of the mathematics materials to be produced by the tional School Mathematics Study Group (SMSG, *Newsletter*, No. 2, '59). This Laboratory is part of the Division of Instruction in the innesota State Department of Education. During its first year, the boratory conducted two experiments, one in the seventh and eighth ades and one in the ninth grade. Twenty-one teachers participated in e first and fifteen in the latter. In 1959–60 the experiment included a tal of 127 teachers from grades six through twelve.

Both standard tests and tests devised by Rosenbloom and Edward . Swanson have been used in evaluating achievement. Below the ninth ade, the School and College Ability Test (SCAT) were given as a easure of aptitude, and in the ninth grade and above the Differential ptitude Tests (DAT) were given. The Sequential Tests of Educaonal Progress (STEP) in Mathematics were given as a pre- and poststs in September and May, respectively. The measure of effectiveness ed in identifying the most and least effective teachers is the regression efficient of the post-test achievement scores of their pupils on the prest achievement and aptitude scores.

Although it is not appropriate to detail here the ambitious and gorous program of the School Mathematics Study Group and the innesota National Laboratory, information concerning their basic obctives are essential to an understanding of the analyses reported herein. hese are interestingly set forth in the following statement from a imeographed leaflet entitled "School Mathematics Study Group":

. . . The number of our citizens skilled in mathematics must be greatly creased; and understanding of the role of mathematics in our society is ow prerequisite for intelligent citizenship. Since no one can predict with rtainty his future profession, much less foretell which mathematics skill ill be required in the future by a given profession, it is important that athematics be so taught that students will be able in later life to learn the w mathematical skills which the future will surely demand of many of them.

Procedures

The data pertinent to this study are the daily logs submitted l teachers participating in the SMSG program during 1958–59 a1 1959–60. Teachers were instructed to pick any two days during the fi1 week. For the next week, they selected any two of the other three da of the week. They continued in this way throughout the term. Th1 were asked to report teacher activities concerning the following:

1. Advance preparation
2. Introduction of present phase of work
3. Demonstrations
4. Questions raised by teacher
5. Explanations to class
6. Explanations to individuals
7. Independent time
8. Homework assigned
9. References assigned
10. Material studied by teacher
11. Suggestions
12. Evaluation of effectiveness of material, teaching, and learni1

They were also asked to consider the following aspects of pu1 activity:

1. Group activities
2. Individual activities
3. Evidence of interest in nonassigned work
4. Class discussions
5. Incidents of discovery or nondiscovery
6. Extra problem solving
7. Math club
8. Fair exhibit
9. Choice of courses for next year

The logs were of a free-response type, some giving an excelle1 picture of the thinking activities of the teacher and his pupils and othe revealing little information concerning this process.

First an attempt was made to categorize the activities reported i 1958–59 according to Guilford's classification (1959a) of mental oper; tions: cognition, memory, convergent thinking, divergent thinking, an evaluation. Under *cognition*, we placed activities involving recognitio1 familiarity, awareness, knowledge about, appreciating, and the lik *Memory* included activities involving memorizing, remembering, reca1 g, knowing thoroughly, learning thoroughly, and the like. Under *nvergent thinking* were included getting the correct answer, solving oblems correctly, having the proper attitude, and the like. Under *vergent thinking*, we counted problem solving where there is no one rrect or accepted best answer, independent thinking, constructive nking, creative thinking, original work, questioning, inquiring, and e like. *Evaluation* included critical thinking, assessing, evaluating, dging, making decisions, comparing, and contrasting.

The logs analyzed according to this procedure were those sub- itted by the five most and five least effective teachers in the 1958–59 periments, as identified by the regression coefficients already de- ribed. The analyses were completed without knowledge of the effec- veness classification of the teacher. Teacher and pupil activities were alyzed separately and compared by means of chi-square.

Our definition of evaluative behavior was elaborated and reported tivities re-analyzed to understand the differentiating characteristics of e evaluative thinking of these two groups of teachers. When the)59–60 data became available, they were similarly analyzed for evalu- ive thinking. Approximately 10 per cent of the teachers at each grade vel were chosen at each extreme. This gave fourteen in each group, ightly over 10 per cent (one in sixth, four in seventh, two in eighth, ie in ninth, two in tenth, two in eleventh, and two in twelfth).

Three categories of evaluative behavior were used: negative evalu- ion, positive evaluation, and trouble-shooting or hypotheses-making pes of evaluation. The following are examples of each:

egative evaluation

Class is too large and abilities too widespread.
They didn't get this lesson very well.
Students had some difficulty rounding off to desired figure.
Pupils showed inability to ferret out method by themselves.
Some students are becoming bewildered as they are confronted by
these proofs.
These materials are very poor.
The wording caused trouble.
Morale is very low.

ositive evaluation

This material is excellent.
The pupils were enthusiastic and had fun.
I like these questions.
Presenting large numbers was very simple and none of the pupils
had any difficulty.

Good response so far.

Many really shouted when they realized what _____ stood f
so it's good for something.

My top five students were real enthusiastic and helped to carry t
class along.

These were easy to understand and teach.

Trouble-shooting; hypothesis making and testing

The pupils are having a very difficult time with proofs. I thi
maybe they have a mental block against three-space ideas.

The students have, I think, in the backs of their minds the id
why don't we do this the way we always have—why make su
a production out of this? My explanations satisfy but not alwa
completely.

I had noticed some difficulty in the writing of congruence in pro
lems such as one and eight in problem set 6-1. As a result of t
observation, I made models of the square, isosceles triangle, a
equilateral triangle. . . . The problem of writing congruenci
seemed to be much less once students had seen concrete e
amples.

Those who have a natural space visualization talent get along re
well but for the others it requires some real hard work.

Students are gradually accustoming themselves to new notatio
the old traditional ideas seem still to linger in their minds.

I believe the students learn better at this point if they present t
proofs than if I do it.

Generally students respond well when information and conclusio
are based on general discussion, assigned work, and relative
simple ideas. When ideas become more general or require
sembling of other ideas to bring out the desired conclusio
then the student flounders.

This class seems very alert to everything in these units, probal
because this is a change from the regular work they had l
year.

My group seems much too "grade-conscious," to the extent th
fear of making a mistake hampers their progress. The boys a
more adventuresome than the girls and have a much more
laxed attitude. The girls are inclined to be tense and wary.

The exercise on page 4 might have worked out better as a blac
board discussion where the student might have "discovered" t
principle that Gauss used.

The basic criteria for assigning an activity to this last category

ιt it must show that the teacher has identified a specific difficulty and
s advanced some hypothesis concerning its cause or remedy, or has
ted such a hypothesis.

Results

MENTAL OPERATIONS OF TEACHERS AND PUPILS

A total of 142 logs of the most effective and 162 logs of the least
ective were available for analysis, or an average of 28.4 and 32.4 per
ιcher, respectively. The number and percentage of activities classified
ιo each of the five types of mental operations reported by the five least
ιd five most effective teachers in the 1958–59 experiment are presented
Figure 14.1. It will be noted that the distribution of activities among
ε five types of mental operations for the two groups differs signifi-
ιntly. The more effective teachers tend to report proportionately fewer

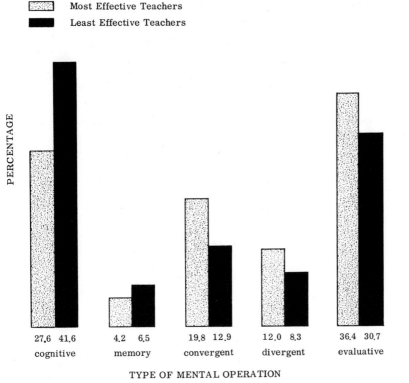

Most Effective Teachers
Least Effective Teachers

PERCENTAGE

| 27.6 41.6 | 4.2 6.5 | 19.8 12.9 | 12.0 8.3 | 36.4 30.7 |
| cognitive | memory | convergent | divergent | evaluative |

TYPE OF MENTAL OPERATION

FIGURE 14.1 *Percentages of Each of Five Types of Mental Operations Reported by Five
ιst and Five Most Effective Teachers in 1958–59 Experiments*

cognitive and memory activities and more of the "thinking" activiti (convergent, divergent, and evaluative).

Figure 14.2 includes a similar set of data for the pupils of the fi

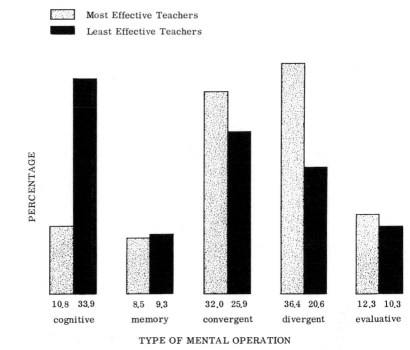

FIGURE 14.2   Percentages of Each of Five Types of Mental Operations of Pupils Repor by Five Least and Five Most Effective Teachers in 1958–59 Experiments

least and five most effective teachers. Here it will be noted that pr portionately more of the thinking and fewer of the cognitive activiti are reported by the most effective teachers.

EVALUATIVE THINKING OF 1958–59 TEACHERS

In classifying and tabulating the activities, I became aware th the behavior classified as evaluative in one group was quite differe from that classified as evaluative in the other group. It was then that decided to re-analyze in greater depth the evaluative thinking of the teachers in an attempt to understand the sensed differences. The da presented in Figure 14.3 summarize the results of this re-analysis. will be observed that in this analysis a larger number of activities we treated as evaluative thinking than in the original analysis. This is d primarily to the fact that some of the activities originally classified

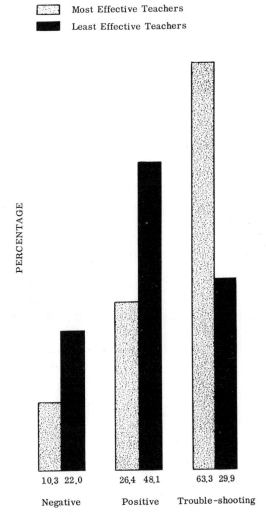

FIGURE 14.3   *Percentages of Each Three Types of Evaluative Thinking Manifested by Five Most and Five Least Effective Teachers in 1958–59 Experiments*

creative thinking" and placed under the divergent thinking category were evaluative in nature. This shift occurred primarily in relation to hypotheses and the suggestion of possibilities for "improving" some aspect of the process.

It will be seen from Figure 14.3 that the effective teachers reported far more of the trouble-shooting and hypothesis-making activities than did the least effective teachers. The less effective teachers tended to report proportionately more negative and positive evaluation than the more effective ones.

The daily logs submitted by the 14 most and 14 least effective teachers in the 1959–60 experiments were analyzed in the same way as those of the five most and five least effective ones in the 1958–59 studies. A total of 607 logs for the most effective group and 616 for the least effective were available for analysis. Thus, we have a mean of 43.4 for the high group and one of 44.0 for the low group, considerably better returns than in 1958–59. The results of this analysis are presented in Figure 14.4. It will be noted that the results are essentially the same as for the 1958–59 analysis. Among the least effective teachers, however, there was a proportionate increase in the trouble-shooting or hypothesis-making activities with an accompanying decrease in negative and positive evaluations.

A closer examination of the activities classified as trouble-shooting or hypothesis-making in the two groups provided several clues for refining the system for analyzing evaluative thinking. Among the least effective teachers, there seems to be a far greater tendency than among the most effective ones to report hypotheses which are so general as to be of little value. The two outstanding favorites of this group of teachers are:

They have difficulty with _____ because they can't read.
The bright ones had no difficulty, but the slow ones found it quite difficult.

These teachers also seemed to depend rather heavily upon tests to do their trouble-shooting diagnoses in a mechanical sort of way. There also seemed to be a characteristic tendency among this low group to report their hypotheses as conclusions or as hypotheses already tested rather than in the hypothesis-making form.

Of special interest are the logs of two teachers who were among the most effective in 1958–59 and among the least effective in 1959–60. Both are classified as among the best qualified teachers in the experiment. Most strikingly different are the logs of Teacher A who, in 1958–59, submitted forty-two logs with a total of eighty-three activities which could be classified as evaluative behavior, and in 1959–60 returned sixty-six logs reporting only twenty-five activities which could be classified as evaluative. In 1958–59, her logs reflected keen sensitivity to the difficulties of her pupils and a wealth of ideas about their nature and treatment. Her 1959–60 logs reflect none of this alertness. The pattern

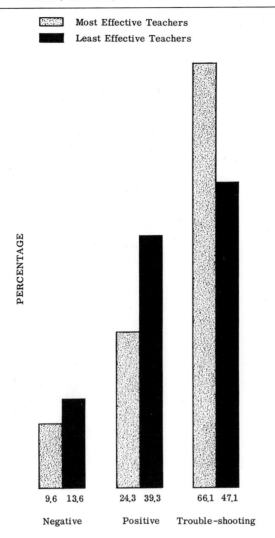

PERCENTAGE

9.6   13.6   24.3   39.3   66.1   47.1

Negative   Positive   Trouble-shooting

TYPE OF EVALUATIVE THINKING

FIGURE 14.4 *Percentages of Each of Three Types of Evaluative Thinking Manifested by ourteen Most and Fourteen Least Effective Teachers in 1959–60 Experiments*

f evaluative thinking is also different. In 1958–59, 17 per cent of her valuative responses were positive; 11 per cent, negative; and 72 per ent, trouble-shooting or hypothesis-making. In 1959–60, 64 per cent 'ere positive; 20 per cent, negative; and 16 per cent, trouble-shooting r hypothesis-making. In other words, the pattern of Teacher A's evalu-tive thinking was typical of her effectiveness category.

Teacher B presents a somewhat different problem. His pattern of valuative thinking is fairly consistent. In 1958–59, his evaluative think-

ing was scored as 63 per cent positive, 4 per cent negative, and 33 pe
cent trouble-shooting or hypothesis-making. In 1959–60, the percentage
were 41, 7, and 52, respectively. His logs for both years reflect suc
enthusiasm and energy that one would expect at first glance that I
would be an effective teacher. His logs are characterized by extreme
positive evaluations, and if we were to rely only upon the net gains
his pupils, he would again be among the most effective teachers. Neve
theless, one might suspect that he is himself so creative and energet
that he gives his pupils little opportunity to learn creatively, and th
his set for positive evaluation is so strong that he may be unaware of th
difficulties which his pupils are experiencing. In 1959–60, there is als
a recurrent note of pressure to "cover material" and a lack of time fc
pupils to discover, solve problems, and think.

Discussion

The major function of this chapter has been to set forth the de
velopment of the author's experiences in trying to discover clues on th
kind of thinking which differentiates the performance of the most an
least effective teachers in experimental courses involving creative think
ing. In spite of the many defects in the data, however, it seems rathe
clear to the author that the most effective teachers do *more thinkin*
than the least effective ones and that their evaluative thinking is cha
acterized by the *trouble-shooting or hypothesis-making* kind of evalu
ation rather than positive or negative evaluations. Since one of th
objectives of the experimental courses is to teach mathematics in such
way that students will be able in later life to learn the new mathematic
skills which will be demanded, such a finding appears to be especiall
salient.

I have no desire, however, to delude the reader concerning th
scientific rigor of the study. There are many defects in the data. Som
teachers submitted logs for two days each week for every week in th
school term, while one teacher in 1958–59 submitted only six logs. Som
logs supplied data which were easy to analyze, while some like those c
Teacher A in 1959–60 supplied very little data which can be analyzec
Thus, categorized activities rather than teachers have been chosen a
the unit for analysis. Logs might also have been chosen.

Evaluation of pupil achievement in terms of the objectives of th
SMSG program also poses difficulties, not only in determining teache
effectiveness, but also in the operation of the experimental progran
Although Professors Rosenbloom and Swanson are developing suc
tests, much importance is apparently being attached to the results c
traditional standardized instruments such as the STEP tests. Many c

ıese difficulties are reflected in the following account of a trouble-
ıooting activity of one of the more effective teachers in the 1958–59
udy:

> I had to use one class period to pep talk students because they were
> ⸀orrying about taking an achievement test in May on the regular funda-
> ıentals. Some of the girls were worked up to the point of crying because
> ıe test is largely traditional material, much of which they will not have had.
> ⸀lost of them scored above grade level last year and they are afraid of the
> omparison this year. They have been assured that the fact that they have
> ⸀ot had this material will be taken into consideration, but they were still
> ⸀orried. I think that I convinced them that this course has increased their
> erception to the extent that they will be able to figure out many things that
> ıey haven't had, partly because they are no longer bewildered by something
> ⸀ery different and are more aggressive and ready to tackle something new
> ⸀ithout as much fear of making a mistake. Without this course they might
> ⸀ot even try to solve something unfamiliar, such as the area of a circle or the
> ⸀imple interest formula.

Professor Rosenbloom has discussed the need for appropriate
ıeasuring instruments in *SMSG Newsletter No. 2* issued in June 1959.
⸀he development of such instruments requires new concepts and time.
⸀hus, it is almost unavoidable that the assessment procedures which
ıust be used during the initial stages of experiments such as these are
ınachronistic. This will be remedied only by time, hard work, and test-
ıaking ingenuity.

Summary

The data analyzed in the study described herein are the daily logs
⸀f teachers participating in the 1958–59 and 1959–60 SMSG experiments
ınder the direction of the Minnesota National Laboratory for the Im-
ırovement of Secondary Mathematics. Teacher effectiveness was deter-
ıined from the regression coefficients of post-test achievement scores
⸀f pupils on pre-test achievement and aptitude scores. Thirty-six teach-
⸀rs of seventh-, eighth-, and ninth-grade mathematics participated in
⸀he 1958–59 experiments, and 127 sixth- through twelfth-grade teachers
⸀ook part in the 1959–60 experiments.

First, the daily logs of the five most and five least effective teachers
⸀n the 1958–59 experiments were analyzed in an attempt to determine
⸀he types of mental operations represented by the teacher and pupil ac-
⸀ivities reported. Guilford's mental operations (cognition, memory, con-
⸀ergent thinking, divergent thinking, and evaluation) were adopted for
⸀his purpose. The analyses indicated that the distribution of activities

MINNESOTA NATIONAL LABORATORY - MATHEMATICS SECTION
DAILY LOG

Teacher _____ Grade _____ Date _____

Material covered on this date:_____ _____

Part I. Teacher Activities

Approximate time spent in preparation of this lesson: SMSG materials_____
_____Other texts, professional literature, etc. _____ Original work_____
Found need to learn more mathematics? Yes _____ No _____

CHECKLIST: Enter in the blanks at the left a single check (✓) for each activity
you engaged in at least once during this lesson and a double check (✓✓) for each
activity which occurred continuously or three or more times.

____ 1. Assigned homework, outside class activities, etc.
    ____ 1.1 Assigned problems from text
    ____ 1.2 Assigned problems from supplementary sources
    ____ 1.3 Assigned problems you developed
    ____ 1.4 Assigned problems requiring a correct solution
    ____ 1.5 Assigned problems requiring divergent solutions
    ____ 1.6 Assigned problems requiring application of rules or principles
    ____ 1.7 Assigned problems requiring discovery of new rules or
             principles
    ____ 1.8 Assigned sustained project requiring three or more days

____ 2. Explained new material
    ____ 2.1 Routinely followed text or teacher commentary
    ____ 2.2 Used special device suggested by SMSG materials
    ____ 2.3 Used special device adapted from colleague or other source
    ____ 2.4 Used original device or procedure you developed
    ____ 2.5 Made quick test (question, problem) to find out if explanation
             had been comprehended

____ 3. Conducted learning and thinking activities of previously assigned material
    ____ 3.1 Answered pupil questions
    ____ 3.2 Gave correct solution to problem(s)
    ____ 3.3 Stimulated pupil(s) to find correct solution
    ____ 3.4 Gave alternative or divergent solution to problem
    ____ 3.5 Stimulated pupil(s) to find alternative or divergent solutions
    ____ 3.6 Asked pupil(s) to reproduce previously presented ideas,
             information, or solutions
    ____ 3.7 Had pupil(s) present solutions to new or assigned problems
             at blackboard
    ____ 3.8 Stimulated competition within class
    ____ 3.9 Had pupils to work in pairs or other small groups

____ 4. Evaluated pupil achievement
    ____ 4.1 Gave test or check-quiz
    ____ 4.2 Discussed or analyzed test results
    ____ 4.3 Pointed out defects in pupil solution(s)
    ____ 4.4 Pointed out other approaches or solutions
    ____ 4.5 Analyzed causes of errors or inability to solve problems
    ____ 4.6 Praised pupil for correct solution
    ____ 4.7 Praised pupil for original solution or unusual idea

____ 5. Used special teaching aid
    ____ 5.1 Film or other commercially produced audio-visual aid
    ____ 5.2 Visual or audio-visual aid you developed
    ____ 5.3 Special reference, magazine article, pamphlet, etc.

____ 6. Other activities (specify): (Use back of page.)

Checklist of Pupil Activities

Enter in the blanks at the left a single check (√) for each activity you observed at least once for one or more pupils, a double check (√ √) for activities observed at least once for a majority of your pupils, and a triple check (√√√) for activities occurring more than once for a majority of the pupils.

Evidences of interest, motivation, curiosity

____ 1. Evidenced having studied assigned material
____ 2. Evidenced having read or studied unassigned material
____ 3. Evidenced having discussed work outside class with one another, parents, etc.
____ 4. Asked question(s) which indicated curiosity
____ 5. Asked question(s) which indicated learning difficulty
____ 6. Took notes on lecture, solution of problems at blackboard, etc.
____ 7. Aggressively kept trying to understand, solve problems, etc.
____ 8. Became frustrated; gave up trying to understand, solve problems, etc.

Evidences of learning

____ 1. Reproduced previously presented ideas and/or solutions
____ 2. Used newly acquired vocabulary
____ 3. Recognized correct principle for solving a problem; applied principle correctly
____ 4. Solved new problems similar to previously explained ones
____ 5. Helped fellow pupils solve problem, learn principle, etc.
____ 6. Organized information, ideas, symbols into an optimal sequence
____ 7. Identified errors or defects in solution proposed by classmate(s)
____ 8. Identified errors or defects in solution by teacher, text, or other authority

Evidences of thinking

____ 1. Discovered relationship between two ideas, concepts, etc.
____ 2. Discovered complex relationship in pattern or system of symbols
____ 3. Visualized what a pattern or set of relationships would look like if rearranged.
____ 4. Explored visually several solutions, courses of action, etc.
____ 5. Saw beyond the immediate and obvious
____ 6. Produced a diversity of possible solutions, applications of principles, etc.
____ 7. Abandoned conventional approach and thought of original solution
____ 8. Produced clever or uncommon responses
____ 9. Worked out the details to develop a general idea, solve a problem, etc.
____ 10. Suggested a symbol (word, letter, number, etc.) that will satisfy a given relationship
____ 11. Used a principle, object, concept in a new way
____ 12. Suggested improved or new way of working, functioning as a class, etc.

Other activities not included above

____ 1. _____
____ 2. _____

If pupils experienced any particular difficulty in learning this material, please indicate the nature of the difficulty and what you did to cope with the problem. Also please add your evaluation and comments concerning the SMSG materials. (Use back of this page.)

among the mental operation categories for the two groups differed si͵
nificantly. The more effective teachers tended to report more thinkir
activities (convergent, divergent, and evaluative) than the less effectiv
ones who reported proportionately more recognitive and memory a
tivities.

A new scheme was then devised for analyzing the evaluative b
havior of these teachers as reflected in their logs. The categories use
were: negative evaluation, positive evaluation, and trouble-shooting ͼ
hypothesis-making and hypothesis-testing evaluation. The more effectiv
teachers were found to report far more of the trouble-shooting or h͛
pothesis-making type of activity, whereas the less effective ones reporte
more negative and positive evaluation. The logs of the fourteen moɪ
and fourteen least effective teachers in the 1959–60 experiments weɪ
analyzed according to the same procedure with essentially the saɪ
results. Detailed examination of the hypothesis-making behavior of theɪ
two groups indicates that the thinking represented by the hypothesi͛
making behavior of the less effective teachers tends to be too generɑ
stereotyped, and vague to be of real value. These teachers also tend ͼ
report conclusions or hypotheses as having been tested rather than a
tual hypotheses about the reasons for difficulties and possibilities coɪ
cerning their solution. It was also suggested that teachers whose evaluɑ
tions are predominantly positive may actually be unaware of the di
ficulties their pupils are having in learning. They may perform ͼ
creatively themselves that they give their pupils no opportunity ͼ
learn creatively.

New reporting forms and procedures were devised in an attemͽ
to collect a more adequate set of data in the future studies, assess tɦ
effects of the experimental SMSG materials, and provide informatic
concerning the characteristics of the evaluative thinking of effectiv
teachers. The basic checklist developed is shown on the two precediɪ
pages. In addition, a different creative problem-solving exercise is givͼ
each month.

HOW
DIFFERENT
CULTURES
EVALUATE
CREATIVE
CHARACTERISTICS

15

Perhaps one of the most powerful ways in which a culture encourages or discourages creative behavior is the way by which teachers and parents encourage or discourage, reward or punish certain personality characteristics as they develop in children—or the behaviors which manifest those characteristics. Usually this encouraging and discouraging process is accomplished in terms of what parents and teachers regard as ideal behavior or the kind of person they would like to see a child become. For this reason, I believe it is tremendously important that we find out what teachers and parents in various cultures consider an ideal personality. Thus, we started asking parents and teachers what kind of persons they would like their children or pupils to become.

From the very outset of this inquiry, we expected to find within each culture some values which encourage creativity and some which discourage it. We also expected to find differences and similarities both within and among different cultures. We believed, however, that it would be useful if we could identify in a culture those values which

The author is indebted to Drs. Alex Osborn and Sidney J. Parnes of the Creative Education Foundation, Buffalo, N. Y.; Dr. Pramila Phatak of Baroda University, India; Dr. Bonifacio Pilapil of the Philippine Normal College, Manila; Mr. John Caroussos of Athens, Greece; Dr. Dietmar Schenitzski of the State University of New York College at Geneseo, New York; and Mr. Wolfgang Koeplin of Berlin, Germany, for their assistance in collecting the data on which this chapter is based.

encourage or discourage creative development and if we could identif
the similarities and differences both within and among cultures. It
the purpose of the study described in this chapter to contribute to th
goal. Although this exploration has for some time been quite out o
hand and will require volumes to report, this chapter will be concerne
with only five cultures or subcultures, one each in the United State
Germany, India, Greece, and the Philippines.

Procedures

THE IDEAL PUPIL CHECKLIST

The Ideal Pupil Checklist, the basic instrument used in this stud
consists of sixty-two characteristics, sixty of which have been foun
through empirical studies to differentiate some group or groups of highl
creative people from a similar group of less creative people. In develoj
ing this instrument we were able to draw from over fifty such empiric
studies. In all of these studies, persons identified as being highly crea
tive on some acknowledged criterion of creative behavior were con
trasted with comparable individuals on personality measures derive
from traditional tests such as the Thematic Apperception Test, th
Minnesota Multiphasic Personality Inventory, the Rorschach Ink Blot
and others. The first checklist derived from a survey of these studie
consisted of eighty-four characteristics, some of which were overlappinj
The list was then pared down to sixty characteristics and then "healthy
and "physically strong" were added for reference purposes.

The characteristics included in the checklist are listed in Tabl
15.1. The following instructions were given to subjects in their ow
language (English, German, Greek, Gujrati).

Check each of the characteristics listed on this page which would de
scribe the kind of person you would like to see the children you teach be
come. Doublecheck the five characteristics which you consider most impor
tant and believe should be especially encouraged. Draw a line through th
characteristics which you consider undesirable and which should be discour
aged or punished.

This procedure has the very desirable advantage of being easy to ad
minister within a very short period of time under individual- or group
testing conditions. Two alternative procedures have been adopted sinc
this study was conducted, one procedure permitting an unlimited num
ber of doublechecks but otherwise identical to that described above
and the other involving Stephenson's Q-sort method which requires th

ubject to rate characteristics according to a forced distribution. For the purpose of obtaining a group picture of what characteristics are most negatively and positively evaluated, however, it is believed that the procedure used in the present study is satisfactory. The instrument is, of course, a rather "coarse-grained" one, but it probably yields about as much precision as is useful for the purposes of this study.

THE CREATIVE PERSONALITY Q-SORT

In order to obtain at least a tentative standard against which sets of group ratings can be compared an Expert Creative Personality Q-Sort was compiled. The sixty-two statements in the Ideal Pupil Checklist were transformed into a Q-sort and rated by a panel of ten judges, all of whom had had advanced graduate courses in personality theory and all of whom had been serious students of the creative personality for at least one year. The judges were given the following instructions:

Use the sixty-two statements on this set of cards to describe your concept of the "ideal" creative personality. At the high end of the scale you should place those characteristics which you regard as most important in the making of a productive creative person. At the low end of the scale you should place those characteristics which you consider least important in the making of a creative personality or which might actually be a liability.

Please follow the following procedure in making your ratings:

1. Pick out the characteristic which you consider most important in the making of a productive, creative personality, and place the card bearing this characteristic in the pile marked "1."
2. Pick out the three characteristics which are the next most important, and place the cards bearing these characteristics in the pile marked "2."
3. Pick out the next five most important characteristics of what you consider the ideal creative personality, and place them in pile "3"; the next nine most important characteristics in pile "4"; and the next thirteen most important ones in pile "5."
4. From the remaining thirty-one characteristics, pick out the one which you consider least important in the making of the ideal creative personality or one which might actually be a liability, and place it in the pile numbered "10."
5. Place the cards bearing the three next least important characteristics in the pile numbered "9," the next five in the pile numbered "8," the next nine in the pile numbered "7," and the remaining thirteen in the pile numbered "6."

The ratings of the ten experts were combined and converted into a

composite Q-sort by adding the ratings received by each item, rankin
the items on the basis of these values, and then placing them into th
original Q-sort distribution (1, 3, 5, 9, 13, 13, 9, 5, 3, 1).

SUBJECTS

The subjects were teachers and other educators from five rathe
distinct cultural groups, tested in their own countries in their own nativ
languages. The United States sample consisted of 264 educators in th
Buffalo, New York, area. The checklist was administered at a meetin
sponsored by the Creative Education Foundation and addressed b
J. P. Guilford of the University of Southern California and mysel
School systems in the northwestern part of the state of New York wer
invited to send representatives to this session, but additional ticket
were supplied some school systems requesting them. Although thi
group may have been somewhat more selected and somewhat bette
oriented to a creative type of education than other groups tested i
the United States, there are reasons to believe that it is fairly representa
tive of United States teachers. The composite rankings of this sampl
correlated .95 with the composite rankings of a sample of 583 teacher
which included groups in the states of Wisconsin, Minnesota, Illinoi
Michigan, California, Georgia, Florida, Nebraska, and Mississipp
The correlations among these several subsamples were all .93 or highe
Thus, we seem to be obtaining a measure which possesses a great de
of cultural commonality within the United States.

The German sample consisted of ninety-four elementary an
secondary teachers in Berlin. The checklist was translated into Germa
by Dietmar Schenitzski, a native of Germany who has lived in th
United States for several years, and Wolfgang Koeplin, who admin
istered the checklist. The responses obtained lead us to believe that
few of the rankings may be peculiar to the Berlin sample. Most of th
rankings, however, appear to be consistent with what are generall
considered to be the cultural values of Germany.

The sample from India consisted of 375 elementary and secondar
teachers in the Baroda area. The checklist was translated into Gujrat
and administered by Pramila Phatak of the faculty of the Department c
Educational Psychology of Baroda University. Subjects were presente
with a checklist which included both the English and Gujrati equiva
lents, since many of the subjects were quite fluent in English. Barod
is a princely state and was formerly a part of the state of Bombay. I
was one of the first states of India to introduce compulsory educatior
Gujrati is the official language of the state, but many of the peopl
speak Marathi. Baroda University is the leading educational center c

ıis rather progressive state, and there is a considerable amount of ducational experimentation under way.

The Greek sample consisted of ninety-four teachers in the area round the city of Volos, coming from such villages, towns, and cities s Gomme, Zagora, Safades, Argalaste, Larissa, Tricala, Elasson, 'saugarada, Sciathos, Velestinan, Calabaca, and Pharsala. The check- st was translated into Greek by John Karoussos, a former student and dvisee of the author and a native of Greece. Subjects were presented checklist containing both the English and Greek words. The teachers ıcluded represent a variety of academic disciplines, grade levels, and ɔcalities.

The Philippine sample consisted of 147 teachers enrolled either ı the Philippines UNESCO National Training Center or the Philippines ʃational Community Training Center. Because all the subjects knew ÿnglish, the checklist was presented to them in English and admin- ;tered by Bonifacio Pilapil, at that time Dean of the Graduate School ıvolved in this UNESCO Center.

ANALYSIS OF DATA

For each of the five cultural groups, an index was obtained for ach of the sixty-two checklist characteristics by weighting responses s follows: two points for a double check, one point for a single check, ero points for no check nor strikethrough, and minus one for each trikethrough. On the basis of these indexes, each characteristic was hen ranked from one (most desirable) to sixty-two (least desirable) or each of the five groups.

In order to measure each set of rankings against the expert ratings or the Ideal Creative Personality, each set of ratings was transformed nto the Q-sort distribution and then correlated with the expert ratings ıy standard Q-sort procedures.

Results

Table 15.1 contains a summary of the composite rankings by the ive cultural groups for each of the sixty-two items. Numerous similari- ıes and differences are noted in these rankings. Some of the major ɔultural values become apparent when we examine the list on page 228 ɔf the ten most valued characteristics of each group.

Even as we examine this list of the ten most favored characteristics ɔf each of the five groups, we begin forming an impression of the cul- ural values which encourage and discourage creative behavior. Missing

TABLE 15.1 Summary of Composite Rankings by Five Different Cultural Groups of Characteristics Contained in Ideal Pupil Checklist

Characteristic	United States (N=264)	Germany (N=93)	India (N=375)	Greece (N=94)	Philippines (N=147)
Adventurous	19	10.5	25	52.5	24.5
Affectionate	40	46	9	18.5	10
Altruistic	36	22	23	8	44
Always asking questions	38.5	30	43	27	37
Attempts difficult tasks	18	5	15	20.5	22
A self-starter	8	14.5	7	30	28
A good guesser	50	45	34	34	54
Bashful	57	53	54	47	59
Becomes preoccupied with tasks	41	12	26	57	43
Considerate of others	4	16	35	13	5
Critical of others	52	29	49	42	46
Courageous in convictions	15	25.5	17	38	15
Courteous	13	18.5	4	10.5	3
Curious	2	7	1	18.5	18.5
Competitive	31	18.5	37	23	32
Desires to excel	24.5	55	11	35	36
Determined	7	27.5	10	14.5	21
Domineering	61	58	50	59	55
Disturbs class organization and procedures	59	62	62	58	60.5
Does work on time	22	10.5	3	12	6
Emotional	54	51	38	23	40.5
Emotionally sensitive	42	42	48	55	51
Energetic	16	31	13	1	11
Fault-finding	58	61	61	52.5	57
Haughty and self-satisfied	62	59	52	62	49
Healthy	14	8.5	5.5	7	4
Independent in judgment	20	6	27	17	23
Independent in thinking	1	4	16	32	18.5
Intuitive	32	37	33	39	42
Industrious	5	3	8	14.5	1
Likes to work alone	43	36	46	23	31

TABLE 15.1 (Cont.)

Characteristic	United States (N=264)	Germany (N=93)	India (N=375)	Greece (N=94)	Philippines (N=147)
Never bored	34	32	19.5	48	30
Nonconforming	48	34.5	55	4.5	53
Negativistic	60	56	57	61	56
Obedient	30	24	2	10.5	2
Popular, well-liked by peers	27	20	28	20.5	27
Persistent	12	23	22	40.5	38.5
Prefers complex tasks	37	38	39	27	38.5
Physically strong	38.5	39	30	36.5	12.5
Quiet	47	34.5	29	25	17
Receptive to ideas of others	6	25.5	44	36.5	26
Regresses occasionally	49	52	59	56	47
Reserved	46	44	47	43.5	33
Remembers well	24.5	13	14	6	8
Self-confident	11	8.5	5.5	9	7
Self-assertive	44	33	45	30	40.5
Self-sufficient	35	42	42	43.5	24.5
Sense of humor	3	2	31	46	14
Sense of beauty	23	27.5	36	16	12.5
Sincere	9	1	18	4.5	20
Spirited in disagreement	45	42	56	40.5	45
Strives for distant goals	21	49	19.5	2	16
Stubborn	55.5	57	58	50	62
Sophisticated	53	50	12	54	50
Timid	55.5	54	53	60	58
Thorough	10	14.5	21	3	35
Talkative	51	60	60	33	60.5
Unwilling to accept say-so	33	47	41	49	52
Visionary	26	48	51	51	48
Versatile, well-rounded	17	17	24	27	34
Willing to take risks	28.5	21	40	45	29
Willing to accept judgments of authorities	28.5	40	32	30	9

from all except the United States and German lists are such characteristics as "independence of thinking" and "independence of judgment." "Curiosity" ranks high in the Baroda, India, group but does not enter the top ten characteristics of the Greek and Philippine teachers. In the Indian list, however, "curiosity" is immediately followed by "obedient," "does work on time," and "courteous." "Remembers well" appears in both the Greek and Philippine lists but not in any of the others.

United States	Germany	India	Greece	Philippines
Independent in thinking	Sincere	Curious	Energetic	Industrious
Curious	Sense of humor	Obedient	Strives for distant goals	Obedient
Sense of humor	Industrious	Does work on time	Thorough	Courteous
Considerate of others	Independent in thinking	Courteous	Sincere	Healthy
Industrious	Attempts difficult tasks	Healthy	Nonconforming	Considerate of others
Receptive to others' ideas	Independent in judgment	Self-confident	Remembers well	Does work on time
Determination	Curious	A self-starter	Healthy	Self-confident
Self-starter	Self-confident	Industrious	Altruistic	Remembers well
Sincere	Healthy	Affectionate	Self-confident	Willing to accept judgments of authorities
Thorough	Adventurous	Determination	Courteous	Affectionate

We obtain a better index of the extent to which the values of each culture conform to creative values as measured by the expert sorts of the Creative Personality when we examine the coefficients of correlation between the composite ratings of each culture with the expert sort. These data are shown in Table 15.2. It will be noted that all of the coefficients of correlation are relatively low, indicating that according to expert judgment, all five of the cultures contain values which are inimical to creative development and behavior. The United States and German groups would appear to have less than the other three groups, however, with India, Greece, and the Philippines following in that order.

Correlations were also run for the composite ratings of the larger sample of 583 United States teachers and for a sample of 257 parents in the Twin Cities area against the expert sort for the Creative Per-

TABLE 15.2 Coefficients of Correlation Between Composite Group Ratings of Five Different Cultural Groups with Composite Q-Sort Ratings of Experts on Creative Personality

Cultural Groups (Teachers)	Number	Coefficient of Correlation
Buffalo, N. Y., United States	264	.51
Berlin, Germany	93	.47
Baroda, India	375	.35
Volos, Greece	94	.32
Manila, Philippines	147	.30

sonality. In both cases, coefficients of correlation of .42 were obtained. This is especially interesting since the ratings of the Buffalo group correlated .95 with those of the diverse group from nine different states. A closer examination of the data indicates, however, that the ratings of the more diverse group do differ from the Buffalo group's ratings on crucial items, such as a greater emphasis on being considerate of others, doing one's work on time, being courteous, and obedient, and less emphasis on courage, criticism, curiosity, emotionality, sensitivity, and independence of thought.

The data contained in Table 15.3 are designed to highlight the specific characteristics which, according to the expert sort on the creative personality, may be encouraged or discouraged more than might be desirable in the interest of the development of creative personalities. It will be noted that some of the overemphases are common to all or almost all the cultures, while others are peculiar to one or two of the cultures. All five cultures, according to this standard, may be unduly punishing the good guesser, the child who is courageous in his convictions, the emotionally sensitive individual, the intuitive thinker, the individual who regresses occasionally and plays or acts childlike, the visionary individual, and the person who is unwilling to accept something on mere say-so without evidence. On the other hand, all of them may be giving unduly great rewards for being courteous, doing work on time, being obedient, being popular and well-liked, and being willing to accept the judgments of authorities.

It is interesting to note that the United States teachers alone are rated as unduly discouraging strong emotional feelings and unduly encouraging being receptive to the ideas of others. They stand together with Germany and Greece on giving a great deal of encouragement to sense of humor and with Germany on encouraging versatility and well-roundedness. They also stand together with Germany on giving an appropriate degree of emphasis to independence in thinking and together with Greece on giving emphasis to talkativeness.

TABLE 15.3 Characteristics More Strongly Approved or Disapproved by Five Different Cultures (by Two or More Standard Deviations) Than Indicated by Expert Ratings of Ideal Creative Personality

Characteristic	United States	Germany	India	Greece	Philippines
Adventurous (4)	-----	-----	-----	Disc.	-----
Affectionate (6)	-----	-----	Encour.	-----	Encour.
Altruistic (7)	-----	Encour.	Encour.	Encour.	-----
Always asking questions (4)	Disc.	-----	Disc.	-----	Disc.
Attempts difficult tasks (4)	-----	-----	-----	-----	-----
A self-starter (4)	-----	-----	-----	-----	-----
A good guesser (5)	Disc.	Disc.	Disc.	Disc.	Disc.
Bashful (7)	-----	-----	-----	-----	-----
Becomes preoccupied with tasks (3)	Disc.	-----	Disc.	Disc.	Disc.
Considerate of others (6)	Encour.	Encour.	Encour.	Encour.	Encour.
Critical of others (6)	-----	-----	-----	-----	-----
Courageous in convictions (1)	Disc.	Disc.	Disc.	Disc.	Disc.
Courteous (8)	Encour.	Encour.	Encour.	Encour.	Encour.
Curious (2)	-----	-----	-----	Disc.	Disc.
Competitive (6)	-----	-----	-----	-----	-----
Desires to excel (6)	-----	Disc.	Encour.	-----	-----
Determined (4)	-----	-----	-----	-----	-----
Domineering (7)	-----	-----	-----	Disc.	-----
Disturbs class organization and procedures (6)	Disc.	Disc.	Disc.	Disc.	Disc.
Does work on time (8)	Encour.	Encour.	Encour.	Encour.	Encour.
Emotional (6)	Disc.	-----	-----	-----	-----
Emotionally sensitive (4)	Disc.	Disc.	Disc.	Disc.	Disc.
Energetic (5)	-----	-----	-----	Encour.	-----
Fault-finding (6)	Disc.	Disc.	Disc.	-----	Disc.
Haughty and self-satisfied (9)	Disc.	-----	-----	Disc.	-----

Note: Number in parentheses indicates composite Q-sort rating of experts

TABLE 15.3   (Cont.)

Characteristic	United States	Germany	India	Greece	Philippines
Healthy (6)	Encour.	Encour.	Encour.	Encour.	Encour.
Independent in judgment (2)	Disc.	-----	Disc.	Disc.	Disc.
Independent in thinking (2)	-----	-----	Disc.	Disc.	Disc.
Intuitive (3)	Disc.	Disc.	Disc.	Disc.	Disc.
Industrious (5)	Encour.	Encour.	Encour.	-----	Encour.
Likes to work alone (5)	-----	-----	-----	-----	-----
Never bored (6)	-----	-----	-----	Disc.	Disc.
Nonconforming (5)	-----	-----	Disc.	Encour.	-----
Negativistic (7)	Disc.	-----	-----	Disc.	-----
Obedient (8)	Encour.	Encour.	Encour.	Encour.	Encour.
Popular, well-liked by peers (7)	Encour.	Encour.	Encour.	Encour.	Encour.
Persistent (4)	-----	Disc.	Disc.	Disc.	Disc.
Prefers complex tasks (5)	-----	-----	-----	-----	-----
Physically strong (7)	-----	-----	Encour.	-----	Encour.
Quiet (7)	-----	-----	Encour.	Encour.	Encour.
Receptive to ideas of others (6)	Encour.	-----	-----	-----	-----
Regresses occasionally (5)	Disc.	Disc.	Disc.	Disc.	Disc.
Reserved (8)	-----	-----	-----	-----	-----
Remembers well (5)	-----	-----	-----	Encour.	Encour.
Self-confident (4)	-----	-----	-----	-----	-----
Self-assertive (4)	-----	-----	-----	-----	-----
Self-sufficient (5)	-----	-----	-----	-----	-----
Sense of humor (5)	Encour.	Encour.	-----	Encour.	-----
Sense of beauty (5)	-----	-----	-----	-----	-----
Sincere (5)	Encour.	Encour.	-----	Encour.	-----
Spirited in disagreement (6)	-----	-----	Disc.	-----	-----
Strives for distant goals (4)	-----	Disc.	-----	Encour.	-----

Note: Number in parentheses indicates composite Q-sort rating of experts

TABLE 15.3 (Cont.)

Characteristic	United States	Germany	India	Greece	Philippines
Stubborn (8)	Disc.	Disc.	Disc.	-----	Disc.
Sophisticated (9)	-----	-----	-----	-----	-----
Timid (9)	-----	-----	-----	-----	-----
Thorough (5)	-----	-----	-----	Encour.	-----
Talkative (7)	-----	Disc.	Disc.	-----	Disc.
Unwilling to accept say-so (3)	Disc.	Disc.	Disc.	Disc.	Disc.
Visionary (3)	Disc.	Disc.	Disc.	Disc.	Disc.
Versatile, well-rounded (6)	Encour.	Encour.	-----	-----	-----
Willing to take risks (3)	Disc.	Disc.	Disc.	Disc.	Disc.
Willing to accept judgments of authorities (10)	Encour.	Encour.	Encour.	Encour.	Encour.

Note: Number in parentheses indicates composite Q-sort rating of experts

Discussion

On the basis of the data which have been presented in this chapter there are a couple of important conclusions about which we can feel rather certain and many about which we can speculate. The data certainly support the conclusion that, insofar as creative values are concerned, all five of the cultures have some features which support creative behavior, while others have questionable value and certain others are downright detrimental. The specific data provide hypotheses about the ways by which each culture might more adequately serve the needs of the creative person and encourage more creative kinds of behavior.

It is interesting to note that the coefficients of correlation of the values of the five cultures with the values of the experts on the creative personality agree rather well with some of the other comparisons which have been made of the creativity of various modern cultures. It will be recalled that the United States and Germany lead, with India, Greece, and the Philippines lagging some distance. Bloom (1958), who has discussed at length some of the factors in the culture of India which work against creative achievement, has given some interesting comparative statistics on a number of criteria. For example, he points out that in the period 1901–1955, in the fields of physics, chemistry, physiology, and medicine, the number of Nobel Prize winners by country are as follows: Germany, forty-one; United States, forty; United Kingdom, thirty-two; France, fifteen; India, one; and Japan, one. None were from Greece or the Philippines. He also cites observations concerning the various kinds of performance by graduate students in United States universities, interviews with Indian "intellectuals" and educational leaders, records of inventions, and the like. Bloom and others have identified a number of factors in the culture of India which work against creative achievement. These and other considerations will be examined in some detail in another report of creative development in India.

Needless to say, the data which have been presented in this chapter possess a number of limitations which should be considered in interpreting the findings. No argument is made for the representativeness of the sample. Our experience indicates, however, that samples as large as the ones which have been used in this study seem to be rather representative of the larger cultures from which they are drawn. For example, correlations among several samples from quite scattered parts of the United States range from .93 to .97, and the Buffalo sample used in this study correlated .95 with a composite sample containing teachers from nine different states. Also, the Baroda sample used herein correlated .86 with the ratings of a group of teachers in New Delhi, India. Regrettably, we do not have similar data for Germany, Greece, and the Philippines. We can, however, compare the data from this study with other knowledge we have about the cultural values of these countries.

Summary

On the basis of empirical studies of creative persons' personalities, a checklist of characteristics important in the creative personality was compiled. This checklist was administered to groups in the general areas of Buffalo, New York, United States; Berlin, Germany; Volos, Greece; Baroda, India; and Manila, Philippines. Rankings were obtained on each of the sixty-two characteristics comprising the checklist for each of these five cultural groups. These rankings were converted to the standard Q-sort distribution and compared with the Q-sort distribution derived from the ratings of a panel of experts on the creative personality. The data for each of the five cultural groups were also factor analyzed to reveal differences with each culture. It was found that the values of the United States and German samples correlate more closely with the ideal creative personality as judged by the panel of experts than the other three cultures. India comes next with Greece and the Philippines lagging. It is clear that all five cultures have some values which support creative behavior and others which are inimical to creative behavior. Specific under- and overemphases were identified for each of the five groups. Teachers need to examine critically their values and ask if the way they encourage and discourage various personality characteristics is in harmony with the development of potentiality.

HELPING
CHILDREN
VALUE
THEIR
IDEAS

16

The great thinkers of the world have had to have confidence that their own thoughts were valuable. Otherwise, they would not have been willing to spend most of their lives bringing into being the great advances in our civilization. Often, this struggle has been without financial profit and in opposition to the established ideas of the day. Can we assume from this that the creative individual knows automatically when his ideas are worthwhile? Although it is true that successful creative people value their ideas and trust in their perceptions, many of our most important scientific discoverers have been tortured by doubts about the worth of their ideas. What is sadder is that in many cases, men have developed important ideas but have not had sufficient faith in their value to develop them fully or to make them known, lest they be scorned. This has unduly delayed progress and robbed the discoverer of his merited reward.

Even when lower levels of creativity and less spectacular creative achievements are involved, the importance of a person's own evaluative behavior is widely recognized. For example Rossman (1931, 1964), in studying the psychology of the inventor, concluded that the noninventor merely "cusses" the deficiencies of the environment, whereas the inventor engages in a more constructive type of behavior—"This is the way to do it." Pepinsky (1959) in three different types of situations

I am indebted to Dr. Kaoru Yamamoto, Mr. Vincent Johnson, and Miss Roberta Hiller for their assistance in preparing this chapter.

found that those persons who were regarded as independent and original in their productivity believed that what they did would make a difference in the organization. Original ideas came from those who place a high value on individualism and see standing out from the crowd as a potential symbol of success rather than failure. Such persons also state criticism in a constructive and depersonalized way. Carl Rogers (1954) has emphasized the importance of the internal locus of evaluation in creativity and trust in one's own organism to perceive reality as one mark of the psychologically healthy person.

Although we do not yet understand fully how a person achieves confidence in the value of his ideas and is able to recognize when his ideas are valuable, it seems rather certain that it has its beginnings in childhood. It is my belief that every person should realize he can do some sort of original work that has some merit. If this realization were cultivated in childhood, we would not have so many adults with a sense of futility about doing something original.

But what can teachers do to encourage this attitude? Out of his own rich experience in helping children gain power by recognizing the value of their ideas, Mearns (1958) suggested five approaches. The first is simple *acceptance*. The teacher must receive each crude product of creative effort, asking only if it is original and sincerely meant. Such a procedure removes fear and sets up hope of success, stimulating the urge to create anew. A second approach is that of *approval*. The teacher must find something to approve in each effort. The approval must be only for the original element, not the parts that are imitations, if confidence is to be built in the worth of the child's own ideas. Mearns holds that correction has no discouraging effect at this stage. Thus, a third approach is *criticism associated with strong general approval*, which he believes to be profitable when mutual trust has been established. The fourth approach he calls "*indirect technique*," maintaining that the best teaching is so indirect that it is not noticeable. For example, he would make no mention of the principles of composition and design until they appeared in the child's own writing. The fifth approach, Mearns called "*the miracle*," a sudden birth of high accomplishment which occurs when all the lines of communication have been opened by a general acceptance of all sincere attempts at creative expression. The worth of the idea is then so strong that almost everyone is aware of its value.

The study described in this chapter is actually the story of one of my own attempts to develop and test one procedure for helping children learn to value their own ideas. As the reader will see, I was perhaps the chief learner, but I believe that through the experience many of the children who participated did learn to value their ideas and those of their classmates.

Procedures

Children whose ideas are respected that their ideas develop confidence. N.B. consider a

SUBJECTS

The subjects of this study were the 100 children enrolled in the third, fourth, fifth, and sixth grades of the University of Minnesota Elementary School, each class being limited to 25 pupils. Although the University Elementary School is not a school specifically for gifted children, a large percentage of the children enrolled would be classified as gifted by most criteria—achievement well above grade level, mean IQ of about 127, and high scores on tests of creative thinking. Their parents possess a high level of education (median education of fathers is five years of college and of mothers, four years of college) and come largely from such professions as university teaching, medicine, law, engineering, journalism, government work, industrial research, and the like. Most of the teachers of the school are young, talented, and provide considerable opportunity for learning in creative ways. Some of the teachers involved in the present study, however, rather definitely preferred the more authoritarian ways of teaching.

EXPERIMENTAL PROCEDURE

The four teachers involved in the study were asked to go ahead with regularly scheduled activities and not to give their pupils any "extra" instruction in creative writing during the six-week period of the study. An attractive magazine consisting of the writings and illustrations of the children involved in the study was used as the medium through which we tried to help the subjects learn to value their own ideas. Through this medium, we hoped to stimulate these 100 children to do a great deal of writing on their own and to form the habit of recording their ideas—something children do not normally do. Most important, it was hypothesized that they would learn to value their own ideas and those of their peers and that this would be reflected by growth in creative writing.

The experiment was launched with the following instructions presented both informally and in mimeographed form:

Your ideas are important! But their value is lost unless you record them—"write them down." People have their best ideas at the funniest times and places. In fact, many of the world's greatest inventors and scientific discoverers say that their great ideas occurred to them when they were in the bathtub, at church, or just walking along. It pays to have an "idea trap"— a small note pad and pencil or something similar for recording your ideas when they occur and before they are forgotten.

During the next six weeks we would like *you* to "trap" your ideas. As ideas for stories, poems, jokes, songs, and the like come to you, write them down. If you think of an idea in the middle of an arithmetic lesson, you may not be able to write it out just that minute, but you can write down just a few words to remind you of your idea later. Then, the first chance you get write it out in detail.

This is the way our creative writing project will work—. . . . Every time you think of a new, interesting, or unusual idea, write it down. You may write it in the form of a story, poem, song, play, joke, game, or in whatever way you like. You might want to illustrate it with a picture. Write about unusual and interesting daily experiences in school, in the neighborhood or at home, weekend experiences, your reactions and feelings about school activities, unusual ideas for new inventions, discoveries, games, and the like.

. . . As soon as you have written down your idea—*trapped it*—put it into the large brown envelope which you have been given. Keep adding to it. Each Friday, you will be asked to choose from your envelope the idea you think others will enjoy most. These will be turned over to me or one of my assistants. We shall pick out the ideas that we think others will enjoy reading and each week, a magazine containing *your* ideas will be "published." You will receive a copy of this magazine and will see your ideas and those of other University Elementary School boys and girls "in print."

In brief, this is what we want you to do:

1. Today, write a 15-minute story just for practice—a brief workout.
2. By tomorrow, try to think of a name for the magazine. Write your suggestion on the white card in your envelope along with your name and give it to your teacher.
3. As you write down your ideas, put them into your envelope.
4. Each Friday for the next six weeks, pick out the writing which you think will be of most interest to others.
5. Don't throw any of your ideas away. You may like some of them better when you read them again in two or three weeks.

Remember—your ideas are important. Others will enjoy reading them, but they become lost if you don't write them down.

Each pupil was presented with a large brown envelope which was to serve as the "bag" for his "trapped" ideas and a copy of the foregoing statement. On Fridays, one of the experimenters visited the four classes and asked each pupil to select from his envelope those productions which he thought others would enjoy most. From these, selections were made for the children's own weekly magazine, named by them *Ideas of the Week.*

Each of the six issues of *Ideas of the Week* had an attractive colored cover whose design was selected from drawings submitted by the children. Items were divided into five sections: Stories, Poems, Inventions, Opinions, and Jokes and Cartoons. The magazine was distributed each Thursday afternoon to help stimulate writing on the evening of the day before new ideas were to be submitted. Much enthusiasm was demonstrated at the time copies were delivered. The deliverer was practically mobbed on each occasion. Interest also ran high among parents, teachers, and members of the research staff. During the six weeks of its publication, *Ideas of the Week* grew from the first issue's eleven pages to twenty-four pages of items in the sixth issue.

ASSESSMENT INSTRUMENTS

To help evaluate the outcomes of the experiment, all subjects were asked to write an imaginative story at the beginning and end of the experiment. As in other experiments on creative writing described in this volume, subjects were asked to write about animals or people with divergent characteristics, such as "The Dog That Doesn't Bark," "The Woman Who Can But Won't Talk," "The Doctor Who Became a Carpenter," and "The Flying Monkey." (The complete lists of subjects are given in Appendix A.) Three scores were chosen as most appropriate in terms of the goals of the study: Yamamoto's Composite Creativity Score, Torrance's Revised Originality Scale, and Torrance's Interest Scale.

At the end of the experiment, each pupil filled out a two-page questionnaire concerning his own experiences during the six-week period and his evaluation of his writing experiences. Each pupil was also interviewed by Miss Roberta Hiller, the editor of the magazine. Except for some highlights from Miss Hiller's analysis, this chapter will be limited to qualitative evaluations and an analysis of the pre- and post-stories written by the subjects.

Results

Some of the research staff's most important learnings from the study are those which occurred in our week-by-week contacts with the 100 children participating in the study. There is no question but that the study generated a great deal of enthusiasm, and almost all the children demonstrated obvious delight with each other's productions and with seeing their own productions in print. The teachers and many of the parents also manifested very clearly their sheer enjoyment of the magazine. The growth in creative writing of some of the children who contributed almost weekly was also obvious. Through the interviews and questionnaires administered at the end of the experiment, it was also clear that even some of the noncontributors came to value the ideas of their peers.

Many of the children's creations yielded fresh insight into the emotional problems and conflicts of creative children. In one of her stories, a highly imaginative fifth-grade girl symbolized what seems to be a central problem of many children in the intermediate grades—a dilemma which causes many to sacrifice their creativity. She called her story "The Green Pig":

> Once upon a time in a far off land there was a magic farm that no one ever visited.
>
> Many different animals lived there. The odd thing about these animals was that they were different colors from regular animals.
>
> The cows were pink, the horses were purple and the hens and chicks were blue! All the pigs were green. That is, all except for one little fellow who was just plain pink. Nobody wanted to be near him or play with him because he wasn't green. And this little pig was very, very sad.
>
> One day, as he was walking along he saw a great big puddle of mud. He splashed and rolled in it because he loved the mud.
>
> When the little pig came out of the puddle, he was all *green!* And he stayed green for all of his life. And all the other pigs began to play with him.

Even the pre-test, however, produced what has come to be a classic symbol of the problems of many highly creative children, the story of "Glob-Blob, the Duck Who Wouldn't Quack" by a sixth-grade girl:

> Whack! Whack! They were after him again—the Ladies Duck Aid Society, with their hair up in pin curls and their screaming, fat ducklings swimming and holding onto their skirts. They never failed. Alas! It was getting too much for little Glob-Blob. Every day there would be quacking and screaming of ducklings while poor Glob-Blob would run as fast as he could to get away from the vicious ducks.
>
> The reason for this was because poor Glob-Blob would not quack. So every day the Ladies Duck Aid Society would chase Glob-Blob, for they said it was for the good of the ducks, and it was not only right but they were doing him a good turn.
>
> It was lucky for Glob-Blob that the ducks were fat and flabby, for if they were limber, I will not mention what would happen. But, one day, these lazy ducks did reduce, and when chasing Glob-Blob dealt him a good many hard blows. And the next day, poor Glob-Blob was at

last doomed. The vicious quackers came and the chase was on. Glob-Blob was failing. It is a shame that so noble a duck should be doomed, but "That is life," said Glob-Blob to himself as, slowly but surely, he dropped to the ground. The quackers, very pleased with themselves, sat down for a chat.

But I shall always remember Glob-Blob and his death. So I shall let him finish his journey, where there will be no more quackers and chasers, and where at last, he may have passionless peace forever.

As the project progressed, the research staff noticed that animals were frequently chosen as main characters of stories and poems by pupils in all four grades. It was also noted that many children used animal behavior to symbolize and to lampoon human behavior. In followup interviews, a sixth-grade girl gave this answer to our query about the reason for her use of animals as main characters, "I can't write stories about people; they don't make sense. People are so limited in what they can do. I'd rather write about animals. I can make them do more things—especially *small* animals." The following story points up what she meant:

Once there was an ant that wasn't very smart, for when winter came he had no chocolate tarts.

The reason is very simple. In the fall who would want to gather them when the weather is so beautiful? So he just played all day and when winter came he had no food.

Oh . . . he must have been hungry and almost starving, the poor little ant.

Have you ever been hungry and starving? . . . Well . . . poor little ant . . . well, have you?

It isn't much fun; the little ant hungry and starving and almost dying.

Have you ever tried gathering chocolate tarts in the winter? Well? . . . Well?

Oh, no! I just found out this ant is just plain lazy and wants sympathy!

He ruined my story!

The editors almost overlooked the merits of this story and included it in the first issue only because so few items had been submitted. They were quite surprised to find that it was voted by the children as one of their favorites, both in the first issue and in the entire set of issues.

In their "Opinion" articles our young authors discussed some of their problems quite frankly. The following editorial, "Parents View of TV," was voted the most popular of the entire writing project:

Ever since the first time I watched television, my parents have told me what it does to me.

When they get mad at my brother or me because we don't do something, they start in about how TV affects us.

When my mother tells us about it she starts with, "You can just sit in front of that box for hours upon hours!!! But do you ever read or go outside?"

Then she answers her own question with "No!"—which of course is not true, because we are forced outside most of the time. And once in a while we go outside on our own!

From here on, the story is different, all except for my dad's opening line, which goes something like this: "Since you are infatuated with the commercials and hypnotized by the shows, you never leave the set. Now this has caused a defect in your hearing and seeing!"

Well, that also is not true because I can see and hear as well as I would like to.

The process of interviewing the subjects at the end of the study proved to be an illuminating one. The subjects seemed to remember quite clearly the source of their ideas. When they sensed that their ideas were being respected and written down, they tried to substantiate in detail their reactions. There was tremendous uniformity of answers both within and between grades. The following are some of the highlights from Miss Hiller's summary:

1. Children in grades three through six can be stimulated to record their ideas on their own. Of the 100 subjects, 90 contributed items. Pupils wrote outside the school's regular curriculum. No special time was set aside by teachers, but youngsters could write and illustrate their ideas when they had completed regular assignments.

2. Third-graders were highest in productivity. Twenty-three of the twenty-five class members contributed fairly regularly, with *poems* submitted more often than any other type of item. (See detailed results later.)

3. Significant sex differences appeared on total number of items contributed during the six weeks of the project. Girls contributed a larger mean number of items than boys, statistically significant at the 5 per cent level of confidence.

4. Majority of the subjects said their ideas occurred to them in school. Reading and arithmetic periods were cited most often.

5. Ideas came in parts, or evolved in "stages," reported the majority. Ideas were rarely "full blown" when the subjects became aware of them.

6. In grades three through five, the majority did their writing in school—after work was completed, at lunchtime, or during recess. Pupils in grade six, however, showed a definite tendency to write at home.

7. When asked whether they "rough draft and rewrite" or "write just once" the items they handed in, third- and fourth-graders tended to write just once. But fifth- and sixth-graders tended to rough draft (as many as two or three times) and then write their final copy.

8. In early stages of writing, pupils sought "evaluation" from outside sources. Evaluation centered on advice on grammar and punctuation. The *final copy* was circulated for praise and assurance that it's "suitable" and "good enough" for handing in.

9. Teachers were sought for evaluation on grammar and punctuation. Parents were mentioned, too. When praise and encouragement were sought, peers of the same sex and same grade were approached most often.

10. Although pupils volunteered they had learned to value their ideas, they stressed the need of a "reason to write." Three weeks after the last issue of the magazine appeared, 67 per cent of the contributors had written nothing at all. Only 33 per cent had written one item or more. A highly creative third-grader represented reactions to this point when he said, "The magazine helps me put my ideas on paper. I think up many thoughts but never put them down before."

11. Students were unanimous in praise of the magazine. They liked the idea of having a unique publication of their own. One third-grade boy summed up the students' sentiment. He said, "I like to write and be like an author." Another third-grade boy said, "I learned how it is to have things in a real magazine. And now I write much more." Said a fifth-grader, "I think many people never knew they could write anything good. But when you've got something to write for, you can write a lot easier."

12. The ten pupils who did not contribute at all gave as their reason, "I have trouble thinking of things." However, later discussions with them revealed them to be "social isolates" who felt their work would be rejected on the basis of their lack of popularity, or the "slow learners" who were fully occupied with completing school work on time.

We found many evidences that the subjects learned to value their ideas. The noncontributors, too, exhibited great enthusiasm for their classmates' creations. Pupils accepted so thoroughly the importance of their ideas that very vocal objections were raised in response to the small amount of editing done by Miss Hiller. She had been instructed to make corrections in spelling and grammar, errors which might prove embarrassing to the author when they appeared in "print." Every effort was made to maintain the integrity of the child's ideas, his style, the flavor of his writing, and the like. During the fourth week of the project several fifth-grade pupils penned very irate complaints. The following sample complaint was published in the fifth issue of the magazine

> Dear Editors:
>
> I don't think you should change our poems, stories, etc. around I know you are trying to make them better, but sometimes the way people write things—no matter whether it makes sense or not—is the way people want them.
>
> In poems this is especially true. Sometimes certain punctuation express an awful lot.
>
> Please try and understand the way we feel about it.

A complaint not selected by the editor, perhaps out of deference and kindness to me, is one which I shall never forget and one which may in some respects give us the most important finding of the study. I reads as follows:

> Dr. Torrance, you told us that our ideas are important. The way ou stories and poems have been changed around makes us wonder.

This experience shows how easy it is for adults unconsciously and un knowingly to communicate to children that their ideas are *not* important As one evidence of this fact, I have presented the Glob-Blob story o the duck that won't quack to at least a dozen audiences and have in cluded it in two or three different journal articles. In each case, the opening has always been "Quack! Quack!" rather than "Whack! Whack! I was not aware of this error until I re-examined the original data in preparing this chapter almost three years later. Now that I see thi error, I think, "Whack! Whack!" makes a much more charming begin ning than "Quack! Quack!" It is certainly more original.

The following response to complaints about overediting by Mis Hiller did little to appease the irate fifth-graders. (They were extremel cold and unresponsive to my efforts to "warm them up" to the tas of writing the final test story. As a result it will be noted in the em pirical data which follow that their writing showed regression on two of the three criteria used.)

> To Readers of *Ideas of the Week:*
>
> Some say "clothes make the man," that a person's appearance i everything. Others believe only the *man* himself is really important. Hi thoughts, his character, his actions are all that really count.
>
> And words are like clothes. Sometimes when you write, your word

may not quite fit! Or there may be a few too many so they bulge out of a space! Or your spelling may need mending. Then *tailoring* (editing) is needed.

Your *IDEAS*, the *body* of your writing, are not altered. Editors try not to meddle with the author's own, individual way of expressing himself.

We believe that your *IDEAS* are the most priceless of treasures. If we didn't, *your* magazine would not be titled *Ideas of the Week.*

Your Editor

During the individual interviews, the editor tried again, as the opportunity presented itself, to clarify the reasons for editing. It became clear that when the children understood the purpose of the editing—that is, to improve the communication value of one's writing and to fulfill one's responsibility to the reader—no disagreement arises. If proofreading and corrections had been made at the time of the writing, the writer's enthusiasm might have made it a manageable task. Since the research staff's only contacts with the subjects was to collect articles and deliver copies of the magazine, this was not possible.

The data which provide the major empirical evidence of outcomes of the experience are presented in Table 16.1. It will be noted that the third grade showed rather marked improvement on all three of the criteria. The fourth-graders started at a higher level and ended at a higher level on both the originality and interest measures. Both of these gains were still significant, however, at the 5 per cent level or better. The fifth-graders showed losses on both originality and the composite index of creativity but showed significant gains on the interest measure. The sixth-graders showed statistically significant gains on originality and interest but a slight loss on the composite index of creativity. It must be noted, however, that the mean pre- and post-test scores of these pupils are usually high in comparison to other sixth-grade groups.

These results become more meaningful when we compare them with a control group composed of fourth- fifth-, and sixth-graders in two other schools. From the data presented in Table 16.2, it will be noted that the control group showed generally rather regressive trends rather than gains, and the loss on interest was statistically significant at the 1 per cent level.

Figure 16.1 presents a record of the number of contributions made by each of the four grades. It will be noted that the third grade contributed the largest number of items and that the fourth grade contributed the smallest number. The difference in percentages between the third and fourth grades is significant at the 1 per cent level. The difference in percentages between the third and all other grades combined is significant at between the 5 per cent and 10 per cent levels, and the difference between the fourth grade and all others is significant at the 1 per cent level. Again, this reflects the tendency of fourth-graders to show a drop in creative activities.

TABLE 16.1 Means, Standard Deviations, and Tests of Significance of Difference in Means on Criterion Measures Derived from Pre- and Post-experimental Imaginative Stories

Grade	Measure	Number	Pre-test Mean	Pre-test St. Dev.	Post-test Mean	Post-test St. Dev.	t-ratio
3	Originality	21	8.05	4.26	15.05	6.19	6.1060***
	Interest	21	3.48	1.89	5.05	1.53	3.3733***
	Composite creativity	21	11.76	4.84	14.33	5.82	1.9051*
4	Originality	25	9.32	3.79	14.52	4.49	5.4312***
	Interest	25	3.52	1.36	4.68	1.65	2.7948**
	Composite creativity	25	14.16	4.41	14.92	4.24	0.7978
5	Originality	25	14.68	6.38	14.60	6.30	-0.0783
	Interest	25	4.28	1.59	5.76	2.05	3.0396***
	Composite creativity	25	17.08	3.57	15.40	5.40	-1.8913*
6	Originality	22	17.23	7.47	19.41	6.12	2.1511**
	Interest	22	5.68	1.36	6.95	1.13	4.9645***
	Composite creativity	22	17.23	4.73	15.59	6.12	-0.9991

* Significant at better than 10 per cent level
** Significant at better than 5 per cent level
*** Significant at better than 1 per cent level

TABLE 16.2 Means of Originality, Interest, and Composite Creativity Scores of Pre- and Post-training Stories by Control Groups in Two Schools and Test of Significance of Difference

Measure	Number	Mean Pre-test	Mean Post-test	t-ratio	Level of Significance
Originality	102	9.49	9.06	-0.956	Not significant
Interest	102	4.45	3.88	-3.944	Less than 1 per cent
Composite creativity	102	14.28	14.63	0.788	Not significant

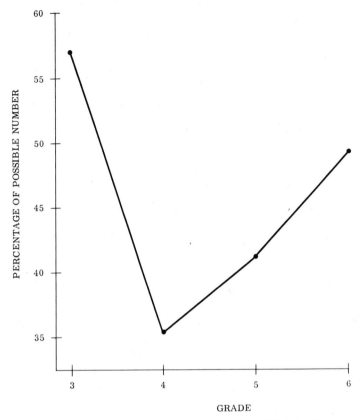

FIGURE 16.1 *Record of Contributions to Ideas of the Week by Grade*

Discussion

The data which have been presented indicate that only in part did the procedures described in this chapter achieve their objectives of helping children learn to value their ideas and improve the creative qualities of their writing. In the case of the regression shown by the fifth grade, it is reasonably certain that the failure was due to negative reactions to overediting. During the first few weeks of the projects, many of these fifth-graders produced some tremendously creative stories, poems, and inventions. Even on the pre- and post-writing measure many of them also showed sizeable gains. The general trend, however, was downward. In the interviews, however, there were at least subjective indications that these children too came to value their ideas. In fact, they resented the fact that others did not seem to value them to the degree that they deserved.

For most of the subjects this seemed to be a new experience and through it they gained a new concept of the meaning of creative writing. The editor was somewhat taken aback by one fourth-grade boy who assured her that he was an "old hand" at creative writing. He reported:

> We do it all the time in our class. In fact, it takes so much of my time that I didn't have a chance to write very often for *Ideas of the Week*. You see, we have to spend our time filling in the blanks in our language workbooks. And it takes the rest of my spare time to write on the blackboard 500 times, "I will not giggle in German class," or "I will not run in the halls."

Quite interestingly the third-graders seemed to respond more favorably to the experimental procedures than any other class. This was of special significance to the research team, since a tentative decision had been made not to include the third grade in the study. A discussion with the third-grade teacher, however, indicated that she felt that these third-graders were ready for such an experience and would profit from it. It will be recalled that they contributed a larger number of items and that they made substantial gains on the three criterion measures of creative qualities.

Summary

Pupils in grades three through six (totaling 100) in one elementary school were encouraged to develop the habit of writing down their ideas over a period of six weeks. At the end of each week, the experimenters visited each classroom and asked that each pupil select one of the ideas from his collection envelope (idea bag) for possible use in a weekly magazine produced by the research staff. The magazine was named *Ideas of the Week* by participants in the study and was issued on Thursday during each of the six weeks of the study. At the beginning and end of the study, each pupil wrote an imaginative story. About one week after the end of the experiment, each pupil was asked to fill out a brief questionnaire giving his reactions to the experience, and each pupil was interviewed about three weeks later by the editor of the magazine. The writings submitted were scored on the scales used in the other creative writing studies already described.

It was found that children in grades three through six can be stimulated to do a great deal of writing on their own, outside the school curriculum. Ninety per cent of the subjects of this study made one or more contributions. Third-graders were highest in productivity and showed significant growth in creative writing as measured by pre- and post-training stories. The fourth and sixth grades also showed growth on two of the three measures. The fifth grade, however, showed fairly regressive trends. In the interviews, a majority of the pupils reported that their ideas occurred to them in school, usually during the arithmetic or reading periods. They also reported that their ideas came in parts or stages. In grades three through five, the majority did their writing in school—after assigned work had been completed, at lunchtime, or during recess. Pupils in the sixth grade, however, showed a definite tendency to do their writing at home. During the early stages, the subjects reported that they sought "evaluation" from outside sources and that the "final copy" was circulated to others for praise and assurance that "it's suitable" and "good enough" for submission. Teachers and parents were sought for evaluation on grammar and punctuation, but praise and encouragement were sought from peers of the same sex and grade. There were many scattered evidences that most of the subjects learned to value more highly their own ideas and those of their peers than they had prior to the experience. They resented most the evaluation represented by minor editing of the items selected for inclusion in the magazine and felt that this was a disavowal of the value of their ideas.

REWARDING
CREATIVE
BEHAVIOR
IN
THE
SCHOOLS

17

Since each of the over twenty small investigations which have been described in this volume have been summarized already, no summary of the separate studies seems to be needed here. Since these studies are interrelated and gain strength from what they add to one another in combination, we do need to ask how all of these studies add up and what they tell us about rewarding creative behavior in schools. Some of the investigations which have been reported have little value, when taken separately. When seen in relation to other investigations, however, they become more powerful and provide guidance in deciding what should be done about rewarding creative behavior in the classroom.

Since a person's way of teaching must be his own personal invention and must come into being through the process of creative thinking, I do not believe that research can ever "tell a teacher what to do." The results of research, however, can serve as a useful guide in the teacher's invention of his way of teaching, just as scientifically developed information can serve as a guide to the inventor of a new machine or the discoverer of a revolutionary, new, scientific principle. It is well known that educational research is a generally neglected resource for improving educational practice. Many of the discoveries of educational research have never been used and it has been estimated (Shane and Yauch, 1954) that it takes between 75 and 100 years for an educational theory to be translated into common practice. Although it cannot be claimed that the findings of the studies reported herein are widely accepted into practice today, we do have considerable testimony from educators throughout the United States that already many of the findings of these studies have been translated successfully into practice. The results of some of these studies were reported to professional groups as early as 1959 and 1960 at national and state meetings and in professional journals. A preliminary summary report was made available in the fall of 1961, and this apparently stimulated a number of people to make interesting applications of the findings. A few of these applications will be reported and discussed as I attempt to discuss the guidance and direction which I believe these studies provide in creating change.

Creating an Environment Which Values Creativity

APPLYING PRINCIPLES
FOR REWARDING CREATIVE THINKING

Although some educators and psychologists have attacked what I have called "principles for rewarding creative thinking" as unvalidated hypotheses, others have attacked them as nothing more than "self-evident truisms or annoyingly pat exhortations." Although I must admit that my observations of classroom teaching made these ideas for rewarding creative thinking seem obvious, I rarely found teachers applying them. If they are self-evident truisms, I was convinced that few teachers acted as though they believed them. Thus, it seemed clear to me that the application of these simple ideas, such as being respectful of children's questions and ideas, could be a very powerful force in bringing about a more creative kind of education. I was also aware of a considerable amount of expert opinion in scattered sources which supported the validity of these ideas.

In my judgment, the data which were presented in Chapter 4 show that many teachers do not understand and accept these ideas and that when they do apply them with fidelity, signs of creative growth are evident. I have been very pleased to note that a number of leaders in the field of creative education have tested and found useful these ideas. Harding (1963) at the Ohio State University reports that he found their experimental application transformed his own teaching. Fine, in his book, *Stretching Their Minds* (1964), described how these ideas have become guiding principles or "rules" at the Sands Point Country Day School of which he is headmaster. He points out that authority prohibits questions but that the rule of the Sands Point Country Day School is:

Treat questions with respect. "Rigid authority deprecates ideas offered by pupils." The Sands Point rule is: *Show pupils that their ideas have value.* "Rigid authority does not provide opportunities for practice and experimentation without evaluation." The rule at Sands Point is: *Encourage opportunities for practice or examination without evaluation, grading, marking.* "Rigid authority does not encourage self-initated learning." The rule at Sands Point is: *Encourage and evaluate self-initated learning. Discuss it, stimulate it, give credit for it* (Fine, 1964, p. 155).

To me, the key concept of Chapter 4 and, to an extent, of all the studies which follow it, is "respect"—respect for the questions and ideas of the child, respect for his right to initiate his own learning effort, and respect for his right to reject, after serious consideration, the adult's ideas in favor of his own. This is a difficult concept to apply consistently. Certainly the teacher should feel free to suggest ideas and to give guidance and direction. The child should be free to reject the suggestion in favor of his own ideas, after considering it and deciding that it is not best for him. Devastating criticism, making fun of the child's remarks, and laughing at his conclusions, however, often hinder the child from expressing himself. It is important that children express themselves, because we will not know what they are thinking unless we let them talk. Neither can we know what children are thinking if we feel that we must "nip in the bud" every idea they initiate.

We can learn some lessons about the role of respect from the studies of engineers and industrial psychologists (Lasswell, 1954). At first, engineers in their investigations of human behavior were primarily concerned with technical factors in production and distribution. Later, they became concerned about the importance of affection and skill. More recently, however, they have been concerned about the importance of respect. They have found that the role of respect is often far more powerful than monetary differences.

In discussing the role of competition among adolescents, Coleman (1961) maintains that the fundamental competition among the members of any group is the competition for respect and recognition from others around them. He found that in different adolescent societies, different achievements bring this respect and recognition. I believe Coleman would say that the removal of creative kinds of achievement as a basis of comparison will not lessen the amount of competition. It only shifts the arena away from creative achievement to other kinds of achievement.

Finally, it should be pointed out that the experiences described in Chapter 4 indicate that our values may cause us to punish creative behavior when we think that we are rewarding it.

IN-SERVICE EDUCATION
FOR REWARDING CREATIVE BEHAVIOR

The in-service education study mentioned in Chapter 5 was inconclusive and illustrates many of the difficulties of conducting research involving this kind of education. Since such studies are expensive, many difficult decisions have to be made regarding the selection of subjects. In this investigation, we chose to randomize the selection of teachers within a single school and run the risk of maximizing the "Hawthorne effect" in the control group. Thus, it seems rather certain from the evidence obtained that the control teachers used as many or more creative activities as the experimental teacher did. At the same time, it also seems rather certain that the experimental teachers fell far short of applying the experimental treatment in a skillful manner.

In spite of the above difficulties, however, there are indications that the in-service education program was successful in a number of ways. The efforts of some of the experimental teachers apparently resulted in one type of creative growth, while those of other teachers resulted in a different kind of creative growth. This is not surprising since the best evidence indicates that creative thinking ability is not a unitary ability. It is to be expected that one type of practice will result in certain types of growth and not in others. The kind of growth may depend in part upon the concept the teacher has of creative thinking. For example, some teachers see elaboration (making things fancy or elaborate) as central to the nature of creative thinking, while others emphasize fluency, perhaps at the expense of elaboration. Still others emphasize originality and give practice in making unusual and clever responses, perhaps at the expense of both fluency (number of responses) and elaboration (detail). With timed tests, such as those used in this study, these differences in emphasis are likely to have strong effects.

Educational change almost always arouses resistance, even when the change is voluntary. In our study, it would have been easy to have gotten one half of the teachers to volunteer for the in-service education program. If we had done this, it is quite likely that we would not have met with resistance. Quite obviously this would not have been fair, however, and the subject teachers accepted this fact. We did encounter resistance, although every teacher appeared cooperative and pleasant throughout the study. Some of the experimental teachers frankly resisted even the notion of rewarding creative thinking. To them, it was "wrong" to reward creative thinking. The formulation of principles such as "Be respectful of the questions of children" and explanations that one of the best rewards for the curious child is to find the answer to his questions perhaps helped somewhat. Some of the teachers felt that creative thinking should not be rewarded and should be engaged in for the pleasure of the process.

Educational researchers conducting in-service education experiments should be prepared to cope with teachers' resistance to change. Adequate time and conditions favorable to continuous interaction between the experimenter and the experimental teachers are needed. Eicholz (1963) has offered an interesting theory on why teachers reject change.

His theory of rejection involves five stages: awareness, disinterest, denial, trial, and rejection. A teacher might be resistant through the early stages and become an accepter, and this occurred in at least one case in our study. The converse may also be true. On the basis of long years of experience and of a study of innovation in five elementary schools, Eicholz believes that five steps are necessary to overcome resistance to change at the various stages in the process of rejection.

First, the ignorance of the teacher about the change must be overcome. We sought to overcome ignorance in the present case by supplying teachers with the manual which had been prepared for the purposes of the in-service education program and by a continuous flow of informative materials and ideas throughout the experiment. These, however, are no guarantee that ignorance was overcome. In fact, it was clear that some of the experimental teachers did not read the materials which were supplied them. Perhaps the best that we can do in schools, however, is to have information about innovations readily available to teachers in lounges and classrooms and to discuss innovations at faculty meetings. Second, the matter of suspended judgment must be considered. Some teachers want to wait and see how good an idea is before they try it. A few teachers, however, are always willing to go ahead and test new materials and ideas. Thus, such teachers should be encouraged to go ahead without trying to involve everybody in the change. A third factor is providing a general environment conducive to experimentation. This is one of the reasons why group or all-school experiments are sometimes useful. A fourth factor, however, grows out of the anxiety of teachers who do not want to change but who witness successful changes among their colleagues. Since this may arouse still greater resistance, it is dangerous to try to force change. A fifth factor arises from the fact that some teachers engage in experimentation to "prove" that the change is harmful. Depending upon the teacher's honesty and objectivity, as well as the desirability of the change, this type of resistance may be transformed into acceptance.

CREATIVE MOTIVATIONS OF TEACHERS

Chapter 5 presents some rather interesting evidence to support the idea that the creative motivations of teachers are a significant factor in the creative growth of pupils. In one study, it was found that the pupils of teachers with high creative motivations made greater gains in creative growth than those in the kindergarten, first, second, and third grades whose teachers had weak creative motivations. This did not occur, however, in the intermediate grades. In another study limited to the intermediate grades, however, it was found that pupils of teachers with high creative motivations made significant gains in creative writing, while those of teachers with weak creative motivations failed to achieve significant growth in this aspect of development. In my opinion, the weight of the evidence in this experiment indicates that efforts to engender greater curiosity and zest for learning among teachers will be worthwhile in terms of the creative growth of their pupils.

In the light of these findings, French's idea (1961) concerning the infusion of the spirit of research into teachers seems quite appropriate. French argues that stimulating habits of questioning orthodoxy, demanding evidence, trying the new or testing the old, and observing what happens should lead to increased teacher effectiveness. This does not mean that teachers should go into the research business but that the adoption of certain habits and attitudes of the researcher is compatible with creative teaching.

CREATIVE ACTIVITIES
IN THE ENVIRONMENT WHICH REWARDS CREATIVITY

The findings reported in Chapter 6 concerning the role of creative activities in the environment which rewards creative behavior may be somewhat disturbing or puzzling to many educators interested in bringing about a more creative kind of education. Of course, there are obviously many facets of this problem which were not considered in these studies. Actually, the results of the studies reported do not tell us that creative thinking activities are unnecessary in bringing about creative growth. They only tell us that something more than creative activities are necessary and that one of the additional factors is the creative motivation of the teacher. This is in spite of the fact that teachers having high creative motivations used more creative thinking activities than their less creatively motivated colleagues.

We cannot ignore the long-standing and widespread advocacy of creative thinking exercises or activities. Binet's "mental orthopedics" undoubtedly played important roles in his work with the mentally retarded child's growth. Marie Montessori's provision for intervals during which children veiled their faces and thought doubtless contributed to creative growth. Dimnet (1930) undoubtedly had good reasons for advocating that children ought to be put through regular thinking exercises in school. Coleman was justified in his objection to the fact that the prescribed exercises of high school students "require not creativity but conformity, not originality and devotion, but attention and obedience" (1961, p. 315). Stein undoubtedly had some empirical basis for his statement that "one of the first things that a college can do is to provide an opportunity for the student to manifest his creative potential" (1958, p. 72). The findings of the studies described in Chapter 6 do not argue against the above conclusions. In fact, they actually support them. They go further, however, in arguing that *creative activities alone are insufficient for producing creative growth*. The suggestion is that the attitudes and values of the teacher and/or of the larger environment must reward creative behavior. *Nothing could be worse than to encourage creative behavior and then to punish such behavior.*

DIFFERENTIAL REWARDS FOR BOYS AND GIRLS

The data presented in Chapter 7 from a variety of sources support in numerous ways the idea that our society rewards boys and girls differently. There seems to be little question but that our society through these differential rewards puts off limits for boys certain areas of awareness and thinking and for girls certain other areas. It seems equally obvious that differential rewards in these ways take a rather heavy toll upon the potentialities of both boys and girls. Specific findings provide clues about what teachers can do to help both boys and girls achieve more fully their potentialities.

It seems rather clear from a number of indications that teachers can improve the education of boys by providing more creative ways of learning and rewarding them for creative behavior. A number of studies have already showed that males in our society excel females in various kinds of problem-solving tasks. Yet observers of classroom behavior rarely find enough problem-solving teaching to record. When we add this to the fact that other measures of educational achievement such as vocabulary, spelling, reading, and the like almost always favor girls, we begin to grasp at least a part of the problem. In one of the studies described in Chapter 7, it was found that when teachers are asked deliberately to reward creative behavior, they usually describe incidents in which boys have been rewarded. This may mean that such a shift in emphasis brings about a better equalization of rewards for boys and perhaps a greater equalization in learning. Of course, it might also mean that teachers reward the creative behavior of boys more frequently than they reward the creative behavior of girls. It might also mean that boys may behave more creatively in the classroom, but even this may mean that girls are rewarded for conforming behavior and are satisfied with this reward.

The results of one of the other studies described in Chapter 7 suggest that we may have been undergoing some social changes which have made it legitimate for girls to be interested in science matters and to enjoy dealing with them. In spite of this change, however, children still value more the science ideas of boys than those of girls. This indicates that many of the preferences of boys and girls are culturally rather than genetically determined.

It is apparent from the data presented that the differential rewards for boys and girls are very pervasive and permeate all areas of their lives. The study of the creative activities done on their own indicates that there are many areas of childhood creative experiencing which seem to be off limits for boys and girls apparently because of their sex. Similar phenomena are found in regard to the occupational goals reported by children and young people. These differential rewards were also shown to be accompanied by differences in such experiencing as manipulation of objects and reading, kinds of experiencing likely to be related to creative achievement. Finally, it was shown that the influence of these differential rewards on the development of the creative thinking abilities is complex but that there are nevertheless differences which can be associated logically with the nature of the differential rewards and their influence on the kinds of experiencing open to boys and to girls.

It would be foolhardy to ask or to expect that boys and girls will be rewarded in the same way. It seems equally foolhardy to place off limits to children so many areas of childhood experiencing and awareness because of their sex.

External Evaluation

ORIGINALITY OF THOUGHT
AND DIFFERENTIAL REWARDS

Although we had anticipated, if not assumed, that rewarding originality would increase the degree of originality found in the creative writing of children and in the number and quality of the original ideas produced by them, we had not expected to find the side effects as complex as they turned out to be. Rather consistently, we found in the studies reported in Chapter 8 and elsewhere that rewarding, encouraging, or otherwise making originality of thinking legitimate does in fact result in greater originality than occurs otherwise. In the writing experiment we found that there was also a tendency for children to write longer stories than otherwise when originality was being rewarded but that they also made more errors, at least in their first drafts. In the other study, it was found that rewarding originality did not interfere with the fluency of ideas and, in fact, tended to increase the number of ideas produced. In still another study not yet reported, it was found that instructions to produce original ideas stimulated greater fluency than instructions to produce a large number of ideas, regardless of their quality. Thus, it seems that making unusual or original ideas legitimate is a more effective way to free individuals of forces which inhibit the production of ideas than is giving instructions to produce a large number of ideas. To add to the complexity of the picture, however, we found in the second study reported in Chapter 8 that flexibility of thinking was unaffected.

Thus, even when we are concerned about creative behavior, we need to decide what kind of creative behavior we want to develop and make our instructions and rewards compatible with the goal.

COMPETITION AS A TYPE OF EXTERNAL EVALUATION

The role of competition in encouraging creative behavior is a complex one, and the studies described in this volume attempt no comprehensive approach to its understanding. In the simple studies reported in Chapter 9, however, it is clear that competition increased the production of ideas, especially original ones. When warm-up or practice experiences were provided, however, much of the advantage which seems to accrue to competition disappeared.

The evidence seems to be sufficiently strong to indicate the need for some reassessment of practices in education regarding competition. It turns out that it is practically impossible to eliminate competition among children. If this proves to be the case, it may then become a matter of maintaining reasonable controls on competition to keep the stresses arising from it from becoming too great and of shifting the focus of competition to other areas or to a variety of areas of behavior.

Many of those who favor scholastic and interscholastic competition in areas other than athletics believe that sporadic and infrequent competition has little effect. The study described in Chapter 9, as well as those described in Chapter 8, suggests that the value of such competition may be underrated insofar as the stimulation of certain types of creative achievements is concerned. They tell us nothing about the long-range effects of continued competition, however. One of the differences between competition as used in Chapter 9 and as used in Chapter 13 is that the former involved individual competition while the latter called for intergroup competition. One of the surprising things about the behavior observed in the intergroup competition, however, was that individual competition still loomed as a powerful force. This was in spite of the fact that deliberate and forceful means were used to make the competition intergroup rather than interindividual. Apparently, at least in our society, interindividual competition is learned very early and appears more natural than intergroup competition.

If we could be successful in schools in stimulating intergroup competition in various kinds of creative achievement, we might thus eliminate or at least reduce one apparently very powerful inhibitor of the development of creative potential. As Coleman (1961) found in his study of adolescent society, the boy who goes all out scholastically is scorned and rebuked for working too hard. The athlete who fails to go all out, however, is scorned and rebuked for not giving his all. Coleman maintains that this is because the scholar's efforts in our present educational structure can bring glory to no one but himself and makes the work of others more difficult. The athlete's achievement, however, appears as a part of a group effort and brings glory to his school or some other group. Thus, he is working for the good of the group.

One factor which worked in favor of competition in both the inter-individual and intergroup competition in these experiments is to be found in the fact that the teacher was not the evaluator. The role of evaluation resided in someone outside the classroom situation and may have been perceived as less threatening than when employed by the classroom teacher. In much of the ordinary competition which goes on within a classroom, the teacher is forced to be the judge as well as the teacher. Perhaps much of the rebellion and conformity which occurs in the classroom may be due to this state of affairs. If an educational system could restore the role of the teacher as teacher and relieve him of the onus of sorting and grading students, we would probably have a higher level of both learning and thinking in schools. It cannot be denied that competition is one means by which challenge occurs, and challenge, if not overwhelming, is apparently conducive to creative achievement.

UNEVALUATED PRACTICE

Although the experiment comparing the effects of unevaluated practice with positive, constructive evaluation was not entirely conclusive, the evidence is strong enough to tip the scales in favor of unevaluated practice. The results suggest that some individuals need the structure given through evaluated practice, while others perform more creatively under conditions of unevaluated practice. In general, the importance of unevaluated practice seems to be clearer in the first four grades than in the fifth and sixth grades. It is interesting to speculate why children in the fifth and sixth grades seem to function at a higher level under the more structured conditions, whereas this is not true in the lower grades. Although the results are not altogether consistent, there are a number of hints that girls may require a higher level of structure than do boys. There are also some indications that some types of creative achievement are more sensitive than others to the influences of unevaluated or evaluated practice. Several different experiments controlling different influences in each will be necessary to elaborate the hypotheses which emerge as side-effects in this study. A number of elementary teachers have reported successful applications of the idea of unevaluated practice. One teacher used it in encouraging creative writing. Whenever a pupil wanted to write without having his work corrected and evaluated, he used a purple pencil from a supply kept on the teacher's desk. The pencils were used frequently at first, and writing became more creative. Soon the pencils were no longer needed, and writing continued to be creative.

CRITICAL AND CREATIVE PEER-EVALUATED PRACTICE

In general, the results of the experiment described in Chapter 11 indicate that pupils in the upper grades do better creative work under creative peer evaluation (suggesting other possibilities) than under critical peer evaluation. To the younger children, differences in the type of peer evaluation appear to make no difference. In fact, the younger children were not very interested in making critical evaluations of one another's work and seemed to pay little or no attention to such evaluations when they were offered. Even in the experiment described in this report, there are indications that consistent use of creative peer evaluation will have more beneficial effects in the lower grades than will critical peer evaluation. In the second task given in the present experiment, both the older and the younger children tended to do better creative work under creative rather than under critical peer evaluation. Even here, however, children in the in-between grades behaved differently. Rather generally the third-grade children tended to perform better under the critical evaluation condition, and the fourth-graders were not differentially affected.

Doubtless, there are conditions under which one type of peer evaluation is more productive than the other. Generally, however, the scales seem to tip in the direction of creative peer evaluation. Developmental differences must be taken into consideration, however.

TALKING WITH CHILDREN
ABOUT THEIR CREATIVE PRODUCTIONS

The study described in Chapter 12 makes no attempt to determine how teachers *should* talk with children about their creative productions. It seeks merely to determine how teachers say that they would talk with children about their creative writing. In my opinion, teachers seriously lack the concepts and understandings necessary to talk with even young children about their creative writing. Teachers tend to oversimplify their comments in terms of generalized praise or criticism, especially insofar as content is concerned. Their concepts about mechanics are somewhat clearer and better defined. This makes teachers hesitant to talk with chil-

lren very constructively about the creative aspects of their writing. It
las occurred to me that teachers might improve their conversations with
hildren about their creative writing by using some of the concepts our
esearch staff developed for use in evaluating the creative qualities of
maginative stories—concepts such as original or surprising endings, un-
isual settings or plots, picturesque speech, vividness, flavor, humor, in-
lividuality of style, imagination, emotions or feelings, curiosity, and the
ike.

Many of the plans offered by teachers for talking with children about
heir creative writing reflect man's strong needs to punish and to pity his
ellow man. Criticism and praise are among the favorite weapons and
lefenses of the respondents. Appeals to the child's own creative resources,
he use of self-evaluative approaches, and the like are rarely used. There
vas little recognition that the mental health of children may interfere
vith both the creativeness and the correctness of their writing. These re-
lections on the data presented in Chapter 12 should not be interpreted
is an admonition against praise or criticism. Both may be necessary and
·ach certainly has its place in talking with children about their writing.
Vly point is that both are probably overused in favor of a more explora-
ory, penetrating, and sensitive thinking together about the creative pro-
luction. Above all, the conversation with the child about his writing
hould encourage him to continue his efforts—efforts which are marked
·y honesty, originality, and freshness of style.

Applegate (1949), who has given sustained and intensive study to
he problem of helping children write, says that she has seen teachers
naim with a red pencil writing that was really brilliant in part. She ex-
)lains that the artist, when writing, is often not a careful person, espe-
·ially during the heat of creation. She also counsels that different
ittitudes should predominate when teachers are talking with children
ibout voluntary stories than when talking with them about assigned
tories. She does not think that voluntary stories should be evaluated un-
ess the writer asks that they be. She feels that such stories were written
or enjoyment and should be enjoyed rather than corrected or evaluated.
;he would talk with children about voluntary stories, if the stories are
)utstanding, show marked improvement, or are far below the level of
he writer's ability. She recommends that children be asked to read as-
;igned stories to the teacher while other pupils are engaged in another
ictivity. During the process the story is discussed with the child.

HOMOGENEOUS AND HETEROGENEOUS GROUPINGS

Neither our results nor those of all of the other studies that have been done on homogeneous and heterogeneous grouping tell us whether homogeneous grouping is "a good thing." In fact, I think these results tell us that the problem is too complex to be answered in this way. I believe, however, that the design of the homogeneous and heterogeneous models developed in the present studies can be used in answering many theoretical questions in such a way as to give useful guidance in exploiting the advantages of both homogeneous and heterogeneous grouping. I believe that the results of the present studies show that homogeneous groups reduce the social stress in groups at all ability levels and elicit all-out responses from children of lower ability, at least for short periods of time.

I suspect that the extremely creative individual will always be rather unpopular among his peers and except in rare circumstances will not become a leader. This is probably "a good thing," since the responsibility of leadership toward other people often prevents a person from experimenting with new and uncertain possibilities and causes him to surrender his imaginative, critical, cynical, devil's advocacy. As Richard Suchman [1] suggests, it may take a lone wolf to penetrate the wall of oversimplification that the nonthinkers build to protect their togetherness. Suchman believes that a classroom full of highly creative youngsters should be highly productive. He says he has found the imaginative and critical hole-pokers are the least disturbed by the hole-poking of others. They welcome this disruptive hole-poking and return the service in kind.

Anyone who has worked with heterogeneous groups of children will report that most highly creative children are difficult to work with in such groups. Frequently, their unusual ideas and brilliant flashes of insight, if communicated, arouse resentment. The resentment and rejection may have either one of two ill-effects on the creative individual. He may become an extremely disruptive influence as a result. Suchman believes that it does not make sense to try to work in a group with highly productive and creative children when the rest of the children simply do not measure up. There does not seem to be any compatible arrangement since the more opportunity you give such a child to exercise his abilities the more hostility you create between him and the others. On the other hand, the more you suppress him, the more he resents you and the entire situation. The highly creative child may also become nonparticipating. In an individual situation, the child may be creative and highly verbal and then may clam up during the group session. It is a considerable risk

---

[1] J. Richard Suchman, Illinois Studies in Inquiry Training, University of Illinois, Urbana, Ill., personal communication, October 21, 1960.

to involve such a child until he feels comfortable in participating. It is a challenge to create a situation in which such a child will become an active participant. If the teacher is able to create a classroom situation in which questions and ideas are respected, nonparticipators may become the most active and valuable contributors.

Two or three school principals have reported very exciting experiments in which they have grouped the classes of certain grades according to the general level of their creative behavior, using a combination of test results and creative achievement as a basis for grouping. In one school, such an experiment is in its third year, and teachers seem to be quite pleased with the outcomes. The problem is a complex one, however. Such a practice certainly cannot be recommended for all schools, and further testing and evaluation are certainly needed.

An example of the type of study needed to determine the differential effects of different approaches to grouping is a study reported by Wanner (1960). This study investigated the differential effects of different seating arrangements on social interaction and independent behavior in sixth-grade classrooms. It was found that if more social interaction is desired, children should be seated next to children of their choice. If more self-reliance is desired, children should be separated from others of their choice. Thus, here as in the studies described in Chapter 13, the decision concerning grouping must be influenced by the type of development which is of concern.

POSITIVE, NEGATIVE, AND TROUBLE-SHOOTING EVALUATION

The study of the evaluative behavior of the more effective mathematics teachers compared with that of the less effective teachers helps to point us away from an obsession with comparisons of the effects of praise and criticism. This study is clearly related to creative thinking, since the experimental mathematics materials used in the study emphasized creative ways of learning mathematics rather than the more authoritarian ways. The results show that these two groups of teachers both offer their students a considerable amount of both praise and criticism, with the less effective teachers offering a greater amount of both praise and criticism than their more effective colleagues. Their more effective colleagues offer instead of praise and criticism a kind of trouble-shooting or hypothesis-making evaluation. These results support the hypothesis of McDonald (1959) that the crucial role of the teacher is that of the hypothesis maker. Having obtained these clues, our task is now one of analyzing more fully the nature of the hypothesis-making evaluations of effective teachers.

CULTURAL DIFFERENCES
IN THE EVALUATION OF CREATIVE CHARACTERISTICS

Using the evaluations of samples of teachers obtained in the general areas of Buffalo, New York, United States; Berlin, Germany; Baroda, India; Volos, Greece; and Manila, Philippines as examples, it was shown that cultures differ rather markedly from one another in terms of the characteristics which they value and encourage or disapprove and discourage. The data indicate that insofar as creative values are concerned, all five of the cultural groups studied have some features which support creative behavior, while others have questionable value and still others are definitely detrimental. The specific data provide hypotheses about the ways in which each culture might more adequately serve the needs of the creative person and encourage more creative kinds of behavior. For example, comparisons with the ratings of experts on the creative personality suggest that all five cultures may be unduly punishing the good guesser, the child who is courageous in his convictions, the emotionally sensitive individual, the intuitive thinker, the individual who regresses occasionally and plays or acts childlike, the visionary individual, and the children who are unwilling to accept things on mere say-so without evidence. All of them may be giving undue rewards for being courteous, doing work on time, being obedient, being popular and well-liked, and being willing to accept the judgments of authorities. The Buffalo, New York, teachers alone are rated as unduly discouraging strong emotional feelings and unduly encouraging receptiveness to the ideas of others. All in all, however, the values of the Buffalo teachers correspond more closely with those of the panel of expert judges and appear to be most compatible with creative development. Germany, India, Greece, and the Philippines follow in that order.

The underlying theoretical rationale developed through work with the Ideal Pupil and Ideal Child Checklists supports the idea that creative people need creative handling, whether in the classroom, home, or factory. Executives who cannot tolerate the independent spirit should not try to supervise the work of creative people. Usually, they will create problems thereby rather than increase productive creativity. Similarly, the teacher who cannot tolerate the independent spirit in children will have difficulty in guiding the learning and thinking of the highly creative child.

Evaluative Behavior of the Individual

HELPING CHILDREN VALUE THEIR IDEAS

Although the experimenters unintentionally committed errors which marred the potential effects of the investigation described in Chapter 15, the experience does indicate that children can be helped to value their ideas and those of their peers. Doubtless this can be accomplished in a variety of ways, but the one used in this instance was encouraging the children to write on their own outside the curriculum and publishing their ideas in an attractive magazine. These experiences were accompanied by creative growth in the third, fourth, and sixth grades. The fifth-grade children became disturbed about the overediting of their writing and, apparently as a result, were unable to rise to their usual heights of creativeness at the time the post-test of creative writing was administered.

One of the serendipitous insights supplied by this investigation is that adults unknowingly communicate to children that they do not regard the ideas of children as valuable without honestly considering them. Perhaps the most important thing that parents, teachers, and other adults can do to communicate to children that their ideas are of value is to listen to their ideas, read them, and try to understand them.

There seem to be many good reasons why we should be concerned about showing children that their ideas have value. The most important motive for creative effort apparently lies within the artist, writer, scientist, or inventor himself. Art educators Conant and Randall (1959) believe that the most effective form of growth measurement insofar as creative art development is concerned is self-evaluation. They believe that this ability can be developed even in the preschool years. Perhaps one of the most important things that educators can do is to recognize that each child can do some kind of original work which has some merit. In-service and preservice education of teachers would be contributing a great deal by removing the erroneous belief that the creative work of teachers and pupils is negligible and not worthwhile. The usual sense of futility about doing something original should give way to feelings of confidence.

Teachers, supervisors, and principals can find many ways of showing children that their ideas have value. Original art work, creative writing, and other productions of children can be displayed in the halls and display cases of the school, in the principal's office, and in the living room of the home. They can be enjoyed in many different ways. Creative writing and other creative achievements outside the curriculum can be used for emotional and intellectual growth among troubled children. The creative achievement may not restore such children to mental health, but it can contribute to such goals.

Children in Defense of Themselves

Almost everyone who has conducted experiments of alternative ways of teaching or learning and has either observed or inquired later about how the subjects *really* learned has been amazed at the extent to which children—and adults too—act in defense of themselves. McConnel (1934), after conducting his well-known study of learning by discovery versus learning through authoritative identification, interviewed many of his subjects. He wrote that he was amazed at the extent to which children acted in their own defense and learned "outside the curriculum" according to their own preferences and "natural ways" of learning. In an experiment involving conditions of boredom, some subjects were not bothered by the boredom because they invented ways of entertaining themselves. Thus, in all the studies described in this volume we can be assured that many of the subjects "acted outside the curriculum" or "outside of the experimental condition" in order to have a better chance to use their best abilities and their preferred ways of learning and thinking. Although we need to learn a great deal more than we now know about what characteristics of learners are most important in planning learning experiences, we believe that the studies reported herein give some anchors to guide our planning, even though some of the anchors are not strong and are not always stable.

INSTRUMENTS
USED
IN
THE
DESCRIBED
STUDIES

Appendix A

Test of Imagination—Form D

The basic test of creative thinking ability used in most of the studies in the present series is the Test of Imagination (Form D). Its evolution and the basic ideas behind it have been described in Chapter 3. The tasks, the instructions for administration, and the available reliability and validity evidence will be presented in this section.

MATERIALS

The materials required for the individual administration of this test include a test booklet for each subject, stop watch, stuffed toy dog (monkey, giraffe, etc. in alternate forms), and print of Tom, the Piper's Son. For the group administration, it is desirable to have colored slides of the toy dog and the picture which are projected on a screen. It is still advantageous to have available for display a model of the toy dog and a copy of the print which is being projected on the screen. This feature is not necessary, however.

ORIENTATION TO THE TEST

An attempt should be made to orient the introduction to the specific group being tested. In general, the orientation to groups usually went something like the following:

The tasks which you will be doing this hour are called tests of imagina
tion. They may also be called tests of your creative thinking ability, your abil
ity to think up ideas. We are finding that this kind of ability is more impor
tant in school success and in life than we used to think. We have given these
tasks to test college students, people in different occupations, elementary
school pupils, high school students, and others. Most of them have enjoyed
doing these tasks and we hope that you will. We also hope that you will do
your very best during this next hour to show how well you can use your
imagination. There are no "right" or "wrong" answers, but we do want you
to give the most imaginative, inventive, and clever ideas you can create. You
will be given several tasks and timed on each. Use your time well and work
as rapidly as you can with comfort.

Now, will you write your name on the face sheet of your booklet, then
the date, and your grade.

TESTING INSTRUCTIONS

Now, I am going to show you a little stuffed toy dog. On the first sheet
of your test booklet, I want you to list the most interesting, clever, and unusual ways you can think of for changing the toy dog so that children would
have more fun playing with it. You will have eight minutes to write down as
many ideas as you can think of. (*Time: Eight minutes after instructions have
been completed.*)

Your time is up on this part. As soon as you have finished the sentence
you are writing, go ahead to Part II. List here the most interesting, clever
and unusual uses you can think of for this toy dog other than as a plaything
These may be uses of it as the toy now is or as it might be changed. For
example, it could be used just as it is for a pin cushion. Or, it could be made
two or three feet tall, and a child could sit on it or ride it. All right, go ahead
and work as rapidly as you can for the next five minutes. (*Time: Five minutes after completion of instructions.*)

All right, your time is up. As soon as you have finished the sentence
you are writing, go ahead to Part III. List on this page the most unusual,
interesting, and clever ideas you can think of for using tin cans. The cans
can be of any size and shape, and you can use as many cans as you like.
You will have five minutes. Go ahead. (*Time: Five minutes after completion
of instructions.*)

Your time is up. As soon as you have finished writing the idea you are
on, go ahead to Part IV. In the next ten minutes, see how many objects you
can sketch which have a circle as the main part. Just use a few lines on the
circles below to identify your ideas which might start: wheel, tire, steering
wheel, etc. Your lines might be either inside or outside the circle, or both
inside and outside. (Demonstrate on blackboard.) If you don't think we'll
be able to guess what object you have sketched, label it. All right, go ahead.
(*Time: Ten minutes after completion of instructions.*)

In individual administration and in testing children in the primary grades, it is necessary for the examiner and his assistants to identify the objects sketched by the subjects.

The remainder of our tasks is what we call the Ask-and-Guess Test. We consider what you do on this part an indication of how well you can use your curiosity about the world in which you live and how good you are at guessing possible causes and consequences of various events. You will be shown a picture and asked to use your imagination about what you see.

On the next sheet, write down all the questions you can think of about the things you see in the picture. Ask questions about any or all parts of the picture and about the events occurring in it. Ask only questions which you cannot answer just by looking at the picture. For example, don't ask, "Is the grass green?" If you are not color blind, you can tell this by looking at the picture. All right, work as rapidly as you can for the next five minutes. (*Time: Five minutes after completion of instructions.*)

All right, your time is up. Turn to the next page as soon as you have finished the question you are writing. In the spaces on this page, list as many possible things as you can think of which might have caused or led up to the action shown in the picture. Make as many guesses as you can of possible causes in the next five minutes. Go ahead. (*Time: Five minutes after completion of instructions.*)

Your time is up. We now come to the last part of the test. On the last page, list as many possibilities as you can of what might happen in the situation pictured. Think of both immediate and long-range consequences. What is going to follow the action shown in the picture? Make as many guesses as you can. Work as hard as you can for the next five minutes. (*Time: Five minutes after completion of instructions.*)

Your time is up. Now pass your booklets to the aisle. We appreciate your hard work and hope that you have enjoyed it. I am sure that we shall learn a great deal from these materials about the way people think.

SCORING

The first four tasks (Product Improvement, Product Utilization, Unusual Uses of Tin Cans, and Circles) were scored for fluency, flexibility, and originality. The Ask-and-Guess Test was scored only for fluency and adequacy of response.

In all cases, *fluency* was determined by counting the number of appropriate or relevant responses given by the subject. Responses reflecting a lack of adaptation to some degree of reality are not counted. For example, responses requiring that the dog be alive are not counted as bona fide responses. The reality requirement is that the resulting product be a toy which would be fun for play.

Flexibility in all cases was determined by counting the number of different categories into which responses can be classified. For each task a scoring guide consisting of an alphabetical list of categories was used. The flexibility categories for the Product Improvement Test are the ones adapted from Osborn's (1957) work: adaptation, addition, changing color, changing shape, combination, division, magnification, minification, motion, multiplication, position, quality of material, rearrangement, reversal, sensory appeal (ear, touch, eye, smell), substitution, and subtraction.

The following are examples of the categories used in scoring the Product Utilization Test: bathroom uses, bedroom uses, business and industrial uses, decorative uses, dining or eating uses, library uses, and living room uses. Examples of the categories for Unusual Uses of Tin Cans are the following: animal waterer or feeder, apparel, art, bank, cage, construction, container, communication, and cooking utensils. The following are illustrative of the categories used in scoring the Circles Test: animal faces, animal parts, animals, audio-visual equipment, balls, buildings, building parts, candy, clocks and watches, coins/money, and containers.

The scoring guides for determining the *originality* index were based on actual tabulations of responses given by subjects covering a broad education span. Approximately 500 records were used in these tabulations and a five-point scale (0, 1, 2, 3, 4) based on the statistical infrequency of the response was used in assigning weights. A few illustrative examples will be given for the Product Improvement Task:

Product Improvement (Toy Dog):

	Weight
Adjustable in length	4
Assemble—dissemble	3
Attach nose loosely	4
Ball to balance on his nose	4
Bark, speak	0
Bark, pull ears to make bark	4
Bark when squeezed	2
Bells on it	3
Bigger	0

The general rule for scoring the *adequacy* of a question on the Ask-and-Guess Test is, "Could the question be answered by looking at the picture?" If the question cannot be answered by looking at the picture, the response is scored as adequate. For example, an inadequate question about the Tom Piper picture would be, "Is the farmer carrying a pitchfork in his hand?" If the subject asked, "Would the farmer really stick the pitch fork in Tom?" he would be credited with an adequate response. The question cannot be answered by looking at the picture. Furthermore, it is a thought-provoking question.

In judging the adequacy of the hypotheses about causation, responses were scored as adequate if they reflect "universal, abstract, necessary causes." Sequences of events of the "this-is-the-way-it-happened" type were not scored as adequate. In the Tom Piper problem, a response such as "Tom and/or his family were hungry or starving" would be judged as adequate. A series of statements such as the following would not be judged as adequate: "Tom ate his breakfast and then he went to school. At recess, he played with Mary and Bill, etc."

The rules for scoring adequacy of consequences are essentially the same as those for scoring causes. The consequence must follow as a logical outcome of the behavior in the picture to be considered adequate. In scoring sequential stories, each action in the story is scored as a separate response and given one point, if it indicates a genuine cause and effect relationship. If the first response in a series is not a logical consequence of the pictured event, the first response is not counted, but succeeding responses are considered adequate if they follow as logical consequences of the others.

INTERSCORER RELIABILITY

Throughout the history of this series of studies, we have experienced little difficulty in maintaining interscorer reliabilities in excess of .90. Yamamoto (1962), for example, reports the following coefficients of interscorer reliability based upon sixty-four test records scored by two independent scorers:

Product Improvement	Fluency	1.00
	Flexibility	.87
	Originality	.98
Unusual Uses (Toy Dog)	Fluency	1.00
	Flexibility	.84
	Originality	.92
Unusual Uses (Tin Cans)	Fluency	1.00
	Flexibility	.87
	Originality	.98
Circles	Fluency	1.00
	Flexibility	.91
	Originality	.98
Ask-and-Guess Test	Fluency	1.00
	Adequacy	.96

In order to maintain quality control, occasional interscorer reliabilit checks are made on each scorer.

TEST-RETEST RELIABILITY

Both as a battery and as separate tasks, Form D has undergone variety of test-retest reliability studies. With a sample of eighty-five stu dent teachers and a time interval of approximately ten weeks betwee tests, Goralski (1964) obtained coefficients of reliability of .82, .78, .5⁹ and .83 on fluency, flexibility, originality, and battery total. Eherts (1961 reported a test-retest reliability coefficient of .88 for twenty-nine fifth grade pupils with an elapsed time of seven months between the tw testings. Sommers (1961) reports reliabilities of .97 and .80 for two dif ferent samples of college students, each about ten weeks apart. With ai elapsed time of two weeks, I obtained a test-retest reliability of .79 with a summer camp population involving subjects ranging from the fourth through ninth grades. The post-testing was conducted under extremely adverse conditions, including extremely hot weather (the warmest expe riences in the area in over five years). Testing samples of 100 to 150 chil dren in each grade from grades two through five, first in the fall and again in the spring, Wodtke (1963) reports reliability coefficients rang ing from .34 to .79.

In a number of studies, test-retest reliabilities have been obtained for separate tasks. Mackler (1962), using three testings and three alter nate forms, each separated by a two-week interval, obtained reliabilitie of .82 (first and second testings), .89 (second and third testings), and .84 (first and third testings) for the fluency score of the Ask-and-Gues Test. Reliabilities of .79, .73, and .68 were obtained for the adequacy scores. With 100 ninth-grade students, McGreevey (1961) obtained alter nate-form reliability coefficients of .79 and .76 on the Ask-and-Gues Test at a single testing. Yamamoto (1962) obtained test-retest reliability coefficients of .83 and .78 on the Ask-and-Guess Test for twenty-two college seniors with an interval of approximately ten weeks between testings.

Mackler (1962), using the same design with the Unusual Uses Tes as he used with the Ask-and-Guess Test (three testings, each two weeks apart), obtained reliabilities of .61, .62, and .71 for fluency, flexibility, and originality between the first and second testings; .75, .74, and .66 between the second and third testings; and .65, .71, and .60 between the first and third testings. Yamamoto (1962a) obtained reliabilities of .75, .60, and .64 for Unusual Uses of Tin Cans and reliabilities of .85, .69, and .77 for Unusual Uses of the Toy Dog/Monkey in the same situation described above.

Yamamoto (1962a) also obtained reliabilities of .69, .64, and .61 on the Product Improvement Test using the toy dog in one case and the toy monkey in another. Rouse (1963), using the Product Improvement Test with thirty-one mentally retarded youngsters with an elapsed interval of about six months, obtained reliabilities of .85, .76, and .68.

The Circles Test has also been subjected to several test-retest reliability studies. Mackler (1962), in the triple testing situation already outlined, obtained reliabilities of .72, .60, and .63 for fluency, flexibility, and originality between the first and second testings; .65, .62, and .81 between the second and third testings; and .47, .60, and .57 between the first and third testings. Yamamoto (1962a), in the situation already specified, obtained reliabilities of .76, .63, and .79. Grover (1963), testing and retesting 101 ninth-grade subjects after an interval of one week, obtained a reliability of .69 on the Circles Test.

VALIDITY

As already indicated in the previous chapter, a deliberate attempt was made in designing tasks, working out instructions for test administration, and developing scoring systems, to build into Form D characteristics which make the best use of what we know about creative behavior. Our general strategy in attempting to establish objective evidences of validity has involved one or the other of the following approaches:

1. Identifying high and low groups on some test measure and then determining whether or not they can be differentiated in terms of behavior which can be regarded as "creative" or personality characteristics which differentiate highly creative persons from their less creative peers

2. Identifying criterion groups on some behavior accepted as creative and then determining whether or not they can be differentiated by test scores

Using the first approach, we formed models of heterogeneous groups on the basis of total scores on Form D and placed them in situations where their behavior could be observed systematically. For example, in a class of twenty-five pupils, the five most creative pupils as identified by this measure were each placed in a different group. Then, the next most creative pupils were each assigned to one of these groups, and so on until all pupils had been so assigned. They were then assigned the task of determining, demonstrating, and explaining the uses, intended and unintended, of a box of science toys. In spite of obvious and sometimes strong social pressures to reduce the productivity of the most creative member of the group, in seventeen of the twenty-five groups (68 per cent) the most creative succeeded in initiating the largest number of ideas during the exploratory phase of the activity. In several other cases, the most creative member initiated only one idea less than the top contender. As a group, they initiated far more ideas than their less creative peers (significant at less than the 1 per cent level of confidence). The observed strategies of the most creative members of these five-person groups in adapting to the pressures of the group were also the same as those generally attributed to creative adults in coping with social pressures in daily life: counteraggressiveness, apparent ignoring of criticism, indomitable persistence in response to frustration, compliance with group demands, clowning, silence and apathy or preoccupation, inconsistent performance, filling the gaps when others falter, and solitary activity of an exploratory and experimental nature.

When matched for intelligence, sex, race, and teacher, the most creative boy and the most creative girl in forty-six classes from grades one through six proved far more frequently than their controls to have reputations for having wild and fantastic ideas, to produce drawings and other products judged as "off the beaten track," and work characterized by humor, playfulness, relative lack of rigidity, and relaxation.

Using most of the tasks contained in Form D (Ask-and-Guess Test, Circles, and Unusual Uses of Tin Cans), Weisberg and Springer (1961) tested a sample of thirty-two gifted (high IQ) fourth-grade children. They made careful personality studies of each of these children and conducted psychiatric interviews with their parents and compared the most creative children in the sample with the least creative. Through psychiatric interviews, the highly creative children were rated significantly higher on strength of self-image, ease of early recall of life experiences, humor, availability of Oedipal anxiety, and even ego development. On the Rorschach Ink Blots, they showed a tendency toward unconventional responses, unreal percepts, and fanciful and imaginative treatment of the blots. Their Rorschach responses also described them as being both more sensitive and more independent than their less creative peers.

Through numerous partial replications of the Getzels and Jackson studies (1962), it has also become clear that tests of creative thinking and tests of intelligence identify different types of gifted individuals. The ways in which they are different describe those high on the measures of creative thinking in a manner which might generally be regarded as "creative." They are perceived by their teachers as less desirable pupils, more difficult to get to know, more playful and less hard-working. They choose occupations which are regarded as unconventional or rare.

Fleming and Weintraub (1962), using essentially the same tasks as are included in Form D, found a coefficient of correlation of −0.41 (significant at the 1 per cent level of confidence) between attitudinal rigidity measured on the Frenkel-Brunswik Revised California Inventory and scores obtained on the creative thinking test battery. The attitudinal rigidity score also correlated $-.37$, $-.40$, and $-.32$ with the originality, fluency, and flexibility scores, respectively. Their subjects were sixty-eight gifted elementary school children in grades three through six.

Yamamoto (1963) obtained coefficients of correlation of .49 and .51 for the fifth and sixth grades, respectively, between composite scores on Form D and a measure of originality based on imaginative stories.

In two as yet unreported studies (Hansen and Blockhus), a group of six high-scoring general business teachers were compared with an equal number of their less creative peers on the basis of intensive observations of classroom behavior and studies of pupils' growth. The more creative teachers behaved in ways which were dramatically different from their less creative peers. They asked more questions—and a greater variety of kinds of questions—gave more illustrations of key concepts, and interacted more with their students. Their pupils also made significantly greater gains in originality on the product improvement, unusual uses of tin cans, consequences, and problem situations.

Using the approach of identifying criterion groups regarded as "highly creative" or "noncreative" on the basis of some independent criterion, several encouraging bits of validity evidence have been accumulated.

As immediate criteria, we have frequently used teacher and peer nominations on various criteria of creative thinking, curiosity, and the like. Quite uniformly we have found that children nominated by their teachers on such criteria achieve higher scores on the tests of creative thinking than do their peers not so nominated or who are nominated as being especially low on the criterion in question. Yamamoto (1962) administered Form D to 569 fifth-grade pupils in one school system. He obtained teacher nominations on such criteria as who thinks of the most ideas, who produces the most original and unusual ideas, who is the first to find another way of meeting a problem, who does the most inventing and developing of new ideas, and who is best at thinking of all the details involved. He used these data to provide a rough validation of the four subscores of Form D. On each criterion, he compared the scores of those nominated with those not nominated. All the differences were clearly significant, except for elaboration, which is not used in the current series of studies.

In the peer nomination studies, results have been consistently significant above the third grade. In other words, pupils receiving a large number of peer nominations on various criteria of creative thinking achieved higher scores on the corresponding measures of creative thinking.

Sommers (1961) used Form D in a validation study which made use of faculty evaluations of industrial arts students who had been observed in courses which provide opportunities for creative achievement. The criterion groups were identified according to faculty nominations based on definitions of creativity and the creative personality. Frequency of nomination and concurrency by other instructors were used. Weightings were assigned nominations from instructors who had made observations of students enrolled in courses permitting substantial creative behavior. Results from Form D were available for ten students about whom there was consensus concerning a high degree of creativity and twelve about whom there was agreement concerning a lack of creativity. The high creatives achieved a mean score of 237 on the battery compared with 179 by the low creatives. The difference in means is significant at less than the 5 per cent level of confidence, and only one of the low creatives achieved a score as high as the mean of the high creative group.

Two additional studies of specially selected groups contribute to the evidence for construct validity. One of these (Wallace, 1961) involves sales production and working in "creative" versus working in "routine, noncreative" departments of a large metropolitan department store. The subjects were sixty-one middle-aged saleswomen who had been working in the department store on an average of about twelve years. According to their sales production (the dollar value of sales per hour of employment) and the amount of customer service required, these saleswomen were divided into four groups: high sales-high service, low sales-high service, high sales-low service, and low sales-low service. When these four groups were compared with each other on their scores on Form D, it was quite clear that the high sales and high service groups scored higher on the measures of creative thinking. Wallace concluded that creative thinking ability does affect sales production and that those who are required to provide a large amount of customer service are more creative than those who provide relatively little customer service. The Ask-and-Guess Test, however, was especially effective in differentiating the high and low sales groups among the low customer service or more routine departments. Apparently the saleswoman who can ask good questions and make good guesses about the customer's needs sells more than the woman who is less skilled in this respect.

Another study (Hebeisen, 1959) was concerned with the thinking abilities of a group of sixty-eight schizophrenic patients in a state mental hospital. These patients were regarded as partially recovered and many of them were being considered by rehabilitation services for employment following their discharge from the hospital. The battery administered was Form A, which was described in Chapter 3, and thus included some of the same tasks included in Form D. The performance of these 68 schizophrenic patients was compared with that of a control group consisting of 100 college students. The disturbed group showed marked impoverishment of imagination and creative thinking abilities. They exhibited far more blocking or inability to respond in any way to the task demands than did the more normal subjects. Their responses were especially lacking in originality, being of an extremely obvious, commonplace, and safe nature.

Forms EP, FP, EI and FI

Forms EP and FP were designed as alternate form tests for kindergarten through third grade, and Forms EI and FI were designed as alternate forms for the fourth, fifth, and sixth grades. Forms EP and FP consist of the following tasks:

Task	Form EP	Form FP
I. Picture Construction	Triangle	Jelly Bean Shape
II. Figure Completion	Set A Figures	Set B Figures
III. Closed Figures	Circles	Square
IV. Ask-and-Guess Test	Tom Piper	Ding Dong Bell

Forms EI and FI consist of the following tasks:

Task	Form EI	Form FI
I. Figure Completion	Set A Figures	Set B Figures
II. Closed Figures	Squares	Circles
III. Product Improvement	Toy Dog	Toy Monkey
IV. Ask-and-Guess Test	Tom Piper	Ding Dong Bell

It will be noted that three of the tasks are common to all four forms, except that there are alternate forms for the pre- and post-tests. It will also be noted that there is considerable overlap between these tasks and Form D.

Some study has been made of the alternate forms through test-retest reliability studies. Testing a sample of fifty summer campers ranging from grades four through nine with an elapsed interval of two weeks between testings, I obtained a coefficient of correlation of .80 with the two sets of incomplete figures. Torrance and Gowan (1963) obtained split-half reliabilities of .88, .85, and .92 with the third, fourth, fifth, and sixth grades, respectively, with samples ranging from forty to fifty-four. With alternate forms of the Ask-and-Guess Test, I obtained a test-retest reliability coefficient of .79 with the summer camp sample already described. Mackler (1962) obtained test-retest reliabilities of .82, .89, and .84 with the Ask-and-Guess Test in the triple testing situation described in the preceding section. McGreevey (1961), also using the Ask-and-Guess Test with 100 ninth-grade students, obtained a reliability coefficient of .76 with alternate forms. Using alternate forms of the Product Improvement Test, Yamamoto (1962) obtained a test-retest reliability coefficient of .83. Rouse (1963) obtained test-retest reliabilities of .85, .76, and .68 for fluency, flexibility, and originality with alternate forms of the Product Improvement Test using a sample of mentally retarded children with an elapsed time of approximately six months. Thus, with the alternate-form-test-retest reliabilities ranging from .68 to .89, it seems reasonably safe to assume some validity for the alternate forms on the basis of the original validity studies with Form D.

The data on the nonverbal, figural tasks which are emphasized in the forms for kindergarten through third grade are less complete than for the verbal tasks. Using an alternate form design in administering the Circles and Squares Tests (Squares-Circles, Circles-Squares) to thirty-one technical college students at a single sitting, Sommers and I obtained test-retest reliability coefficients of .68, .60, .65, and .72 for fluency, flexibility, originality, and elaboration, respectively. Circles and Squares cannot be considered as equivalent forms insofar as difficulty is concerned, however, as indicated by the means for the thirty-one technical college students in Table A.1.

TABLE A.1   Mean Scores of Thirty-one Technical College Students on Circles and Squares Tests

Measure	Circles	Squares
Fluency	16.7	15.0
Flexibility	13.6	11..9
Originality	18.7	15.3
Elaboration	30.5	37.4

Apparently it is easier to elaborate on the Squares Test and easier to obtain high scores on fluency, flexibility, and originality on the Circles Test.

In general, I have conceded that the verbal tasks of creative thinking are more likely to yield satisfactory validity evidence than figural ones in most educational settings, since success and perceptions of success in most situations are so strongly influenced by a person's verbal skills. At least one study (Hart, 1962) yields encouraging evidences of validity for the three figural tasks included in these forms where the verbal tasks failed to do so. Hart tested fifty-three senior nursing students who had been carefully rated by a school of nursing staff according to their effectiveness in the performance of nursing functions. Comparing the more effective nursing students with the less effective ones, she found that all three of the nonverbal tasks (Picture Construction, Incomplete

Figures, and Circles) differentiated the less effective students from the more effective ones at less than the 5 per cent level of confidence. Three of the factor scores (flexibility, originality, and elaboration) derived from the nonverbal tasks also differentiated these three groups at better than the 5 per cent level of confidence. Only the fluency score failed to discriminate these two groups of nursing students at a significant level.

Using a carefully developed set of teacher ratings of creative pupil characteristics, Nelson (1963) obtained statistically significant differentiations between creative and uncreative criterion groups of fifth- and sixth-grade children on the measures of figural originality and elaboration but not on fluency and flexibility.

Imaginative Stories:
Tests of Creative Writing

Two different forms of the Imaginative Stories Test have been used, Forms A and B. On each of these forms, ten topics are given, and subjects are asked to choose one of them and to write the most interesting and exciting story they can think of about that topic. Subjects are urged not to be preoccupied with their handwriting, spelling, and the like. Instead, they are asked to use their energy to put as many good ideas as they can into their stories. A time limit of twenty minutes was established in the administration of the test.

The general instructions given subjects are as follows:

In the next twenty minutes, I would like you to write the most interesting and exciting story you can think of about one of the topics listed below. Try to write legibly but do not worry too much about your handwriting, spelling, and the like. Instead, try to put into your story as many good ideas as you can. Choose any one of the following topics or make up a similar one of your own.

The following titles are suggested in Form A:

The Dog That Doesn't Bark
The Man Who Cries
The Woman Who Can But Won't Talk
The Cat That Doesn't Scratch
Miss Jones Stopped Teaching
The Doctor Who Became a Carpenter
The Rooster That Doesn't Crow
The Horse That Won't Run
The Duck That Doesn't Quack
The Lion That Doesn't Roar.

In Form B, the following titles were suggested:

The Teacher Who Doesn't Talk
The Hen That Crows
The Dog That Won't Fight
The Flying Monkey
The Boy Who Wants to Be a Nurse
The Girl Who Wants to Be an Engineer
The Cat That Likes to Swim
The Woman Who Swears Like a Sailor
The Man Who Wears Lipstick
The Cow That Brays Like a Donkey

It will be noted that all the titles involve an animal or a person who possesses some divergent characteristic. This was deliberate, since we were interested in investigating the ways in which children value divergency and how children perceive their society's pressures against divergency. As we had planned and as was demonstrated in pilot studies, the titles appealed to the interest and imagination of the children. In fact, a child almost has to create in order to produce a story about the titles given. Very few recalled stories from their experiences.

Depending upon the purposes of the investigation in which the Imaginative Stories Test was used, the results are evaluated according to different schemes. Only the two methods used in two or more different studies will be described here. It seems better to describe the others in connection with the specific study, since the methods of analysis flow so naturally from the objectives of the specific studies.

One of the more elaborate scoring schemes is one developed by Yamamoto (1961) and includes scales for the following six general criteria: organization, sensitivity, originality, imagination, psychological insight, and richness. Each of these six general criteria was then divided into five components. The more detailed guide provides a definition of each component and gives illustrative scoring examples. Only the definitions of the components will be given here.

Organization (Score one point for the presence of each component)

1. *Balance (Integration).* Is the production well balanced in its organization? Is it well integrated in that all of the parts contribute something to the story?
2. *Arrangement (Order).* Is the production skillfully arranged in terms of its temporal and/or special sequence? Here score one point whenever the author reports events in the order in which they would be

expected to occur. If the production is very short (arbitrarily, less than fifty words), score zero on this dimension. A production need not be well balanced to rate high here.

3. *Consistency.* Is the production consistent in its efforts to give a story about one of the topics presented? Here score zero only in those cases where there is explicit contradiction or inconsistency in any part or parts of the production.

4. *Conciseness.* Is the production wordy or parsimonious? It is not the length of the production itself which is to be considered but rather its length in relation to its meaningfulness—how much it says.

5. *Clarity (Communication).* Does the production clearly convey the writer's idea? Is the communication good? If you understand what the author is trying to say, score one point here.

Sensitivity (Score one point for the presence of each component)

1. *Stimulus perception.* Is the subject sensitive to the original stimulus, namely the presented title? Did he grasp what is required of him? Here also pay attention to the way the subjects responded to the verb(s) used in the suggested topic. Remember that the dog is a dog that *does not* bark, not a dog that *will not* bark or *cannot* bark. The woman is a woman who *can but won't* talk, not a woman who *simply cannot talk.* When the subject ignores or overlooks this subtle but important phase, give him a zero score.

2. *Association.* Did the subject react adequately to the stimuli which came up in his own production? Did he permit one thing to lead naturally to another? Was his association smooth and relevant? Usually score one point unless the production is unusually queer or incoherent in its association.

3. *Relevancy of ideas.* Is the idea presented relevant? Are the ideas contributing something to the over-all production? Are they essential? Are they marginal, peripheral, or totally irrelevant, or are they central? If most of the presented ideas are relevant, score one here.

4. *Specificity.* Is the production specific in its important details? Is it detailed in its exposition of the central ideas?

5. *Empathy.* Does the subject show some empathy with the principal character in his production? Score one here whenever there is explicit description of how the character feels or felt (He was very sad, She was afraid of . . .). When some emotion or feeling is explicitly ascribed to a character in the story, or when the character, in direct narration, expresses his emotion, a score of one is given.

Originality (Score one point for the presence of each component)

1. *Choice of topic.* Scoring of this criterion is entirely dependent upon the frequency of each topic chosen out of the ten possible choices (based on a sample of 1061 subjects in the third through sixth

grades). In Form A, the most common titles for boys are numbers 1, 2, 6, 8, and 10, and the use of any of these titles is scored zero. The most common titles used by girls are 1, 2, 3, 5, 8, and 10. In Form B, the most common titles for boys are 1, 3, 4, 7, 8, and 9. The most commonly used by girls are 1, 4, 7, and 9. The remaining topics and self-produced topics are scored one point.

2. *Ideas.* Is the main idea novel or unusual? Is it stereotyped? The following recurring ideas and schemes seem to be so obvious and commonplace as to rate a score of zero and can be used as a guide until a more detailed one can be developed:

The dog couldn't bark. He tried and tried but he couldn't bark.

The doctor quit medicine because he didn't like it. He became a carpenter.

The man cries because he peeled onions.

The lion got so mad he finally roared.

The lion could only squeak and everybody made fun of him.

Miss Jones stopped teaching because she couldn't stand her naughty, noisy, unruly children.

The man wears lipstick because he couldn't get it off.

3. *Organization.* Is the writer's way of organizing his materials governed by traditional story-telling form? A score of zero should be given whenever some stereotyped form (Once upon a time there was . . . , . . . and they lived happily ever after, or So this is the end of the story) is used in the production. (About 80 per cent of the productions of children from the third through the fifth grades use at least one of these common forms.)

4. *Style of writing.* Are there any signs of an original style of writing? This dimension has no objective rationale yet and is sometimes difficult to judge. Give a score of one whenever the subject uses direct narrative sentences or quoted dialogues.

5. *Sense of humor.* Is the production humorous or surprising? There could be much discussion on what constitutes humor. Granted this criterion is fairly subjective, we construe it as meaning surprising, pleasantly surprising, escape from the pedestrian and trivial aspects of reality, or the juxtaposition of the incongruous.

Imagination

1. *Imagination.* Does the subject show rich imagination or is his imaginative ability scarce and limited? Is the subject able to "associate away from" the original stimulus, or is he bound to it? Score one whenever the subject develops the topic to some extent and does not appear to be "in a rut."

2. *Fantasy.* Is the production strictly on a factual basis or is it rich in fantasy? The question to be asked in scoring this dimension is: Could this really happen? A production in which animals talk to each other or to people is worth a score of one. It must be pointed

out that there may be "imagination" without "fantasy," but by definition, "fantasy" implies "imagination."

3. *Abstraction.* Is the production high on the abstraction ladder? Is it attached to natural phenomena or is it logically more abstract? Give a score of one to all generalizations (All lions roar, or Cats don't like water). Also score one when the characters involved are named in a manner symbolic of their roles. For example, a nurse might be named Miss Getwell, or the lion that does not roar might be named Silence or Roarless.

4. *Identification.* Did the subject identify the principal character(s) in his story with proper name(s)?

5. *Reasoning.* Did the subject give any reason for the phenomenon described in the stimulus sentence, or did he simply accept it as it was? In some self-developed topics this dimension may not be applicable. In such cases, give a score of zero.

Psychological insight

1. *Causal explanation.* Did the subject give a physical (organic) cause to explain the phenomenon described in the stimulus sentence or a nonphysical (functional) reason? There is often some doubt as to whether a given reason is organic or functional. In such a case, give a score of zero.

2. *Perspective.* Did the subject show any perspective in terms of how and when—"the dog that doesn't bark" would start barking again? This might be termed "restoration of equilibrium." Also score a point whenever the subject states the long-term perspective about his principal character(s), whether this "normalizes" or not. "Living happily ever after" is not enough, incidentally, unless the subject shows how this is possible.

3. *Meaningfulness.* Is the production meaningful as a whole? Here we are most dramatically confronted with a choice situation between social and psychological, or adult and child, criteria of creativeness, and, unfortunately, we have no clear-cut answer. Score, therefore, one point here unless the production is totally incoherent and nonsensical. The following and similar stereotypes should, however, be scored zero on this dimension.

Once there was a man who cried. He didn't know why. Then all of a sudden he stopped crying.

There was a lion who couldn't roar. He tried and tried but he couldn't.

4. *Ego-involvement.* Is there any self-reference? Does the subject speak of his own experience?

5. *Understanding.* Does the production show deep understanding of the life situation described? Here the subject is judged for his insight into complex interpersonal (be it expressed in terms of animals involved) relationships. This calls for a kind of reality testing on the part of the subject.

Richness

1. *Expression.* Literally speaking, is the production rich in its expression? Does it describe things carefully and/or colorfully?
2. *Ideas.* Is the subject rich in ideas? Does he have a large number of ideas? The number, rather than quality or integrity, of ideas is to be considered here.
3. *Emotion.* Is the production rich in its expression of emotion? Score one point here whenever the subject shows commiseration with his characters and/or his story. On the *empathy* dimension, we look for explicit emotion *ascribed* to principal characters, but on *emotion* we are interested primarily in direct expression of the subject's own emotion. Expression of emotion might be either explicit or implicit.
4. *Curiosity.* Does the production show keen curiosity? Is anyone in the story chiefly concerned with finding out why, what, how, or when?
5. *Fluency.* Is the subject fluent in his production? Here we are interested in fluency in the sense of number of words, and an arbitrary cutting score of 150 words has been established for the twenty-minute time limit. As the scale is developed, it will probably be necessary to establish different cutting scores for each grade.

RELIABILITY OF SCORING

To check the interscorer reliability of scoring, three judges were given the same set of eighty-five protocols and asked to score them independently according to the manual. All three judges were new to the task of rating creative writing. Interscorer reliabilities of .79, .80, and .76 were obtained.

RELATIONSHIPS WITH OTHER MEASURES

The product-moment coefficients of correlation between the composite scores obtained from the foregoing scales and other measures of intellectual performance were obtained by Yamamoto for a class of twenty fifth-graders and a class of twenty sixth-graders. (See Table A.2.)

Although all of the relationships between this measure of creative writing and other measures of intellectual performance are positive and many of them are statistically significant, they are low enough to indicate that this measure is tapping a somewhat different kind of ability and/or achievement from the others, except perhaps the scales for Originality and Interest which will now be described.

TABLE A.2 Product-Moment Coefficients of Correlation Between Composite Creativity Scores and Other Measures

Measure	Fifth Grade	Sixth Grade
Form D, creative thinking ability	.56*	.28
Originality of writing	.65*	.80*
Interest score on writing	.70*	.72*
Mental age (IQ)	.27	.31
Reading achievement (Iowa)	.60*	.38
Work-study skills (Iowa)	.35	.53*
Language skills (Iowa)	.62*	.46
Arithmetic skills (Iowa)	.38	.47

* Significant at 5 per cent level or better

EVALUATION OF ORIGINALITY AND INTEREST

The instructions for the writing of the imaginative stories were designed to encourage originality and interest. The relevant literature was surveyed in an attempt to determine what characteristics of compositions had been considered by others in rating them on originality and interest. These were then listed, and nine characteristics for each were selected as being appropriate for relatively objective scoring. Most of the criteria for Interest were obtained from the work of Flesch and his associates (Flesch, 1948; Flesch and Lass, 1955). The others were gleaned from a variety of sources (Colvin, 1902; Hinton, 1940; Applegate, 1949).

Originality

In determining the Originality score, the following nine points or characteristics are considered, and one point is given for the occurrence of each in the story:

1. *Picturesqueness.* Writing may be said to be picturesque if it suggests a picture, is colorful, strikingly graphic, or objectively descriptive.
2. *Vivid.* A vivid story is told with liveliness and intenseness. The description is so interesting, or even exciting, that the reader may be stirred emotionally. It is vigorous, fresh, alive, spirited, lively.
3. *Flavor.* A story may be said to have flavor if it possesses a

noticeable, characteristic element or taste, or appeals to the sense of taste, smell, touch, or feel.

4. *Personal element.* A story may be rated as having the personal element if the author involves himself in the account or expresses his personal feelings or opinions about the events described.

5. *Original solution or ending, surprising.* What we are looking for here essentially is the "punch line." It need not be funny, though it may, but it must be unexpected, unusual, surprising.

6. *Original setting or plot.* This category is scored if the setting, plot, or theme is unusual or original, unconventional, or new.

7. *Humor.* Stories are scored for humor if they have the quality of portraying the comical, the funny, the amusing. One simple criterion would be to score a story for this category if it makes the rater laugh or smile. This is not altogether dependable, however, when one is rating a large number of stories at a single sitting. Thus, it is useful to take clues from the works of some of the better-known humorists: frequently bringing together certain incongruities which arise naturally from the situation or character, so as to illustrate some fundamental absurdity in human behavior or character.

8. *Invented words or names.* When parts of two or more words are combined to express some concept, when animals and persons are given amusing names or names appropriate to their character, or the like, credit is given in this category.

9. *Other unusual twist in style of content.* This category was added primarily for the purpose of giving a bonus credit for a high type of originality not adequately reflected in the eight foregoing categories.

Interest

The following nine characteristics were used in scoring interest:

1. *Conversational tone.* Many children tell a story just as though they were carrying on a conversation with the reader. Others write more formally and thereby spoil the reader's interest.

2. *Naturalness.* Usually, but not always, stories written in a conversational tone are also "natural." The conversation, however, may be stilted and artificial; it might still be "conversational in tone" but not "natural." A story may also have naturalness without being conversational.

3. *Use of quotations.* A score for "use of quotations" is given whenever the direct words of the speaker are given. Many children in the early grades (third and fourth) have not been taught to use quotation marks, although some use them with-

out being taught. Thus, credit is given whether quotation marks are used or not. Almost all stories credited with "use of quotation marks" have a "conversational tone." Many having a "conversational tone," however, do not use quotations.

4. *Variety in kind of sentence.* Two types of variety or kind of sentence can be considered and either gives credit in this category. (In one study, it was decided to give a point for each kind of variety.) Sentences may vary according to use: declarative, interrogative, or exclamatory. They may also vary according to form: simple, compound, complex, and compound-complex. In a short story (under 150 words) any variation of either type qualifies the story for credit. In longer stories, there must be three or more variations in form and/or use.

5. *Variety in length of sentence and structure.* If there is a mixture of short and long sentences, this category is scored. Also credit is given for any variation in the structure of sentences, such as predicate before subject, dependent clause before independent clause, and the like.

6. *Personal touch.* Same as "Personal touch" under "Originality."

7. *Humor.* Same as "Humor" under "Originality."

8. *Questions and answers.* Two types of question-and-answer techniques are scored for this category. There may be questions and answers in the direct quotations of speakers, or the writer may ask the reader a question and then answer the question. Either is scored for this category.

9. *Feelings of characters.* If the feelings of characters in the story are given either through their own words or through the writer, this category is credited.

Reliability of Scoring

Three judges were involved in the initial determination of interscorer reliability. The scoring task was new to all three judges, but Judge A was an established research worker with more than three years' experience in creative thinking research. Judge B had had only two months' experience with creative writing projects. Judge C had had no training whatsoever when he was asked to perform the judging task.

The resulting interscorer reliabilities are shown in Table A.3.

Relationship with Other Measures of Intellectual Performance

With a class of twenty fifth-graders and one of twenty sixth-graders the coefficients of correlation were obtained between these two measures and other measures of intellectual performance. (See Table A.4.)

TABLE A.3 Interscorer Reliability Coefficients of Three Judges in Scoring Imaginative Stories for Originality and Interest

Judges	Number of Records	Originality	Interest
A and B	25	.88	.84
A and C	30	.84	.82

TABLE A.4 Product-Moment Coefficients of Correlation of Measures of Originality and Interest with Other Measures

Measure	Fifth Grade		Sixth Grade	
	Originality	Interest	Originality	Interest
Composite measure of creative writing	.65*	.70*	.80*	.72*
Total score on Form D, creative thinking test	.49*	.53*	.51*	.45*
Mental age (Stanford-Binet)	.44*	.29	.44*	.30
Reading achievement (Iowa)	.63*	.58*	.26	.32
Study-work skills (Iowa)	.54*	.44*	.40	.41
Language skills (Iowa)	.61*	.57*	.37	.13
Arithmetic skills (Iowa)	.60*	.52*	.57*	.32*

* Significant at 5 per cent level or better

In the fifth grade there was a coefficient of correlation of .85 between Originality and Interest, and in the sixth grade there was one of .75. As in the case of the Composite Creative Writing Score, all the coefficients are positive, and many of them are statistically significant.

The Personal-Social Motivation Inventory

At the very outset of the Minnesota Studies of Creative Thinking, it became obvious that certain motivations facilitated or hampered the production of original or otherwise creative ideas. In both individual and group testing, some children became productive if we employed one means of motivation (such as competition for a prize, seeing how well you can do, or just for fun), while others responded to another. This led us to a concern about the motivations which might be involved in becoming a creative person or making optimum use of one's creative talents.

After making an analysis of reported research on creative persons, the biographies of eminent creative persons, and the theoretical work in this area, we attempted to develop the structure for an inventory.

It was planned that a scale to be called "Creative Motivation" would be the central measure. For this scale, we attempted to develop items which would show an inquiring, searching, reaching-out, and courageous attitude. Knowing that one must be sensitive to defects, problems, gaps in knowledge, and the like, we also felt that we needed a measure of "Critical Motivation." We did not want to combine these items with the "Creative Motivation" items because we know only too well that many people can recognize and identify defects but are not themselves able to produce constructive ideas and are unable to see other possibilities. Furthermore, some of them are simply not interested in going beyond the identification of defects. In fact, we were not certain that this scale would even differentiate between highly creative and less creative persons. We believed, however, that the critical motivation must be assessed in order to understand the motivations of creative people. It might provide us with useful clues in guiding individuals in the better use of their creative talents. Some individuals are unable to produce original ideas because they are too critical, while others fail because they are not critical enough to perceive deficiencies.

Another very obvious motivation of creative persons seemed to be their "Intellectual Autonomy." They are able to reach conclusions independently from their observations and other data, and have the courage to stick to their judgments. This is highly essential because the person who produces original ideas is always in the very beginning a minority of one, and it takes a great deal of strength to withstand the discomfort engendered thereby. Thus, we sought to select and construct items which would operationally define the need or motivation for "Intellectual Autonomy."

In a very provocative article by Tumin (1954), we found a most interesting theoretical rationale concerning the obstacles to creativity. These obstacles, as formulated by Tumin, include:

1. An excessive quest for certainty
2. An excessive quest for power
3. An excessive quest for meaning
4. An excessive quest for social relations
5. A pathological rejection of social relations

Since much of the data that we had collected from the observation of children and from the analysis of the biographies of eminent creative people fitted this theoretical formulation, we undertook the task of selecting and constructing items which would operationally define each of these variables.

Many sources were used in assembling items for the eight scales identified above. The work of Runner (1954) proved to be the most useful source of items for the "Creative Motivation" scale. Other instruments such as the Minnesota Multiphasic Personality Inventory, the Bernreuter Personality Inventory, and the like were also surveyed as sources of possible items. Others were constructed from data collected from various sources about creative persons.

EXPLORATORY DEVELOPMENTS

The initial pool of items was judged by eight members of the staff of the Bureau of Educational Research, all of whom had been familiarized with the research concerning creative persons. On the basis of these judgments, Som Nath Ghei and I assembled a 189-item inventory with the eight scales identified in the Introduction. Preliminary work seemed to indicate that the scales for Creative Motivation, Critical Motivation, and Quest for Power or Power Motivation were likely to be of the greatest value. Item analyses were then conducted to select items for a 100-item inventory which would provide scores on these three motivations (creative, critical, and power).

EVIDENCES OF VALIDITY

Neither of the instruments can be regarded as adequately validated, although the scattered bits of evidence available are quite promising and will be summarized herein.

Research Workers

The first group to whom the instrument was administered consisted of research assistants and fellows and senior researchers in the College of Education at the University of Minnesota. Five of this group of seventeen persons were identified as being unimaginative in their work, uninterested in educational research, each more or less working at the tasks of research to earn money to help finance graduate study. Not one member of this group attained a score in excess of 18 on the Creative Motivation scale. None of these five persons is now doing any research. None of the remaining twelve persons tested in this original group achieved a score less than 20 on this scale. All members of this group have continued to do research and have been fairly productive of professional publications, research ideas, and the like.

Graduate Students Who Produce Original Ideas

Students in a course entitled "Personality Development and Mental Hygiene" are required to develop some original ideas as a part of the course requirements. These ideas are rated on five ten-point scales, as follows: newness and freshness, a push forward in knowledge, surprisingness, usefulness, and creative intellectual energy expended in developing the idea. The materials to be evaluated included a statement of the student's idea, a description of the process by which the idea occurred and was developed, a rationale for the idea, a plan for testing the idea, and a statement of the possible consequences of the idea should it be found valid.

Comparisons were made between the means of those ranking in the upper 27 per cent of the class on the originality projects with those ranking in the lower 27 per cent on this criterion. The results are shown in Table A.5. It will be noted that "Creative Motivation" scores

TABLE A.5 Means, Standard Deviations, and *t*-Ratios for Measures on the Personal-Social Motivation Inventory Comparing the More Creative Students with the Less Creative Students as Judged by Original Projects

Scale	High Creatives (N=20)		Low Creatives (N=20)		t-ratio	Level of Significance
	Mean	St. Dev.	Mean	St. Dev.		
Creative motivation	20.05	3.30	17.40	4.10	2.23	Less than 3 per cent
Critical motivation	6.60	2.03	7.95	2.80	1.73	Less than 10 per cent
Obstacles of creativity	10.95	2.73	11.65	1.96	0.70	Not significant

differentiate fairly well between these two criterion groups. There is a nonsignificant tendency for the "Critical Motivation" score to discriminate in a negative direction. The scales developed from Tumin's formulation did not discriminate between the criterion groups, but the trend was in the expected direction.

Critical and Creative Reading of Research Reports

Another requirement of the author's course in Educational Psychology 159 is to read critically one research article and to submit a report identifying defects in the statement of the problem, hypotheses, data collection, analysis of data, and interpretation of findings, and to read another, creatively pointing out possibilities in the statement of the problem and the like. These reports were evaluated independently by Judson A. Harmon, teaching assistant for the course, who had no knowledge of scores achieved on the Inventory. Scores on the Inventory were analyzed to determine "creative" or "critical" dominance for each student. After students were dichotomized in this way, a comparison was made of their ratings on the critical and creative reports of their reading. It was determined whether they achieved a higher score on the creative than the critical, the critical than the creative, or scored the same on both. The results as shown in Table A.6 indicate

TABLE A.6 Relative Superiority of Critical and Constructive (Creative) Research Reviews Prepared by Students Expressing Dominance of Critical and Creative Motivations on Personal-Social Motivation Theory

	Number			
Dominant Motivation	Better on Creative	Better on Critical	Same	Total
Creative motivation	24	3	13	40
Critical motivation	23	29	16	68
Total	47	32	29	108

Note: Chi-square $= 15.219$, significant at .1 per cent level

that students dominated by a creative attitude tend to do a better job in reading research creatively or constructively than they do in reading research critically. The reverse is true of students dominated by a critical motivation. Results are statistically significant at the .1 per cent level.

FACTORIAL GROUPINGS

Scores achieved by 100 graduate students in Educational Psychology were factor analyzed along with scores on the need scales of the Stern Activity Index, tests of creative thinking, ratings on original projects, and various achievement measures in "Personality Development and Mental Health." The Creative Motivation score loaded most heavily in a factor which included the following scales from the Stern Activity Index: humanism, counteraction, energy, nurturance, understanding, reflectiveness, and scientism. *Humanism* is defined by Stern (1958) as the manipulation of external social objects or artifacts through empirical analysis, reflection, and discussion. *Counteraction* involves a restriving to overcome experienced frustration, failure, and humiliation. *Energy* is defined as an intense, sustained, vigorous effort as opposed to sluggish inertia. *Nurturance* involves the giving of support to others by providing love, assistance, and protection. *Understanding* represents an interest in intellectual activity, problem solving, analysis, or abstraction as an end in itself. *Reflectiveness* is defined as an introspective preoccupation with private psychological, spiritual, esthetic, or metaphysical experience. *Scientism* involves the need to manipulate external physical objects through empirical analysis, reflection, and discussion. Placement in this cluster of variables would seem to give some construct validity to the Creative Motivation scale, since all the characteristics represented by these variables are commonly associated with the creative process and the creative personality.

The Critical Motivation variable is a part of a factor which includes also quest for absolute certainty, pathological rejection of social relations, and excessive quest for social relations. Placement in this cluster helps to identify that aspect of the Critical Motivation represented by the items in this inventory and helps to explain why scores on this scale tend to favor the relatively noncreative groups rather than the creative groups. This factor correlates .0018 with the factor in which Creative Motivation is placed.

Power Motivation is a part of a third factor which includes also the needs for dominance, narcissism, achievement, and fantasied achievement. Stern (1958) defines *dominance* as an assertive manipulative control over others. *Narcissism* is a preoccupation with the self. *Achievement* is defined as a surmounting of obstacles and proving personal worth, while *fantasied achievement* involves daydreams of success in achieving personal recognition and narcissistic aspirations for personal distinction. Again, we have evidence of construct validity, since all of these features are involved in the rationale on which the Power Motivation scale was constructed.

Responses of Creative Leaders

At the 1962 Creative Problem-solving Institute conducted by the Creative Education Foundation at the University of Buffalo, thirtynine members of the Creative Leaders Convocation were administered the short form consisting of thirty of the most promising items in the Creative Motivation scale. These creative leaders for the most part have impressive records as inventors, creative educators, creative writers, creative businessmen, and the like. The mean score attained by this group is significantly higher than that attained by any other group to which these items have been administered (differences significant at better than the 1 per cent level of confidence). With the exception of one item, a majority of the creative leaders answered the items correctly. In most cases, the majority was overwhelming and generally much higher than in any of the other groups tested. Only 49 per cent of the creative leaders reacted positively to the statement, "My interest is often caught up in ideas that may never lead to anything." It would have been interesting to have inquired further into reactions to this item. It is likely that many of these leaders are accustomed to achieving success when they work in this way. They have confidence that such ideas will lead to something worthwhile.

Sex Differences in Harmony with Cultural Expectations

A peripheral kind of validity is to be found in the fact that sex differences are rather consistently in the expected direction and that most of these differences are statistically significant. In Table A.7 which

TABLE A.7 Means and Standard Deviations of Graduate Students in Educational Psychology on the Eight Scales of the Personal-Social Motivation Inventory

Scale	Males (N=125)		Females (N=177)	
	Mean	St. Dev.	Mean	St. Dev.
Creative motivation	18.77*	5.94	17.68	5.25
Critical motivation	7.47*	1.86	6.26	1.85
Intellectual autonomy	23.96*	4.43	22.23	5.93
Quest for certainty	13.15	5.21	13.74	4.90
Quest for power	10.42*	3.69	7.99	3.80
Quest for meaning	6.83	1.83	6.63	1.83
Quest for social relations	11.55	3.70	12.24	3.61
Rejection of social relations	7.96	4.19	8.29	4.34

*Differences between males and females significant at 1 per cent level or better

presents norms for fairly large samples of graduate students in Educational Psychology, it will be noted that men have higher creative motivations, critical motivations, intellectual autonomy, and need for power. Although the differences are not statistically significant, there is a trend for the women to have a stronger need for certainty, a stronger need for social relations, as well as a stronger rejection of social relations.

STUDENT PREFERENCES
IN PROFESSOR-STUDENT RELATIONS

Another interesting bit of validity evidence comes from a study reported by Drabek (1963) involving 740 undergraduate students in a large midwestern university. Drabek identified from this sample two criterion groups according to their preference in professor-student relationships: an active group and a passive group. The 185 students scoring in the upper quartile of the Professor-Student Relations Inventory (indicating a preference for an active professor-student relationship) scored higher on the creative attitude scale ($t = 2.93$, significant at less than the 1 per cent level of confidence) than the 185 students scoring in the lower quartile of this measure and indicating a preference for a passive professor-student relationship. Students preferring an active professor-student relationship were also less dogmatic, subscribed to a less orthodox religious ideology, participated more in intellectual extracurricular activities, more frequently discussed issues of national and international importance with their parents, and more frequently used public and private libraries.

CONCLUDING STATEMENT

Although considerable work needs to be done in refining some of the scales and in validating the scales by systematic observation, experiments, and personality studies, it is believed that the results thus far obtained are promising enough to warrant further research.

DEVELOPING
CREATIVE
THINKING
THROUGH
LANGUAGE
ARTS

Appendix B

In Plato's *Phaedus,* Thamus, the king, attacked the invention of the alphabet on the grounds that it would produce forgetfulness in the minds of those who learn to use it, because they would not practice their memories. Since that time, most of the peoples of the earth have adopted some kind of alphabet. Until quite recently, however, almost as much importance has been placed on the development of the memory abilities as in the days of Plato. In fact, we still admire one who *recites* a poem more than one who reads it or explains its meaning. We admire the pupil who *knows* the answer more than one who *knows where to look it up or how to figure it out.*

It has long been the proclaimed aim of education to develop all of an individual's mental abilities. Generally, we have thought of the IQ as somehow representing the sum total of an individual's mental abilities. The school curriculum has been developed in such a way as to exercise and develop the kinds of abilities reflected in the IQ, and the IQ has continued to be a good predictor of school achievement, although it has not been a very good predictor of vocational success. Many other school practices have been based on measures obtained from intelligence tests. It has almost always been one of the measures

---

The materials included in this appendix were presented as a mimeographed monograph in the in-service education projects discussed in Chapters 4, 5, 6. They are offered in this volume as an example of what can be done in one specific field to develop guided, planned experiences in creative thinking in that field.

used in identifying intellectual giftedness. Some schools place children with IQ's of 135, 140, or the like in special classes. Some base their grading systems on it. A child is considered to be doing satisfactory work if he is measuring "up to his IQ," that is, if his achievement quotient is equal to his IQ. A child whose achievement quotient is lower than his IQ is regarded as an underachiever and is urged to study harder and learn more rapidly. One whose achievement quotient is above his IQ is regarded as overachieving and is urged not to study so hard and to play more.

There is now a growing recognition that the IQ attempts to measure only a small number of man's thinking abilities. We don't know yet just how many of these thinking abilities there are and how many of them are important in education. Guilford has theorized that there are 120 such abilities, and he has thus far been able to identify and measure approximately 60 of them. He represents these 120 abilities by the cube shown in Figure B.1. You will note that there are five major groups of abilities and that each of these may be expressed in a variety of ways.

First, there are the cognitive abilities, those used in recognizing

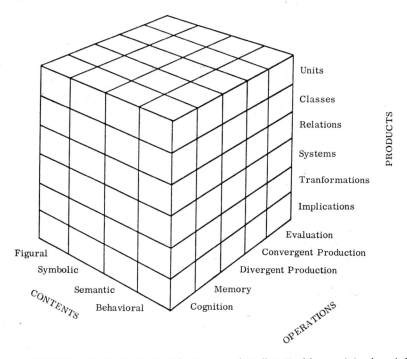

FIGURE B.1 *Guilford's Model of the Structure of Intellect. Used by permission from J. P. Guilford and P. R. Merrifield, The Structure of Intellect Model: Its Uses and Implications (Los Angeles: University of Southern California, 1960).*

facts, discovery, and rediscovery. Then, there are the memory abilities, those used in retaining what has been cognized. Then, we have two kinds of productive thinking abilities which are used in generating new information from known information and remembered information. One type, the convergent thinking abilities, leads to one right answer, recognized best answer, or conventional answer. The other, the divergent thinking abilities, leads to new and divergent directions. Finally, there are the evaluation abilities, which are used in reaching decisions as to goodness, suitability, or adequacy, of what we know, remember, and produce through productive thinking.

The IQ and most of our measures of educational achievement emphasize the first three types: cognition, memory, and convergent thinking.

Thus far, the evidence indicates that the creative thinking abilities are important in healthy personality development and mental hygiene, the acquisition and application of knowledge and basic intellectual skills, vocational success, invention and scientific discovery, and in coping with all of life's demands. We have found that many of these thinking abilities can be measured and studied. It now seems clear that all individuals possess, to some degree, the abilities involved in doing creative thinking, that these abilities can be increased or decreased by education, and that it is a legitimate role of education to provide experiences which will develop said abilities.

We cannot yet be certain how many creative thinking abilities there are. In this booklet, suggested activities have been collected for developing seven of these abilities discovered by Guilford (1950, 1951, and 1959a) and an eighth, curiosity. Ideas will be presented for developing each of the following:

1. Ideational fluency
2. Associational fluency
3. Spontaneous flexibility
4. Adaptive flexibility
5. Originality
6. Elaboration
7. Sensitivity
8. Curiosity

Following the presentation of ideas for developing these abilities, a few general suggestions will be made for developing creativity in the language arts and for rewarding creative thinking in school situations.

Developing Ideational Fluency

Ideational fluency involves the production of many ideas where free expression is encouraged and where quality is not evaluated. We are able to assess this ability by asking individuals or groups to produce as many ideas as possible for the improvement of a product or new uses of it. In teaching language arts in the intermediate grades, children can be given practice in using this ability by having pupils suggest as many titles as possible for a story, as many endings as possible for an uncompleted story, diverse uses of a word, diverse ways of describing an object or scene, and the like. Students could be required to describe in diverse ways a certain situation or make a certain appeal in such a way as to communicate most effectively to several different audiences, such as children, teenagers, old people, college students, and others.

DEVELOPING IDEATIONAL FLUENCY
THROUGH GROUP METHODS ("BRAINSTORMING")

We know that the expression of one idea stimulates other ideas, often of better quality. We also know that those who are most fluent in a group are the ones who exert the most influence on the group and the decisions it makes. There are a number of group methods which language arts teachers can use in developing this skill. One such widely used method in business and industry has been called "group brainstorming" (Clark, 1958; Osborn, 1957, 1963). In applying this method, pupils would be asked to think of as many solutions as possible to some problem, ways of improving a product, new uses of a product, and the like. In doing this, four rules would be invoked:

1. *Judgment is temporarily ruled out.* Negative criticism of ideas is withheld until later, since this "puts on the brakes" in thinking of new ideas. The teacher or leader can use a bell to remind pupils when they start using negative criticism, which they surely will at first.
2. *"Freewheeling" is welcomed.* The more unusual the idea, the better. It is easier to tame down a wild idea than to make a dull idea exciting or interesting.
3. *Quantity is wanted.* The greater the number of ideas, the more the likelihood of winners.
4. *Combination and improvement are sought.* In addition to contributing ideas of their own, children should learn how to use the ideas of others by building on to them or combining them with other ideas. A wild idea suggested by one may not be practical, but by changing it a little or by combining it with another idea, it may become both practical and exciting.

Of course, the ideas collected should finally be evaluated and selections made of the most promising ones. The first problem though is to stimulate the flow of ideas and to improve their quality by combination or addition. Particularly to be avoided during this first stage are the well-known "killer phrases" used by teachers and pupils to dampen enthusiasm for thinking of original ideas.

DEVELOPING IDEATIONAL FLUENCY
THROUGH "PROPS" AND "STARTERS"

During the early stages of training children to think of a larger number of ideas, it may be helpful to give them some props and starters through a set of familiar principles. Here are some of the questions which can be asked in most situations to generate new ideas or solutions:

1. What would happen if we add something?
2. What would happen if we take something away?
3. What would happen if we multiplied it (made more, made pairs, arranged in sets)?
4. What would happen if we divided it?
5. What would happen if we made it bigger?
6. What would happen if we made it smaller?
7. What would happen if we made it of different material? Changed its membership or composition?
8. What would happen if we took something away and put something else in its place?
9. What would happen if we took it apart and rearranged or reorganized it?
10. What would happen if we changed its position?
11. What would happen if we gave it a different sensory or emotional appeal (light, touch, odor, motion, sound)?
12. What would happen if we adapted it to another use (Osborn, 1963, pp. 175-176)?

In one of our experiments (Torrance, 1963a), these principles were taught with significant effects as early as the second grade by first having children suggest for about ten minutes all the ideas they could think of for improving a fire truck. They were then led to generalize these principles to "almost anything" by taking a square and modifying it according to the principles and pointing out the relationships to the ideas they had suggested for improving the fire truck. Although this experiment emphasized concreteness even in establishing the generalization principle through the use of squares, the same principles can be applied to more abstract problems, including human relation problems, organizational malfunctioning, and the like.

DEVELOPING IDEATIONAL FLUENCY
THROUGH DICTATION OF IDEAS

Research has shown that competition can greatly increase ideational fluency, and there are many devices available to language arts teachers for combining competition with the development of ideational fluency. An example of such a device is a modification of the format of the TV program in which representatives of two teams compete in jointly telling a story, with each trying to work in a quotation given secretly at the outset.

Various types of role playing can also be used to develop ideational fluency and spontaneity. One very promising idea has been suggested by one of the author's students who calls his plan Competitive Team Role Playing. Under this plan, a class is divided into four teams. Each of the protagonists in a role playing situation is supported by a team of advisers. The other two teams each observe one of the protagonists. Roles can, of course, be rotated.

Scholars in the field disagree on the merits of using competition, some maintaining that the teacher should never show preference for any child's creative productions. The fact remains, however, that competition does stimulate a larger number and higher quality of ideas among children.

Developing Associational Fluency

Associational fluency involves the production of words or ideas from a restricted area of meaning. A simple test item would require a subject to suggest several words as synonyms for a specific word, such as "intelligent." Responses might include smart, bright, sharp, and keen.

Teaching the use of such references as Roget's *Thesaurus*, encouraging variety in the choice of words in composition, making pupils aware of such variety in effective writing, and the like are some of the simple methods available to the teacher to develop associational fluency. I have enjoyed seeing first-grade children have fun with words, playing games which require them to keep thinking of words that rhyme, words having a certain kind of ending or a certain kind of beginning, and the like. Crosby (1954), in one of the leaflets in the portfolio of the National Council of Teachers of English on *Creative Ways in Teaching the Language Arts*, describes many ways of having fun with words which may be expected to develop associational fluency.

She especially emphasizes the importance of creating opportunities which help youngsters:

1. Recognize word relationships
2. Recognize words of similar meaning
3. Recognize words of opposite meaning
4. Extend word meanings
5. Select appropriate definitions
6. Detect irrelevant words
7. Select words with precise meanings

DEVELOPING ASSOCIATIONAL FLUENCY THROUGH WORD PLAY

Word play or activities involving attempts to invent new words can be useful in developing associational fluency. Reid's *Ounce, Dice, Trice* (1958) should give the imaginative teacher many ideas for such activities. For example, think of names for times of day when there are no clocks. Examples would include daypeep and dusk owlcry. Children can be encouraged to make up words for ideas, objects, collections of objects, and the like. One teacher describes some interesting outcomes from having children define nonsense words. Reid's book will suggest the possibility of having children think of as many words as they can, or having them make up words which communicate certain feelings or moods. Examples include squishy words, light words, heavy words, moving words, big words, and the like.

Developing Flexibility

SPONTANEOUS FLEXIBILITY

Spontaneous flexibility is used in the production of a diversity of ideas in a relatively unrestricted situation. This kind of thinking enables a person to keep out of ruts by jumping readily from one train of thought to another in thinking of new uses for some device or product. We found an extreme lack of this kind of ability among schizophrenics administered one of our tests. On the task requiring them to think of uses of tin cans, 87 per cent of their responses were in one category—*container*. Only about 33 per cent of the responses of normal adult groups fall in this category, and only about 15 per cent of the responses of fourth-, fifth-, and sixth-grade pupils can be classified as *container* responses.

The application of the aforementioned principles of addition, combination, substitution, and the like provides one deliberate method of stimulating increased flexibility. In fact, we use these principles as the categories for assessing spontaneous flexibility in evaluating responses to tasks requiring subjects to think of ways of improving a product, such as a toy.

ADAPTIVE FLEXIBILITY

Adaptive flexibility requires that the conventional problem-solving methods which have become unworkable be abandoned in favor of original solutions. In the field of invention, an example would be putting the eye in the point of the needle to make possible the invention of the sewing machine. One of the tasks we are now experimenting with along this line requires the subject to make varying arrangements of a series of three or more pictures in such a way as to tell different stories. He is then required to create stories according to each of the various arrangements. There are a number of exercises in the language arts which could be constructed along these lines. The principles of reversal and changing position are especially useful in stimulating adaptive flexibility.

Developing Originality

Originality involves the production of clever or uncommon responses to specific situations. An example would be writing "It's time to retire" as a caption for a picture of a sleepy child standing near a worn tire (Guilford, 1959a). English exercises in writing captions for cartoons and pictures, titles for stories, headlines for news items, plot titles, and the like would be expected to contribute to the development of this ability. In our own research, we are finding that the instruction to think of "unusual, clever, or original" ideas serves as an effective spur to the production of original ideas. Instructions to think of something no one else in the class will think of has also been productive. Such instructions are likely to be ineffective, however, if original or unusual ideas are not rewarded.

Herein lies one of the serious difficulties in developing creative thinking. Original ideas are likely to be upsetting to both teacher and pupils. Because of their very novelty, there are no standards by which to judge them. In fact, history suggests that the more original the idea the more it is likely to be considered by contemporaries as evil, "crackpot," or "silly." The teacher who would develop an environment which values creative thinking, however, must alter this tendency to immediately consider new ideas erroneous, bad, or foolish without first examining them. The habit of testing systematically such ideas should be developed early.

In most classrooms, the child who expresses an unusual idea or offers an unusual production takes a calculated risk! In such a setting, it takes a great deal of courage for a youngster to press for presentation of his unusual ideas.

DEVELOPING ORIGINALITY
THROUGH UNUSUAL INCIDENTS

A necessity for any kind of creative act is some kind of "warm-up" experience—something to wake up the creator, make him more sensitive, and alive. Any unusual incident provides such a "warm-up." It may be some unusual event in the community or in the school, some unusual achievement of one of the members of the class, or the like. Such events have stimulated most of our ballads. Or, it may be a snowstorm, the wind, falling leaves, a woodpecker on a tree outside the window, the harvest, squirrels playing in the trees—any unusual incident. These can become the materials for poems, songs, stories, and plays. To take advantage of some of these, however, the teacher may have to modify the schedule.

The creative teacher can create opportunities through field trips, special days, pictures, dramatizations, pets and animals, growing plants, and the like. The creative teacher causes ideas to develop, and these ideas can become the substance of the creative productions of children.

DEVELOPING ORIGINALITY
THROUGH BOOK REPORTS

Giving book reports can be an occasion for originality. One way to do this is to eliminate the usual method of presentation, the oral or written summary. You will then get a variety of techniques of presentation. Another method is to present the book report as a sales talk, trying to see the book or sell the remainder of the class on reading it. Wilson (1959) has described a number of variations developed by pupils in the intermediate grades—posters, skits, displays, and other unusual devices. One boy had everyone puzzled for a while. He had arrived ahead of time and had painted huge footprints leading from outside to the teacher's desk. He had read *Robinson Crusoe,* and the footprints were Friday's.

DEVELOPING ORIGINALITY
THROUGH AUDIO-VISUAL AIDS

Another way of "warming up" pupils is through various audio-visual aids. These too make him more alive, more spontaneous, more ready for creative acts. Both commercial and homemade recordings can be used for this purpose. Pictures, films, a radio broadcast, a TV program, and similar media are also useful. Spontaneous role playing also provides a common experience for all the members of the group and the raw materials for the creative production. In listening to and watching the audio-visual material, pupils can be encouraged to try to see and hear things which they think others will miss and use these as the basis for their productions. The ability to elaborate can also be developed, if pupils are encouraged to get an idea from the audio-visual material and then to build upon it themselves.

DEVELOPING ORIGINALITY AND SENSITIVITY
THROUGH HUMOR

Children from ages nine through twelve usually have a well-developed sense of humor. They enjoy jokes and surprises of their own and humor in stories. Getzels and Jackson (1962) and Torrance (1962a) have shown that highly creative children excel highly intelligent ones in this respect. This interest and enjoyment of humor can be used by teachers in the intermediate grades to motivate children to develop their originality and sensitivity.

One of the more obvious ways of developing originality and sensitivity through humor is to give children assignments requiring them to tell and write humorous stories, including jokes, anecdotes, amusing accounts of their own experiences, and imaginary stories. They can be asked to think up funny endings or titles for stories they read.

Work on humorous writing may also be used as a way of introducing advanced language arts skills, improvement in spelling, and other writing skills. It provides an opportunity to help children become aware of sense-appealing words through which humor can be expressed. It is a good time to give them an appreciation of sentence structure as a means of conveying emotion.

Limericks with their play on words and surprise endings are enjoyed by boys and girls in the intermediate grades.

A study of the works of some of our humorists can be used in teaching sensitivity to words, sentence structure, organization, and other characteristics used in communicating emotions to produce humor. The following are a few of the many writers whose works might be appropriate: Mark Twain, Lewis Carroll, James Whitcomb Riley, Willie Snow Etheridge, Cornelia Otis Skinner, James Thurber, and P. G. Wodehouse.

Developing Sensitivity

Almost all the recent studies of highly creative individuals in a variety of fields emphasize the importance of being sensitive and open to some kind of environmental stimuli. Apparently it is a matter of being sensitive to the kind of stimuli which furnish the raw materials for the idea to be developed. For example, a person can be creative about interpersonal relations by being sensitive to human feelings, emotions, and needs; it may not matter that he is not sensitive to chemical phenomena. The creative research chemist, however, must be highly sensitive to chemical phenomena, and it apparently does not matter that he is insensitive to many interpersonal phenomena, at least insofar as his creative ability as a research chemist is concerned.

There is a need, however, to make young children more sensitive to a wide range of environmental stimuli. Research has already shown that they can be helped to sense such stimuli more clearly and vividly and that this affects the quality of their creative productions. In one experimental validation of this idea, Littwin (1935) tried three methods of developing imaginative writing with three matched groups of seventh- and eighth-grade pupils. Over a ten-week period, one group practiced writing vivid descriptions of pictures which they had previously studied; the second studied literary models containing words of sound, color, and movement; the third group practiced describing all the possible sensations, such as sight, smell, touch, and hearing, that they could experience in examining an object or situation. The group emphasizing perception through the various senses showed significantly greater gains on composition tests than did the other two groups.

DEVELOPING SENSITIVITY
THROUGH CONSTRUCTIVE CRITICISM

A study of the psychology of inventors (Rossman, 1931) indicates that an important difference between the inventor and the noninventor is that the latter tends only to "cuss" the defects of his environment and the former tends to say, "This is the way to do it." These two kinds of thinking are apparent in the responses of children even in the kindergarten. For example, some can think of endless defects in a toy, a picture, or an action, but no constructive response seems to occur to them. Many say that the toy dog used in the test should be able to move without suggesting how it could be made to move. Others would put wheels on it, tie a string on it to pull it along, put a motor or battery in it, place a magnet in its nose, install a winding apparatus, and the like.

We have some evidence that the habits and skills of this type of constructive criticism can be developed even in adults. Certainly the criticism of the work of pupils and of published works provides an appropriate vehicle for developing such skills. In a class of graduate students, the author assigned students the task of reading and analyzing five journal articles related to the course. One group was instructed to read the article *critically* and in its written reports to point out defects in the statement of the problem, the underlying assumptions, hypotheses, data-collection procedures, techniques of analysis and reporting, conclusions, interpretations, and the like. The second group was asked to read the articles *imaginatively* and in its reports to point out other possibilities in the statement of the problem, the underlying assumptions, hypotheses, and the like. During the second half of the course, students were required to develop a "new idea" in the field. The "new ideas" of those who had read the articles imaginatively were judged to be of higher quality than those of the students who had read the research articles critically.

Reading creatively involves either a heightening of anticipation or doing something with what has been read. Both of these approaches involve some degree of elaboration of what is read. First, even though the goal is to reproduce what has been read, it can and should be done with imagination. Next to reproducing imaginatively what one has read comes elaborating or spelling out what has been read. Third is the transformation or rearrangement of what is read. Shakespeare's creativity was of this type. Fourth is the stage of going beyond what is read. A good story, biography, or other reading material is likely to evoke many ideas and questions which can send the reader far beyond what is read.

DEVELOPING SENSITIVITY
THROUGH CRITICAL AND CREATIVE READING OF COMIC BOOKS

"Teachers can cope most successfully with the comic book problem when they face it frankly, as a reality . . . ," says deBoer (Herrick and Jacobs, 1955, p. 375). Critical and creative reading of comic books would appear to be a promising technique for exploiting the nine- to twelve-year-olds' increasing interest in reality. Have him criticize the material in the comic books from the standpoint of reality as he has experienced it, as he has observed it in the behavior of others, and as he has found it in history, geography, and other courses in the elementary school. Use this method to teach constructive criticism. How could the author have handled a sequence more realistically? What would a certain character have really said or done?

DEVELOPING SENSITIVITY
THROUGH THE TAPE RECORDER

Listening skills are important in the development of sensitivity. A very important device for teaching these skills is the tape recorder. Its possibilities are almost infinite in variety. For example, many of us are extremely poor listeners in face-to-face conversation. Record a conversation between two members of the class and then play it back. Have the children listen to one another and catch the things they had not heard at first. The teacher can also prepare tape recordings of school and community events, special programs, and the like. The class can then be given experience in listening for information, ideas, attitudes, or the like. The teacher can also encourage a creative set in listening by asking pupils as they listen to consider how the speaker is really feeling and what he is really thinking. The teacher can also record the pupils' own story telling and have this replayed for their analysis and reactions.

DEVELOPING SENSITIVITY
BY EXPLOITING INCREASED INTEREST IN REALISM

Children between the ages of nine and twelve have a wide range of interests and show decreased interest in imaginative play and increased interest in realism and in "proving things." This characteristic helps to explain a sharp decrement in most of the creative thinking abilities between the third and fourth grades. If this characteristic is recognized and exploited, however, it is likely that much of this decrement will be eliminated.

The exploitation suggested is entirely in line with the legitimate aims of education. In fact, one of the most widely accepted objectives of education is to teach the young to test reality, to give them a realistic picture of the world in which they live. The trouble is that we try too hard to achieve this realistic perception of the world by memorizing facts and tend to neglect experiences through which boys and girls learn to test their perceptions against reality and to trust their own perceptions of reality. Teachers and classmates reject brilliant and imaginative ideas without testing.

Some of the more obvious kinds of testing would be in the realm of science, but language arts would seem to have a role in this process as well. Certainly the ability to hear more, see more, smell more, feel more, and the like are related to the development of language skills. A legitimate kind of activity would seem to be assignments in which children express creatively ideas and feelings stimulated by literature, music, painting, and the like.

Children between nine and twelve can also weigh evidences and draw conclusions based on information secured from several sources. Thus, another kind of exercise would involve giving facts from several sources and having pupils write conclusions, giving their reasoning for the conclusions. Controversial topics in the press and radio are frequently suitable for this purpose. The process of selecting questions, analyzing the issues, gathering data, and appraising the data should also have value in developing both the creative and evaluative thinking abilities.

DEVELOPING SENSITIVITY AND FLUENCY THROUGH WORD GAMES

In addition to their value in teaching spelling and vocabulary, word games can also be used to develop fluency and sensitivity. Baker (1955) has described a number of such games designed primarily to improve spelling. These include alphabet games, writing games, dictionary games, word authors, and word lotto. The writing games described by Baker would appear to be suited to the purpose of developing fluency and sensitivity among children in the intermediate grades. Included are such activities as making new words by adding letters, making new words by leaving off letters, finding little words in big words, making new words by rearranging letters, finding words that have the opposite meaning, and the like. Dictionary games are also appropriate. One variation is to list in alphabetical order the names of fruits or vegetables or some other class of objects, beginning with each letter of the alphabet.

DEVELOPING SENSITIVITY AND FLUENCY
THROUGH CREATIVE DRAMATICS

Creative dramatics in its many forms can be useful in developing fluency and sensitivity. In reading or listening to a story, play, or book, have your pupils pick out one of the characters, telling them to try and imagine themselves as this character as they listen and read. Afterwards, have them dramatize some part of the story or put the same characters in a somewhat different situation. They would of course play the parts with which they had identified. Those who compose the audience could then discuss how accurate the various portrayals were.

Children in the intermediate grades also have sufficient development to compose original plays. Swickhard (Herrick and Jacob, 1955) presents many valuable suggestions in her chapter on "Children's Experiences in Dramatic Interpretation." She includes the following as the processes which release dramatic interpretation: dramatic play, play making, finger plays, puppets and marionettes, choral verse, television and radio shows, pantomime and flannel boards, play writing and creative stories. She maintains that these types of activity develop sensitivity to color, drama, meaning, use, and origin of words. More detailed helps will be found in Ward's *Playmaking with Children* (1957) and Siks' *Creative Dramatics: An Art for Children* (1958).

Developing Ability· to Elaborate

Elaboration requires the specification of details that contribute to the development of a general idea. An example would be the task of listing the specific steps that should be taken in planning a class party or producing a class play. It is important that children form the habit of working out the full implication of their ideas. Often original thinkers fall short of their potential achievement because they fail to follow through on their ideas and work out their full implications. As a result, their work may have obvious defects which could have been eliminated easily. Or, such individuals may fail to reach an important discovery just because they did not press their thinking far enough. Children should begin learning early a willingness to follow through on ideas and do some of the tedious work of implementing ideas. Later, they should develop a willingness to submit their ideas to the standard tests of art, literature, science, and the like. They must learn that this may take days, weeks, or even months, and that the process which they must follow may not be completely evident at any one time.

There is much that the language arts teacher can do to contribute to the development of the habit of working out the implications of ideas. In his own field, he can help make available the resources for working out ideas. Otherwise, frustration and a feeling of purposelessness are likely to result. There is value in the excitement which comes from seeing the embodiment of one's idea in some concrete form or product. This may be a letter written and mailed to accomplish a certain purpose, a news story published in the school paper or local paper, a play produced by the class, a song sung by one's classmates, copy for an advertisement converted into a poster or billboard, or any one of many other such products.

It is this need for training children to elaborate upon their ideas which makes so valuable such sustained projects as writing a play, a book, or some other literary work.

DEVELOPING ABILITY TO ELABORATE
THROUGH WRITING A BOOK

Stegall in *Creative Ways in Teaching the Language Arts,* prepared by a subcommittee of the Elementary Section Committee of the National Council of Teachers of English, describes a very exciting experience in which fourth-graders wrote a book. Through this creative vehicle they learned about outlining, organizing, paragraphing, capitalizing, punctuating, usage, and the like. In the process, these fourth-graders also prepared a volume entitled *My Own English Book* which contained all the rules applied in writing the book after they had been evolved, tested, and accepted. The first book was a cooperative class project, but at the end of the first semester *each child* in the class clamored to write his own—his very own—novel during the second semester.

Such an activity provides one of the few kinds of activities which has a continuity not broken up by schedules, bells, and the like. It gives children a chance to carry out an idea to completion. This need is a strong one and brings with it much satisfaction.

DEVELOPING ABILITY TO ELABORATE
THROUGH AUTHOR ILLUSTRATIONS

Research (Burrows, 1959) shows that elaboration can be improved in the early school years by having children illustrate their stories or tell whole stories through pictures. For example, one third-grade class was instructed to fold paper into parts and plan a sequence of pictures to narrate a story. As a result, they expressed more ideas and wrote more words and sentences than when they planned and merely wrote. Apparently the "spelling out," or elaboration, of ideas in a visual medium stimulates children to cross the threshold from oral communication to use of written symbols. It seems to be the manipulation and playing around with ideas that make the difference.

Developing Curiosity

LEARNING SKILLS OF ASKING AND GUESSING

Children need help in keeping alive their curiosity and ability to ask questions. They need help in learning how to ask good questions and to improve their ability to ask better questions by making good guesses about the possible answers.

One way to develop such skills would be to follow a procedure similar to one used in testing these skills. Use an interesting picture of almost any kind. First, have your pupils ask as many questions as they can think of which cannot be answered just by looking at the picture. Have the class test the quality of each question by asking such questions as "Can the question be answered by looking at the picture?" "Can the question be answered?" and "Would the answer be of any use, if we knew it?" Afterwards, they can make guesses about the causes of the events and/or conditions shown in the picture and the consequences, both immediate and long-range. After the guesses, have them ask additional questions to determine whether or not their guesses are accurate. Finally, you might have them write a paragraph stating which guess they think is most likely to be correct and why they think so.

At times, it is not enough just to ask questions and make guesses. There must be a "right" answer against which questions and guesses are directed. There are a number of interesting and effective ways for doing this. One would be a variation of the old "twenty questions game." The object might be to guess the ending of a story, an object in the room, or the like. Instead of "twenty questions," the contest might be to discover the answer using the fewest possible questions. After discovering the correct answer, individuals or groups can be encouraged to take a look at their thought processes, trying to discover how they might have asked better questions.

DEVELOPING OR KEEPING ALIVE CURIOSITY
THROUGH READING

There are some evidences that curiosity decreases at about the fourth grade. This is a time, however, when the child's interest in reality increases and when his reading skills reach a relatively high level. These two developmental factors can be used to develop and keep alive his curiosity. Reading can be used both to stimulate and to satisfy his curiosity. One of the greatest rewards to the curious person is to find answers to his questions. Reading can provide some of the answers and thus keep alive this valuable quality.

General Suggestions

USING CREATIVE WRITING FOLDERS

Our most creative thinking does not occur as the result of conscious effort; nor is it a function of the unconscious. It is a function of the preconscious. Important ideas occur to some people in the heat of various kinds of activities. Quiet periods of relaxation are also conducive to creative thinking. The bathtub, the church, the bed, and the like have been named repeatedly by inventors and scientific discoverers as the birthplace of great ideas.

The best compositions are not likely to be written in a scheduled thirty-minute period or even for tomorrow's homework. It is a good idea to encourage children to keep all their creative writing in a folder and then have them submit their best work. Along with this, it would be a good idea to encourage them to establish the "idea-trap" habit. Some of their best ideas for poems, stories, and songs will occur at times and places not suitable for working on them. If they jot down the idea in a notebook, this will "trap the idea," and they can return to it later and work it into a poem, story, play, or the like.

EVOLVING AND TESTING
RULES OF GRAMMAR AND COMPOSITION

A creative method of teaching rules of grammar and composition tested successfully by some teachers in the intermediate grades involves a process of evolving and testing rules. One approach is to have pupils watch for examples in their reading. If they observe a certain usage frequently enough, they are urged to make a rule about it and present it to the class for consideration. A rule must be *proved* by ten examples. Each such discovery may be rewarded for example by "three points." Since superior pupils are likely to be the ones who push the hunt for rules and proof, less aggressive pupils can be encouraged by awarding them one point for further strengthening the rule.

DEVELOPING CREATIVE THINKING
THROUGH DIFFICULT OR CHALLENGING PROBLEMS AND ASSIGNMENTS

One of the chief requirements for the occurrence of creative thinking is that the problem be sufficiently difficult in relation to the resources of the individual. If the problem is too easy, perception or a short reasoning process will be enough to give the answer, and creative thinking will not occur. If a problem is complex enough, the thinker will not be able to reach an easy solution at once by memory, perception, or a short reasoning process. A difficult problem must be approached from all angles and cannot be solved immediately. The thinker must continue to wrestle with it. It is only in this way that a high level of creative thinking is elicited.

Most teachers are far too conservative in what they expect of children's creative problem solving.

Principles for Rewarding Creative Thinking

Research tells us that children and adults learn and develop along the lines which they find rewarding. In our classrooms, children are rewarded for spelling words correctly, memorizing the multiplication tables, getting the correct solution to an arithmetic problem, giving the correct answer on a geography test, dotting *i*'s, and crossing *t*'s. They are rewarded for being neat, polite, clean, cooperative, honest, and punctual. In other words, most of the rewards in education go to those who meet "behavioral norms"—get the right answers, hit the right note, keep in step. It is not suggested that we abandon rewarding these behaviors. It is only suggested that we *also* reward creative thinking.

There are two major obstacles to achieving this goal. These two obstacles need to be understood and mastered. The first is in recognizing and appreciating the child's creative ideas or productions. It is particularly difficult for a conventional teacher to recognize and appreciate the contribution of an unconventional or an unloved and unlovely child. It is not difficult to understand why the highly creative child with his eternal questioning, manipulating, experimenting, and unexpected answers is disturbing to the class and the teacher.

A second obstacle to valuing creativity is our tendency to overrate the finished product—the finished poem, the masterpiece of music or art, the balanced interpersonal relationship, the organized behavior of the championship team. We are too easily deceived by the comparative perfection and smoothness of these masterpieces and evaluate them as if they were the immediate deliveries of a creative act. We also tend in our society to withhold rewards for new creative works of all kinds. For example, almost all concert programs are filled with a preponderance of old music. Copland (1959) has recently called our concert halls "auditory museums of a most limited kind." He maintains that this obsession with old music makes music listening safe and unadventurous, since it deals only with the accepted masters. The danger, of course, is that this tendency extended into many fields will eventually result in a depletion of creative talent.

The following six tentative principles are offered for rewarding creative thinking in the classroom:

1. Be respectful of children's questions.
2. Be respectful of imaginative and unusual ideas.
3. Show pupils that their ideas have value.
4. Give opportunities for practice or experimentation without evaluation.
5. Encourage and evaluate self-initiated learning.
6. Tie in evaluations with causes and consequences.

Each of these will now be discussed briefly with suggestions for applying them.

TREAT QUESTIONS WITH RESPECT

One of the first requirements for creative thinking is the capacity to be puzzled. Children have this capacity to be puzzled, and their curiosity impels them to ask questions and in one way or another to find the answers. The world, however, does not much like curiosity. As Morgan (1959) says:

> The world says that curiosity killed the cat. The world dismisses curiosity by calling it idle, or *mere* idle, curiosity—even though curious persons are seldom idle. Parents do their best to extinguish curiosity in their children, because it makes life difficult to be faced every day with a string of unanswerable questions about what makes fire hot and why grass grows, or to have to halt Junior's investigations before they end in explosion and sudden death (Morgan, 1959, p. 13).

The teacher who is respectful of the child's questions will use the child's poor questions as an opportunity to teach the class how to ask good questions. She will help and/or show him how to find the answers to his questions. The most important reward for the curious child is to find the answers to his questions.

BE RESPECTFUL OF IMAGINATIVE, UNUSUAL IDEAS

In most classrooms, the child who expresses a new or unusual idea not in the books takes a calculated risk. In such a setting, it takes a great deal of courage for a child to press for presentation of his unusual ideas. Such ideas are frequently hooted at with disbelief and branded as "silly" or "screwy." He hesitates to risk interrupting the orderly classroom procedure and sequence in suggesting ideas different from those in the book.

Children should be taught early not to be afraid to express their ideas. They themselves can be taught to evaluate some of them, and these can be tested or considered further by the group and evaluated on the basis of the evidence. This testing can take place in a sympathetic and constructive manner.

The teacher who is respectful of imaginative ideas will avoid making fun of the child's ideas, the gadgets and other objects he produces, or the conclusions he draws from his experiences. This teacher will show the child how to test his ideas for reasonableness against what he and others already know. He will try to establish in the class the habit of considering and testing ideas. He will encourage the three-stage process of asking questions, making guesses, and testing the guesses.

SHOW PUPILS THEIR IDEAS HAVE VALUE

It is important that the child learns early to place value on his own ideas and to trust his perceptions of reality. One approach to this is to have him form the habit of recording what he thinks. This helps him to appreciate the value of his imagination and at the same time discourages excessive daydreaming. As the child sees his ideas expressed in some concrete form, he should be encouraged to continue his efforts. The "idea-trap" habit already described helps to prevent good ideas from slipping away from us. Even though the idea may at the time seem a little far-fetched and it is not possible to determine its real significance, it is wise to record it. The idea can be criticized, modified, or rejected at a later time, or it may stimulate another really important idea.

The language arts teacher who shows her pupils that their ideas have value will do the following:

1. Write the ideas down or have them record the ideas in some way
2. Consider the ideas of pupils and adopt some of them for use in classroom activities
3. Help the students find opportunities to try out some of their ideas
4. Display creative work on bulletin boards, or in some other way communicate the results of their testing

The teacher must recognize that the drive to communicate the answer once it has been discovered is about as strong as the drive to ask questions. Providing opportunities for communicating ideas is an important reward.

Most writers in the language arts field, such as Laura Zirbes (1959) and Mauree Applegate (1962), emphasize that children's writings should serve some real purposes which they can recognize. They should write letters that can be mailed, songs that can be sung, poems and stories that can be read and enjoyed, and plays that can be enacted. Various devices should be developed so that their writings can be read, used, shared, and enjoyed by one another. This can be done in a number of ways. Copies can be duplicated and distributed, or the original or rewritten version can be placed in a class folio or book. Writings can also be placed on the bulletin board, in the school paper, or displayed in other ways. Their creative dramatics and discussions can be replayed and discussed or transcribed and edited so they can be enjoyed by others. Zirbes suggests that it can be useful to have an older student or adult give an appreciative reading of an original poem or story before a group of friends or peers.

GIVE OPPORTUNITIES FOR PRACTICE OR EXPERIMENTATION WITHOUT EVALUATION

External evaluation is always a threat and as such brings out defensiveness and cuts off awareness of some portion of experience. Experiments (Hemphill, 1961) show that rejection of ideas by the group is a powerful inhibitor of efforts to initiate ideas. At the same time, research also indicates that we tend to learn along whatever lines are evaluated in determining grades, rate of pay, and the like. Thus creative productions need to be evaluated, but the process should be nonthreatening, especially in the learning or trying-out stage.

It would seem that this condition could be created by providing a practice period which "doesn't count." Children would be encouraged to experiment, to try out different ideas, and to explore possibilities. They would be told not to be afraid of messing up their paper or other materials and assured that "it won't count on the record." Later, of course, they will be given a similar task which will be evaluated.

In some of our earlier testing of children, we noted again and again that some terribly inhibited children whose creativity seemed to be paralyzed became tremendously productive when urged to think of ideas just for fun. We have recently conducted an experiment in which we tried to test the effects of such a practice session as opposed to the effects of immediate evaluation even in the practice session.

ENCOURAGE AND EVALUATE SELF-INITIATED LEARNING

Apparently the first signs of creative thinking occur in the spontaneous accompaniment of other activities. One mark of the highly creative individual is his exceptional self-starting ability. The strong curiosity of the child and his exploratory tendencies suggest that all or almost all children have this self-starting ability. The problem of parents and teachers is to keep it alive. It seems quite possible that too much reliance is placed upon prescribed curricula and that we need to make more efforts to appraise and credit growth resulting from the student's own initiative.

Since it is quite apparent that the rate of change in our society has increased and that we can expect ever increasing rates of change, it would seem that more emphasis might be placed on the task of learning how to learn, the development of self-motivation, and the like. Perhaps we would develop a higher level of creative thinking if we did not try to teach such a large number of subjects and allowed time for self-initiated learning, thinking creatively about the materials taught, carrying out some of the new ideas developed, and the like. Above all, we should provide some time for pupils to think.

TIE IN EVALUATIONS WITH CAUSES AND CONSEQUENCES

It is important that children learn to use their imagination to understand the relationship between what happens to them and cause and consequence. It is this kind of thinking that we try to obtain through the causes and consequences parts of our *Ask-and-Guess Test.* This ask-and-guess approach can also be developed into a very powerful teaching design, as Mork (1959) has set forth in a recent article.

The relationship of behavior to causes and consequences can also be taught when the defects of ideas or solutions are criticized or when naughty or dangerous behavior is punished. The teacher who ties in evaluation with causes and consequences helps the child to see this relationship and thus learn from his experiences.

Five Principles for Rewarding Creative Thinking in Children

We know that all teachers to some extent apply the principles listed below. In this field experiment, however, we are urging teachers to seek systematically and consciously to apply them in a reasonable and appropriate way.

1. *Treat questions with respect.* Use poor questions as an opportunity to teach how to ask good ones. Try to help the child or teach him how to find answers to questions. One of the most important rewards for the curious child is to find the answers to his questions.

2. *Treat imaginative ideas with respect.* Do not make fun of the child's ideas or conclusions from his experiences. Show him how to test his ideas for reasonableness against what he already knows. Try to establish, in the class, habits of considering and testing ideas.

3. *Show your pupils that their ideas have value.* Have them write down their ideas (or dictate them in the lower grades); adopt some of them or try them out in classroom activities; display them on the bulletin board. Above all, give them time to think.

4. Occasionally have pupils *do something "for practice" without the threat of evaluation,* to try something out, and later do a similar task for the record, for keeps.

5. *Tie in evaluation with causes and consequences.* In criticizing defects in ideas or in punishing naughty or dangerous behavior, explain the response in such a way as to foster the ability to see causes and consequences of behavior. Do not say, "This is good" or "This is bad." Say, "I like this because . . ." or "This could be made better by . . ."

All these principles must, of course, be applied within the limitations of the age group you teach. The applications should be continued and consistent rather than just "one-shot" treatments.

You might find it useful sometime soon to write out a description of specific instances in which you applied each of these principles. You can then review them and consider your behavior more insightfully than when it occurred. You might also find it useful to discuss your descriptions with a colleague.

REPORT OF INCIDENT OF REWARDING CREATIVE THINKING

Grade:_____ Date:_____ PRINCIPLE: Treat questions with respect.

Describe an incident in which you as the teacher or the pupils in the
class showed respect for an unusual question, a silly question, a
difficult question, an annoying question, etc.

1. What was the question, who asked it, and what were the general
   conditions under which it was asked?

2. What was your immediate reaction?

3. What was the immediate reaction of the class, if observable?

4. In what way was respect shown for the question?

5. What, if any, were the observable effects (immediate and/or long-
   range)?

REPORT OF INCIDENT OF REWARDING CREATIVE THINKING

Grade:_____ Date:_____ PRINCIPLE: Treat imaginative ideas with respect.

Describe an incident in which you as the teacher or the pupils in your class showed respect for an unusual idea, a silly or wild idea, a dangerous idea, etc.

1. What was the idea, who expressed it, and what were the general conditions under which the idea was suggested?

2. What was your immediate reaction to the idea?

3. What was the immediate reaction of the class, if observable?

4. In what way was respect shown for the idea?

5. What, if any, were the observable effects (immediate and/or long-range)?

REPORT OF INCIDENT OF REWARDING CREATIVE THINKING

Grade:_____ Date:_____ PRINCIPLE: Show pupils that their ideas
                                      have value.

Describe an incident in which you were able to communicate to one of
your pupils that his ideas have value.

1. What was the occasion which provided the opportunity to show a
    pupil that his ideas are valuable? Who was the child? What did
    he do? How did he seem to feel about his idea(s)?

2. What did you do to try to show him that his ideas are of value?

3. How did he react to what you did (immediate and/or long-range)?

4. What was the reaction of the class, if observable?

REPORT OF INCIDENT REWARDING CREATIVE THINKING

Grade:_____ Date:_____ PRINCIPLE: Do something for practice
                                        and later for record.

Describe below an incident in which you had pupils do something for
practice, just experimenting, with no threat of evaluation, and later
had them perform a similar task "for the record."

1. Describe the initial assignment and the general situation in which
    it was given.

2. How did you communicate to them that they were free to experiment,
    that it didn't count, etc.?

3. What happened during the "practice" period?

4. What happened immediately after the practice period?

5. What was the nature of the similar task given for "the record?"

6. How was it rewarded, if rewarded?

REPORT OF INCIDENT REWARDING CREATIVE THINKING

Grade:_____ Date:_____ PRINCIPLE: Tie evaluation to cause and
effect.

Describe below some incident in which you tied in evaluation with
causes and consequences.

1.   What was the nature of the behavior to be evaluated? Who was
     involved?

2.   What was your personal evaluation of the behavior?

3.   How did you or the class show the relationship of the behavior to
     cause and/or consequence?

4.   What were the effects, if observable (immediate and/or long-
     range)?

REFERENCES

Abramson, J., "Essai d'Etalonnage de Deux Tests d'Imagination et d'Observation," *Journal de Psychologie*, XXIV (1927), 370-379.

Allen, A., "Five-year Olds Can Think: Try Them Out in Discussion Situations," *Elementary English*, XL (1963), 72-74f.

Allen, M. S., *Morphological Creativity*. Englewood Cliffs, N.J.: Prentice-Hall, Inc., 1962.

Anderson, H. H., "Domination and Social Integration in the Behavior of Kindergarten Children and Teachers," *Genetic Psychology Monographs*, XXI (1939), 289-385.

————, ed., *Creativity and Its Cultivation*. New York: Harper and Row, Publishers, 1959.

————, "Developing Creativity in Children." Paper prepared for the 1960 White House Conference on Children and Youth, 1960. Mimeographed.

Andrews, E. G., "The Development of Imagination in the Pre-School Child," *University of Iowa Studies of Character*, Vol. III (1930), No. 4.

Applegate, M., *Helping Children Write*. Scranton, Pa.: International Textbook Co., 1949.

————, *Easy in English*. Evanston, Ill.: Harper & Row, Publishers, 1962.

Ashton-Warner, S., *Teacher*. New York: Simon and Schuster, Inc., 1963.

Baker, Z. W., *The Language Arts, The Child, and The Teacher*. San Francisco: Fearon Publishers, Inc., 1955.

Barbe, W. B. and T. S. Waterhouse, "An Experimental Program in Reading," *Elementary English*, XXX (1956), 102-104.

Barchillon, J., "Creativity and Its Inhibition in Child Prodigies," in *Personality Dimensions of Creativity*. New York: Lincoln Institute for Psychotherapy, 1961.

Barkan, M., *Through Art to Creativity*. Boston: Allyn and Bacon, Inc., 1960.

Barnes, F. R., "We Are All Researchers," *Instructor*, LXI (1960), 6-7.

Barron, F., "Originality in Relation to Personality and Intellect," *Journal of Personality*, XXV (1957), 730-742.

————, "The Psychology of Imagination," *Scientific American*, CXCIX (1958), 151-166.

————, *Creativity and Psychological Health*. Princeton, N.J.: D. Van Nostrand Co., Inc., 1963.

Bartlett, Sir F., *Thinking*. New York: Basic Books, Inc., 1958.

Baskin, S. and Ruth Churchill, "Experiments in Independent Study," *Antioch College Reports*. Yellow Springs, Ohio: Antioch College, March 1961.

Benson, K. R., *Creative Crafts for Children*. Englewood Cliffs, N.J.: Prentice-Hall, Inc., 1958.

Bentley, J. C., "The Creative Thinking Abilities and Different Kinds of Achievement." M.A. research paper. Minneapolis, Minn.: University of Minnesota, 1961.

Binet, A., *Les Idées Modernes sur les Enfants*. Paris: E. Flamarion, 1909.

Bloom, B. S., "Some Effects of Cultural, Social, and Educational Conditions on Creativity," in C. W. Taylor, ed., *The Second (1957) University of Utah Research Conference on the Identification of Creative Scientific Talent*. Salt Lake City: University of Utah Press, 1958, pp. 55-65.

Boraas, J., *Teaching to Think*. New York: The Macmillan Company, 1922.

Bosselman, B. C., *The Troubled Mind*. New York: The Ronald Press Company, 1953.

Bremer, N., "First-grade Achievement under Different Plans of Grouping," *Elementary English*, XXXV (1958), 324-326.

Bruner, J. S., *The Process of Education*. Cambridge, Mass.: Harvard University Press, 1960.

Buhl, H. R., *Understanding the Creative Engineer*. New York: American Society of Mechanical Engineers, 1961.

Burkhart, R. C., *Spontaneous and Deliberate Ways of Learning*. Scranton, Pa.: International Textbook Company, 1962.

Burkhart, R. C. and G. Bernheim, *Object Question Test Manual*. University Park, Pa.: Department of Art Education, Pennsylvania State University, 1963.

Burrows, A. T., *Teaching Composition*. Washington, D.C.: National Education Association, 1959.

Canfield, J. K., "Flexibility in Grouping in Reading," *Reading Teacher*, XI (1957), 91-94.

Chassell, L. M., "Tests for Originality," *Journal of Educational Psychology*, VII (1916), 317-328.

Clark, C. H., *Brainstorming*. Garden City, N.Y.: Doubleday & Company, Inc., 1958.

Clark, E. J., "The Relationship Between the Personality Traits of Elementary School Teachers and Their Evaluations of Objectional Pupil Behavior," *Journal of Educational Research*, XLV (1951), 61-66.

Cochran, W. W., "Elementary Patent Law," in *Training Manual for Patent Examiners*. Washington, D.C.: Patent Office, U. S. Department of Commerce, 1955.

Cogan, M. L., "The Behavior of Teachers and the Productive Behavior of Their Pupils; I: Perception Analysis," *Journal of Experimental Education*, XXVII (1958), 89-124.

Cole, N. R., *The Arts in the Classroom*. New York: The John Day Company, Inc., 1940.

Coleman, J. S., *The Adolescent Society*. New York: Free Press of Glencoe, Inc., 1961.

Colvin, S. S., "Invention Versus Form in English Composition: An Inductive Study," *Pedagogical Seminary*, IX (1902), 393-421.

Compton, A. H., "Case Histories: Creativity in Science," in *The Nature of Creative Thinking*. New York: Industrial Relations Institute, Inc., 1953.

Conant, H. and A. Randall, *Art in Education*. Peoria, Ill.: Chas. A. Bennett Co., Inc., 1959.

Copland, A., *Music and Imagination*. New York: Mentor Books, 1959.

Crutchfield, R. S., "Male Superiority in 'Intuitive' Problem Solving," *American Psychologist*, XV (1960), 429. Abstract.

———, "Conformity and Creative Thinking," in H. E. Gruber, G. Terrell, and M. Wertheimer, eds., *Contemporary Approaches to Creative Thinking*, pp. 120-140. New York: Atherton Press, 1962.

Cunnington, B. F., P. Buckland, and R. Peterson, *Giovanni and the Giant*. Minneapolis, Minn.: Bureau of Educational Research, University of Minnesota, 1962. Mimeographed.

Cunnington, B. F. and E. P. Torrance, *Sounds and Images*. Minneapolis, Minn.: Bureau of Educational Research, University of Minnesota, 1962. Mimeographed.

Darnell, D., *Effects of Three Different Methods of Evaluating Writings upon Creativity in Writing*. Ann Arbor, Mich.: University Microfilms, Inc., 1962.

Datta, L., "Test Instructions and the Identification of Creative Scientific Talent." Unpublished paper. New York: General Electric Co., 1963.

Dimnet, E., *The Art of Thinking*. New York: Simon and Schuster, Inc., 1930.

Dinkmeyer, D. and R. Dreikurs, *Encouraging Children to Learn*. Englewood Cliffs, N.J.: Prentice-Hall, Inc., 1963.

Drabek, T. E., "Student Preferences in Professor-Student Classroom Role Relations." Paper read at annual meeting of the Ohio Valley Sociological Association, Toledo, Ohio, May 4, 1963.

Drews, E. M., "Recent Findings about Gifted Adolescents," in E. P. Torrance, ed., *New Ideas: Third Minnesota Conference on Gifted Children*. Minneapolis: Center for Continuation Study, University of Minnesota, 1961a.

———, "A Critical Evaluation of Approaches to the Identification of Gifted Students," in A. Traxler, ed., *Measurement and Evaluation in Today's Schools*, pp. 47-51. Washington, D.C.: American Council on Education, 1961b.

Dykstra, R., "An Investigation of the Reading Vocabulary of Beginning Second-grade Pupils with Special Emphasis Given to Words Not Introduced in the First Grade." M.A. research report. Minneapolis, Minn.: University of Minnesota, 1959.

✗ Eherts, A. S., "An Experimental Investigation of the Effect of Extraneous Motivation on the Development of Creative Thinking," M.A. research paper. Stetson, Fla.: Stetson University, 1961.

✗ Eicholz, G. C., "Why Do Teachers Reject Change?" *Theory into Practice*, II (1963), 264-268.

Emrich, R. L., *Style of Thinking: A Cross-cultural Study of Cognition*. Ann Arbor, Mich.: University Microfilms, Inc., 1962.

Ferebee, J. D., "Learning Form Through Creative Expression," *Elementary English*, XXVII (1950), 73-78.

Ferren, J., "The Problem of Creative Thinking in Painting," in *The Nature of Creative Thinking*. New York: Industrial Relations Institute, Inc., 1953.

Fiedler, F. E., W. Meuwese, and S. Oonk, *Performance on Laboratory Tasks Requiring Group Creativity: An Exploratory Study*. Urbana, Ill.: Center for Research in Social Psychology, University of Illinois, 1960.

✗ Fine, B., *Stretching Their Minds*. New York: E. P. Dutton & Co., Inc., 1964.

Flanagan, D., "Creativity in Science," in P. Smith, ed., *Creativity*, pp. 103-109. New York: Hastings House, Publishers, Inc., 1959.

Flanagan, J. C., "The Definition and Measurement of Ingenuity," in C. W. Taylor and F. Barron, eds., *Scientific Creativity: Its Recognition and Development*, pp. 89-98. New York: John Wiley & Sons, Inc., 1963.

Fleming, E. S. and S. Weintraub, "Attitudinal Rigidity as a Measure of Creativity in Gifted Children," *Journal of Educational Psychology*, LIII (1962), 81-86.

Flesch, R., "A New Readability Yardstick," *Journal of Applied Psychology*, XXXII (1948), 221-233.

Flesch, R. and A. H. Lass, *The Way to Write*. New York: McGraw-Hill Book Company, 1955.

Fredericksen, N., *Development of the Test "Formulating Hypotheses": A Progress Report*. Princeton, N.J.: Educational Testing Service, 1959.

Freedman, R., *Teenagers Who Made History*. New York: Holiday House, 1961.

✗ French, R. L., "Research as a Basis for Creative Teaching," *Educational Horizons*, XI (Fall 1961), 28-34.

Friedenberg, E. Z., *The Vanishing Adolescent*. New York: Dell Publishing Company, 1959.

✗ Gainsberg, J. C., "Critical Reading Is Creative Reading and Needs Creative Teaching," *Reading Teacher*, VII (1953), 19-26.

Getzels, J. W., "Non-IQ Intellectual and Other Factors in College Admission," in *The Coming Crisis in the Selection of Students for College Entrance*. Washington, D.C.: American Educational Research Association, 1960.

✓ Getzels, J. W. and P. W. Jackson, *Creativity and Intelligence*. New York: John Wiley & Sons, Inc., 1962.

Gibbs, E., *The Teaching of Art in School*. New York: John de Graff, Inc., 1958.

Ginn, O., "Should Boys and Girls Go to School Together?" *Parade*, October 21, 1962, pp. 8-9.

Goertzel, V. and M. G. Goertzel, *Cradles of Eminence*. Boston: Little, Brown & Co., 1962.

Goralski, P. S., "Creativity: Student Teachers' Perceptions of Approaches to Classroom Teaching." Doctoral Dissertation. Minneapolis, Minn.: University of Minnesota, 1964.

Gordon, W. J. J., *Synectics: The Development of Creative Capacity*. New York: Harper and Row, Publishers, 1961.

Griffiths, R., *A Study of Imagination in Early Childhood*. London: Routledge & Kegan Paul, Ltd., 1945.

Grippen, V. B., "A Study of Creative Artistic Imagination in Children by the Constant Contact Procedure," *Psychological Monographs*, XLV (1933), 63-81.

Grover, B. L., "Some Effects and Correlates of Different Types of Practice Used in Studying a Topic in Ninth-grade Classrooms." Doctoral Dissertation. Minneapolis, Minn.: University of Minnesota, 1963.

Grozinger, W., *Scribbling, Drawing, Painting*. New York: Frederick A. Praeger, Inc., 1955.

Guilford, J. P., "Creativity," *American Psychologist*, V (1950), 444-454.

——, "Structure of Intellect," *Psychological Bulletin*, LIII (1956), 267-293.

——, *Personality*. New York: McGraw-Hill Book Company, 1959a.

——, "Three Faces of Intellect," *American Psychologist*, XIV (1959b), 469-479.

——, "Basic Conceptual Problems of the Psychology of Thinking," in E. Harms, ed., *Proceedings of the New York Academy of Sciences*. New York: New York Academy of Sciences, 1960.

——, "Some New Looks at the Nature of the Creative Processes." Paper presented at a Symposium on Psychological Measurement at the Dedication of Thurstone Hall, Educational Testing Service, Princeton, New Jersey, April 14, 1962.

Guilford, J. P. and P. R. Merrifield, *The Structure of Intellect Model: Its Uses and Implications*. Los Angeles: University of Southern California, 1960.

Guilford, J. P., P. R. Merrifield, and Anna B. Cox, *Creative Thinking at the Junior High School Level*. Los Angeles: University of Southern California, 1961.

Guilford, J. P., R. C. Wilson, P. R. Christensen, and D. J. Lewis, *A Factor-analytic Study of Creative Thinking; I: Hypotheses and Descriptions of Tests*. Los Angeles: University of Southern California, 1951.

Hammer, E. F., *Creativity*. New York: Random House, 1961.

Handlin, O., "Are Colleges Killing Education?" *Atlantic*, CCIX (1962), 41-45.

Harding, H. F., "Is There a Vital Need for a More Creative Trend in American Education?" Address at the Symposium on Developing Creative Potential Through Education, Webber College, Babson Park, Florida, February 21, 1963.

Hargreaves, H. L., "The 'Faculty' of Imagination," *British Journal of Psychology, Monograph Supplement*, Vol. III (1927), No. 10.

Harms, E., "A Test for Types of Formal Creativity," *Psychological Bulletin*, XXXVI (1939), 526-527.

Harris D., "The Development and Validation of a Test of Creativity in Engineering," *Journal of Applied Psychology*, XLIV (1960), 254-257.

Harris, R. H. and A. L. Simberg, *AC Test of Creativity Ability: Examiner's Manual*. Chicago: Education-Industry Service, 1225 East 60th Street, 1959.

Hart, A. M., "A Study of Creative Thinking and Its Relation to Nursing." Doctoral Dissertation. Indianapolis, Ind.: Indiana University, 1962.

Hebeisen, A. A., "The Performance of a Group of Schizophrenic Patients on a Test of Creative Thinking," M.A. research paper. Minneapolis, Minn.: University of Minnesota, 1959.

Hemphill, J., "Why People Attempt to Lead," in L. Petrullo and B. M. Bass, eds., *Leadership and Interpersonal Behavior*, pp. 201-215. New York: Holt, Rinehart & Winston, Inc., 1961.

Henry, J., "The Problem of Spontaneity, Initiative, and Creativity in Suburban Classrooms," *American Journal of Orthopsychiatry*, XXIX (1959), 266-279.

―――, *Culture Against Man*. New York: Random House, 1963.

Herrick, V. E. and L. B. Jacobs, eds., *Children and the Language Arts*. Englewood Cliffs, N.J.: Prentice-Hall, Inc., 1955.

Heyl, H. H., "Grouping Within the Classroom," *National Elementary Principal*, XXXV (1955), 83-86.

Heys, F., Jr., "The Theme-a-Week Assumption: A Report of an Experiment," *English Journal*, LI (1962), 320-322.

Hinton, E. M., *An Analytical Study of the Qualities of Style and Rhetoric in English Composition*. New York: Bureau of Publications, Teachers College, Columbia University, 1940.

Hoffman, L. R. and N. R. F. Maier, "Sex Differences, Sex Composition, and Group Problem Solving," *Journal of Abnormal and Social Psychology*, LXIII (1961), 453-456.

Holland, J. L., "Creative and Academic Performance Among Talented Adolescents," *Journal of Educational Psychology*, LII (1961), 136-137.

Holland, J. L. and L. Kent, "The Concentration of Scholarship Funds and Its Implications for Education," *College and University*, XXXV (Summer 1960), 471-483.

Hourd, M. L. and G. E. Cooper, *Coming into Their Own*. London: William Heinemann, Limited, 1959.

Hyman, R., *Some Experiments in Creativity*. New York: General Electric Co., 1960.

———, "On Prior Information and Creativity," *Psychological Reports*, IX (1961), 151-161.

Jefferson, B., *Teaching Art to Children*. Boston: Allyn and Bacon, Inc., 1959.

Julian, J. W. and I. D. Steiner, "Perceived Acceptance as a Determinant of Conformity Behavior," *Journal of Social Psychology*, LV (1961), 191-198.

Kirkpatrick, E. A., "Individual Tests of School Children," *Psychological Review*, V (1900), 274.

Kubie, L. S., *Neurotic Distortion of the Creative Process*. Lawrence, Kan.: University of Kansas Press, 1958.

LaPiere, R., *The Freudian Ethic*. New York: Duell, Sloan & Pearce, Inc., 1959.

Lasswell, H. D., "New Horizons in Human Relations," in R. M. MacIver, ed., *New Horizons in Creative Thinking*, pp. 139-146. New York: Harper & Row, Publishers, 1954.

Lichter, S. O., E. B. Rapien, F. M. Seibert, and M. A. Sklansky, *The Drop-Outs*. New York: Free Press of Glencoe, Inc., 1962.

Littwin, M. F., "Experimental Investigation of the Effect of Method of Presentation Upon the Imaginative Quality of Descriptive Writing among Elementary-School Pupils," *Journal of Experimental Psychology*, IV (1935), 44-49.

Lowenfeld, V., *Creative and Mental Growth*. New York: The Macmillan Company, 1952.

McCardle, H. J., *An Investigation of the Relationship Between Pupil Achievement in First-Year Algebra and Some Teacher Characteristics*. Ann Harbor, Mich.: University Microfilms, Inc., 1959.

McCarty, S. A., *Children's Drawings: A Study of Interest and Abilities*. Baltimore: The William & Wilkins Co., 1924.

McCloy, W. and N. C. Maier, "Re-creative Imagination," *Psychological Monographs*, LI (1939), 108-116.

McConnell, T. R., "Discovery vs. Authoritative Identification in the Learning of Children," *University of Iowa Studies in Education*, IX (1934), 13-62.

McDonald, F. J., *Educational Psychology*. Belmont, Calif.: Wadsworth Publishing Company, Inc., 1959.

McGreevey, P., Personal communication to author, Olympia, Washington, November 27, 1961.

McGuire, C., E. Hindsman, F. J. King, and E. Jennings, "Dimensions of Talented Behavior," *Educational and Psychological Measurement*, XXI (1961), 3-38.

McKeachie, W. J., "How Do Students Learn?" in R. Cooper, ed., *The Two*

Ends of the Log. Minneapolis, Minn.: University of Minnesota Press, 1958.

X MacKinnon, D. W., "Characteristics of the Creative Person: Implications for the Teaching-Learning Process," in *Current Issues in Higher Education*, pp. 89-92. Washington, D.C.: Association for Higher Education, National Education Association, 1961.

———, ed., *The Creative Person.* Berkeley, Calif.: University of California General Extension, 1962.

McMillan, M., *Education Through the Imagination.* New York: Appleton-Century-Crofts, 1924.

McPherson, J. H., "A Proposal for Establishing Ultimate Criteria for Measuring Creative Output," in C. W. Taylor and F. Barron, eds., *Scientific Creativity: Its Recognition and Development*, pp. 24-29. New York: John Wiley & Sons, Inc., 1963.

Mackler, B., "Creativity and Life Style." Doctoral Dissertation. Lawrence, Kan.: University of Kansas, 1962.

Markey, F. V., *Imaginative Behavior in Pre-School Children.* New York: Bureau of Publications, Teachers College, Columbia University, 1935.

Marshall, M., "Helping Children Write Better Themes," *Peabody Journal of Education*, XXXVIII (1960), 96-99.

Maslow, A. H., *Motivation and Personality.* New York: Harper & Row, Publishers, 1954.

———, *Toward a Psychology of Being.* Princeton, N.J.: D. Van Nostrand Co., Inc., 1962.

Maw, W. and E. W. Maw, "The Relationship Between Curiosity and Scores on a Test of General Information," *Journal of the Association for Research in Growth Relationships*, II (1960), 27-34.

Maxwell, J., "What to Do About the Boys?" *NEA Journal*, XLIX (March 1960), 26.

Mayer, M., *The Schools.* New York: Harper & Row, Publishers, 1961.

Mead, M., "Bringing Up Children in the Space Age," *Air Force*, XLII (1959), 71-73.

———, "Where Education Fits In," *Think*, XXVIII (November–December 1962), 16-22.

Meadowcroft, W., *The Boy's Life of Edison.* New York: Harper & Row, Publishers, 1949.

Mearns, H., *The Creative Adult.* Garden City, N.Y.: Doubleday & Company, Inc., 1941.

———, *Creative Power* (Reprint). New York: Dover Publications, Inc., 1958.

Mednick, S. A., "Development of Admission Criteria for Colleges and Universities That Will Not Eliminate Such Applicants as the Bright and Non-conformist, the Under-challenged, and the Individual with Highly Specialized Ability," in *Current Issues in Higher Education*, pp. 86-88. Washington, D.C.: National Educational Association, 1961.

————, "The Associative Basis of the Creative Process," *Psychological Review*, LXIX (1962), 220-232.

Morgan, E. S., "What Every Yale Freshman Should Know," *Saturday Review*, XLIII (1960), 13-14.

Mork, G. M. A., "A Science Lesson on Rocket Satellites," *University of Kansas Bulletin of Education*, XIII (1959), 86-91.

Murphy, G., *Human Potentialities*. New York: Basic Books, Inc., 1958.

————, *Freeing Intelligence Through Teaching*. New York: Harper & Row, Publishers, 1961.

Mussen, P. H. and J. J. Conger, *Child Development and Personality*. New York: Harper & Row, Publishers, 1956.

Myers, R. E. and E. P. Torrance, "Can Teachers Encourage Creative Thinking?" *Educational Leadership*, XIX (1961), 156-159.

National Council of English Teachers, *Creative Ways in Teaching the Language Arts, a Portfolio of Elementary Classroom Procedures*. Champaign, Ill.: National Council of Teachers of English, 1954.

Nelson, J. F., "The Construction of a Scale of Teacher Judgment of Pupil Creativity." M.A. research report. Duluth, Minn.: University of Minnesota, 1963.

O'Brien, M. A., R. A. Elder, P. Putnam, and M. R. Sewell, "Developing Creativity in Children's Use of Imagination: Nursery, Ages Two and Three," *Union College Studies in Character Research*, Vol. 1, No. 5, January 1954.

Oetzel, R., "Selected Bibliography on Sex Differences." Mimeographed paper compiled with the sponsorship of the Social Science Research Council, Stanford University, California, 1962.

Ojemann, R. H., "Are Creativity and Mental Health Compatible?" in M. F. Andrews, ed., *Creativity and Psychological Health*. Syracuse, N.Y.: Syracuse University Press, 1961.

Osborn, A. F., *Your Creative Power*. New York: Charles Scribner's Sons, 1948.

————, *Applied Imagination*. New York: Charles Scribner's Sons, 1957.

Osgood, C. E., "The Nature and Measurement of Meaning," *Psychological Bulletin*, XLIX (1952), 192-237.

Overstreet, H. and B. Overstreet, *The Mind Alive*. New York: W. W. Norton & Company, Inc., 1954.

Owens, W. A., C. F. Schumacher, and J. B. Clark, "The Measurement of Creativity in Machine Design," *Journal of Applied Psychology*, XLI (1957), 297-302.

Palm, H. J., "An Analysis of Test-score Differences Between Highly Creative and High Miller Analogies Members of the Summer Guidance Institute." M.A. research report. Minneapolis, Minn.: University of Minnesota, 1959.

Parloff, M. B. and J. H. Handlon, "The Influence of Criticalness on Creative Problem-solving in Dyads," *Psychiatry*, XXVII (1964), 17-27.

Parnes, S. J. and A. Meadow, "Effects of 'Brainstorming' Instructions on Creative Problem-solving by Trained and Untrained Subjects," *Journal of Educational Psychology*, L (1959), 171-176.

————, "Evaluation of Persistence of Effects Produced by a Creative Problem-solving Course," *Psychological Reports*, VII (1960), 357-361.

Patri, A., *The Questioning Child*. New York: Appleton-Century-Crofts, 1931.

Patrick, C., *What Is Creative Thinking?* New York: Philosophical Library, 1955.

Payne, J. N., "Teaching Mathematics to Bright Pupils," *University of Michigan School of Education Bulletin*, XXIX (1958), 97-102.

Pepinsky, P. N., *Originality in Group Productivity; I: Productive Independence in Three Natural Situations*. Columbus, Ohio: Research Foundation, Ohio State University, 1959.

————, "Study of Productive Nonconformity," *Gifted Child Quarterly*, IV (Winter 1960), 81-85.

Pepinsky, P. N., J. K. Hemphill, and R. N. Shevitz, "Attempts to Lead, Group Productivity, and Morale under Conditions of Acceptance and Rejection," *Journal of Abnormal and Social Psychology*, LVII (1958), 47-54.

Pepinsky, P. N. and H. B. Pepinsky, *Originality in Group Productivity*. Annual Summary Report, Project NR 170-396, Contract NONR 495. The Ohio State University Research Foundation, November 15, 1958.

Piers, E. V., J. M. Daniels, and J. F. Quackenbush, "The Identification of Creativity in Adolescents," *Journal of Educational Psychology*, LI (1960), 346-351.

Pitcher, E. G., "Male and Female," *Atlantic*, CCXI (March 1963), 87-91.

Pitcher, E. G. and E. Prelinger, *Children Tell Stories: An Analysis of Fantasy*. New York: International Universities Press, Inc., 1963.

Punsalan, V. J., "Reading Habits and Interests of Sixth-Grade Pupils," M.A. research paper. Minneapolis, Minn.: University of Minnesota, 1961.

Reid, A., *Ounce, Dice, Trice*. Boston: Little, Brown & Co., 1958.

Rhodes, M., "An Analysis of Creativity," *Phi Delta Kappan*, XLII (1961), 305-310.

Ribot, T., *Essay on the Creative Imagination*. London: Routledge & Kegan Paul, Ltd., 1906.

Riessman, F., *The Culturally Deprived Child*. New York: Harper & Row, Publishers, 1962.

Roe, A., *The Making of a Scientist*. New York: Dodd, Mead & Co., 1962.

————, "Personal Problems and Science," in C. W. Taylor and F. Barron, eds., *Scientific Creativity: Its Recognition and Development*. New York: John Wiley & Sons, Inc., 1963.

Rogers, C. R., *Client-centered Therapy*. Boston: Houghton Mifflin Company, 1951.

————, "Toward a Theory of Creativity," *ETC: A Review of General Semantics,* XI (1954), 249-260.

Rossman, J., *The Psychology of the Inventor.* Washington, D.C.: Inventors Publishing Co., 1931.

————, *Industrial Creativity: The Psychology of the Inventor.* New Hyde Park, N.Y.: University Books, Inc., 1964.

Rouse, S. T., "Effects of a Training Program on the Productive Thinking of Educable Mental Retardates." Doctoral Dissertation. Nashville, Tenn.: George Peabody Teachers College, 1963.

Rousseau, H. J., "Ability in a Multi-cultural Community: Rhodesia and Nyasaland," in G. Z. F. Bereday and J. A. Lauwerys, eds., *The Gifted Child: The Yearbook of Education.* New York: Harcourt, Brace & World, Inc., 1962.

Rubin, L. J., "Creativity and the Curriculum," *Phi Delta Kappan,* XLIV (1963), 438-440.

Runner, K., "Some Common Patterns," *Adult Leadership,* III (December 1954), 15-17.

Russell, D. H., "The Development of the Thinking Process," *Review of Educational Research,* XXIII (1953), 137-145.

————, *Children's Thinking.* Boston: Ginn & Company, 1956.

Schwartz, G. and P. W. Bishop, eds., *Moments of Discovery,* Vols. I and II. New York: Basic Books, Inc., 1958.

School Mathematics Study Group, *Newsletter No. 2,* June 1959. New Haven, Conn.: School Mathematics Study Group, Yale University.

Sears, P. S., "The Pursuit of Self-esteem: The Middle Childhood Years." Unpublished paper, Laboratory of Human Development, Stanford University, California, 1960. Dittoed.

Selye, H., "The Gift for Basic Research," in G. Z. F. Bereday and J. A. Lauwerys, eds., *The Gifted Child: The Yearbook of Education,* pp. 339-408. New York: Harcourt, Brace & World, Inc., 1962.

Shane, H. G. and W. A. Yauch, *Creative School Administration.* New York: Holt, Rinehart & Winston, Inc., 1954.

Sigel, I., "Sex Differences in Cognitive Functioning Re-examined: A Functional Point of View." Paper presented at the 1962 Biennial Meeting of the Society for Research in Child Development, Berkeley, California, 1962.

Siks, G. B., *Creative Dramatics.* New York: Harper & Row, Publishers, 1958.

Simpson, R. M., "Creative Imagination," *American Journal of Psychology,* XXXIII (1922), 234-243.

Smith, M. C., "Does Correcting Errors Discourage Creativeness?" *Elementary English Review,* XX (1943), 7-12.

Sommers, W. S., *The Influence of Selected Teaching Methods on the Development of Creative Thinking.* Ann Arbor, Mich.: Dissertation Abstracts, 1961.

Spearman, C. E., *Creative Mind*. London: Cambridge University Press, 1930.

Stein, M. I., "Creativity and Culture," *Journal of Psychology*, XXXVI (1953), 311-322.

————, "Toward Developing More Imaginative Creativity in Students," in R. M. Cooper, ed., *The Two Ends of the Log*, pp. 69-75. Minneapolis, Minn.: University of Minnesota Press, 1958.

Stephenson, W., *Testing School Children*. New York: David McKay Co., Inc., 1949.

Stern, G. G., *Preliminary Manual: Activities Index and College Characteristics Index*. Syracuse, N.Y.: Psychological Research Center, Syracuse University, 1958.

Stevens, L. A., "Experience Is Not the Best Teacher," *Pageant*, XIX (September 1963), 54-60.

Stewart, G. W., "Can Productive Thinking Be Taught?" *Journal of Higher Education*, XXI (1950), 411-414.

Strang, R., "Developing Creative Powers of Gifted Children," in *Creativity of Gifted and Talented Children*, pp. 20-31. New York: Bureau of Publications, Teachers College, Columbia University, 1959.

Strevell, W. H. and P. Oliver, "Grouping Can Be Flexible Within the Classroom," *Nations Schools*, LIX (1957), 89-91.

Sullivan, H. S., *Interpersonal Theory of Psychiatry*. New York: W. W. Norton & Company, Inc., 1953.

Taton, R., *Reason and Chance in Scientific Discovery*. New York: Philosophical Library, 1957.

Taylor, C. W., ed., *Creativity: Progress and Potential*. New York: McGraw-Hill Book Company, 1964.

Taylor, I. A., "The Nature of Creative Process," in P. Smith, ed., *Creativity*, pp. 51-82. New York: Hastings House, 1959.

Thoreau, H. J., *Walden* (Reprint). New York: The New American Library of World Literature, Inc., 1942.

Thurstone, L. L., "Creative Talent," in L. L. Thurstone, ed., *Applications of Psychology*, pp. 18-37. New York: Harper & Row, Publishers, 1952.

Torrance, E. P., "Current Research on the Nature of Creative Talent," *Journal of Counseling Psychology*, VI (1959), 309-316.

————, ed., *Education and Talent*, Minneapolis, Minn.: University of Minnesota Press, 1960a.

————, "Creative Thinking Through the Language Arts," *Educational Leadership*, XVIII (1960b), 13-18.

————, "Evaluation of the Creative Outcomes of a Science and Arts Camp." Unpublished data. University of Minnesota, Minneapolis, Minn., 1960c.

————, "Factors Affecting Creative Thinking in Children: An Interim Research Report," *Merrill-Palmer Quarterly*, VII (1961a), 171-180.

————, ed., *New Educational Ideas: Third Minnesota Conference on Gifted Children*. Minneapolis, Minn.: Center for Continuation Study, University of Minnesota, 1961b.

————, "Priming Creative Thinking in the Primary Grades," *Elementary School Journal*, LXII (1961c), 34-41.

————, "Can Grouping Control Social Stress in Creative Activities?" *Elementary School Journal*, LXII (1961d), 139-145.

————, *Guiding Creative Talent*. Englewood Cliffs, N.J.: Prentice-Hall, Inc., 1962a.

————, "Developing Creative Thinking Through School Experiences," in S. J. Parnes and H. F. Harding, eds., *A Source Book for Creative Thinking*, pp. 31-47. New York: Charles Scribner's Sons, 1962b.

————, *Education and the Creative Potential*. Minneapolis, Minn.: University of Minnesota Press, 1963a.

————, *What Research Says to the Teacher: Creativity*, Pamphlet No. 28. Washington, D.C.: National Education Association, 1963b.

————, "Changing Reactions of Pre-Adolescent Girls to Tasks Requiring Creative Scientific Thinking," *Journal of Genetic Psychology*, CII (1963c), 217-223.

————, "The Creative Personality and the Ideal Pupil," *Teachers College Record*, LXV (1963d), 220-226.

————, "Education and Creativity," in C. W. Taylor, ed., *Creativity: Progress and Potential*, pp. 49-128. New York: McGraw-Hill Book Company, 1964a.

Torrance, E. P. and J. C. Gowan, *The Reliability of the Minnesota Tests of Creative Thinking*. Minneapolis, Minn.: Bureau of Educational Research, University of Minnesota, 1963.

Torrance, E. P. and Staff, *Role of Evaluation in Creative Thinking*. Minneapolis, Minn.: Bureau of Educational Research, University of Minnesota, 1964b.

Toynbee, A., "Has America Neglected Its Creative Minority?" *California Monthly*, LXXII (February 1962), 7-10.

Triandis, H. C., A. R. Bass, R. B. Ewen, and Eleanor Hall Mikesell, "Team Creativity as a Function of the Creativity of the Members." Urbana, Ill.: Group Effectiveness Research Laboratory, University of Illinois, 1962.

Tumin, M., "Obstacles to Creativity," *ETC: A Review of General Semantics*, XI (1954), 261-271.

Veatch, Jeanette, "The Structure of Creativity," *Journal of Educational Sociology*, XXVII (1953), 102-107.

Vernon, Margaret D., "The Development of Imaginative Construction in Children," *British Journal of Psychology*, XXXIX (1948), 102-111.

Wallace, H. R., "Creative Thinking: A Factor in Sales Productivity," *Vocational Guidance Quarterly*, IX (Summer 1961), 223-226.

Wanner, P. W., "Social Interaction, Independent Behavior, and Industry as Affected by Two Different Seating Arrangements in Sixth-grade Classrooms." Paper presented to California Educational Research Association, Bakersfield, California, March 11-12, 1960.

Ward, Winifred, *Playmaking with Children*, 2nd Ed. New York: Appleton-Century-Crofts, 1957.

Weisberg, P. S. and Kayla J. Springer, "Environmental Factors in Creative Function," *Archives of General Psychiatry*, V (1961), 554-564.

Welch, L., "Recombination of Ideas in Creative Thinking," *Journal of Applied Psychology*, XXX (1946), 638-643.

Whipple, G. M., *Manual of Mental and Physical Tests; Part II: Complex Processes*. Baltimore: Warwick & York, 1915.

Wilson, R. C., "The Program for Gifted Children in the Portland, Oregon, Schools," in C. W. Taylor, ed., *The 1955 University of Utah Research Conference on the Identification of Creative Scientific Talent*, pp. 14-22. Salt Lake City: University of Utah Press, 1956.

————, "Creativity," in *Education for Gifted Children*, 57th Yearbook of the National Society for the Study of Education, pp. 108-126. Chicago: University of Chicago Press, 1958.

————, "Developing Creativity in Children," *Education*, LXXXI (1960), 19-23.

Wilt, M., *Creativity in the Elementary School*. New York: Appleton-Century-Crofts, 1959.

Wodtke, K. H., "A Study of the Reliability and Validity of Creativity Tests at the Elementary School Level." Doctoral Dissertation. Salt Lake City, Utah: University of Utah, 1963.

Wylie, R. C., "Children's Estimates of Their Schoolwork Ability as a Function of Sex, Race, and Socioeconomic Level," *Journal of Personality*, XXXI (1963), 203-224.

Yamamoto, K., "Creativity and Sociometric Choice Among Adolescents." M.A. research report. Minneapolis, Minn.: University of Minnesota, 1960.

————, *Scoring Manual for Evaluating Imaginative Stories*. Minneapolis, Minn.: Bureau of Educational Research, University of Minnesota, 1961. Mimeographed.

————, *A Study of the Relationships Between Creative Thinking Abilities of Fifth Grade Teachers and Academic Achievement*. Ann Arbor, Mich.: University Microfilms, Inc., 1962.

————, "Creative Writing and School Achievement," *School and Society*, XCI (October 19, 1963), 307-308.

Zigler, E. and P. Kanzer, "The Effectiveness of Two Classes of Verbal Reinforcers on the Performance of Middle- and Lower-Class Children," *Journal of Personality*, XXX (1962), 157-163.

Zirbes, L., *Spurs to Creative Teaching*. New York: G. P. Putnam's Sons, 1959.

Zubin, J., "Nomographs for Determining the Significance of the Difference Between the Frequencies of Events in Two Contrasted Series of Groups," *Journal of American Statistical Association*, XXXIV (1939), 539-544.

INDEX

NAME
INDEX

SUBJECT INDEX